Poverty and the Government in America

Poverty and the Government in America

A Historical Encyclopedia

VOLUME 2

Jyotsna Sreenivasan

A B C ☉ C L I O

Santa Barbara, California • Denver, Colorado • Oxford, England

Every reasonable effort has been made to trace the owners of copyright materials
in this book, but in some instances this has proven impossible. The editors
and publishers will be glad to receive information leading to more complete
acknowledgments in subsequent printings of the book and in the meantime extend their
apologies for any omissions.

Library of Congress Cataloging-in-Publication Data
Poverty and the government in America : a historical encyclopedia /
[edited by] Jyotsna Sreenivasan.
       p. cm.
    Includes bibliographical references and index.
    ISBN 978-1-59884-168-8 (hardcopy : alk. paper) – ISBN 978-1-59884-169-5 (ebook)
1.   Poverty–Government policy–United States–Encyclopedias. 2.   Public welfare–United
States–Encyclopedias.   I. Sreenivasan, Jyotsna.

    HC110.P6P595 2009
    362.5'561097303–dc22

                                                                2009029704

ISBN: 978-1-59884-168-8
EISBN: 978-1-59884-169-5

13   12   11   10   09   1   2   3   4   5

This book is also available on the World Wide Web as an eBook.
Visit www.abc-clio.com for details.

ABC-CLIO, LLC
130 Cremona Drive, P.O. Box 1911
Santa Barbara, California 93116-1911

This book is printed on acid-free paper ∞

Manufactured in the United States of America

Contents

W

Preface

Although the poverty rate was high and often growing throughout much of the history of the American colonies and the United States, since the beginning of the twentieth century, the country has made considerable progress in combating poverty. Yet, since the early 1970s, the poverty rate in the United States has remained the same or even increased, instead of continuing to decrease.

During colonial times and the early part of the United States, few people were interested in preventing poverty; they saw poverty as a permanent part of society and simply wanted to deal with the poor in the easiest and most efficient way. Poor people were considered to be the responsibility of the local governments, who cared for them by apprenticing poor children to employers; by auctioning off poor adults to the lowest-bidding family; and by forcing the elderly, the unemployed, and the disabled to live in poorhouses or workhouses. At that time, state governments provided money for the poor only during times of war or disaster, and the federal government rarely took an interest in the poor (see the entry on Poor Laws for more on this topic).

By the mid-1800s, however, the needs of the poor began to overwhelm the eastern cities, and they turned to the states for help. Some states wrote reports on how to prevent poverty (see the entry on the Quincy Report for more information on this). The states' solution—constructing more poorhouses—did not work, but nevertheless this method of dealing with the poor lasted until the early twentieth century.

Since the early twentieth century and especially since the New Deal of the 1930s, the federal government has come up with some effective programs to alleviate and prevent poverty. Gradually over the years the state and federal governments joined towns and cities in providing money and help to the unemployed, elderly, disabled, and children in the form of Social Security, unemployment insurance, minimum-wage legislation, free and reduced-price lunches in schools, food stamps, and cash aid to families with children. The spread of public education, public libraries, and public playgrounds and parks has benefited everyone, but especially those with low incomes who cannot afford to pay for private education and private recreation clubs.

These measures have helped raise the standard of living of the lowest economic classes of society. As Loyola University law professor William Quigley points out, "American poor people are rich beyond the wildest dreams of the poor in impoverished countries, where one billion people survive on about a dollar a day." However, Quigley goes on to say, "Our citizens … are constantly inundated by a culture that equates dignity with income, possessions, and the ability to be self-supporting" (2003, 39). In other words, just because American poor people have more food, better housing, and access to higher-quality education than poor people in some other countries, that does not mean that they are not poor by American standards.

It is true, however, that the percentage of the truly poor people has gone down in the United States, due in large part to government programs. "Using some contemporary definitions of poverty … it is roughly accurate to say that 40% of Americans were poor in 1900, 33–40% in the Great Depression, 25% in the mid-1950s, and 6 to 15% between 1970 and 1980," says James Patterson, a history professor at Brown University. Furthermore, the idea of what a person needs to escape poverty has become more generous over the years. Patterson points out that, by 1977 standards, most Americans at the beginning of the twentieth century would have been considered poor (1994, 12–13).

As the overall standard of living has risen in the United States, so has the minimum standard of living that the public has been willing to grant to the poor and needy. Diana Karter Appelbaum (1977) surveyed a number of "poverty lines" throughout the twentieth century. She found that the pre-1929 poverty-line budgets provided a less well-balanced diet, and allowed for smaller housing and fewer comforts, than the poverty-line budgets of the 1960s and after (for more on this issue, see the entry on the Poverty Line).

Although this is certainly good news, others see the glass as "half empty" and point out that the federal poverty line is set far too low to actually meet the basic needs of real families. In 2007, the official percentage of people living below the poverty line in the United States was around 12.5 percent; however, this statistic masks the fact that the government recognizes that its poverty line is too low: many government programs provide benefits to people above the poverty line. For example, almost half the schoolchildren in this country are eligible for a free school lunch, meaning that they live in a family with an income of less than 130% of the federal poverty line. The official percentage of people living in poverty, even given the fact that the poverty line is set too low, has stayed the same or risen somewhat since the early 1970s. The United States seems to be stagnating in its progress against poverty.

What does work in the battle against poverty? To read about laws and government programs that have been fairly successful at decreasing poverty and unemployment, or at increasing access to jobs, education, money, food, housing, health care, political participation, and other necessities, see the following entries (note that some of these programs were temporary and are no longer in effect): Affirmative Action; Child Support Enforcement Program; Civilian Conservation Corps; Civil Rights Act of 1964; Civil Works Administration; Community Action Programs; Earned Income Tax Credit; Elder Nutrition Programs; Fair Labor Standards Act of 1938; Federal Emergency Relief Act; Food Stamp Program; GI Bill; Head Start; Home Visitation Programs; Housing, Low-Income; Indian New Deal; Indian Self-Determination; Job Corps; Living-Wage Laws; Manpower Development and Training Act of 1962; Maternal and Child Health Services; Medicaid; Medicare; Minimum-Wage Laws; National Service; National Voter Registration Act of 1963; New Deal Cooperative Communities; Public Libraries; Public Schools; Public Works Administration; Reconstruction Era; Sheppard-Towner Maternity and Infancy Act of 1921; Social Security Act; Supplemental Security Income; Temporary Assistance to Needy Families; Tennessee Valley Authority; Title IX of the 1972 Educational Amendments; Unemployment Insurance; Vocational Education; Voting Rights Act of 1965; Workers' Compensation; and Works Progress Administration.

The following entries deal with laws or government programs that have had mixed results in terms of helping the poor: Aid to (Families with) Dependent Children; Comprehensive Employment and Training Act; Elementary and Secondary Education Act of 1965; Freedmens' Bureau; Higher Education Act of 1965; Homestead Act of 1862; Indian Reorganization Act of 1934; McKinney-Vento Homeless Assistance Act; Model Cities; Mothers' Pensions; National School Lunch Act; Orphanages; and Poorhouses.

To read about government laws and programs that have not been successful in combating poverty, and that in some cases made the problem worse, take a look at the following entries: Agricultural Adjustment Act; General Allotment Act of 1887; Indian Removal Act of 1830; National Recovery Administration; Prohibition; Termination and Relocation; and Urban Renewal.

Which government programs are currently the most successful at lifting people above the poverty line? The following figure from the Center on Budget and Policy

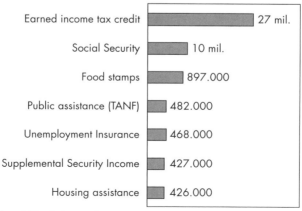

FIGURE 1. Children Lifted above the Poverty Line by Selected Benefits, 2002. Source: Center on Budget and Policy Priorities tabulations of the March 2003 Current Population Survey.

Priorities, a nonprofit organization researching fiscal policy and public programs that affect low-income people, shows that the most effective government program to lift children above the poverty line is the Earned Income Tax Credit, followed by Social Security payments to the retired or disabled, or to their dependent heirs.

This book concentrates on the history of government programs dealing with poverty in the United States, but readers may be curious about what economists and activists for the poor believe the government should do in the future. For ideas that could be implemented in the future, see the following entries: Guaranteed Annual Income; Kerner Commission; National Health Insurance; Reparations for Slavery; Roosevelt, Franklin Delano (he proposed an "Economic Bill of Rights" in 1944); and United Nations Human Rights Treaties.

SOURCES

Appelbaum, Diana Karter. "The Level of the Poverty Line: A Historical Survey." *Social Service Review* (September 1977): 514–523.

Patterson, James T. *America's Struggle Against Poverty, 1900–1994*. Cambridge, MA: Harvard University Press, 1994.

Quigley, William P. *Ending Poverty as We Know It*. Philadelphia, PA: Temple University Press, 2003.

WEB SITES

Center on Budget and Policy Priorities. http://www.cbpp.org/pubs/socsec.htm (accessed May 2008).

U.S. Census Bureau. Report on Poverty and Income. http://www.census.gov/hhes/www/income/income07.html (accessed September 2008).

Acknowledgments

I thank my editors, Holly Heinzer and Kim Kennedy-White, for their support and help. I also thank the University of Idaho Inter-Library Loan department for bringing in some of the more unusual and hard-to-find books I needed to complete this book.

K

KELLEY, FLORENCE (1859–1932)

Florence Kelley was one of the major leaders of a movement to force governments in the United States to address child labor and human welfare issues. Kelley investigated sweatshop labor in Illinois and served as the first chief factory inspector of Illinois, "one of the most powerful posts held by a woman in the industrial world" at that time, according to a biographer (Sklar 1995, 242).

She also became the first leader of the National Consumers League, an organization that asked consumers not to purchase products made with child labor or under inhumane working conditions.

Kelley was born in Philadelphia on September 12, 1859, the third child of eight. Her father was a judge and served as a member of the U.S. House of Representatives from 1861 to 1890. Kelley was ill often as a child, and her education was interrupted because of this. She made use of her father's extensive library to educate herself. When she was twelve, her father took her to see a steel factory and a glass factory. While her father marveled at the industrial advances of his country, the young Florence was horrified to see dozens of little boys working in the middle of the night.

At the age of sixteen, Kelley entered Cornell University, which had recently started admitting women students. Despite ill health, which caused her to miss years of classes, she managed to graduate six years later, in 1882. She wrote a thesis on the changing legal status of children.

In 1883, she decided to study at the University of Zurich. There, she became interested in socialism as an answer to the poverty and child labor that distressed her. In 1884, she married a fellow student, a Russian man who was also interested in socialism. She began translating from German into English a book by Friedrich Engels, a leading Socialist. Her translation of *The*

INVISIBLE CHILD LABOR

In 1872, Florence Kelley's father wanted his daughter to see a new steel-making process, the Bessemer process, which allowed much more steel to be made in America. Instead of feeling pride in her country's industrial advances, Florence noticed what the adults seemingly did not: the presence of children working in the factories. In her unfinished autobiography she explains her first impression of the

> presence and activity of boys smaller than myself . . . carrying heavy pails of water and tin dippers, from which the men drank eagerly.. . . The attention of all present was so concentrated on this industrial novelty that the little boys were no more important than so many grains of sand in the [steel] molds. For me, however, they were a living horror, and so remained.

Source: Sklar, Kathryn Kish. *Florence Kelley and the Nation's Work: The Rise of Women's Political Culture, 1830–1900.* New Haven, CT: Yale University Press, 1995, 45–46.

Condition of the Working Classes in England in 1844 was published in London and New York in the late 1880s.

Florence Kelley was a consumer movement leader and labor reformer who devoted her life to securing laws that would protect children and women in the workplace. (Library of Congress)

Kelley continued to study, translate, and write as she started a family, giving birth to three children. At this time, she also began collecting statistics on child labor. The family moved to New York in 1886, and in 1891, she left her husband because of physical abuse and his inability to support the family. They had been relying on money from Kelley's father to get by. She took her three children to Chicago, Illinois, where she moved into a small room in the Hull House settlement, and arranged for her children and their nanny to live at the home of wealthy friends (Sklar 1995, 167–168, 178–179).

While at Hull House, she proposed to the Illinois State Bureau of Labor Statistics that she conduct an investigation of the "sweating system" in Chicago—the practice of contracting out work to be done in the homes of the poor. She was appointed a Special Agent of the Bureau. During her months of work, she visited as many as 1,000 homes and shops. Her report disclosed that some workers—many of them women and their children—toiled for sixteen hours a day, seven days a week. Wages were sometimes so low that the workers were not able to support themselves, let alone any other family members (Sklar 1995, 223, 230–233).

In 1893, the state legislature followed Kelley's recommendations and passed a law that created a state factory inspection system, and set a minimum age of fourteen for workers and an eight-hour day for women and children. Kelley was appointed the chief factory inspector of the state of Illinois. She chose five women and six men to assist her. One of her biographers points out that "nowhere else in the Western world was a woman entrusted to enforce the labor legislation of a city, let alone of a large industrial region the size of Illinois" (Sklar 1995, 237).

As a result of the law, even before the inspections began, many factories stopped using employees under fourteen years of age. In addition to inspecting workplaces, Kelley pursued court cases against employers who violated the law. She was especially interested in enforcing the eight-hour work day for women. Unfortunately, this section of the law was declared unconstitutional by the Illinois Supreme Court in 1895, because it restricted a woman's right to enter into a work contract for longer hours (Blumberg 1966, 139; Sklar 1995, 281).

In 1897, a new Illinois governor took office who selected as chief factory inspector a man who had been on the payroll of the Illinois Glass Company, which Kelley had targeted because they were the state's largest employer of children. Kelley was out of a job. She took on evening work at a library, and began to write articles for a German Socialist magazine.

In 1899, she was invited to become the head of a new organization, the National Consumers League, which aimed to educate the public to buy only from factories that had earned the National Consumers League label. She moved to New York City and began living at the Henry Street settlement house. She traveled around the country, encouraging states to set up state consumer leagues, and inspecting factories to find those that did not employ workers under sixteen, that did not use home workers, and that obeyed all state labor laws (Goldmark 1953, 57–63).

Kelley led the National Consumers League until her death in 1932. During this time, she also worked for the passage of national child labor laws, championed the formation of a federal agency to oversee children's welfare (this was realized in 1912, as the U.S. Children's Bureau), and worked for minimum-wage laws.

See also: Addams, Jane; Child Labor Laws; Children's Bureau; Lathrop, Julia; National Consumers League; Settlement Houses; Socialism; Wald, Lillian

Sources

Blumberg, Dorothy Rose. *Florence Kelley: The Making of a Social Pioneer.* New York: Augustus M. Kelley, 1966.

Goldmark, Josephine. *Impatient Crusader: Florence Kelley's Life Story.* Urbana, IL: University of Illinois Press, 1953.

Sklar, Kathryn Kish. *Florence Kelley and the Nation's Work: The Rise of Women's Political Culture, 1830–1900.* New Haven, CT: Yale University Press, 1995.

Web Site

National Consumers League. http://www.nclnet.org/ (accessed December 2007).

KERNER COMMISSION (NATIONAL ADVISORY COMMISSION ON CIVIL DISORDERS)

The Kerner Commission was set up by President Lyndon Johnson in 1967, to study the 1967 urban race riots, discover the causes of the riots, and make recommendations as to how such riots could be prevented in the future. Because it was chaired by Illinois governor Otto Kerner, Jr., it is familiarly named after him.

Urban riots began in 1964. Store windows were smashed, stores were looted, bricks and bottles thrown, and people injured and sometimes killed. Sometimes the violence was the result of protest rallies which spiraled out of control: "Despite exhortations of Negro community leaders against violence, protest rallies became uncontrollable" (*Report* 1968, 36).

One of the worst riots took place in Los Angeles. The violence started in August 1965, after a police officer arrested a black man for speeding. Two days later, crowds gathered in the business district of Watts (a poor black neighborhood): "the principal intent of the rioters now seemed to be to destroy property owned by whites, in order to drive white 'exploiters' out of the ghetto." Four thousand people were arrested, and thirty-four people were killed. The rioters caused $35 million in damage (*Report* 1968, 38).

The riots continued in 1966 and 1967. On a hot summer day in Chicago in 1966, violence erupted after several black youths were arrested for turning on a fire hydrant to play in the water.

By the time the rioting had been controlled, more than 500 people had been arrested and three blacks were killed (*Report* 1968, 39).

When President Johnson set up the Kerner Commission in July 1967, he stressed that, while the country would not tolerate violence, "just saying that does not solve the problem." He wanted the commission to answer three basic questions: "What happened? How did it happen? What can be done to prevent it from happening again and again?" (*Report* 1968, 536).

Johnson was criticized at first because most members of the Kerner Commission were fairly conservative politically. Only one of the eleven commission members was part of a black organization: Roy Wilkins of the National Association for the Advancement of Colored People. Nevertheless, as Tom Wicker of the *New York Times* points out, the commission's report had a powerful impact precisely because its members were politically moderate:

> A commission made up of militants, or even influenced by them, could not conceivably have spoken with a voice so effective, so sure to be heard by white, moderate, responsible America. And the importance of this report is that it makes plain that white, moderate, responsible America is where the trouble lies. (*Report* 1968, v)

To study the riot situation and make recommendations, the commissioners and their staff heard testimony from 130 people—ghetto residents, civil rights leaders, government officials, sociologists, reporters, historians, police officers, the Federal Bureau of Investigation, and the National Guard. The commissioners personally visited eight cities that had suffered from riots. Their staff visited and surveyed more than 1,000 people in twenty-three cities where riots had occurred in 1967.

The Kerner Commission concluded that black rioting was caused, in large part, by poverty and unequal economic opportunity. According to the Kerner Commission, "what the rioters appeared to be seeking was fuller participation in the social order and the material benefits enjoyed by the majority of American citizens. Rather than rejecting the American system, they were anxious to obtain a place for themselves in it" (*Report* 1968, 7).

The Kerner Commission made a series of sweeping recommendations to address inequality in employment, education, and housing. As a long-term goal, the Commission recommended setting up a national system of income supplementation so that everyone would have an adequate income to meet basic needs. The commission recognized that it would cost money to really solve the problem, but believed that the resources were there: "The great productivity of our economy, and a federal revenue system which is highly responsive to economic growth, can provide the resources. The major need is to generate new will—the will to tax ourselves to the extent necessary to meet the vital needs of our nation" (*Report* 1968, 23).

Johnson stated, when setting up the commission, that "the work that you do ought to help guide us not just this summer, but for many summers to come and for many years to come" (*Report* 1968, 537). The Kerner Commission's report has had a long-term impact, with its work being continued by the Milton S. Eisenhower

Foundation, a nonprofit organization based in Washington, D.C. In February 2008, the Foundation released a forty-year update on the work of the Kerner Commission. According to the Eisenhower Foundation, "America has, for the most part, failed to meet the Kerner Commission's goals of less poverty, inequality, racial injustice and crime." Poverty and unemployment rates for blacks remained much higher than for whites (2008, 2).

However, the Foundation also acknowledges positive results: "Compared to the late 1960s, substantial African American and Latino middle classes have emerged, the number of minority entrepreneurs has greatly expanded, and there are large numbers of minority local and state elected officials" (2008, 5). The Foundation recommends that the United States strengthen full-employment laws; increase the federal minimum wage; enact universal health care; put more resources into job training; and ensure that all public schools across the country have comparable funds (2008, 6–7).

See also: Civil Rights Movement; Full Employment; Johnson, Lyndon; King, Martin Luther, Jr.; Minimum-Wage Laws; Model Cities; National Health Insurance; Poor People's Campaign

Sources

Eisenhower Foundation. Executive Summary of *What We Together Can Do: A Forty Year Update of the National Advisory Commission on Civil Disorders.* Washington, DC: Eisenhower Foundation, 2008. http://www.eisenhowerfoundation.org/kerner.php (accessed July 2008).

Report of the National Advisory Commission on Civil Disorders, with special introduction by Tom Wicker. New York: Bantam Books, 1968.

PRIMARY DOCUMENT 16

Excerpt from Report of the National Advisory Commission on Civil Disorders

SUMMARY OF REPORT

INTRODUCTION

The summer of 1967 again brought racial disorders to American cities, and with them shock, fear and bewilderment to the nation. The worst came during a two-week period in July, first in Newark and then in Detroit. Each set off a chain reaction in neighboring communities.

On July 28, 1967, the President of the United States established this Commission and directed us to answer three basic questions:

What happened?

Why did it happen?

What can be done to prevent it from happening again?

To respond to these questions, we have undertaken a broad range of studies and investigations. We have visited the riot cities; we have heard many witnesses; we have sought the counsel of experts across the country.

This is our basic conclusion: Our nation is moving toward two societies, one black, one white—separate and unequal.

Reaction to last summer's disorders has quickened the movement and deepened the division. Discrimination and segregation have long permeated much of American life; they now threaten the future of every American.

This deepening racial division is not inevitable. The movement apart can be reversed.

Choice is still possible. Our principal task is to define that choice and to press for a national resolution.

To pursue our present course will involve the continuing polarization of the American community and, ultimately, the destruction of basic democratic values. The alternative is not blind repression or capitulation to lawlessness. It is the realization of common opportunities for all within a single society.

This alternative will require a commitment to national action—compassionate, massive and sustained, backed by the resources of the most powerful and the richest nation on this earth. From every American it will require new attitudes, new understanding, and, above all, new will. The vital needs of the nation must be met; hard choices must be made, and, if necessary, new taxes enacted.

Violence cannot build a better society. Disruption and disorder nourish repression, not justice. They strike at the freedom of every citizen. The community cannot—it will not—tolerate coercion and mob rule.

Violence and destruction must be ended—in the streets of the ghetto and in the lives of people.

Segregation and poverty have created in the racial ghetto a destructive environment totally unknown to most white Americans.

What white Americans have never fully understood but what the Negro can never forget—is that white society is deeply implicated in the ghetto. White institutions created it, white institutions maintain it, and white society condones it.

It is time now to turn with all the purpose at our command to the major unfinished business of this nation. It is time to adopt strategies for action that will produce quick and visible progress. It is time to make good the promises of American democracy to all citizens-urban and rural, white and black, Spanish-surname, American Indian, and every minority group.

Our recommendations embrace three basic principles:

- To mount programs on a scale equal to the dimension of the problems;

- To aim these programs for high impact in the immediate future in order to close the gap between promise and performance;

- To undertake new initiatives and experiments that can change the system of failure and frustration that now dominates the ghetto and weakens our society.

These programs will require unprecedented levels of funding and performance, but they neither probe deeper nor demand more than the problems which called them forth. There can be no higher priority for national action and no higher claim on the nation's conscience. . . .

PART I—WHAT HAPPENED?
Chapter 2—Patterns of Disorder

The "typical" riot did not take place. The disorders of 1967 were unusual, irregular, complex and unpredictable social processes. Like most human events, they did not unfold in an orderly sequence. However, an analysis of our survey information leads to some conclusions about the riot process. In general:

- The civil disorders of 1967 involved Negroes acting against local symbols of white American society, authority and property in Negro neighborhoods—rather than against white persons.

- Of 164 disorders reported during the first nine months of 1967, eight (5 percent) were major in terms of violence and damage; 33 (20 percent) were serious but not major; 123 (75 percent) were minor and undoubtedly would not have received national attention as "riots" had the nation not been sensitized by the more serious outbreaks.

- In the 75 disorders studied by a Senate subcommittee, 83 deaths were reported. Eighty-two percent of the deaths and more than half the injuries occurred in Newark and Detroit. About 10 percent of the dead and 38 percent of the injured were public employees, primarily law officers and firemen. The overwhelming majority of the persons killed or injured in all the disorders were Negro civilians.

- Initial damage estimates were greatly exaggerated. In Detroit, newspaper damage estimates at first ranged from $200 million to $500 million; the highest recent estimate is $45 million. In Newark, early estimates ranged from $15 to $25 million. A month later damage was estimated at $10.2 million, over 80 percent in inventory losses. . . .

- What the rioters appeared to be seeking was fuller participation in the social order and the material benefits enjoyed by the majority of American citizens. Rather than rejecting the American system, they were anxious to obtain a place for themselves in it.

- Numerous Negro counter-rioters walked the streets urging rioters to "cool it." The typical counter-rioter was better educated and had higher income than either the rioter or the noninvolved.

- The proportion of Negroes in local government was substantially smaller than the Negro proportion of population. Only three of the 20 cities studied had more than one Negro legislator; none had ever had a Negro mayor or city manager. In only four cities did Negroes hold other important policy-making positions or serve as heads of municipal departments.. . .

- Although specific grievances varied from city to city, at least 12 deeply held grievances can be identified and ranked into three levels of relative intensity:'

First Level of Intensity
1. Police practices
2. Unemployment and underemployment
3. Inadequate housing

Second Level of Intensity
4. Inadequate education
5. Poor recreation facilities and programs
6. Ineffectiveness of the political structure and grievance mechanisms

Third Level of Intensity
7. Disrespectful white attitudes
8. Discriminatory administration of justice
9. Inadequacy of federal programs
10. Inadequacy of municipal services
11. Discriminatory consumer and credit practices
12. Inadequate welfare programs. . . .

PART II—WHY DID IT HAPPEN?
Chapter 4—The Basic Causes
In addressing the question "Why did it happen?" we shift our focus from the local to the national scene, from the particular events of the summer of 1967 to the factors within the society at large that created a mood of violence among many urban Negroes.

These factors are complex and interacting; they vary significantly in their effect from city to city and from year to year; and the consequences of one disorder, generating new grievances and new demands, become the causes of the next. Thus was created the "thicket of tension, conflicting evidence and extreme opinions" cited by the President. Despite these complexities, certain fundamental matters are clear. Of these, the most fundamental is the racial attitude and behavior of white Americans toward black Americans.

Race prejudice has shaped our history decisively; it now threatens to affect our future. White racism is essentially responsible for the explosive mixture which has been accumulating in our cities since the end of World War II. Among the ingredients of this mixture are:

- Pervasive discrimination and segregation in employment, education and housing, which have resulted in the continuing exclusion of great numbers of Negroes from the benefits of economic progress.

- Black in-migration and white exodus, which have produced the massive and growing concentrations of impoverished Negroes in our major cities, creating a growing crisis of deteriorating facilities and services and unmet human needs.

- The black ghettos where segregation and poverty converge on the young to destroy opportunity and enforce failure. Crime, drug addiction, dependency on welfare, and bitterness and resentment against society in general and white society in particular are the result.

At the same time, most whites and some Negroes outside the ghetto have prospered to a degree unparalleled in the history of civilization. Through television and other media, this affluence has been flaunted before the eyes of the Negro poor and the jobless ghetto youth.

Yet these facts alone cannot be said to have caused the disorders. Recently, other powerful ingredients have begun to catalyze the mixture:

- Frustrated hopes are the residue of the unfulfilled expectations aroused by the great judicial and legislative victories of the Civil Rights Movement and the dramatic struggle for equal rights in the South.

- A climate that tends toward approval and encouragement of violence as a form of protest has been created by white terrorism directed against nonviolent protest; by the open defiance of law and federal authority by state and local officials resisting desegregation; and by some protest groups engaging in civil disobedience who turn their backs on nonviolence, go beyond the constitutionally protected rights of petition and free assembly, and resort to violence to attempt to compel alteration of laws and policies with which they disagree.

- The frustrations of powerlessness have led some Negroes to the conviction that there is no effective alternative to violence as a means of achieving redress of grievances, and of "moving the system." These frustrations are reflected in alienation and hostility toward the institutions of law and government and the white society which controls them, and in the reach toward racial consciousness and solidarity reflected in the slogan "Black Power."

- A new mood has sprung up among Negroes, particularly among the young, in which self-esteem and enhanced racial pride are replacing apathy and submission to "the system."

- The police are not merely a "spark" factor. To some Negroes police have come to symbolize white power, white racism and white repression. And the fact is that many police do reflect and express these white attitudes. The atmosphere of hostility and cynicism is reinforced by a widespread belief among Negroes in the existence of police brutality and in a "double standard" of justice and protection—one for Negroes and one for whites.

To this point, we have attempted to identify the prime components of the "explosive mixture." In the chapters that follow we seek to analyze them in the perspective of history. Their meaning, however, is clear: In the summer of 1967, we have seen in our cities a chain reaction of racial violence. If we are heedless, none of us shall escape the consequences.. . .

PART III—WHAT CAN BE DONE?
Chapter 10—The Community Response

Our investigation of the 1967 riot cities establishes that virtually every major episode of violence was foreshadowed by an accumulation of unresolved grievances and by widespread dissatisfaction among Negroes with the unwillingness or inability of local government to respond.

Overcoming these conditions is essential for community support of law enforcement and civil order. City governments need new and more vital channels of communication to the residents of the ghetto; they need to improve their capacity to respond effectively to community needs before they become community grievances; and they need to provide opportunity for meaningful involvement of ghetto residents in shaping policies and programs which affect the community.

The Commission recommends that local governments:

- Develop Neighborhood Action Task Forces as joint community government efforts through which more effective communication can be achieved, and the delivery of city services to ghetto residents improved.

- Establish comprehensive grievance-response mechanisms in order to bring all public agencies under public scrutiny.

- Bring the institutions of local government closer to the people they serve by establishing neighborhood outlets for local, state and federal administrative and public service agencies.

- Expand opportunities for ghetto residents to participate in the formulation of public policy and the implementation of programs affecting them through improved political representation, creation of institutional channels for community action, expansion of legal services, and legislative hearings on ghetto problems.

In this effort, city governments will require state and federal support. The Commission recommends:

- State and federal financial assistance for mayors and city councils to support the research, consultants, staff and other resources needed to respond effectively to federal program initiatives.

- State cooperation in providing municipalities with the jurisdictional tools needed to deal with their problems; a fuller measure of financial aid to urban areas; and the focusing of the interests of suburban communities on the physical, social and cultural environment of the central city.. . .

Chapter 16—The Future of the Cities

By 1985, the Negro population in central cities is expected to increase by 72 percent to approximately 20.8 million. Coupled with the continued exodus of white families to the suburbs, this growth will produce majority Negro populations in many of the nation's largest cities.

The future of these cities, and of their burgeoning Negro populations, is grim. Most new employment opportunities are being created in suburbs and outlying areas. This trend will continue unless important changes in public policy are made.

In prospect, therefore, is further deterioration of already inadequate municipal tax bases in the face of increasing demands for public services, and continuing unemployment and poverty among the urban Negro population.

Three choices are open to the nation:

- We can maintain present policies, continuing both the proportion of the nation's resources now allocated to programs for the unemployed and the disadvantaged, and the inadequate and failing effort to achieve an integrated society.

- We can adopt a policy of "enrichment" aimed at improving dramatically the quality of ghetto life while abandoning integration as a goal.

- We can pursue integration by combining ghetto "enrichment" with policies which will encourage Negro movement out of central city areas.

The first choice, continuance of present policies, has ominous consequences for our society. The share of the nation's resources now allocated to programs for the disadvantaged is insufficient to arrest the deterioration of life in central city ghettos.

Under such conditions, a rising proportion of Negroes may come to see in the deprivation and segregation they experience, a justification for violent protest, or for extending support to now isolated extremists who advocate civil disruption. Large-scale and continuing violence could result, followed by white retaliation, and, ultimately, the separation of the two communities in a garrison state.

Even if violence does not occur, the consequences are unacceptable.

Development of a racially integrated society, extraordinarily difficult today, will be virtually impossible when the present black ghetto population of 12.5 million has grown to almost 21 million.

To continue present policies is to make permanent the division of our country into two societies; one, largely Negro and poor, located in the central cities; the other, predominantly white and affluent, located in the suburbs and in outlying areas.

The second choice, ghetto enrichment coupled with abandonment of integration, is also unacceptable. It is another way of choosing a permanently divided country. Moreover, equality cannot be achieved under conditions of nearly complete separation. In a country where the economy, and particularly the resources of employment, are predominantly white, a policy of separation can only relegate Negroes to a permanently inferior economic status.

We believe that the only possible choice for America is the third—a policy which combines ghetto enrichment with programs designed to encourage integration of substantial numbers of Negroes into the society outside the ghetto.. . .

Chapter 17—Recommendations For National Action

INTRODUCTION

No American—white or black—can escape the consequences of the continuing social and economic decay of our major cities.

Only a commitment to national action on an unprecedented scale can shape a future compatible with the historic ideals of American society.

The great productivity of our economy, and a federal revenue system which is highly responsive to economic growth, can provide the resources.

The major need is to generate new will—the will to tax ourselves to the extent necessary, to meet the vital needs of the nation.

We have set forth goals and proposed strategies to reach those goals. We discuss and recommend programs not to commit each of us to specific parts of such programs but to illustrate the type and dimension of action needed.

The major goal is the creation of a true union—a single society and a single American identity. Toward that goal, we propose the following objectives for national action:

- Opening up opportunities to those who are restricted by racial segregation and discrimination, and eliminating all barriers to their choice of jobs, education and housing.

- Removing the frustration of powerlessness among the disadvantaged by providing the means for them to deal with the problems that affect their own lives and by increasing the capacity of our public and private institutions to respond to these problems.

- Increasing communication across racial lines to destroy stereotypes, to halt polarization, end distrust and hostility, and create common ground for efforts toward public order and social justice.

We propose these aims to fulfill our pledge of equality and to meet the fundamental needs of a democratic and civilized society—domestic peace and social justice. . . .

THE WELFARE SYSTEM

Our present system of public welfare is designed to save money instead of people, and tragically ends up doing neither. This system has two critical deficiencies:

First, it excludes large numbers of persons who are in great need, and who, if provided a decent level of support, might be able to become more productive and self-sufficient. No federal funds are available for millions of men and women who are needy but neither aged, handicapped nor the parents of minor children.

Second, for those included, the system provides assistance well below the minimum necessary for a decent level of existence, and imposes restrictions that encourage continued dependency on welfare and undermine self-respect.

A welter of statutory requirements and administrative practices and regulations operate to remind recipients that they are considered untrustworthy, promiscuous and lazy. Residence requirements prevent assistance to people in need who are newly arrived in the state. Regular searches of recipients' homes violate privacy. Inadequate social services compound the problems.

The Commission recommends that the federal government, acting with state and local governments where necessary, reform the existing welfare system to:

- Establish uniform national standards of assistance at least as high as the annual "poverty level" of income, now set by the Social Security Administration at $3,335 per year for an urban family of four.

- Require that all states receiving federal welfare contributions participate in the Aid to Families with Dependent Children Unemployed Parents program (AFDC-UP) that permits assistance to families with both father and mother in the home, thus aiding the family while it is still intact.

- Bear a substantially greater portion of all welfare costs-at least 90 percent of total payments.

- Increase incentives for seeking employment and job training, but remove restrictions recently enacted by the Congress that would compel mothers of young children to work.
- Provide more adequate social services through neighborhood centers and family-planning programs.
- Remove the freeze placed by the 1967 welfare amendments on the percentage of children in a state that can be covered by federal assistance.
- Eliminate residence requirements.

As a long-range goal, the Commission recommends that the federal government seek to develop a national system of income supplementation based strictly on need with two broad and basic purposes:

- To provide, for those who can work or who do work, any necessary supplements in such a way as to develop incentives for fuller employment;
- To provide, for those who cannot work and for mothers who decide to remain with their children, a minimum standard of decent living, and to aid in the saving of children from the prison of poverty that has held their parents.

A broad system of implementation would involve substantially greater federal expenditures than anything now contemplated. The cost will range widely depending on the standard of need accepted as the "basic allowance" to individuals and families, and on the rate at which additional income above this level is taxed. Yet if the deepening cycle of poverty and dependence on welfare can be broken, if the children of the poor can be given the opportunity to scale the wall that now separates them from the rest of society, the return on this investment will be great indeed. . . .

Source

Eisenhower Foundation. "Report of the National Advisory Commission on Civil Disorders, Summary of Report." www.eisenhowerfoundation.org/docs/kerner.pdf (accessed July 2008).

KING, MARTIN LUTHER, JR. (1929–1968)

Martin Luther King, Jr. was the most prominent leader of the civil rights movement for equal rights for African Americans that took place during the 1950s and 1960s. In addition to equal political and legal rights, King was also concerned about the problem of poverty. Shortly before his assassination, he launched the Poor People's Campaign, which he believed to be the next step of the civil rights movement.

Martin Luther King, Jr. was born on January 15, 1929, in Atlanta, Georgia. His father was a Baptist preacher, and the family lived a comfortable middle-class life. King first became aware of racial segregation when, at the age of six, a white friend was not allowed to play with him anymore. Throughout his childhood and young adulthood he experienced segregation and racism: he

Martin Luther King Jr. speaks at a press conference in Birmingham, Alabama, on May 16, 1963. King led the African American struggle to achieve full rights of U.S. citizenship. He eloquently voiced the hopes and grievances of African Americans before he was assassinated in 1968. His powerful speeches and message of nonviolence have continued to inspire people of all races and generations. (Library of Congress)

and his family were required to sit in separate places in stores and on buses. King and other black children could not use the same swimming pools or public parks as white children. As a child he also became aware of poverty: some of his playmates were poor, and as a teenager he worked with poor black and white people (King 1998, 7–12).

While attending Morehouse College in Atlanta, King read Henry David Thoreau's 1849 essay "On Civil Disobedience," which details Thoreau's

refusal to pay taxes because those taxes supported slavery and a war he considered to be unjust (the Mexican-American War). This essay was the first time King had encountered the theory of nonviolent resistance. "Fascinated by the idea of refusing to cooperate with an evil system, I was so deeply moved that I reread the work several times," King wrote (1998, 14).

He studied to be a minister first at Crozer Theological Seminary in Pennsylvania, and then at Boston University's School of Theology. While at

LIFE IN THE GHETTO

In 1966, Martin Luther King, Jr., his wife, and four children moved to the Chicago ghetto of Lawndale to work with the people there. King writes of his experiences:

Our own children lived with us in Lawndale, and it was only a few days before we became aware of a change in their behavior. Their tempers flared, and they sometimes reverted to almost infantile behavior. During the summer, I realized that the crowded flat in which we lived was about to produce an emotional explosion in my own family. It was just too hot, too crowded, too devoid of creative forms of recreation. There was just not space enough in the neighborhood to run off the energy of childhood without running into busy, traffic-laden streets. And I understood anew the conditions which make of the ghetto an emotional pressure cooker.

Source: King, Martin Luther, Jr. *Autobiography of Martin Luther King, Jr.*, ed. Clayborne Carson. New York: Warner Books, 1998, 302.

Crozer, he learned more about the work of the Indian nonviolent leader Mahatma Gandhi. "As I delved deeper into the philosophy of Gandhi, my skepticism concerning the power of love gradually diminished, and I came to see for the first time its potency in the area of social reform" (King 1998, 23).

In 1954, King took a job as pastor of the Dexter Avenue Baptist Church in Montgomery, Alabama. In 1955, after Rosa Parks was arrested for refusing to yield her seat to a white man, the Montgomery civil rights community decided to hold a bus boycott to get rid of the law that black passengers had to sit at the back of the bus and yield seats to white passengers. They also decided to form a new organization and elect a new leader to include all the different people and groups who supported the boycott. King was asked to lead this new organization, the Montgomery Improvement Association, and he agreed.

The boycott lasted 382 days and ended only after the U.S. Supreme Court ordered the city of Montgomery to end their segregated seating on buses. This was the beginning of the civil rights movement. In 1957, King and other civil rights leaders formed the Southern Christian Leadership Conference (SCLC). The purpose of this organization was to help local groups around the country to hold nonviolent protests in favor of equal treatment and equal rights. Despite the fact that King and his family were the targets of violence (their home was shot at and bombed, for example), and despite the fact that police sometimes responded to peaceful protesters by using dogs and fire hoses, King continued to insist that the civil rights movement be nonviolent. In 1959, he spent a month in India learning more about Gandhi's nonviolent techniques.

After the civil rights movement won important victories—the passage of the

Civil Rights Act of 1964 and the Voting Rights Act of 1965—King decided to turn his attention to the problem of poverty. Violent riots were breaking out in cities around the country. In August 1965, King visited the Watts area of Los Angeles just after riots caused thirty deaths. While he was disturbed by the violence, he understood the desperation of the people: "it was my opinion that the riots grew out of the depths of despair which afflict a people who see no way out of their economic dilemma" (King 1998, 291).

He began to see that the civil rights movement thus far had not adequately addressed the issue of poverty. "The civil rights movement had too often been middle-class oriented and had not moved to the grassroots levels of our communities," he wrote (1998, 299). So in 1966, at the invitation of a Chicago-based civil rights group, he and his family moved to Chicago for several months. He invited other SCLC leaders to move there with him. King and the SCLC were largely unsuccessful in Chicago. King wrote, "in all frankness we found the job greater than even we imagined." Still, King remained committed to the issue of addressing poverty (King 1998, 312).

He began urging the SCLC to make poverty its next big campaign. In late 1967, King and the SCLC launched the Poor People's Campaign. He believed poverty could be conquered through a nonviolent movement. Despite the fact that some black activists were turning their backs on nonviolence, King stood firm. "Riots just don't pay off," he said in January 1968 to SCLC staff. "For if we say that power is the ability to effect change, or the ability to achieve purpose, then it is not powerful to engage in an act that does not do that—no matter how loud you are, and no matter how much you burn" (quoted in Branch 2006, 671).

King was assassinated on April 4, 1968, as he was helping sanitation workers in Memphis organize as part of the Poor People's Campaign. The civil rights movement and the Poor People's Campaign declined soon after. But King's commitment to nonviolence continues to inspire social justice activists around the world.

See also: Civil Rights Movement; Civil Rights Act of 1964; Guaranteed Annual Income; Kerner Commission (National Advisory Commission on Civil Disorders); Poor People's Campaign; Segregation Laws; Voting Rights Act of 1965

Sources
Branch, Taylor. *At Canaan's Edge: America in the King Years, 1965–1968.* New York: Simon and Schuster, 2006.
King, Martin Luther, Jr. *Autobiography of Martin Luther King, Jr.* edited by Clayborne Carson. New York: Warner Books, 1998.

Web Site
The King Center. http://www.thekingcenter.org/ (accessed July 2008).

L

LABOR UNIONS

One major cause of poverty is low wages. To press for higher wages, shorter working hours, and other benefits, workers have formed unions to negotiate as a group with employers. Over the years, governments and employers have sought to suppress unions, arguing that walk-outs and strikes hindered the smooth flow of commerce. In 1935, with the passage of the National Labor Relations Act, unions were finally recognized as not only legal, but as beneficial to the nation's economy.

Workers in America first united temporarily in protest of low wages: Maine fishermen in 1636 protested when wages were withheld, and in the 1700s, workers in a number of trades—tailors, shoemakers, seamen, printers—staged protests or strikes. The first permanent workers' organizations were mutual-aid societies, commonplace by the late 1700s. They were designed not to press for higher wages, but to set up cooperative sickness and death benefits funds for workers of a certain trade. By the beginning of the 1800s, some of these mutual-aid societies had begun pressuring employers for higher wages and shorter hours. These early labor unions were limited to members of a particular craft or trade, such as weavers, carpenters, or shoemakers (Dulles and Dubofsky 1984, 22–27).

In the mid-1800s, many trades formed national unions, although often these lasted only a few years. The Knights of Labor, started in 1869, was the first national union that was active for more than a few years. It included not only wage-earners, but also farmers and merchants. It reached its peak membership of 700,000 in 1886. In 1881, the American Federation of Labor (AFL) started. It included only skilled wage-earners as members. In 1905, the Industrial Workers of the World was formed—a Socialist union that sought to replace the capitalist U.S. government with a Socialist government. In 1938, the Congress of

361

Demonstrator wears an Industrial Workers of the World hat card that says, "Bread or Revolution," April 13, 1914. (Library of Congress)

Industrial Organizations (CIO) formed to organize the unskilled factory workers who were not eligible for membership in the AFL. In 1955, the AFL and the CIO joined forces to create the AFL-CIO. In the 1960s, agricultural laborers—many of them immigrants from Mexico and the Philippines—organized into the United Farm Workers.

In addition to negotiating with employers for higher wages and better working conditions for their members, labor unions also engage in political activities, forming their own local political parties, helping to elect politicians who were sympathetic to their causes, and pushing for the passage of laws to regulate working conditions. During the 1800s, the labor parties encouraged states to establish bureaus of labor to collect statistics on workers.

In 1884, due to pressure from labor unions, the federal government set up the Bureau of Labor (Dulles and Dubofsky 1984, 37; Dubofsky 1994, 13–14).

Starting in the late 1800s, employers began to oppose unions. They created "blacklists" (lists of union members) and refused to hire them. Factory owners hired their own police forces to break up strikes. Company police forces shot at striking workers with pistols and machine guns, and threw tear bombs. According to Pennsylvania Governor Gifford Pinchot, in 1923, police forces employed by iron and coal companies were twenty times larger than the state police force (Brandes 1976, 2).

During much of the 1800s, the relationship between worker and employer was assumed to be something that government ought not to interfere with. However, in the 1870s, an economic depression caused widespread unemployment and wage cuts. Workers across the country engaged in strikes and even violent conflicts with employers. Railroad workers refused to work after their wages were cut repeatedly. When governors of Maryland and Pennsylvania said that state police forces could not end the strikes, President Rutherford Hayes sent federal troops to Baltimore and Pittsburgh to control angry striking workers (Dubofsky 1994, 6–9).

Some members of Congress wanted to define the government's role in relation to strikes. In 1882, a Senate committee was formed to investigate the causes of strikes, and to recommend laws to remove those causes. However, during the two years of the committee's existence, the senators did not introduce any laws to help workers or to address the cause of strikes. Meanwhile, judges began to restrict union activities. "Federal judges viewed strikes as disorderly by definition and as threats to the social order," explains Melvyn Dubofsky (Dubofsky 1994, 12–13, 15–16).

In 1902, a U.S. president was for the first time at least partly on the side of the workers. Members of the United Mine Workers were on strike in Pennsylvania. President Theodore Roosevelt asked the workers and employers to meet to come to an agreement. When the mine owners refused to meet, Roosevelt threatened that the army would seize the mines. As a result, mine owners agreed to negotiate and the mine owners got a pay raise. However, the agreement did not require employers to recognize or negotiate with union leaders. The agreement also acknowledged that employers had the right to hire anyone they wanted—not just union members (Dubofsky 1994, 41–42).

During the 1920s, labor unions lost membership, perhaps because the country was enjoying a period of prosperity and many workers did not see a need for unions. Some employers engaged in "welfare capitalism," providing good pay and benefits to keep workers. At the same time, employers continued to discriminate against union members, and courts continued to prohibit certain union activities, such as "secondary boycotts" (efforts by workers to support strikers in another company by boycotting that company's products) (Dulles and Dubofsky 1984, 236–245).

With the start of the Great Depression in 1929, unemployment became a nationwide problem. The benefits of welfare capitalism evaporated as

businesses struggled to survive. President Franklin Roosevelt knew that great measures were needed to save the struggling American economy. The National Labor Relations Act of 1935 protected unions and strikes, and even stated that union organizing was beneficial to the economy. The Fair Labor Standards Act of 1938 set minimum wages and maximum work hours, and prohibited child labor. In the words of historians Foster Rhea Dulles and Melvyn Dubofsky, "Heretofore, labor unions had been tolerated; now they were to be encouraged" (1984, 256).

See also: Fair Labor Standards Act of 1938; Great Depression; National Labor Relations Act of 1938; Roosevelt, Franklin Delano; Socialism; Welfare Capitalism

Sources

Brandes, Stuart. *American Welfare Capitalism, 1880–1940.* Chicago, IL: University of Chicago Press, 1976.

Dubofsky, Melvyn. *The State and Labor in Modern America.* Chapel Hill, NC: University of North Carolina Press, 1994.

Dulles, Foster Rhea, and Melvyn Dubofsky. *Labor in America: A History.* Arlington Heights, IL: Harlan Davidson, 1984.

LATHROP, JULIA
(1858–1932)

In 1912, when Julia Lathrop was named to head the U.S. Children's Bureau, she became the first woman to head a federal agency. She was also instrumental in starting the first juvenile court in the United States, in Cook County, Illinois.

Lathrop was born on June 29, 1858, in Rockford, Illinois. Her father was a lawyer, member of the Illinois legislature, and a representative in the U.S.

Congress from 1877 to 1879. Her mother was the first valedictorian of nearby Rockford College. Lathrop graduated from Vassar College in 1880, after which she worked at her father's law office and studied law. In 1890, she moved into a new settlement house in Chicago, Hull House, which had been started in 1889, by Jane Addams. Settlement houses were located in poor neighborhoods and allowed college-educated women and men to live among the needy, learn from them, and offer help. During her twenty years at Hull House, Lathrop volunteered as a Cook County visiting agent, inspecting county poorhouses, hospitals, and other institutions for the poor. In 1892, the Illinois governor appointed her to the State Board of Charities. Her friend and Hull House co-resident Jane Addams describes her work: "She visited every one of the 102 county farms or almshouses, discussing conditions with their superintendents and ameliorating for the inmates as best she might the evil effects which unjust suffering always produces" (1935, 83). She advocated for transferring the insane from poorhouses to state hospitals.

She was disturbed by the political corruption she encountered. Trustees of poorhouses were not hired for their skills or experience, but rather were appointed based on political favoritism. In turn, the trustees rewarded their political allies by giving them contracts to supply coal and food to the poorhouses, and by handing out jobs at the poorhouses. Because the poorhouse suppliers were interested only in making a profit from state money, and because the attendants were generally not trained for the work, this system resulted in "insufficient heating for people who are old and ill, poor food for growing children and, worst of all, neglect for the helplessly insane. If only because the attendants do not know how properly to care for their charges, they constantly yield to the temptation of roughness and cruelty," Lathrop noted. In response, Lathrop worked to ensure that jobs at poorhouses and state hospitals would go to those who were most qualified (Addams 1935, 94, 99).

In 1901, Lathrop resigned from the State Board of Charities in protest, because the new Illinois governor had refused to pass a bill that would offer jobs and contracts on a merit basis. She returned to the Board in 1905, with the election of a new governor, and remained until 1909 (Addams 1935, 109–113).

While she was serving on the State Board of Charities, Lathrop was also a leader in the movement to set up the first juvenile court in the country. Lathrop had noticed that children who were convicted of crimes often had no appropriate place to go. At that time, children over ten years of age who were arrested could be held with adults in police stations and tried in the same courts as adults. If found guilty, they could be sent to an adult prison. Often, to avoid exposing children to the harsh prison conditions, judges would simply let them go or would send them to a school for orphans. Lathrop and others proposed a law, passed in 1899, that set up a special court system in Cook County for young people, including a detention home and school equipped with classrooms and a gymnasium (Addams 1935, 132–136).

To better train the attendants of the insane in state hospitals, Lathrop helped arrange for summer classes for attendants at the Chicago School of Civics and Philanthropy, starting in 1908. These classes eventually grew into the school of social work at the University of Chicago (Addams 1935, 151–158).

Lathrop was appointed in 1912 to head the newly created U.S. Children's Bureau. She became the first woman to lead a federal government bureau. Although she had not been active in promoting the formation of the Bureau, the founder of Hull House, Jane Addams, urged President Taft to appoint Lathrop as the head of the Bureau (Addams 1935, 189–204; Lindenmeyer 1997, 28–29).

Lathrop began her work at the Bureau by researching infant mortality around the country. She was also careful about selecting her staff: she wanted to hire based strictly on merit, and not on political favoritism. The Bureau's initial budget was a tiny $25,000 per year, enough for about fifteen staff members. Lathrop found this budget outrageous when the government could afford to spend hundreds of thousands on agricultural issues such as hog cholera. When, in 1914, the House of Representatives denied Lathrop's request for more money, she asked her friends Florence Kelley, Lillian Wald, and others for help. They arranged for a nationwide letter-writing campaign, and a few weeks later, the House of Representatives agreed to a much larger yearly budget—growing to between $250,000 and $350,000 during Lathrop's time at the Bureau. Lathrop was able to hire seventy-six employees in 1915. Most Bureau staff members were women (Lindenmeyer 1997, 38, 53–58).

In 1917, Lathrop helped write and push for the passage of a law, the Sheppard-Towner Act, to provide money to states for maternal and infant health. In 1921, just as the Sheppard-Towner Act was going into effect, Lathrop resigned at the age of sixty-three from the Bureau. She suggested as her replacement Grace Abbott, another former Hull House resident, and Abbott was appointed by President Harding (Lindenmeyer 1997, 76–92).

After her retirement, Lathrop built a house for herself and her widowed sister in Rockford, Illinois. She became active in a campaign against capital punishment and worked to save the life of a seventeen-year-old who had been convicted of murder. A year after Lathrop's death, the governor of Illinois commuted the sentence of the young man to ninety-nine years of imprisonment (Addams 1935, 219–224).

See also: Addams, Jane; Children's Bureau; Juvenile Justice System; Kelley, Florence; Poorhouses; Settlement Houses, Sheppard-Towner Maternity and Infancy Act of 1921

Sources
Addams, Jane. *My Friend, Julia Lathrop.* New York: The Macmillan Company, 1935.

Lindenmeyer, Kriste. *A Right to Childhood: The U.S. Children's Bureau and Child Welfare, 1912–1946.* Urbana, IL: University of Illinois Press, 1997.

LEGAL SERVICES FOR THE POOR

The Sixth Amendment to the U.S. Constitution, ratified in 1791, guarantees people accused of a crime the right to a lawyer. The Fourteenth Amendment to

Lawyers for the National Association for the Advancement of Colored People celebrate outside the Supreme Court after successfully challenging school segregation in Brown v. Board of Education *(1954). From left to right are: George E. Hayes, Thurgood Marshall, and James Nabrit. (Library of Congress)*

the U.S. Constitution, ratified in 1868, guarantees every citizen "the equal protection of the laws." However, people who are too poor to pay for a lawyer may find themselves at a real disadvantage when working within the legal system.

Since the early 1930s, courts have been required to provide poor people with free defense lawyers, if the accused person is at risk of going to jail. Some states also appoint lawyers for poor people who are not faced with jail—such as in child custody cases. Since the late 1800s, private organizations have provided free legal services to the poor. The federal government began providing legal services for the poor starting in 1965, through the Office of Economic Opportunity

(OEO), which was created by the Economic Opportunity Act of 1964. In 1973, the U.S. Congress passed a law to establish the Legal Services Corporation, to provide free legal services to the poor (Hershkoff and Loffredo 1997, 315–316, 320; Houseman and Perle 2007, iv–v).

The first short-lived government effort to provide legal aid to the needy was the Freedmen's Bureau, which was set up in 1865, to help the newly freed slaves. However, this federal bureau ended in 1869. The first private organization to provide legal services to the poor was the German Immigrants' Society, founded in 1876, in New York City. Private legal aid organizations spread across the country. The National Alliance of Legal Aid Societies was formed in 1911 (this later became the National Legal Aid and Defender Association). By 1965, there were 157 legal aid organizations—at least one in almost every major U.S. city. Some of these organizations were run by private lawyers, others were part of law schools, and some were funded by city governments. However, these legal aid services could not provide services to all those who needed it. Legal aid services probably reached only 1 percent of those in need (Houseman and Perle 2007, 3).

In the 1960s, advocates for the poor began promoting a new model for legal aid to the poor. Instead of simply helping the poor to navigate through existing laws, legal aid to the poor could actually be used to change those laws so they helped the poor, rather than punished the poor. The National Association for the Advancement of Colored People, which was founded in 1909, pioneered this form of legal advocacy on behalf of

African Americans. Their most famous victory was the racial desegregation of American public schools (Houseman and Perle 2007, 4–5).

As legal services advocates, Edgar and Jean Cahn wrote in an influential 1964 article in the *Yale Law Journal,*

> The assertion of a right in even a single case can have community-wide ramifications: police may begin to act more circumspectly; welfare workers may consult their regulations more regularly; credit companies may be slower to repossess articles or to sell them without affording proper opportunity for payment; and landlords may become prompter in making repairs. (Cahn and Cahn 1964, 1338)

In 1964, the Economic Opportunity Act created the OEO. This law aimed to eliminate poverty by providing federal funding for a wide variety of programs and projects. Although legal aid to the poor was not specifically mentioned in the law, Jean and Edgar Cahn persuaded the OEO to fund legal services for the poor. Because the Economic Opportunity Act emphasized that poor people should have a voice in how programs for the poor were run, the OEO required legal services organizations to include poor people on their boards of directors and required that offices be located in poor neighborhoods. The federal government made "law reform" a priority of these programs—in other words, reforming the law and addressing areas where the law hindered rather than helped the poor. The OEO also funded national and state support centers and training programs. By 1968, forty-nine states had legal services programs funded by the OEO (Houseman and Perle 2007, 7–12).

These legal services programs not only helped individual clients to gain their own legal rights in court but also helped the poor in general by winning important court cases that set precedents for how the poor should be treated. For example, legal services lawyers won court cases that ensured that welfare recipients could not be denied benefits arbitrarily. *King v. Smith,* a U.S. Supreme Court case decided in 1968, struck down the "substitute parent" rule that many states used to deny welfare benefits. That rule stated that if any man lived in the house—even a casual boyfriend who was not the father of the children—then the family could be denied benefits. The Supreme Court ruled that states could not deny benefits to eligible children just because of the mother's behavior.

Legal advocates also helped the poor by speaking on their behalf in front of the U.S. Congress and state legislatures. Legal advocates influenced laws creating or changing the Food Stamp Program, Supplemental Security Income, Special Supplemental Nutrition Program for Women, Infants and Children (WIC), and Medicaid, among others.

Lawyers have helped make sure the regulations and rules adopted by welfare offices and other poor-relief services were beneficial to the poor, and that government officials treated the poor with respect. For example, legal services programs helped ensure that police officers took seriously the complaints of women who suffered domestic violence and that these women were treated as criminal victims by police, instead of as partners in a domestic squabble (Houseman and Perle 2007, 13–14).

Over the years, some presidents and members of Congress have tried to cut

SUCCESS STORY FROM LEGAL SERVICES OF GREATER MIAMI

Katrina was struggling to get off welfare and gain employment at a stable job to support her two young children. However, because of the geographic size of Miami-Dade County, where she lives and works, she needed a reliable automobile to reduce her three-hour commute on public transportation and remain employed.

While Florida state law allowed welfare recipients in such a situation to purchase an automobile, there was no formal application form or procedure for Katrina to submit her request. Therefore, she asked her supportive services caseworker to provide her with an automobile. Following several months of waiting, her request was verbally denied.

Katrina then turned to Legal Services of Greater Miami (LSGMI), who agreed to find her transportation. LSGMI found that not only was there no application form or procedure, but there were also no policies or procedures to guarantee due process protections for people like Katrina. As a result, LSGMI filed an action in the Florida Third District Court of Appeals. Due to negotiations, Katrina eventually received $8,500 toward the purchase of an automobile, as allowed by law. Additionally, LSGMI assisted in developing an application process for others in Katrina's situation, which included standards to evaluate requests, and a detailed client-accessible grievance procedure.

Source: Legal Services Corporation. Client Success Stories. http://www.lsc.gov/about/clientstories.php (accessed September 2008).

funding for legal services to the poor, and even to end the program. Because of this, advocates for the poor soon realized that legal services needed to be separated from direct control by the president and politicians. In 1974, Congress passed and President Richard Nixon signed a bill to create the Legal Services Corporation (LSC), which is a private, nonprofit corporation. Its board of directors is appointed by the U.S. president and confirmed by the U.S. Senate, but the board members must be balanced between the two political parties.

LSC funds 138 legal programs with 900 offices across the country. Programs also receive funds from state and local governments, and private businesses and organizations. Seventy-five percent of

clients are women, and most are women with children. Almost 40 percent of LSC cases involve family issues such as domestic violence or child custody. Almost 25 percent of cases involve housing, such as preventing foreclosures or forcing landlords to make necessary repairs. In 2005, LSC conducted a two-month survey of people who came to legal aid offices for help, and found that, because of limited funding, legal programs for the poor were able to help only half of those who sought help and were eligible for aid (Legal Services Corporation Web site).

See also: Criminal Justice System and Poverty; Economic Opportunity Act of 1964; Food Stamp Program/Supplemental Nutrition Assistance Program; Freedmen's Bureau;

PRIMARY DOCUMENT 17

Excerpt from "The War on Poverty: A Civilian Perspective," by Edgar S. and Jean C. Cahn, *Yale Law Journal*, July 1964

III. IMPLEMENTING THE CIVILIAN PERSPECTIVE - A PROPOSAL FOR A NEIGHBORHOOD LAW FIRM

.... [T]here is a need for supplying impoverished communities the means with which to represent the felt needs of its members. The remainder of the article details a proposal for the establishment of one kind of institution - a university affiliated, neighborhood law firm - which could serve as a vehicle for the "civilian perspective" by placing at the disposal of a community the services of professional advocates and by providing the opportunity, the orientation, and the training experience to stimulate leadership amongst the community's present inhabitants.. . .

Thus there are at least four areas in which legal advocacy and legal analysis may prove useful in implementing the civilian perspective: traditional legal assistance in establishing or asserting clearly defined rights; legal analysis and representation directed toward reform where the law is vague or destructively complex; legal representation where the law appears contrary to the interests of the slum community; and legal representation in contexts which appear to be non-legal and where no judicially cognizable right can be asserted.

A. Traditional legal assistance in establishing or asserting clearly defined legal rights

The potential of extended legal services, including legal representation, legal education, and preventive counselling for the poor is only now coming to be appreciated. Effective legal representation for the indigent accused of a crime is but one part of this need; of equal importance for the poor are the assertion of rights in areas of the law involving landlord and tenant, installment purchase contracts, and domestic relations. Of still greater import for the poor is representation to insure the equitable and humane application of administrative rules and regulations under such programs as aid for dependent children, welfare, and unemployment compensation. The assertion of a right in even a single case can have community-wide ramifications: police may begin to act more circumspectly; welfare workers may consult their regulations more regularly; credit companies may be slower to repossess articles or to sell them without affording proper opportunity for payment; and landlords may become prompter in making repairs.. . .

The neighborhood law firm, if it is to affect the respect which members of a community are accorded, must not only assert rights; it must also create a widespread consciousness of such rights within the community. . . .

Of even more far-reaching import is the capacity of individuals acting in concert to create associations and binding legal obligations. This can take the form of an association of tenants, of recipients of welfare, of consumers whose purchases are bought through certain finance companies. It can even include the incorporation of a block, neighborhood, or community with retained "house counsel" to safeguard the interests of the community and to keep officials and private parties dealing with the community under continuous surveillance. Ultimately the power to create legal relationships is a form of political power—its utilization by slum communities is one way of revitalizing the democratic process. . . .

B. Legal analysis and representation directed toward reform where the law is vague, uncertain, or destructively complex

The poor live in a legal universe which has, by and large, been ignored by legal scholars. Low visibility decisions decide their destiny; official discretion determines their fate; and rights, even with lawyers to assert them, take a destructively long time to ascertain and vindicate. . . .

Here intervention and advocacy on behalf of the poor must be accompanied by extended scholarly considerations of the policies, alternatives, and costs involved. A neighborhood law firm concerned with this dimension of the law as it affects the poor should have some formal nexus with the academic world. The law, as experienced by one stratum of society, must be made known to legal scholars so that it can be scrutinized, so that knowledge of it can be disseminated through the law school curriculum and the evolution of what we might term "urban law" proceed rationally and at an accelerated pace.

C. Legal representation where the law appears contrary to the interests of the slum community

Here skillful representation can often mitigate the harsher effects of the law, can delay or nullify its operation, and on occasion can prompt reassessment and change.

In a society interlaced with governmental welfare and rehabilitative programs, much of the law encountered by slum dwellers is the rules of eligibility which entitle them to partake of the benefits of numerous governmental and quasi-governmental programs. Violation of or failure to fulfill such conditions operates to bar participation. Many of these rules not only work hardship but often operate to defeat the underlying purposes which the program was instituted to achieve.

Typical of these rules are those which deny benefits to families where an adult male capable of supporting the family is present, which prohibit participation in job retraining programs by persons with police records, and which call for the expulsion of families from low income projects if the families' income rises above a specified amount. The value of such rules, particularly when sporadically and punitively enforced, is certainly dubious. The "man in the house" rule, for example, creates a financial incentive for the break-up of low-income families, undermines the male ego attuned to our society's work ethic, and increases the likelihood of promiscuity, illegitimacy, evasion, and crime. Eviction from housing projects of families whose income has risen above a certain level imposes a sanction on upward mobility and operates to deprive the project community of those members who have roots there and who might provide leadership, stability, and role-models for their neighbors. Refusal to make job retraining available to persons with police records operates quantitatively to exclude much of the potential target population and qualitatively to bar precisely that group which has already manifested some alienation from the law and which is most likely to be in need of intensive vocational training and personal therapy.

Such rules are symptomatic of a failure to provide responsiveness to the conditions and needs of the groups purportedly served, and are indicative of the lack of leverage and articulateness possessed by such groups. Where the rule, statute, or regulation works a hardship, legal representation may be able to suspend or postpone its operation, permit a period of transition, and otherwise mitigate its hardship. . . . The effect of representation, however, can go beyond simply securing a delay in eviction from a housing project or a single exception to the rule barring persons with police records from a job retraining program. It may, for instance, result in an administrative qualification of the rule to the effect that eviction shall not be required until the city has discharged its obligation to relocate the family in suitable quarters, or lead to a construction of the eligibility requirement to the effect that juvenile offenses and misdemeanors do not constitute a "police record" within the meaning of the criteria.

Administrative power to classify and construe can be exercised in other creative ways. The family whose income is too high to continue living in a low income project may be eligible for a middle income project unit if one is available. Besides seeking to obtain a preferred position on the waiting list for vacancies, an attorney can also explore the possibility of having specific apartments in the low income housing project reclassified as apartments for middle income families. But until proposals for the use of unexercised powers are made by skilled advocates who know the desires and needs of the neighborhood and who can devise possible ways of implementing them, there is little likelihood that such possibilities will even be explored by officials. . . .

D. Legal representation in contexts which appear to be non-legal

Often we are blinded to the efficacy of legal representation as a potential route to a desired result because other modes of communication, organization, pressure, and protest suffice - at least for the middle class. The need for extensive pressure to force official compliance can often be significantly reduced by a legal determination of whether alleged fiscal or administrative barriers really exist. And in some situations the simple communication of legal authority for certain action may be sufficient to get officials to respond and to change a policy which inertia, timorousness, or lack of imagination appeared to have firmly ensconced.

Such representation may be of critical help in nurturing the growth of embryonic civic organizations in neighborhoods where apathy and defeatism prevail. It may prove virtually impossible in slum communities to mount a major extended campaign to persuade local officials to permit the community to use school facilities and recreational areas during summer months, evenings, or afternoon hours. Here legal representation can conceivably supplement local pressure in overcoming official reluctance to expend funds for lighting, janitorial services, and police protection against vandalism. Denial of access to such facilities for periods of time might arguably constitute a deviation from a plan submitted by a redevelopment agency to obtain federal funds where that plan committed the city to maintain minimal recreational and other community facilities and where that plan treated the school building and yard as partially fulfilling that commitment. While it by no means follows that such a commitment could be enforced by court action, the mere threat of publicity or litigation or consultation with federal officials may suffice. Or local officials may be quite willing to cooperate once presented with a theory to defend expenditures which they would otherwise have feared to make. . . .

Source

Cahn, Edgar S., and Jean C. Cahn. "The War on Poverty: A Civilian Perspective." *Yale Law Journal* 73, no. 8 (July 1964): 1317–1352.

Medicaid; National Association for the Advancement of Colored People; Special Supplemental Nutrition Program for Women, Infants and Children; Supreme Court and Poverty

Sources

Cahn, Edgar S., and Jean C. Cahn. "The War on Poverty: A Civilian Perspective." *Yale Law Journal* 73, no. 8 (July 1964): 1317–1352.

Hershkoff, Helen, and Stephen Loffredo. *The Rights of the Poor: The Authoritative ACLU Guide to Poor People's Rights.* Carbondale, IL: Southern Illinois University Press, 1997.

Houseman, Alan W., and Linda E. Perle. *Securing Equal Justice for All: A Brief History of Civil Legal Assistance in the United States.* Center for Law and Social Policy, 2007. www.clasp.org/publications/legal_aid_history_2007.pdf (accessed September 2008).

Web Site

Legal Services Corporation. http://www.lsc.gov/ (accessed September 2008).

Legal Services Corporation. Fact Sheet. http://www.lsc.gov/about/factsheet_whatislsc.php (accessed September 2008).

LIVING-WAGE LAWS

A living wage refers to a minimum wage that is high enough to allow a full-time worker to support a family and keep them out of poverty. Originally, the minimum-wage movement in the United States was a living-wage movement, designed to keep a family out of poverty. However, the first federal minimum-wage law that managed to pass Congress, the Fair Labor Standards Act of 1938, specified a minimum wage of only $0.25 per hour, which was not enough to support a family, according to government studies. And although the national minimum wage has risen significantly over the years, since 1968, the real dollar value of the federal minimum wage has fallen so that, as of 2007, the national minimum wage would not keep even a family of two above the federal poverty line.

In response to the falling value of the federal minimum wage, many states have passed higher minimum wages. There have also been movements in cities and counties to pass laws mandating a true living wage. The modern living-wage movement started in Baltimore, Maryland, in 1995, with the passage of a law requiring companies providing services to the city government to pay their employees a wage of $6.10 per hour starting in 1996 (at that time, the national minimum wage was $4.75 per hour). In other words, any business that is paid by the city government to provide services to the city has to pay this living wage. Starting in 1999, the Baltimore wage has risen each year to keep pace with inflation. As of 1999, the Baltimore living wage was enough to keep one full-time worker with one child above the poverty line, but it was about 10 percent less than needed to keep a family of four above the poverty line. The law had a limited affect on the overall wages of the city, because less than 1,000 workers were affected by the initial wage increase (Pollin and Luce 1998, 2–3, 46–47, 51).

The living-wage movement took off after the success of the Baltimore campaign. By 1998, twelve other cities had passed similar living-wage laws and, as of 2008, according to the Living Wage Resource Center Web site, a total of 140 similar living-wage ordinances have passed in cities and counties across the country. The idea behind these laws is that businesses that benefit from public funds must pay their employees enough to keep those employees above the poverty line. "Our limited public dollars should not be subsidizing poverty-wage work," says the Living Wage Resource Center's Web site. "When subsidized employers are allowed to pay their workers less than a living wage, tax payers end up footing a double bill: the initial subsidy and then the food stamps, emergency medical, housing and other social services low wage workers may require to support themselves and their families even minimally."

While most cities limit their living-wage laws only to those companies that have contracts with the government, or that receive government tax credits, a handful of cities have passed living-wage laws for almost all employees within the city. Santa Fe, New Mexico, passed a law in 2003, requiring every business in the city with at least twenty-five employees to pay $8.50 per hour. This wage increased $1 every two years until 2008, when it began to keep pace with inflation. Other cities with citywide minimum wages that are higher than the federal minimum wage include Washington, D.C.; San Francisco, California; and Albuquerque, New Mexico (Gertner 2006; Living Wage Resource Center Web site).

A relatively small number of workers have benefited from the living-wage laws—less than 250,000 as of 2002, according to estimates. And in some cases, living-wage ordinances are not strongly enforced. Nevertheless, these kinds of laws are important because they send the message that it is immoral and unjust to pay an employee less than is needed to stay above the poverty line. As Jon Gertner points out, living-wage supporters ask, "should an employer be allowed to pay a full-time employee $5.15 an hour ... if that's no longer enough to live on? Is it just under our system of government?" The local laws are examples and models for the ultimate goal of a significant increase in the federal minimum wage, preferably one that keeps pace with inflation, so lawmakers do not have to fight minimum-wage battles over and over again. Cities with living-wage laws are like "economic laboratories" to test the feasibility and impact of a minimum wage that actually keeps families out of poverty (Luce 2004, 53, 76; Gertner 2006).

See also: Fair Labor Standards Act of 1938; Minimum-Wage Laws; Poverty Line

Sources

Gertner, John. "What Is a Living Wage?" *New York Times Magazine,* January 15, 2006. http://www.nytimes.com/2006/01/15/magazine/15wage.html?_r=1&oref=slogin (accessed April 2008).

Luce, Stephanie. *Fighting for a Living Wage.* Ithaca, NY: Cornell University Press, 2004.

Pollin, Robert, and Stephanie Luce. *The Living Wage: Building a Fair Economy.* New York: The New Press, 1998.

Web Site

Living Wage Resource Center http://www.livingwagecampaign.org/ (accessed April 2008).

LONG, HUEY (1893–1935)

Huey Long was an influential U.S. Senator from Louisiana during the Great Depression. He created and promoted the "Share Our Wealth" program to

Louisiana senator Huey Long (1932–1935) was a flamboyant orator and referred to himself as the "Kingfish." (Library of Congress)

radically redistribute wealth in the nation as a way to end poverty. Although his plan was considered unworkable by many experts, the popularity of his ideas helped push President Franklin Roosevelt to enact more programs to redistribute wealth and help the poor.

Huey Pierce Long was born on August 30, 1893, in Winn Parish, one of the poorer counties of Louisiana. His family was well-off, however, and by the time Long was in high school, they lived in one of the largest houses in the county. Long dropped out of high school in 1910, and for the next four years worked as a door-to-door salesman. He attended law school at Tulane for a year and passed the bar exam in 1915, after which time he moved back to his hometown of Winnfield to practice law.

Long wanted to get involved with politics, but was too young to run for most offices. In 1918, he discovered that the Railroad Commission had no minimum age for its commissioners. He ran, won, and became a commissioner at the age of twenty-five. The Commission was in charge of not only railroads, but also telephone companies and other utilities. Long worked to lower utility rates and improve service. He also called for heavier taxes on corporations. In 1924, he ran for governor and lost that year, but he won four years later.

As governor, he pushed through laws to provide help to the poor and improve Louisiana's economy: free textbooks for students, paved highways, and low-cost natural gas for New Orleans. He increased taxes on wealthy oil and gas companies. He expanded public-health facilities, improved treatment of the mentally ill, and founded a medical school. He began night schools for illiterate adults. "Louisiana's legislature before Long moved at the pace of a snail," according to biographer Glen Jeansonne. "Under Long, it became hyperactive" (1993, 6; also see Brinkley 1983, 30–31).

At the same time, Long was working to consolidate his power in Louisiana by providing jobs and favors to more people. He instituted a system of deducting 5 to 10 percent from state employees' salaries to pay for publicity for his own programs and to reward his friends. Employees who refused to pay were fired. "Patronage—the giving and taking away of jobs—remained the cornerstone of the Long machine," explains biographer Alan Brinkley (1983, 26; White 2006, 91).

Long ran for and won a seat in the U.S. Senate in 1930, just after the start of the Great Depression. In the Senate, Long began speaking about the idea of redistributing the country's wealth. When Franklin Roosevelt was elected president in 1932, Long supported him at first. He soon complained, however, that Roosevelt's first proposals to lift the country out of the Great Depression were too conservative and too favorable to the wealthy. Long introduced three bills that limited the personal incomes and private fortunes of the wealthy, and he began speaking on the radio about the idea of wealth redistribution. Roosevelt began receiving letters from around the country, asking him to support Long's legislation (Brinkley 1983, 59–64; Jeansonne 1993, 112–113).

Long aimed to run for president in 1936, and as such, he cultivated a national audience. He started a national newspaper called *American Progress,* which he mailed for free to hundreds of thousands of people. In February 1934, Long started an organization called the Share Our Wealth Society and invited people around the country to form local clubs. Long's plan called for confiscating income above $1 million and wealth in excess of $5 million. This money would be used to provide every family with a house, car, radio, and an annual income of $2,500. Long also proposed to guarantee a job for every American, give old-age pensions, institute a thirty-hour work week, and provide a free college education to anyone who passed entrance examinations. By the end of the year, the organization had 3 million members, and by the spring of 1935, 7.5 million members. Long was receiving more mail than all the other senators combined (Brinkley 1983, 70–71; Jeansonne 1993, 114–117).

Long's plan was one of several popular plans that aimed to go farther than Roosevelt's New Deal programs. The Townsend Movement, which called for old-age pensions, and Father Charles Coughlin, a Catholic priest who spoke about monetary reform, were popular as well.

Critics charged that Long's plan was unrealistic, that there were simply not enough millionaires in the country to provide all the benefits Long proposed. However, Long did not seem disturbed by the impracticality of his plan. He told a reporter that his plan was just a way to attract votes (Jeansonne 1993, 123–125).

Although Long's plan was not practical, it was popular, and perhaps in response to this, President Roosevelt introduced legislation to greatly expand federal help to the needy. Roosevelt confessed that he felt the need to "steal Long's thunder" (quoted in Jeansonne 1993, 163). The Social Security Act of 1935 provided old-age pensions and money to single mothers. The National Labor Relations Act legalized labor unions. The Works Progress Administration, the largest public-works project of the New Deal, was proposed by Roosevelt in 1935. Roosevelt also proposed the Wealth Tax Act to redistribute wealth. The bill that finally passed increased the tax rate on the highest individual incomes to 75 percent, although many other provisions had been removed, and the bill no longer did much to redistribute wealth. Still, these new laws and programs proved popular, and many of Long's supporters turned their support toward the president (Brinkley 1983, 246–247; Davis 1986, 544–548).

Long was assassinated on September 8, 1935, and his influence on national politics ended.

See also: Coughlin, Charles; Great Depression; New Deal; Roosevelt, Franklin Delano; Townsend Movement; Works Progress Administration

Sources

Brinkley, Alan. *Voices of Protest: Huey Long, Father Coughlin, and the Great Depression.* New York: Vintage Books, 1983.

Davis, Kenneth S. *FDR: The New Deal Years, 1933–1937.* New York: Random House, 1986.

Jeansonne, Glen. *Messiah of the Masses: Huey P. Long and the Great Depression.* New York: HarperCollins College Publishers, 1993.

White, Richard D., Jr. *Kingfish: The Reign of Huey P. Long.* New York: Random House, 2006.

LOWELL, JOSEPHINE SHAW (1843–1905)

Josephine Shaw Lowell was one of the most prominent and respected charity organizers of the late 1800s. She was a leader of the "scientific charity" movement, which sought to bring objectivity, organization, and investigation to poverty relief. She was the first woman in New York to be appointed to an official state position, as a State Board of Charities commissioner, and she helped found the New York Consumers League to bring consumer pressure to bear on inhumane working conditions. While she started her career with typical Victorian attitudes toward the poor—that is, that poverty was caused by moral failings such as laziness—her open mind and willingness to learn led her to new ideas and solutions to the problem of poverty.

Josephine Shaw was born on December 16, 1843, in Roxbury, Massachusetts, and soon moved with her family to Staten Island, New York. Her father was a wealthy gentleman farmer, and both her parents were abolitionists (they worked to end slavery). She was educated at private girls' schools in New York City and Boston. She and her sisters were not expected to attend college. She supported the Civil War effort by volunteering for the Women's Central Organization in New York City, coordinating and sending donations to the soldiers. In late 1863, she married a soldier, Charles Lowell. About ten months later, her husband was killed in battle.

Lowell gave birth to her only child, a daughter, about a month after her husband's death. She relied on nannies and her parents to help her care for the child. In 1866, she became active in the New York branch of the American Freedmen's Union Commission, a group of private charities that raised money for schools and teachers for the newly freed slaves. Lowell interviewed and hired teachers, and traveled to Virginia to visit schools.

In 1873, she began volunteering with a friend's new organization, the State Charities Aid Association (SCAA), which was designed along the principles of "scientific charity." The SCAA set up volunteer committees to visit poorhouses throughout the state of New York. Lowell not only visited poorhouses, but also wrote reports and made recommendations to state authorities. She wanted charity relief to be well organized and efficient. She recommended that the state remove the mentally ill from poorhouses and place them in separate institutions, that the able-bodied be put to work, and that prisoners be given vocational training.

In 1876, as a result of her impressive work with the SCAA, the New York State Board of Charities appointed her as one of its commissioners. As a member of the State Board of Charities, Lowell attacked another public menace: the corruption of city government that wasted money on poverty relief and did not actually reform the poor. She wanted poor relief in the city to be honest and organized, and above all to care for the public welfare, instead of being concerned mostly with political gain. She was concerned with the plight of women prisoners. In 1881, she submitted a bill to the New York legislature to fund and build separate prisons for women, to ensure their safety and help them reform. The bill finally passed in 1884.

In 1882, she started her own organization, the Charity Organization Society (COS) of New York City. Its goal was to follow "scientific charity" principles to organize and coordinate the private relief efforts throughout the city, and also to offer moral uplift to the poor. Hers was not the first COS in the United States—that had been started in 1877, in Buffalo—but Lowell's COS was located in the largest city of the United States.

In 1884, she wrote a book to publicize her principles, *Public Relief and Private Charity*. She believed that the government in general should not provide "outdoor relief," or aid to the poor in their own homes. The government should confine its help to institutions, such as poorhouses and orphanages, which should be run efficiently and honestly. Private relief should help the needy who are not in institutions, and private relief also should provide moral guidance to the poor, through well-off "friendly visitors." Her book, speeches, and articles were influential in the field of scientific charity.

At the same time, she was studying the causes of poverty. She read a popular book by Henry George, *Progress and Poverty,* which advocated a "single tax" on land only as a remedy for economic inequality. She corresponded with leaders of the labor movement.

Despite her interest in the roots of economic inequality, she continued to view pauperism in a harsh light. In the late 1880s and 1890s, she led campaigns to end the practice of providing free lodging for tramps (unemployed men traveling in search of work) in police stations and other city buildings. Her organization hired a special agent who was empowered by the city to arrest beggars. Her attitude toward the poor was so stern that critics charged that her COS was an "organization for the prevention of charity" (quoted in Waugh 1997, 163).

Ironically, although she preached that COSs ought not to dispense relief themselves, but simply should refer the needy to the appropriate private agency, she often gave freely to the poor who visited her office and told her their stories. She funded salaries for women staff members of the women's prisons she had helped to set up (Waugh 1997, 170).

By the late 1880s and early 1890s, she became more aware of low wages and unemployment as causes of poverty. She often hired working-class women as paid agents for her organization, and she struggled with the wealthy, male leaders of her COS to be able to pay these agents a fair wage. She wrote articles defending the right of workers to hold strikes. She became advisor to the Working Women's Society of New York, which investigated the conditions of work in department stores and, in 1891, she set up the Consumers League of the City of New York, with herself as its first president. In response to the depression of 1893, which caused about 20 percent of American workers to become unemployed, Lowell formed the East Side Relief-Work Committee, a temporary organization to offer jobs to the unemployed.

See also: Freedmen's Bureau; George, Henry; National Consumers League; Outdoor Relief; Scientific Charity

Source

Waugh, Joan. *Unsentimental Reformer: The Life of Josephine Shaw Lowell.* Cambridge, MA: Harvard University Press, 1997.

M

MANN, HORACE
(1796–1859)

Horace Mann has been called the "father of the American public school" (Morgan 1936, 3). In the early 1800s, as the head of the first state board of education in the United States, he pushed Massachusetts to improve the quality of teachers and schools. His belief in the importance of schooling for all influenced schools across the country. He believed a good education should be accessible to everyone—not just to those with the money to pay school tuition.

Horace Mann was born in Franklin, Massachusetts, on May 4, 1796. His parents owned a small farm. During the winters, Horace attended a one-room schoolhouse with a leaking roof. He and his family also braided straw for hats and sold these to a nearby hat factory. At the age of twenty, he entered Brown University and graduated in 1819, at the top of his class. He found work as a legal apprentice, but within a year he was back at Brown, this time as an instructor. In 1822, he started law school in Litchfield, Connecticut, and in 1823, began practicing law in Dedham, Massachusetts.

In 1827, Mann was elected a representative to the Massachusetts General Court (House of Representatives), where he served until 1833. Mann worked on the issue of humane care for the insane, who were often housed in filthy, unhealthy surroundings. He managed to push through a law in 1830, to build a state hospital for the insane. He was elected to the Massachusetts Senate in 1833. He advocated for more government money for schools—he believed that all children should have the opportunity for education. "My creed is that God made of one blood all children of men, and that circumstances have caused the diversities among them," he said in a speech to the Senate (quoted in Messerli 1972, 226). However, he was not successful at

In 1837, Horace Mann abandoned a successful law practice and promising political career to become the first secretary of Massachusetts' new state board of education. He then set out to reform the public school system in Massachusetts; eventually, it became a model for the rest of the United States. (Library of Congress)

convincing the other Senators to spend more money on education.

In 1837, he accepted an appointment as secretary of the Massachusetts Board of Education, the country's first state board of education. The board of education was to study the schools and make recommendations for improvement. Mann decided to devote all his time to his new job, and to give up his law practice. Some friends were baffled as to why he would give up a successful career as a state senator and a lucrative law practice to accept such a powerless position, but Mann was enthusiastic about the possibilities of the new job. In his journal he wrote, "Henceforth, so long as I hold this office, I devote myself to the supreme welfare of mankind on earth" (quoted in Morgan 1936, 13).

Mann rode a horse all over Massachusetts, inspecting schools and giving speeches to groups of parents, teachers, and interested citizens. He stressed that education was necessary for a democratic government; and that education had the potential to equalize differences in wealth and social class. He encouraged local people to form organizations for the improvement of the "common schools," as the county elementary schools were called. After his horseback tour, Mann wrote the first of twelve annual reports for the school board. Mann's annual reports were read widely, and over the years, they influenced states and schools across the country (Morgan 1936, 37).

In Mann's first report, he detailed the fact that Massachusetts schools were of uneven quality. While most Massachusetts schools at that time were supported by taxes, and so were free to students, if a town ran short of money it would simply shorten the school term to as little as four weeks per year. In towns with inadequate schools, well-off parents chose to send their children to private schools. Parents usually had to provide the books, so students in the same school studied from different books. School buildings were often too small and badly ventilated (Messerli 1972, 263–275, 285–292).

Mann began speaking to members of the Massachusetts legislature and proposed new laws regarding many school details, such as textbook purchases and schoolhouse repairs. In 1838, the legislature approved money for teacher training. In July 1839, the first teacher training school in the country was opened in Lexington, Massachusetts.

The idea behind these schools was to establish teaching "norms," and so they were called "normal" schools. He started a magazine called the *Common School Journal,* and in 1840, began a speaking tour across the eastern states.

In 1943, he toured schools in Europe and learned about modern methods of education. He was especially impressed with the education system of Prussia (now part of Germany). In his seventh annual report, he recommended changes to the Massachusetts school system to conform more with the Prussian system, such as professionally trained teachers, standardized curriculum, and centralized supervision of schools. A group of Boston schoolmasters became incensed at this report and put out a report of their own, attacking Mann's recommendations. Mann then issued a "Reply" to the Boston schoolmasters. The publicity resulting from this fight helped focus the public's attention on the issue of education. Incompetent teachers were replaced and corporal punishment, which had been widespread in schools, was reduced, although it was still legal (Morgan 1936, 23–24; Messerli 1972, 416–421).

Meanwhile, more normal schools were opening throughout the state. In 1846, Mann proposed two-week training institutes for people already working as teachers, and the Massachusetts legislature provided funding for these. As a result of Mann's work, government money for Massachusetts public schools doubled, and teacher wages increased by more than 50 percent. Public schools were in session on average for one month longer (Morgan 1936, 35).

Mann was elected to the U.S. House of Representatives in 1848, where he was active in the antislavery cause. In 1852, Mann was appointed president of Antioch College, a new college in Ohio.

See also: Mental Illness and Poverty; Public Schools

Sources
Messerli, Jonathan. *Horace Mann: A Biography.* New York: Alfred A. Knopf, 1972.
Morgan, Joy Elmer. *Horace Mann: His Ideas and Ideals.* Washington, DC: National Home Library Foundation, 1936.

MANPOWER DEVELOPMENT AND TRAINING ACT OF 1962

The Manpower Development and Training Act (MDTA) provided federal funds to help unemployed workers retrain for a new job. When this law was signed by President John F. Kennedy, he called it "perhaps the most significant legislation in the area of employment since the Employment Act of 1946" (quoted in Woolley and Peters n.d.).

The MDTA was passed in response to automation in American factories during the 1950s, which meant that factories needed fewer employees, as well as employees with different skills. Businesses were investing some money in retraining, but not enough. Starting in 1952, some states began funding retraining programs for the unemployed. Pennsylvania was the first; however, states did not have enough money to retrain everyone in need (Kremen 1974).

By 1961, the unemployment rate was 7 percent. Some economists feared that, unless they were retrained, some of the unemployed would never again be able to find work. In 1961, the MDTA was introduced into Congress, and it passed in March 1962. Under this law, the Department of Labor was in charge of planning and coordinating training programs, establishing standards, and deciding who could participate. Training programs could last up to one year. Heads of families were provided with an allowance so they could support their families during the training period (Kremen 1974; Ginzberg 1980, p 4).

The MDTA was in place from 1963 to 1974. Very soon, it became apparent that the law would need to target not the recently unemployed, but those who were hard to employ. "The problem was the bottom of the labor barrel, not the top," said an assistant secretary at the Department of Labor (quoted in Mucciaroni 1990, 60). The MDTA thus began to be seen more as a poverty program, than as a labor program. The training was being offered not because it was necessarily good for the economy, but because it was definitely good for the unemployed (Mucciaroni 1990, 60–61).

The MDTA offered both classroom training and on-the-job training. At first, married white men were the main targets of the MDTA—because it was assumed they were the heads of families and needed to support their families. Soon, however, the MDTA also began targeting young African American men. Women also received some training through the MDTA: they accounted for 45 percent of participants in classroom training, and 30 percent of participants in on-the-job training. Women tended to be trained for clerical work and tended not to be trained for technical work (Rose 1995, 79–80).

From 1963 to 1974, an average of 126,000 people participated in the MDTA each year. MDTA was successful in placing its graduates in jobs. About 70 percent of participants obtained jobs for which they had been trained, and the MDTA dropout rate was less than the high school dropout rate. The taxes paid by those employed after the MDTA training repaid the cost of this training within five years (Franklin and Ripley 1984, 8–9; Mucciaroni 1990, 11).

Still, the MDTA had its opponents. Some people objected to the fact that the program was too centralized—too controlled by the federal government. Others complained that it was too expensive. In 1974, the MDTA was replaced by the Comprehensive Educational and Training Act. This Act called for programs that were more decentralized than the MDTA—it provided federal funding, but allowed communities to plan their own training programs (Ginzberg 1980, 6–7).

See also: Comprehensive Employment and Training Act; Full Employment; Public Works Projects

Sources

Franklin, Grace A., and Randall B. Ripley. *CETA: Politics and Policy, 1973–1982.* Knoxville, TN: University of Tennessee Press, 1984.

Ginzberg, Eli, ed. *Employing the Unemployed.* New York: Basic Books, 1980.

Kremen, Gladys Roth. "MDTA: the Origins of the Manpower Development and Training Act of 1962." U.S. Department of Labor, 1974. http://www.dol.gov/oasam/programs/history/mono-mdtatext.htm (accessed September 2008).

Mucciaroni, Gary. *The Political Failure of Employment Policy, 1945–1982.*

Pittsburgh, PA: University of Pittsburgh Press, 1990.

Rose, Nancy E. *Workfare or Fair Work: Women, Welfare and Government Work Programs.* New Brunswick, NJ: Rutgers University Press, 1995.

Woolley, John T., and Gerhard Peters. *The American Presidency Project* [online]. Santa Barbara, CA: University of California (hosted), Gerhard Peters (database), n.d. http://www.presidency.ucsb.edu/ws/?pid=9106 (accessed September 2008).

MATERNAL AND CHILD HEALTH SERVICES

The Maternal and Child Health Services program was established in 1935 by Title V of the Social Security Act. According to the Maternal and Child Health Bureau, Title V is the nation's longest-lasting public health legislation. It is also one of the nation's largest federal block grant programs. A block grant is a federal grant given to the states with limited requirements as to how the money should be used (*Title V: A Snapshot of Maternal and Child Health* 2000, 23; Maternal and Child Health Bureau Web site).

While it aims to serve the poor, the Maternal and Child Health Services program is different from Medicaid, which provides health insurance directly to poor individuals. In contrast, the funds through Title V are provided to the medical service suppliers (such as clinics, and state and local health departments). Rural areas and poor areas of the country are targeted. Within those areas, services are provided free of charge to everyone, regardless of income (Davis and Schoen 1978, 120–121).

The Maternal and Child Health Services program grew out of the Sheppard-Towner Maternity and Infancy Act of 1921, which for eight years set up clinics around the country for pregnant women and young children. Funding for this program expired in 1929, just as the Great Depression was starting. Advocates for poor women and children managed to ensure that the Social Security Act of 1935 included provisions for maternal and child health (Davis and Schoen 1978, 122).

State governments must match federal Title V money—they must provide $3 in funds or resources for every $4 in federal money that they receive. The purpose of the maternal and child health services money is to reduce infant mortality and birth defects; to provide comprehensive health care to women; to provide immunizations, health screenings, and other preventive and primary care services for children, including children with special health care needs; to reduce adolescent pregnancy; and to prevent injuries and violence to children. The Maternal and Child Health Bureau also manages other federal health programs, including Healthy Start, which targets communities with high infant mortality rates. As of 2009, the Maternal and Child Health Bureau served more than 34 million women and children a year (Maternal and Child Health Bureau Web site).

Each state operates its Maternal and Child Health Services programs differently. To find people who need help, outreach workers funded by Title V might be sent out to canvas neighborhoods and ask about mothers and children with health care needs. An outreach worker might first visit a

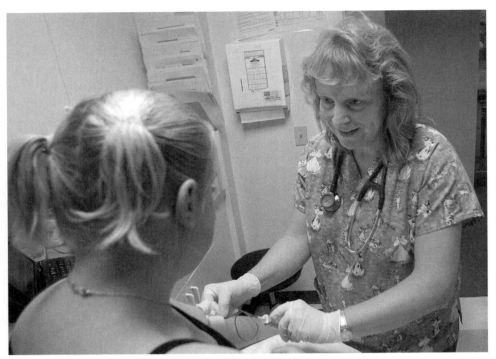

A healthcare worker gets blood samples from a young patient at the Avis Goodwin Community Health Center in Rochester, New Hampshire, in June 2005. (AP/Wide World Photos)

woman in her own home. Women are informed about the nearest health clinic and the services it can provide, and are encouraged to make an appointment. In addition to health services, poor women might also receive information about Medicaid, food stamps, education programs about nutrition and parenting, and employment services (*Title V: A Snapshot of Maternal and Child Health* 2000, 20–22).

In addition to general grants to states, Title V also provides money for "special projects of regional and national significance" (SPRANS). In 1997, SPRANS grants were used, for example, to help children with sickle-cell disease and hemophilia; to provide care for rural children with special

health needs; to set up genetic clinics for Spanish speakers; to identify and provide help to substance-abusing parents; and to build and maintain the self-esteem, health, and career aspirations of girls (*Title V: A Snapshot of Maternal and Child Health* 2000, 6–7, 31–270).

Title V is helping to improve the health of poor women and children. As of 1998, the infant mortality rate (the number of infants who died before their first birthday) in the United States was 7.2 per 1,000 live births, compared with sixty-eight per 1,000 in 1929, when the Sheppard-Towner Maternity and Infancy Act ended, and twenty-five per 1,000 as of 1961. While this is a positive trend, the Maternal and Child

Health Bureau points out that the 1998 figure is still higher than the infant mortality rate in many other wealthy countries. Also as of 1998, 79 percent of children nationwide between the ages of nineteen and thirty-five months were immunized against nine diseases; and 83 percent of infants nationwide were born to mothers who had received prenatal care in the first trimester (Davis and Schoen 1978, 148; *Title V: A Snapshot of Maternal and Child Health* 2000, 13–17).

See also: Children's Bureau; Great Depression; Medicaid; Medicare; Sheppard-Towner Maternity and Infancy Act of 1921; Social Security Act

Sources

Davis, Karen, and Cathy Schoen. *Health and the War on Poverty: A Ten-Year Appraisal.* Washington, DC: The Brookings Institution, 1978.

Title V: A Snapshot of Maternal and Child Health, 2000. Rockville, MD: Maternal and Child Health Bureau, December 2000. http://mchb.hrsa.gov/programs/blockgrant/ snapshot2000.htm (accessed July 2008).

Web Site

Maternal and Child Health Bureau. http:// mchb.hrsa.gov/ (accessed July 2008).

MCKINNEY-VENTO HOMELESS ASSISTANCE ACT

The McKinney-Vento Homeless Assistance Act, also called the Steward B. McKinney Homeless Assistance Act, provides federal funds to help the homeless. It was passed in 1987, in response to the growing number of homeless individuals and families during the 1980s.

When more people began to suffer from homelessness in the early 1980s, local governments, churches, and non-profit agencies were the first to respond by providing more homeless shelters and emergency food programs such as food pantries and soup kitchens. At that time, President Ronald Reagan and others within the federal government did not believe that homelessness was a problem with which the national government needed to get involved. In 1983, the National Governors' Association released a report arguing that the problem of homelessness was too large and widespread for the state governments to handle, and asking the national government to get involved.

In 1983, Congress appropriated $140 million in federal funds to help provide emergency food and shelter to the homeless. These funds were provided as part of existing disaster relief programs—no new law was passed to help the homeless at that time. In 1984, Congress appropriated an additional $70 million for homeless relief.

By 1985, many members of Congress were starting to realize that the federal government needed to pay more attention to the issue of homelessness. In that year, thirty-two separate bills to help the homeless were introduced. Some members of Congress decided to combine these bills into one, which was introduced into Congress in 1986. The American public had also become aware of the problem of homelessness: millions participated in Hands Across America in May 1986, to raise money for hungry and homeless people. Parts of the homeless bill were passed in October 1986. One law made it easier for homeless people to participate in existing aid programs such as Supplemental Security Income, food stamps, and Aid to (Families with) Dependent Children. (Previously, these programs had required people to have a permanent address to participate). Another law provided federal funds for emergency homeless shelters and transitional housing. In 1987, a larger bill to help the homeless was passed and named after Stewart B. McKinney, the main Republican sponsor of the bill, who died that year from AIDS (Foscarinis 1996, 160–161; Watson 1996, 172; Wright, Rubin, and Devine 1998, 1–2).

The McKinney Act provided up to $1 billion in 1987 and 1988 for emergency food and shelters, transitional housing, health care (including care for the mentally-ill homeless, and drug and alcohol treatment programs), job training, and other services for the homeless. Funding could be used to prevent homelessness by providing rental assistance and to build or renovate permanent low-income housing in the form of "single-room occupancy" units— essentially, small studio apartments. For homeless people with mental or physical disabilities, funding could be used to establish permanent housing that included supportive services. One section of the law made available unused or underused buildings and land owned by the federal government. State and local governments and private nonprofit organizations could use these buildings and land at no cost to help the homeless. The law specified that public schools and state education authorities had to ensure that homeless children received an education.

For many years, funding for the Homeless Assistance Act grew until it reached a high of $1.49 billion in 1995. Since then, funding has declined by 28 percent, and some programs have been eliminated, such as job training for the homeless, and adult literacy and education programs. In 2000, the law was renamed the McKinney-Vento Homeless Assistance Act after Representative Bruce Vento, a longtime supporter of the law who died that year. From 2001 to 2005, funding was dramatically increased to make sure homeless children had access to public schooling ("McKinney-Vento Act" 2008).

While the McKinney-Vento Act has helped state and local governments and private nonprofit organizations to more effectively help homeless people, the main problem with the law is that it targets most of its efforts toward emergency measures—that is, its helps people after they have already become homeless, rather than trying to prevent people from becoming homeless in the first place. According to the National Coalition for the Homeless, a nonprofit organization dedicated to ending homelessness, "The McKinney-Vento Act was intended as a first step toward resolving homelessness; in the absence of legislation containing farther-reaching measures, homelessness can only be expected to increase" ("McKinney-Vento Act" 2008).

See also: Aid to (Families with) Dependent Children; Emergency Food Programs; Food Stamp Program/Supplemental Nutrition Assistance Program; Homelessness; Homeless Shelters; Housing, Low-Income; Supplemental Security Income

Sources
Foscarinis, Maria. "The Federal Response: The Stewart B. McKinney Homeless Assistance Act." In *Homelessness in*

America, ed. Jim Baumohl, 160–171. Phoenix, AZ: Oryx Press, 1996.

"McKinney-Vento Act." National Coalition for the Homeless Fact Sheet No. 18, June 2008. http://www.nationalhomeless.org/publications/facts.html (accessed September 2008).

Watson, Vicki. "Responses by the States to Homelessness." In *Homelessness in America,* ed. Jim Baumohl, 172–178. Phoenix, AZ: Oryx Press, 1996.

Wright, James D., Beth A. Rubin, and Joel A. Devine. *Beside the Golden Door: Policy, Politics and the Homeless.* New York: Aldine de Gruyter, 1998.

MEDICAID

Medicaid is a government-funded health insurance program for the poor that started in 1965, as part of President Lyndon Johnson's Great Society initiative. It was added, along with Medicare (health insurance for the elderly), as an amendment to the Social Security Act.

The federal government first got involved with health care for the needy when it began providing health care to the poor under the Sheppard-Towner Maternity and Infancy Act of 1921, which set up 3,000 clinics across the country for poor women and children. Funding for this program expired in 1929, and in 1935, the Social Security Act included funding for a similar program of health clinics: Maternal and Child Health Services. However, poor people who lived far from these clinics still had to struggle to pay for health care and still could not afford hospitalization. By 1965, the federal government was providing health care to the poor through Head Start preschool children, Cuban refugees, migrant farmworkers, and people who lived in the poor regions of the Appalachian Mountains (David 1985, 54–55; Andrew 1998, 96; Engel 2006, 31–37).

In 1964, President Lyndon Johnson set up a panel of health care experts that revealed that many Americans could not afford basic medical care. A number of different health insurance bills were proposed, emphasizing health care for the elderly. The Medicare plan passed in July 1965. Title XIX of this law created Medicaid, which provided medical care to poor children who did not have support from their parents, and those children's caretakers, as well as to the blind, people with disabilities, and poor elderly people who could not afford to pay Medicare's co-payments. The original Medicaid program provided federal money to states if they wished to create a Medicaid program, but states did not have to do so. In addition, Medicaid excluded families with working fathers, even if the family's income was below the poverty line. Advocates for children pointed out that because Medicaid's requirements were so strict, many families still would not be able to afford basic health care for their children (Engel 2006, 48–51).

By 1972, all states had set up Medicaid programs. Over the years, Medicaid has been expanded to include more people. In 1986, pregnant poor women and infants under one year became eligible for Medicaid, if their states chose to offer this program. In 1987, states were allowed to cover women and infants with incomes of up to 185 percent of the federal poverty line. In 1989, states were required to cover poor pregnant women below 133 percent of the poverty line and children under six years old. Young people between six and eighteen who lived

President Lyndon B. Johnson signs the Medicare program into law on July 30, 1965. On the right is former president Harry Truman, who became the first person to apply for the federal health care program. (Lyndon B. Johnson Library)

below the poverty line became eligible for Medicaid starting in 1990. In 1994, the federal government passed the Vaccines for Children program, which provides free childhood vaccines (Gruber 2003, 17–19). States are required to include the Vaccines for Children program in their state Medicaid plan.

According to Jonathan Gruber, Medicaid is really "four public insurance programs in one." Medicaid offers insurance for four different populations: poor women and children; poor elderly (for health care expenses not covered by Medicare); poor people who are disabled; and poor elderly people who are in nursing homes (2003, 15–16).

Until 1996, Medicaid was linked to Aid to (Families with) Dependent Children (AFDC): when families stopped receiving AFDC payments, they also automatically stopped being eligible for Medicaid. This discouraged low-income families from seeking jobs, because the jobs they were likely to get were low paid and usually did not offer health insurance. So by opting for a job, a family might have found itself worse off financially. When AFDC was replaced with Temporary Assistance to Needy Families (TANF) in 1996, families still could be eligible for Medicaid even if they did not receive TANF payments (CMS, "Key Milestones in CMS Programs").

In 1997, the State Children's Health Insurance Program (SCHIP) was created to offer health care to children whose families had a low income but were not poor enough to be eligible for Medicaid. This program provides coverage to children whose families have an income of up to 200 percent of the federal poverty line. Some states have chosen to cover entire families and not just the children in those families. According to the SCHIP Web site, this program is "the single largest expansion of health insurance coverage for children since the initiation of Medicaid in the mid-1960s" (State Children's Health Insurance Program Web site).

Medicaid has helped the poor to live healthier lives. According to Jonathan Engel, "poor people are in better health today, and receive better health care, than had Medicaid not been created" (2006, 249). Still, Engel points out that because some doctors and hospitals refuse to take Medicaid patients (because Medicaid generally pays lower fees to doctors and hospitals), some poor people have trouble finding doctors (2006, 250).

In 1973, Medicaid covered 21 million people. By 2000, Medicaid covered almost 43 million people. About half of the people covered under Medicaid are children (CMS, Medicaid Facts and Figures).

See also: Great Society; Head Start; Health Care for the Poor; Johnson, Lyndon; Maternal and Child Health Services; Medicare; National Health Insurance; Poverty Line; Sheppard-Towner Maternity and Infancy Act of 1921; Social Security Act

Sources
Andrew, John A. III. *Lyndon Johnson and the Great Society.* Chicago, IL: Ivan R. Dee, 1998.
Cohn, Jonathan. *Sick: The Untold Story of America's Health Care Crisis—and the People who Pay the Price.* New York: HarperCollins, 2007.
David, Sheri I. *With Dignity: The Search for Medicare and Medicaid.* Westport, CT: Greenwood Press, 1985.
Engel, Jonathan. *Poor People's Medicine: Medicaid and American Charity Since 1965.* Durham, NC: Duke University Press, 2006.
Gruber, Jonathan. "Medicaid." in *Means-Tested Transfer Programs in the United States,* ed. Robert A. Moffit. Chicago, IL: The University of Illinois Press, 2003.

Web Sites
CDC (Centers for Disease Control and Prevention). Vaccines for Children Program. http://www.cdc.gov/vaccines/programs/vfc/default.htm (accessed September 2008).
CMS (Centers for Medicare and Medicaid Services). Key Milestones in CMS Programs. Medicare and Medicaid History. http://www.cms.hhs.gov/History/ (accessed July 2008).
CMS (Centers for Medicare and Medicaid Services). Medicaid. http://www.cms.hhs.gov/home/medicaid.asp (accessed September 2008).
CMS (Centers for Medicare and Medicaid Services). Medicaid Facts and Figures. http://www.cms.hhs.gov/TheChartSeries/05_Medicaid_Facts_Figures.asp (accessed September 2008).
State Children's Health Insurance Program. http://www.cms.hhs.gov/MedicaidGenInfo/05_SCHIP%20Information.asp#TopOfPage (accessed July 2008).

MEDICARE

Medicare is a government-funded health insurance program for the elderly, which started in 1965, as part of President Lyndon Johnson's Great Society initiative. Medicare covers everyone over sixty-five years of age. It was added as an amendment to the Social Security Act.

In 1957, Congress considered a bill that would have provided hospitalization and nursing home coverage for anyone who received Social Security payments for the elderly. This bill never made it out if its congressional committee. In 1960, Congress passed the Kerr-Mills Act, which provided care to the elderly poor. States could choose whether or not to join this program. In 1961, President John F. Kennedy proposed legislation that would have provided hospital and nursing home care for the elderly (David 1985, 54–55; Andrew 1998, 96).

In 1964, President Lyndon Johnson set up a panel of health care experts that revealed that many Americans could not afford basic medical care. A number of different health insurance bills were proposed to offer health care for the elderly. The American Medical Association, which historically ha opposed any government funding of health care or health insurance, proposed their own plan, which was a voluntary program available to individuals only if their states signed up for it. The plan that passed in July 1965 was a combination of two of the original bills, and included Part A, a program in which every state had to participate that provided hospital coverage for the elderly, and Part B, a voluntary insurance program for the elderly that paid for medical bills. This was called Medicare, and was added as Title XVIII of the Social Security Act. Working people pay for Part A through payroll taxes. Those who wish to participate in Part B pay a monthly premium (Andrew 1998, 97–100; CMS, "Key Milestones in CMS Programs"; CMS, "Your Medicare Benefits").

At first, no cost controls were built into Medicare. Doctors and hospitals could charge as much as they wanted, and the government would pay. The Johnson administration believed that including cost controls would have

killed the bill. According to Wilbur Cohen, who was undersecretary of health, education, and welfare at that time, "It wasn't possible in 1965 to put cost controls in. It would have never passed Congress. That would have been federal control, which was the whole political issue at that time" (quoted in Andrew 1998, 105).

However, the costs of Medicare grew so rapidly that even conservative politicians came to agree that cost controls were needed. In the 1980s, President Ronald Reagan's administration and the Congress limited the amount Medicare would pay for physician services and hospital fees (Cohn 2007, 93–94).

Over the years, Medicare has been expanded to include more people and more benefits. In 1972, those under sixty-five years of age with long-term disabilities were also able to participate in Medicare. In 2003, the Medicare Prescription Drug, Improvement, and Modernization Act "made the most significant changes to Medicare since the program began," according to the Centers for Medicare and Medicaid Services Web site. This new program provides coverage for prescription drugs. In addition, elderly people with an income of less than 150 percent of the poverty line are eligible for prescription drug subsidies, and those with high incomes pay more premiums under Part B. This law also initiated a program called Medicare Health Support, which helps people with chronic illnesses, such as heart disease and diabetes, follow a plan to reduce their health risks (CMS, "Key Milestones in CMS Programs").

Medicare does not pay for every medical cost. While most people are automatically enrolled for free in Part A (hospital insurance), some people— those who did not have jobs that required them to pay Medicare taxes— are not automatically enrolled. Those people must pay a monthly premium of up to $423 (as of 2008) to enroll themselves in Medicare Part A. The monthly premium in 2008 for those who wished to enroll in Part B was about $96.40, or more depending on income level. Individuals also have to pay a "deductible" (which was $135 as of 2008) before Medicare began covering services under Part B (which covers doctor's visits and other non-hospital care). If a Medicare beneficiary is hospitalized, as of 2008, they paid a $1,024 deductible, plus $256 per day for days sixty-one to ninety, and $512 per day for days 91 to 150. Beneficiaries must pay all costs after 150 days. Medicare does not pay for private nurses, private rooms, or televisions and telephones in the hospital room. Poor elderly people who cannot afford the costs of Medicare can get help from Medicaid, the government health insurance for the poor (CMS, "Your Medicare Benefits").

Before Medicare coverage went into effect, only half of those over age sixty-five had insurance coverage. As of 2005, 95 percent of those over age sixty-five are covered by Medicare, according to the Center for Medicare Advocacy's Web site.

See also: Great Society; Johnson, Lyndon; Medicaid; National Health Insurance; Social Security Act

Sources

Andrew, John A. III. *Lyndon Johnson and the Great Society.* Chicago, IL: Ivan R. Dee, 1998.

Cohn, Jonathan. *Sick: The Untold Story of America's Health Care Crisis—and the People who Pay the Price.* New York: HarperCollins, 2007.

David, Sheri I. *With Dignity: The Search for Medicare and Medicaid.* Westport, CT: Greenwood Press, 1985.

Web Sites

Medicare. http://www.medicare.gov/ (accessed July 2008).

CMS (Centers for Medicare and Medicaid Services)."Key Milestones in CMS Programs." Medicare and Medicaid History. http://www.cms.hhs.gov/History/ (accessed July 2008).

CMS (Centers for Medicare and Medicaid Services). "Your Medicare Benefits." http://www.medicare.gov/Library/PDFNavigation/PDFInterim.asp?Language=English&Type=Pub&PubID=10116 (accessed September 2008).

Center for Medicare Advocacy. Quick Facts. http://www.medicareadvocacy.org/FAQ_QuickStats.htm (accessed July 2008).

MENTAL ILLNESS AND POVERTY

Mental illness can be a cause of poverty, because many people who are mentally ill are not able to support themselves. During colonial times and the 1800s, governments often dealt with the mentally ill in the same way that they dealt with other poor people. Medical treatment was rarely offered, since no one really knew what to do to cure mental illness or alleviate its symptoms. The early American "poor laws" specified that towns and counties could raise taxes to care for the poor, and the mentally-ill poor were included in this needy population.

Well-off families could afford to care for their insane relatives at home

Patient cell at the Public Hospital for Persons of Insane and Disordered Minds at Williamsburg, Virginia. The hospital was the first of its kind in the country. (The Colonial Williamsburg Foundation)

and perhaps provide humane treatment. The poor insane were viewed with suspicion and were beaten, chained, and confined. Sometimes they were cared for in private homes, with the towns paying the expenses of the insane poor person. If they were violent or a threat to others, they were placed in jails or sometimes in a specially built cell in their own homes. Guards sometimes sold tickets to the general public to view the mentally ill (Baxter and Hathcox 1994, 1; Grob 1994, 6–17).

While most towns were too small to have special buildings just for the mentally ill, in the mid-1700s, Philadelphia built the first hospital for the mentally ill. It was funded through private donations and accepted poor people. It also accepted well-off patients who could pay for their care. In 1773, the state of Virginia opened the first government-

funded hospital to care for poor people who were mentally ill. These early hospitals used chains, whips, physical restraint, cold showers, and bloodletting. Patients were half-naked and slept on straw in unheated rooms (Bell 1980, 5; Grob 1994, 18–21).

In the 1800s, asylums for the mentally ill were founded in northeastern states. By 1844, twenty-four small hospitals for the mentally ill in the United States were supported by both government funds and private funds. Although these institutions were supposed to serve the poor as well as the wealthy, in fact, they preferred to accept people who could pay. Increasingly, asylums began to use humane care and compassion with the mentally ill. This was called "moral treatment" and was believed to provide a cure for mental illness. Starting in about 1830, there was a movement to have state governments build asylums for the insane to provide this "moral treatment" to more people in need (Bell 1980, 15; Baxter and Hathcox 1994, 29–31; Grob 1994, 31–39).

Horace Mann, a member of the Massachusetts House of Representatives, pushed through a bill to establish the Worcester State Lunatic Hospital, which opened in 1833. Other states followed the lead of Massachusetts. Dorothea Dix was one of the main leaders of the movement to have state governments build more asylums. She was a Massachusetts teacher and writer who took on the cause of the mentally ill after seeing their condition in a Massachusetts jail where she taught Sunday school to the inmates. As a result of her work, thirty-two mental hospitals in the United States and abroad were established, and even more were enlarged. By the late 1800s, almost every state had at least one public institution for the mentally ill. These institutions offered the inmates opportunities for work and leisure in comfortable settings (Baxter and Hathcox 1994, 29, 51–74).

From 1920 to 1950, funding for state hospitals decreased. The state hospitals became crowded, staff were underpaid, and buildings were deteriorating. Patients again were found to be naked and chained. After 1950, more modern treatments allowed many mentally ill patients to return to their homes and families. The patient population at state institutions dropped from 500,000 in 1950, to 100,000 in 1990. Some states decided to close their mental hospitals. In 1963, the U.S. Congress passed the Community Mental Health Centers Act to provide funding for community care of the mentally ill. However, starting in the late 1970s, government funding for community care was reduced, resulting in a rise of homelessness among the mentally ill.

Sometimes these mentally ill homeless are picked up and put in jail. The United States appears to have come full circle, returning to the colonial era, during which time poor mentally ill people roamed the streets or were put in jail. According to William Baxter and David Hathcox, "it has been said that the Los Angeles County Jail is the largest mental institution in the country" (Baxter and Hathcox 1994, 99, 106, 110, 121, 129).

See also: Dix, Dorothea; Homelessness; Mann, Horace; Poor Laws, Early American

Sources
Baxter, William E., and David W. Hathcox. *America's Care of the Mentally Ill: A Photographic History.* Washington, DC: American Psychiatric Association, 1994.

Bell, Leland. *Treating the Mentally Ill from Colonial Times to the Present.* New York: Praeger Publishers, 1980.

Grob, Gerald N. *The Mad Among Us: A History of the Care of America's Mentally Ill.* New York: The Free Press, 1994.

MINIMUM-WAGE LAWS

When people concerned about poverty realized that low wages were a major cause of poverty, they sought to persuade states to pass laws specifying a minimum hourly wage. The first minimum-wage laws in the United States were state laws that applied only to women and children. Adult males did not gain a legal minimum wage until 1938, with the passage of the federal Fair Labor Standards Act.

The National Consumers League was one of the first organizations to promote the idea of a minimum wage. In the early 1900s, they decided to support minimum-wage legislation for women and children only. This was partly because the U.S. Supreme Court had invalidated laws that specified the working hours and wages of men workers, because these laws supposedly violated the workers' freedom to enter into any kind of contract they wanted. However, the Supreme Court did uphold an Oregon maximum-hour law for women, on the grounds that women were different from men and the state had a responsibility to protect women's health. The Consumers League hoped the Court would uphold minimum-wage laws for women (Waltman 2000, 11–12).

In 1912, with the help of the National Consumers League, Massachusetts became the first state to pass a minimum-wage law for women and children. This law created "wage boards" to set minimum wages for various industries. The law stipulated that the wages had to be enough to supply the necessities of life and to maintain the worker's health. Compliance with this law was essentially voluntary: employers that refused to abide by the minimum wages were punished only by having their names printed in the newspaper.

The next year, eight more states adopted minimum-wage laws. By 1923, a total of fourteen states plus the District of Columbia had enacted minimum-wage laws. Some of these laws formed wage boards to set minimum wages, and others specified a certain minimum wage in the law itself. Most of the laws were not voluntary:

employers who refused to comply faced fines or imprisonment.

In 1923, the U.S. Supreme Court dropped a bomb: it invalidated the District of Columbia's minimum-wage law, arguing that it violated the liberty of contract of both the employee and the employer. Based on this ruling, federal courts struck down many of the other minimum-wage laws, and even the laws that were not struck down were no longer being enforced (Nordlund 1997, 11; Waltman 2000, 28–29).

In 1929, the Great Depression began, and the federal government began to think about how it could help prevent sliding wages. The first federal minimum-wage law was the Davis-Bacon Act, passed in 1931, which applied to only one industry. It set wage standards for construction firms working on government contracts. The federal government did not want construction firms to bid low to be awarded the contract and then to hire inexperienced workers at low wages. Many states also had similar laws for construction workers on government contracts—the first such state law was passed in Kansas in 1891.

Two other similar federal minimum-wage laws are the Walsh-Healey Act, passed in 1936, and the Federal Service Contract Act of 1965. Like the Davis-Bacon Act, these laws apply only to firms that have government contracts—in this case, contracts to supply the government with goods or services. Such companies are required to pay the "prevailing wage"—the normal wage for workers in that field (Pollin and Luce 1998, 28–29).

In 1933, the federal government passed the first national law that sought to regulate wages in many different industries. This was the National Industrial Recovery Act, the first part of which set up the National Recovery Administration (NRA) to create trade associations to come up with "codes of fair competition" in their fields, including minimum wages. These codes were to be approved by the U.S. president. The law was enforced only for two years before the U.S. Supreme Court declared the NRA to be unconstitutional in 1935, because it gave too much power to the president.

States were also reacting to the Great Depression by passing new minimum-wage laws. They tried to word their laws in different ways to get around the Supreme Court decision on the District's law. By 1938, twenty-five states had adopted minimum-wage laws. Oklahoma's law applied to men as well as women. In 1937, the U.S. Supreme Court upheld Washington State's minimum-wage law. This was good news, because in 1938 the federal government passed the Fair Labor Standards Act, which provided for a national minimum wage. This law was upheld by the U.S. Supreme Court in 1941 (Nordlund 1997, 25–26; Waltham 2000, 29–34).

As of 2008, according to the U.S. Department of Labor, thirty-two states mandate minimum wages higher than the federal minimum. In these cases, the state law supersedes the national law. Three states have lower minimum-wage rates (applicable only to those workers not covered by the federal minimum-wage law).

Over the years, critics have argued against minimum wages because they believed that raising wages would cause unemployment: if an employer has to pay more for workers, then fewer workers would be hired. However, this theory has not proven to be true. According to David Card and Alan Krueger, who studied what happened when minimum wages were increased in a number of states, an increase in minimum wages often had no impact on the unemployment rate, and sometimes employment opportunities increased at the same time that minimum wages went up (1995, 1–2).

In examining whether the minimum wage reduces poverty, Card and Krueger found that the poorest families do earn more when the minimum wage is increased. But an increase in the minimum wage does not specifically target poverty. "The minimum wage is a blunt instrument for reducing overall poverty ... because many minimum-wage earners are not in poverty, and because many of those in poverty are not connected to the labor market" (1995, 3).

The real dollar value of the federal minimum wage has been falling since about 1968. Many activists for the poor point out that a full-time job at the federal minimum wage will no longer keep a family out of poverty, as it could in the late 1960s. In 2007, the federal minimum wage was raised to $5.85, which translates into a full-time salary of about $12,000. In contrast, the federal poverty threshold in 2007 for a family of two (one adult and one child) was $14,291, according to the U.S. Department of the Census. So even by working full-time at a minimum-wage job, a parent with only one child would still be considered poor (Pollin and Luce 1998, 23; Economic Policy Institute, Issue Guide on the Minimum Wage, Figure 1).

In response, activists have worked in many states and cities to pass "living-wage" laws, which mandate higher minimum wages to ensure that workers earn enough to keep themselves and their families above the federal poverty line. Furthermore, many experts point out that the federal poverty line is itself set too low to account for basic needs, so that even if the minimum wage were raised to allow a worker to support a family above the poverty line, that worker still may not be able to meet the costs of all basic needs.

See also: Fair Labor Standards Act of 1938; Great Depression; Living-Wage Laws; Minimum-Wage Laws—Supreme Court Cases; National Consumers League; National Recovery Administration; Poverty Line; Progressive Era

Sources

Card, David, and Alan B. Krueger. *Myth and Measurement: The New Economics of the Minimum Wage.* Princeton, NJ: Princeton University Press, 1995.

Nordlund, Willis J. *The Quest for a Living Wage: The History of the Federal Minimum Wage Program.* Westport, CT: Greenwood Press, 1997.

Pollin, Robert, and Stephanie Luce. *The Living Wage: Building a Fair Economy.* New York: The New Press, 1998.

Waltman, Jerold. *The Politics of the Minimum Wage.* Urbana: University of Illinois Press, 2000.

Web Sites

Census Bureau. Poverty Threshold 2007. http://www.census.gov/hhes/www/poverty/threshld/thresh07.html (accessed April 2008).

Economic Policy Institute. Issue Guide on the Minimum Wage. http://www.epi.org/content.cfm/issueguides_minwage (accessed April 2008).

U.S. Department of Labor. History of Minimum Wage Laws. http://www.dol.gov/esa/minwage/coverage.htm (accessed April 2008).

U.S. Department of Labor. Minimum-Wage Laws in the States—January 2008. http://www.dol.gov/esa/minwage/america.htm (accessed April 2008).

MINIMUM-WAGE LAWS—SUPREME COURT CASES

One major obstacle to federal and state minimum-wage laws in the first part of the twentieth century was the U.S. Supreme Court. Until the late 1930s, the Court tended to believe that any government regulation of work, such as minimum wages or maximum hours, was unconstitutional, because it violated the Constitution's supposed guarantee of "freedom of contract"—a worker's freedom to enter into any kind of contract he or she desired. In addition, at that time, the Court took a narrow view of the federal government's role in regulating business, believing that the national government could get involved only in aspects of business that directly related to interstate commerce—shipping goods between states.

In 1923, the U.S. Supreme Court heard arguments in *Adkins v. Children's Hospital*. In 1918, Congress created a board to set minimum wages for women and children in the District of Columbia to protect them from poverty, which could lead to ill health and immoral behavior. Children's Hospital in Washington, D.C., wanted the law removed because they did not want to pay all employees the minimum wage. The Supreme Court agreed with the Children's Hospital in a ruling of five to three. Justice George Sutherland declared that although the government had the right to use its police powers to prevent specific evils, in this case, freedom of contract took precedence. Sutherland said that a woman's freedom of contract should not be limited any more than a man's freedom, and also found that the law was unjust to employers because it only considered workers' needs (Hall 1992, 9; Lewis and Wilson 2001, 11).

In 1933, the federal government passed minimum-wage regulations in the form of Title I of the National Industrial Recovery Act (NIRA), which required industries to come up with "codes of fair competition" in their fields, including minimum wages. These codes were to be approved by the U.S. president and had the force of law. In 1935, the Supreme Court heard the case *Schechter Poultry Corp. v. United States*. Schechter Poultry of Brooklyn, New York, was accused of violating the wage and hour regulations of the slaughterhouse industry, and of selling diseased chicken. The Court, in a unanimous decision, declared that Title I of the NIRA was invalid because it gave too much power to the executive branch of the government by allowing industry groups and the president to create regulations that affected the nation's entire economy. Although the court did not specifically rule on whether or not the federal government could enact minimum-wage laws, this ruling had the effect of nullifying what was the first federal attempt to mandate minimum wages (Hall 1992, 757; Lewis and Wilson 2001, 832–833).

Despite the Adkins decision, states continued to try to pass minimum-wage laws, varying the language slightly to get around the Court's views. In 1936,

a New York state minimum-wage law was challenged and ruled unconstitutional by the New York Supreme Court. The U.S. Supreme Court agreed with the New York decision in a five-to-four vote in *Morehead v. New York*. Again, the majority of the justices argued that the government should not interfere with freedom of contract. However, the court was divided and Justice Harlan Fiske Stone wrote in his dissenting opinion that "there is grim irony in speaking of the freedom of contract of those who, because of their economic necessities, give their services for less than is needful to keep body and soul together" (quoted in Hall 1992, 562). The very next year, however, the Supreme Court overturned the *Adkins* decision in a five-to-four vote in *West Coast Hotel v. Parrish*. Elsie Parrish was being paid less than the minimum wage at the West Coast Hotel in Washington State. She sued to recover the wages that should have been paid to her under the law. The Washington State Supreme Court ruled in favor of Parrish, and the hotel appealed the case to the U.S. Supreme Court. Chief Justice Charles Evans Hughes, writing for the majority, argued that the government had the power to restrict freedom of contract in the interest of the community, and that women, because of their physical differences from men and their role as mothers, required state protection to "preserve the strength and vigor of the race" (quoted in Hall 1992, 924; also see Lewis and Wilson 2001, 1018).

In 1938, the federal government passed the Fair Labor Standards Act, which set a national minimum wage for both women and men. This law was challenged in *United States v. Darby*

PRIMARY DOCUMENT 18

Excerpt from *United States v. Darby Lumber Company,* Supreme Court Opinion No. 82; Argued: December 19, 20, 1940; Decided: February 3, 1941

In the opinion below, the U.S. Supreme Court finally agreed that the federal government had the right to issue laws regulating the minimum wages, maximum hours, and other aspects of work, as they relate to products or services destined for interstate commerce. This opinion on behalf of the unanimous decision of the Court was written by Chief Justice Harlan Fiske Stone. The "appellee" referred to below is the Darby Lumber Company, which was charged with being in violation of the Fair Labor Standards Act of 1938.

MR. JUSTICE STONE delivered the opinion of the Court.

The two principal questions raised by the record in this case are, first, whether Congress has constitutional power to prohibit the shipment in interstate commerce of lumber manufactured by employees whose wages are less than a prescribed minimum or whose weekly hours of labor at that wage are greater than a prescribed maximum, and, second, whether it has power to prohibit the employment of workmen in the production of goods "for interstate commerce" at other than prescribed wages and hours. A subsidiary question is whether, in connection with such prohibitions, Congress can require the employer subject to them to keep records showing the hours worked each day and week by each of his employees including those engaged "in the production and manufacture of goods, to-wit, lumber, for 'interstate commerce.'" ...

The Fair Labor Standards Act set up a comprehensive legislative scheme for preventing the shipment in interstate commerce of certain products and commodities produced in the United States under labor conditions as respects wages and hours which fail to conform to standards set up by the Act. Its purpose ... is to exclude from interstate commerce goods produced for the commerce and to prevent their production for interstate commerce under conditions detrimental to the maintenance of the minimum standards of living necessary for health and general wellbeing, and to prevent the use of interstate commerce as the means of competition in the distribution of goods so produced, and as the means of spreading and perpetuating such substandard labor conditions among the workers of the several states. The Act also sets up an administrative procedure whereby those standards may from time to time be modified generally as to industries subject to the Act or within an industry in accordance with specified standards, by an administrator acting in collaboration with "Industry Committees" appointed by him.

Section 15 of the statute prohibits certain specified acts, and § 16(a) punishes willful violation of it by a fine of not more than $10,000, and punishes each conviction after the first by imprisonment of not more than six months or by the specified fine, or both. Section 15(1) makes unlawful the shipment in interstate commerce of any goods "in the production of which any employee was employed in violation of section 6 or section 7," which provide, among other things, that, during the first year of operation of the Act, a minimum wage of 25 cents per hour shall be paid to employees "engaged in [interstate] commerce or the production of goods for [interstate] commerce," § 6, and that the maximum hours of employment for employees "engaged in commerce or the production of goods for commerce" without increased compensation for overtime, shall be forty-four hours a week. § 7.

Section 15(a)(2) makes it unlawful to violate the provisions of §§ 6 and 7, including the minimum wage and maximum hour requirements just mentioned for employees engaged in production of goods for commerce. Section 15(a)(5) makes it unlawful for an employer subject to the Act to violate § 11(c), which requires him to keep such records of the persons employed by him and of their wages and hours of employment as the administrator shall prescribe by regulation or order.

The indictment charges that appellee is engaged, in the State of Georgia, in the business of acquiring raw materials, which he manufactures into finished lumber with the intent, when manufactured, to ship it in interstate commerce to customers outside the state, and that he does, in fact, so ship a large part of the lumber so produced. There are numerous counts charging appellee with the shipment in interstate commerce from Georgia to points outside the state of lumber in the production of which, for interstate commerce, appellee has employed workmen at less than the prescribed minimum wage or more than the prescribed maximum hours without payment to them of any wage for overtime. Other counts charge the employment by appellee of workmen in the production of lumber for interstate commerce at wages at less than 25 cents an hour or for more than the maximum hours per week without payment to them of the prescribed overtime wage. Still another count charges appellee with failure to keep records showing the hours worked each day a week by each of his employees . . . .

The motive and purpose of the present regulation are plainly to make effective the Congressional conception of public policy that interstate commerce should not be made the instrument of competition in the distribution of goods produced under substandard labor conditions, which competition is injurious to the commerce and to the states from and to which the commerce flows. The motive and purpose of a regulation of interstate commerce are matters for the legislative judgment upon the exercise of which the Constitution places no restriction, and over which the courts are given no control. . . . Whatever their motive and purpose, regulations of commerce which do not infringe some constitutional prohibition are within the plenary power conferred on Congress by the Commerce Clause. Subject only to that limitation, presently to be considered, we conclude that the prohibition of the shipment interstate of goods produced under the forbidden substandard labor conditions is within the constitutional authority of Congress.

In the more than a century which has elapsed since the decision of *Gibbons v. Ogden,* these principles of constitutional interpretation have been so long and repeatedly recognized by this Court as applicable to the Commerce Clause that there would be little occasion for repeating them now were it not for the decision of this Court twenty-two years ago in *Hammer v. Dagenhart,* . . . In that case, it was held by a bare majority of the Court, over the powerful and now classic dissent of Mr. Justice Holmes setting forth the fundamental issues involved, that Congress was without power to exclude the products of child labor from interstate commerce. The reasoning and conclusion of the Court's opinion there cannot be reconciled with the conclusion which we have reached, that the power of Congress under the Commerce Clause is plenary to exclude any article from interstate commerce subject only to the specific prohibitions of the Constitution.

Hammer v. Dagenhart has not been followed. The distinction on which the decision was rested, that Congressional power to prohibit interstate commerce is limited to articles which in themselves have some harmful or deleterious property—a distinction which was novel when made and unsupported by any provision of the Constitution—has long since been abandoned . . . . The thesis of the opinion—that the motive of the prohibition or its effect to control in some measure the use or production within the states of the article thus excluded from the commerce can operate to deprive the regulation of its constitutional authority—has long since ceased to have force. . . .

The conclusion is inescapable that *Hammer v. Dagenhart* was a departure from the principles which have prevailed in the interpretation of the Commerce Clause both before and since the decision, and that such vitality, as a precedent, as it then had, has long since been exhausted. It should be, and now is, overruled.

Validity of the wage and hour requirements. Section 15(a)(2) and §§ 6 and 7 require employers to conform to the wage and hour provisions with respect to all employees engaged in the production of goods for interstate commerce. As appellee's employees are not alleged to be "engaged in interstate commerce," the validity of the prohibition turns on the question whether the employment, under other than the prescribed labor standards, of employees engaged in the production of goods for interstate commerce is so related to the commerce, and so affects it, as to be within the reach of the power of Congress to regulate it.

To answer this question, we must at the outset determine whether the particular acts charged in the counts which are laid under § 15(a)(2) as they were construed below constitute "production for commerce" within the meaning of the statute. As the Government seeks to apply the statute in the indictment, and as the court below construed the phrase

"produced for interstate commerce," it embraces at least the case where an employer engaged, as is appellee, in the manufacture and shipment of goods in filling orders of extrastate customers, manufactures his product with the intent or expectation that, according to the normal course of his business, all or some part of it will be selected for shipment to those customers.

Without attempting to define the precise limits of the phrase, we think the acts alleged in the indictment are within the sweep of the statute. The obvious purpose of the Act was not only to prevent the interstate transportation of the proscribed product, but to stop the initial step toward transportation, production with the purpose of so transporting it. Congress was not unaware that most manufacturing businesses shipping their product in interstate commerce make it in their shops without reference to its ultimate destination, and then, after manufacture, select some of it for shipment interstate and some intrastate, according to the daily demands of their business, and that it would be practically impossible, without disrupting manufacturing businesses, to restrict the prohibited kind of production to the particular pieces of lumber, cloth, furniture or the like which later move in interstate, rather than intrastate, commerce.

The recognized need of drafting a workable statute and the well known circumstances in which it was to be applied are persuasive of the conclusion, which the legislative history supports, . . . that the "production for commerce" intended includes at least production of goods which, at the time of production, the employer, according to the normal course of his business, intends or expects to move in interstate commerce although, through the exigencies of the business, all of the goods may not thereafter actually enter interstate commerce.

There remains the question whether such restriction on the production of goods for commerce is a permissible exercise of the commerce power. The power of Congress over interstate commerce is not confined to the regulation of commerce among the states. It extends to those activities intrastate which so affect interstate commerce or the exercise of the power of Congress over it as to make regulation of them appropriate means to the attainment of a legitimate end, the exercise of the granted power of Congress to regulate interstate commerce. . . .

Our conclusion is unaffected by the Tenth Amendment, which provides:

> The powers not delegated to the United States by the Constitution, nor prohibited by it to the States, are reserved to the States respectively, or to the people.

The amendment states but a truism that all is retained which has not been surrendered. There is nothing in the history of its adoption to suggest that it was more than declaratory of the relationship between the national and state governments as it had been established by the Constitution before the amendment, or that its purpose was other than to allay fears that the new national government might seek to exercise powers not granted, and that the states might not be able to exercise fully their reserved powers. . . .

From the beginning and for many years, the amendment has been construed as not depriving the national government of authority to resort to all means for the exercise of a granted power which are appropriate and plainly adapted to the permitted end. . . .

Validity of the requirement of records of wages and hours. § 15(a)(5) and § 11(c). These requirements are incidental to those for the prescribed wages and

hours, and hence validity of the former turns on validity of the latter. Since, as we have held, Congress may require production for interstate commerce to conform to those conditions, it may require the employer, as a means of enforcing the valid law, to keep a record showing whether he has, in fact, complied with it. The requirement for records even of the intrastate transaction is an appropriate means to the legitimate end. . . .

Validity of the wage and hour provisions under the Fifth Amendment. Both provisions are minimum wage requirements compelling the payment of a minimum standard wage with a prescribed increased wage for overtime of "not less than one and one-half times the regular rate" at which the worker is employed. Since our decision in *West Coast Hotel Co. v. Parrish,* . . . it is no longer open to question that the fixing of a minimum wage is within the legislative power, and that the bare fact of its exercise is not a denial of due process under the Fifth more than under the Fourteenth Amendment. Nor is it any longer open to question that it is within the legislative power to fix maximum hours . . . . Similarly, the statute is not objectionable because applied alike to both men and women . . . .

The Act is sufficiently definite to meet constitutional demands. One who employs persons, without conforming to the prescribed wage and hour conditions, to work on goods which he ships or expects to ship across state lines is warned that he may be subject to the criminal penalties of the Act. No more is required.

Source

United States v. Darby, 312 U.S. 100 (1941). U.S. Supreme Court Decision.

Lumber Company. Fred Darby's company shipped its goods out of state. Darby was charged with paying less than the minimum wage. Darby claimed that, according to a 1918 Supreme Court ruling in a child labor law case, the federal government had authority to regulate only the interstate commerce aspect of business, and had no authority to regulate matters such as minimum wages that were not directly related to interstate commerce. This time, the Court unanimously upheld the Fair Labor Standards Act. Chief Justice Harlan Fiske Stone wrote that Congress had the authority to regulate any activity that directly or indirectly had an effect on interstate commerce (Lewis and Wilson 2001, 264–265).

See also: Child Labor Laws—Supreme Court Cases; Minimum-Wage Laws; Supreme Court and Poverty

Sources

Hall, Kermit L., ed. *The Oxford Companion to the Supreme Court of the United States.* New York: Oxford University Press, 1992.

Lewis, Thomas, and Richard Wilson, eds. *Encyclopedia of the U.S. Supreme Court.* Pasadena, CA: Salem Press, 2001.

MODEL CITIES

The "model cities" program was a federal government initiative started in 1966, as part of President Lyndon Johnson's efforts to create a Great Society by addressing the country's social and economic ills. The law creating this program was called the Demonstration Cities and Metropolitan Development Act. Its goal was to set up "model cities" that would use federal money to address "urban blight"—slums and deteriorating conditions in the inner cities.

The federal government had been providing money to improve poor urban areas since 1949, through the "urban renewal" program. Urban renewal aimed at destroying slum areas—areas of inferior and dilapidated housing where poor people lived. Urban renewal was supposed to provide better housing for the poor, but in fact it destroyed much more housing than it created.

Starting in 1964, poor people started or participated in violent riots in many cities around the country. Realizing that something needed to be done to help urban areas and that urban renewal was not the answer to poverty in cities, President Johnson set up a Task Force on Urban Problems in 1965 to study possible solutions. This task force recommended establishing an experimental program involving sixty-six cities of different sizes. The federal government was to concentrate money and resources in the poor areas of these cities so that problems of poverty and urban blight could be solved. Cities were to use the money to establish not just better housing, but all sorts of programs and services to help the poor people living in those neighborhoods. The results of these demonstration projects, it was hoped, would point the way to future government programs and would lead to increased funding for all cities (Haar 1975, 45–46).

However, this idea for a limited number of experimental cities, and a concentration of funding in the poor areas of these cities, did not come to pass. The Model Cities bill that passed into law in 1966, allowed almost any city to apply to participate in the program. This was done to gain the support of enough members of Congress so the bill would pass. Therefore, federal money ended up being spread thinly around the country, instead of being concentrated in the poor areas of a limited number of cities.

By 1967, the U.S. Department of Housing and Urban Development had received 193 applications for grants, and sixty-three cities were selected as the first model cities. Each city had to set up a City Demonstration Agency. Cities first had to prepare a plan of what they wanted to do, and then could request additional funding to implement their plan. By April of 1968, 168 additional cities applied for the model cities program, and from this group, seventy-five cities were approved. In December 1968, Seattle, Washington, was the first city to have its Comprehensive Development Plan approved, and by June 1969, thirty-five city plans were approved (Frieden and Kaplan 1975, 260–264).

Local residents were supposed to play a large role in the model cities plans, and so each City Demonstration Agency had an advisory board made up of local citizens who were elected. In addition, the model cities project were asked to recruit, train, and hire local residents, as a way to create jobs in the area. Although model cities money was supposed to help the poor, in fact, cities did not necessarily use the money in this way. According to John Andrew, "All too often [local officials] saw Model Cities as an opportunity to secure funds rather than as a chance to restructure their urban environment through social engineering" (1998, 145–146). For example, Newark, New

Jersey, decided to use its model cities funds to demolish 150 acres of slum housing and to build a medical and dental college.

Cities had trouble achieving the goals of the model cities program, because their local governments were not always set up to efficiently channel the funding to areas where it was needed. New York City was able to spend only half of its model cities grant by 1973, because internal bureaucracy held up the process of getting things done within the city. For example, model city assistants had to go through ten different city agencies in New York City even to accomplish simple tasks such as buying office equipment (Haar 1975, 208).

Cities were not able to make much progress in terms of reducing unemployment or offering more affordable housing. Job-training programs were often not terribly successful because few job openings were available for the people who were trained. Because constructing and renovating housing is expensive, the model cities generally were not able to provide much affordable housing (Washnis 1974, 37, 43).

Nevertheless, the model cities program did have some successes. Many cities set up neighborhood health centers with the funds, and some cities started model neighborhood schools and employment training centers. Chicago started seven community schools that offered free meals and adult classes, and that emphasized parental involvement. The students at these schools increased their achievement test scores. Cities created parks, playgrounds, and community centers with model cities funds. They also put money into law enforcement, creating community policing programs and half-way houses for drug addicts (Washnis 1974, 15–16, 35–36, 44–45).

The model cities program was over almost before it had begun. In 1974, Congress combined the model cities program with urban renewal and created a new program called the Community Development Block Grant. These grants allowed cities that already had started working on their model cities plans to complete five years of the plan (Frieden and Kaplan 1975, 266–268).

Despite the fact that the model cities program was underfunded and ended too soon to show results, it did have some long-lasting effects. According to Charles Haar, a Harvard Law School professor who worked on the model cities program as assistant secretary for Metropolitan Development, the model cities program helped shape the viewpoint within the U.S. Department of Housing and Urban Development. Housing began to be seen not just as a physical, bricks-and-mortar issue, but also as an issue related to job opportunities, schools, and community participation (1975, 196).

See also: Great Society; Johnson, Lyndon; Kerner Commission (National Advisory Commission on Civil Disorders); Urban Renewal

Sources

Andrew, John A. III. *Lyndon Johnson and the Great Society.* Chicago, IL: Ivan R. Dee, 1998.

Frieden, Bernard J., and Marshall Kaplan. *The Politics of Neglect: Urban Aid from Model Cities to Revenue Sharing.* Cambridge, MA: The MIT Press, 1975.

Haar, Charles M. *Between the Idea and the Reality: A Study in the Origin, Fate and Legacy of the Model Cities Program.* Boston, MA: Little, Brown and Company, 1975.

Washnis, George J. *Community Development Strategies: Case Studies of Major Model Cities.* New York: Praeger Publishers, 1974.

MOTHERS' PENSIONS

Mothers' pensions, also called widows' pensions, were in the early 1900s a popular means of providing government support to women with dependent children, and to women without a husband who could provide income. This system was designed to allow women to stay at home with their children, rather than be forced to leave them alone while working, or to place them in an orphanage.

President Theodore Roosevelt expressed support for pensions for "deserving mothers" in a 1909 speech calling for the formation of the Children's Bureau. However, the conference resolution called for pensions to be provided by private charity, and not by the government.

The first government pensions for widows was established at the urging of juvenile court judges, because they saw a connection between delinquent children and poor mothers who were forced to work and leave their children unsupervised. Judge E. E. Porterfield convinced the Missouri legislature to pass a law in 1911, providing money to widows or women whose husbands were imprisoned. This law applied only to Jackson County, and would be given only to women who were deemed fit to bring up their children. Also in 1911, a judge in Illinois worked to pass a similar law. A judge in Colorado ran a

MOTHERS' PENSIONS

OVER 20 STATES
ARE HELPING TO PRESERVE THE HOME

BY KEEPING CHILDREN IN SCHOOL
UNTIL QUALIFIED TO WORK

Exhibit panel promoting mothers' pensions, ca. 1914. (Library of Congress)

successful campaign to pass a mothers' pension law in 1912.

At about this time, leaders of the private charity movement, such as the Charity Organization Societies that were widespread around the country, came out in opposition to government funding of mothers' pensions. These leaders believed that the government should not provide aid to poor people in their own homes, but should only fund poorhouses and other institutions. They believed that mothers' pensions ought to be funded solely through private charity. However, not all leaders of private charitable movements felt this way. Jane Addams, a leader of the settlement-house movement, was in

favor of government funding of mothers' pensions, as were many of her settlement-house associates, such as Florence Kelley and Julia Lathrop (Skocpol 1992, 428–430).

Despite some opposition, state after state continued to pass legislation in favor of mothers' pensions. By 1919, thirty-nine states had enacted mothers' pension laws, and by 1935, all but two states had such laws. Although they were passed by state legislatures, these laws gave control of these programs to counties and cities, which were allowed to provide payments to women who were deemed worthy parents (for example, in 1913, divorced women were not eligible for help in Illinois). Eventually some pension programs became mandatory, and were provided with at least some state funding. In addition, some laws were expanded to apply to all needy women with children, even those with illegitimate children. However, the pensions provided were generally small (Trattner 1994, 225–226; Katz 1996, 133).

One reason for the widespread passage of these mothers' pension laws was the strong support of women's organizations and women's magazines, according to Theda Skocpol, a professor of government and sociology at Harvard University. A fashion magazine called the *Delineator,* which was owned by the Butterick sewing-pattern company, carried articles about legal and charitable issues of interest to women. The magazine was widely circulated, reaching 1 million readers through the mail. An editor of this magazine, William Hard, was a former settlement-house worker and friend of Jane Addams and Julia Lathrop. In

1912, he began to promote the idea of mothers' pensions in the magazine. The General Federation of Women's Clubs, a national network of women's clubs, supported and promoted the idea of mothers' pensions. The National Congress of Mothers and the National Consumers League also publicized mothers' pensions. Skocpol concludes that the women's groups worked with juvenile court judges and with women's magazines to pass such legislation in almost every state (1992, 432–465).

Mothers' pensions were to be given to women who maintained a "suitable home" for their children. Advocates for the poor did not want to provide government support to women who might raise children who would be a burden to society when they grew up. Each state interpreted the idea of a "suitable home" differently. Widows, or wives of men who were permanently disabled, were generally considered capable of providing a suitable home. Women who were ill or who engaged in extramarital affairs were deemed unsuitable in some states. Children's behavior was a key in some states: mothers of children who did not do well in school, or who were juvenile delinquents, were sometimes found to be unsuitable. In Minnesota, immigrant mothers were instructed to learn English and to speak English in the home. Many states denied aid to almost all black mothers (Bell 1965, 7–13).

Did the mothers' pensions allow poor women to stay at home and nurture their children? Skocpol argues that the funding was inadequate to really support all eligible families. In some states, all eligible women received small amounts of money, and because

the women were not supposed to work full-time outside the home, they were forced to take poorly paid work that could be done at home, or part-time work outside the home. In other states, some families received a decent amount of money, while many more were put on waiting lists. "Indeed, mothers' pensions in practice truly boomeranged on the intention of their original supporters by pushing poor women into the marginal wage-labor market," Skocpol notes (1942, 476). She goes on to say that the women who had supported the laws in the first place did not generally have the political power to make sure they were adequately funded (1992, 469–479).

During the Great Depression, which began in 1929, states had even less money for mothers' pensions, and finally, in 1935, the federal government started providing help to poor mothers with dependent children in the form of Aid to Dependent Children, part of the Social Security Act. This program later became Aid to Families with Dependent Children. As society has grown more comfortable with the idea of mothers working outside the home, support has lessened for providing aid to mothers to allow them to stay at home with their children. Starting in the 1960s, recipients of Aid to Families with Dependent Children were encouraged to find work. In 1996, the Aid to Families with Dependent Children program ended, and was replaced with Temporary Assistance for Needy Families, which places time limits on aid and requires parents receiving aid to participate in some work activities (which could include job training or education as well as actual work).

See also: Addams, Jane; Aid to (Families with) Dependent Children; Children's Bureau; Juvenile Justice System; Kelley, Florence; Lathrop, Julia; National Consumers League; Progressive Era; Scientific Charity; Settlement Houses; Social Security Act; Temporary Assistance for Needy Families

Sources

Bell, Winifred. *Aid to Dependent Children.* New York: Columbia University Press, 1965.

Katz, Michael. *In the Shadow of the Poorhouse: A Social History of Welfare in America.* New York: Basic Books, 1996.

Skocpol, Theda. *Protecting Soldiers and Mothers: The Political Origins of Social Policy in the United States.* Cambridge, MA: Harvard University Press, 1992.

Trattner, Walter I. *From Poor Law to Welfare State: A History of Social Welfare in America.* New York: The Free Press, 1994.

N

NATIONAL AND COMMUNITY SERVICE TRUST ACT OF 1993

The National and Community Service Trust Act of 1993 was introduced into Congress by President Bill Clinton, and passed with support from both Democratic and Republican members of Congress. The goal of the law was to expand national service programs. "National service" refers to government-funded programs that provide a stipend or other incentive for people to volunteer in areas that help the community. National service programs provide services to help low-income people; and also provide a way for anyone— including those with low income—to serve the community, learn job skills, and gain work experience.

The National and Community Service Trust Act created the Corporation for National and Community Service to manage all the federal government's national service programs. Some of these programs, such as Volunteers in Service to America (VISTA) and the Foster Grandparent Program, had been created in the 1960s. The service learning program to encourage schools to provide volunteer opportunities to students was created in 1990. The National and Community Service Trust Act also created a new program: AmeriCorps.

The Corporation for National and Community Service encompasses five different general programs: AmeriCorps State and National, AmeriCorps-VISTA, AmeriCorps National Civilian Community Corps (NCCC), Senior Corps, and Learn and Serve America. In addition, the agency manages grants for a number of special initiatives, such as the Martin Luther King, Jr. Day of Service and the President's Volunteer Service Award.

AmeriCorps State and National, the broadest of the programs, provides funding to nonprofit organizations, schools, colleges, and public agencies to hire and train AmeriCorps volunteers

An *AmeriCorps member clears debris inside a house damaged by Hurricane Katrina in St. Bernard Parish, Louisiana, 2006. More than 35,000 national service participants contributed 1.6 million hours of volunteer service during the first year of hurricane relief and recovery efforts along the Gulf Coast. (Corporation for National and Community Service)*

Conservation Corps of the 1930s. Young people ages eighteen to twenty-four live together and receive training at one of four different camps around the country. Then teams of people are sent out to help throughout the country at nonprofit organizations, schools, cities, parks, and American Indian tribes. More than 70,000 people participate in the AmeriCorps programs each year.

Senior Corps includes the Foster Grandparent program, linking seniors with children who need one-on-one attention and help; the Senior Companion Program, linking seniors with adults who have trouble with the tasks of everyday living; and Retired Senior Volunteer Corps, which provides volunteer opportunities to anyone fifty-five and older. Learn and Serve America provides grants to schools, colleges, and community-based organizations to get young people involved with service-learning projects (Corporation for National and Community Service Web site).

Since 1994, more than 540,000 people have participated in the AmeriCorps programs. A long-term study of 2,000 people who participated in either AmeriCorps State and National, or AmeriCorps NCCC looked at the impact of the AmeriCorps programs. The results showed that even eight years after enrolling, participants were more engaged with their community, more likely to choose careers in public service, and more satisfied with their lives, than a similar group of people who were interested in national service but did not serve. According to the researchers, "Not only does AmeriCorps provide individuals with

who work in the areas of education, public safety, health, and environmental protection. AmeriCorps members who work full-time for one year receive $4,725 toward college tuition or to pay back student loans. In addition, many members receive a modest living allowance while volunteering. AmeriCorps VISTA is similar, but provides volunteers specifically to help people and communities out of poverty. The AmeriCorps NCCC program is a ten-month program modeled on the Civilian

COOKIES FOR BOOKWORMS

An AmeriCorps National Civilian Community Corps (NCCC) volunteer, Elon Danziger, tells how he and his teammates created a reading program at an elementary school in a low-income county in California. This reading program continued even after the AmeriCorps volunteers left.

A child's motivation and achievement depends most of all on their parents' influence. This was the premise of an after-school parent-child reading program that we had observed at another school, in a much more prosperous district, where my teammates and I had served as mentors for a week.... I suggested at our next team meeting that we start a similar program at Palmer Way.... We presented it to the principal.... After she pointed out that offering food would be a major draw, we finally agreed on the rather un-hip name she proposed: "Cookies for Bookworms."...

The day finally arrived. A little before the school day ended, we helped the janitor unfold the cafeteria tables. We brought over baskets of books in English and Spanish.... We set up a station for food, which would be brought out after half an hour of reading (principal's orders). We waited. Parents began to arrive. More parents arrived, and a few grandparents. Fifteen minutes after the announced starting time, 80 people filled the room.... There they were, beaming 6- and 7-year-olds reading books they had chosen to patient parents. Even after the much-awaited cookie distribution, kids returned to the tables, cookies and Kool-Aid cups in hand, to finish a chapter or to find out what happened next....

Later, I received a letter from a Palmer Way teacher mentioning that Cookies for Bookworms was still going on. It felt great to know that my team had left a legacy and that families were continuing to connect through reading.

Source: *Pass the Fire: Stories about Service in America.* Washington, DC: Ameri-Corps, August 2003.

opportunities to help address their communities' most pressing needs, but the program also spurs individuals to be agents of positive change in their communities long after their AmeriCorps service (Corporation for National and Community Service 2008, 1).

Corporation for National and Community Service, Office of Research and Policy Development. *Still Serving: Measuring the Eight-Year Impact of AmeriCorps on Alumni*, Executive Summary. Washington, DC, 2008. http://www.abtassociates.com/page.cfm?PageID=40739 (accessed October 2008).

See also: National Service

Sources

Perry, James L., and Ann Marie Thomson. *Civic Service: What Difference Does It Make?* Armonk, NY: M.E. Sharpe, 2004.

Web Site

Corporation for National and Community Service. http://www.nationalservice.org/ (accessed October 2008).

PRIMARY DOCUMENT 19

Remarks on National Service at Rutgers University in New Brunswick, President Bill Clinton, March 1, 1993

In this speech, President Clinton makes the claim that national service has been part of American culture since the beginning of the country.

I came here to ask all of you to join me in a great national adventure, for in the next few weeks I will ask the United States Congress to join me in creating a new system of voluntary national service, something that I believe in the next few years will change America forever and for the better.

My parents' generation won new dignity working their way out of the Great Depression through programs that provided them the opportunity to serve and to survive. Brave men and women in my own generation waged and won peaceful revolutions here at home for civil rights and human rights and began service around the world in the Peace Corps and here at home in VISTA.

Now, Americans of every generation face profound challenges in meeting the needs that have been neglected for too long in this country, from city streets plagued by crime and drugs, to classrooms where girls and boys must learn the skills they need for tomorrow, to hospital wards where patients need more care. All across America we have problems that demand our common attention.

For those who answer the call and meet these challenges, I propose that our country honor your service with new opportunities for education. National service will be America at its best, building community, offering opportunity, and rewarding responsibility. National service is a challenge for Americans from every background and walk of life, and it values something far more than money. National service is nothing less than the American way to change America.

It is rooted in the concept of community: the simple idea that none of us on our own will ever have as much to cherish about our own lives if we are out here all alone as we will if we work together; that somehow a society really is an organism in which the whole can be greater than the sum of its parts, and every one of us, no matter how many privileges with which we are born, can still be enriched by the contributions of the least of us; and that we will never fulfill our individual capacities until, as Americans, we can all be what God meant for us to be.

If that is so, if that is true, my fellow Americans, and if you believe it, it must therefore follow that each of us has an obligation to serve. For it is perfectly clear that all of us cannot be what we ought to be until those of us who can help others, and that is nearly all of us, are doing something to help others live up to their potential.

The concept of community and the idea of service are as old as our history. They began the moment America was literally invented. Thomas Jefferson wrote in the Declaration of Independence, "With a firm reliance on the protection of Divine Providence, we mutually pledge to each other our lives, our fortune, and our sacred honor."

In the midst of the Civil War, President Lincoln signed into law two visionary programs that helped our people come together again and build America up. The Morrill Act helped States create new land grant colleges. This is a land grant university. The university in my home State was the first land grant college west of the Mississippi River. In these places, young people learn to make American agriculture and industry the best in the world. The legacy of the Morrill Act is not only our great colleges and universities like Rutgers but the American tradition that merit and not money should give people a chance for a higher education.

Mr. Lincoln also signed the Homestead Act that offered 100 acres of land for families who had the courage to settle the frontier and farm the wilderness. Its legacy is a nation that stretches from coast to coast. Now we must create a new legacy that gives a new generation of Americans the right and the power to explore the frontiers of science and technology and space. The frontiers of the limitations of our knowledge must be pushed back so that we can do what we need to do. And education is the way to do it, just as surely as it was more than 100 years ago.

Seven decades after the Civil War, in the midst of the Great Depression, President Roosevelt created the Civilian Conservation Corps, which gave 2 1/2 million young people the opportunity to support themselves while working in disaster relief and maintaining forests, beaches, rivers, and parks. Its legacy is not only the restoration of our natural environment but the restoration of our national spirit. Along with the Works Products Administration, the WPA, the Civilian Conservation Corps symbolized Government's effort to provide a nation in depression with the opportunity to work, to build the American community through service. And all over America today you can see projects, even today in the 1990's, built by your parents or your grandparents with the WPA plaque on it, the CCC plaque on it, the idea that people should be asked to serve and rewarded for doing it.

In the midst of World War II, President Roosevelt proposed the GI bill of rights, which offered returning veterans the opportunity for education in respect to their service to our country in the war. Thanks to the GI bill, which became a living reality in President Truman's time, more than 8 million veterans got advanced education. And half a century later, the enduring legacy of the GI bill is the strongest economy in the world and the broadest, biggest middle class that any nation has ever enjoyed.

For many in my own generation, the summons to citizenship and service came on this day 32 years ago, when President Kennedy created the Peace Corps. With Sargent Shriver and Harris Wofford and other dedicated Americans, he enabled thousands of young men and women to serve on the leading edge of the new frontier, helping people all over the world to become what they ought to be, and bringing them the message by their very lives that America was a great country that stood for good values and human progress. At its height, the Peace Corps enrolled 16,000 young men and women. Its legacy is not simply good will and good works in countries all across the globe but a profound and lasting change in the way Americans think about their own country and the world.

Shortly after the Peace Corps, Congress, under President Johnson, created the Volunteers In Service To America. Senator Jay Rockefeller, whom I introduced a moment ago, and many thousands of other Americans went to the hills and hollows of poor places, like West Virginia and Arkansas and Mississippi, to lift up Americans through their service.

The lesson of our whole history is that honoring service and rewarding responsibility is the best investment America can make. And I have seen it today. Across this great land, through the Los Angeles Conservation Corps, which took the children who lived in the neighborhoods where the riots occurred and gave them a chance to get out into nature and to clean up their own neighborhoods and to lift themselves and their friends in the effort; in Boston with the City Year program; with all these programs represented here in this room today, the spirit of service is sweeping this country and giving us a chance to put the quilt of America together in a way that makes a strength out of diversity, that lifts us up out of our problems, and that keeps our people looking toward a better and brighter future.

National service recognizes a simple but powerful truth, that we make progress not by governmental action alone, but we do best when the people and their Government work at the grass roots in genuine partnership. . . .

The plan can help to rebuild our cities and our small communities through physical investments that will put people to work. But Americans still must work to restore the social fabric that has been torn in too many communities. Unless people know we can work together in our schools, in our offices, in our factories, unless they believe we can walk the streets safely together, and unless we do that together, governmental action alone is doomed to fail.

The national service plan I propose will be built on the same principles as the old GI bill. When people give something of invaluable merit to their country, they ought to be rewarded with the opportunity to further their education. National service will challenge our people to do the work that should and indeed must be done and cannot be done unless the American people voluntarily give themselves up to that work. It will invest in the future of every person who serves.. . .

We'll ask young people all across this country, and some who aren't so young who want to further their college education, to serve in our schools as teachers or tutors in reading and mathematics. We'll ask you to help our police forces across the Nation, training members for a new police corps that will walk beats and work with neighborhoods and build the kind of community ties that will prevent crime from happening in the first place so that our police officers won't have to spend all their time chasing criminals.

We'll ask young people to work, to help control pollution and recycle waste, to paint darkened buildings and clean up neighborhoods, to work with senior citizens and combat homelessness and help children in trouble get out of it and build a better life.

And these are just a few of the things that you will be able to do, for most of the decisions about what you can do will be made by people like those in this room, people who run the programs represented by all of those wearing these different kinds of tee-shirts. We don't seek a national bureaucracy. I have spoken often about how we need to reinvent the Government to make it more efficient and less bureaucratic, to make it more responsive to people at the grass roots level, and I want national service to do just that. I want it to empower young people and their communities, not to empower yet another Government bureaucracy in Washington. This is going to be your programs at your levels with your people.. . .

I ask you all, my fellow Americans, to support our proposal for national service and to live a proposal for national service, to learn the meaning of America at its best, and to recreate for others America at its best. We are not just another country. We have always been a special kind of community, linked by a web of rights and responsibilities and bound together not by bloodlines but by beliefs. At an age in time when people all across the world are being literally torn apart by racial hatreds, by ethnic hatreds, by religious divisions, we are a nation, with all of our problems, where people can come together across racial and religious lines and hold hands and work together not just to endure our differences but to celebrate them. I ask you to make America celebrate that again.

I ask you, in closing, to commit yourselves to this season of service because America needs it. We need every one of you to live up to the fullest of your potential, and we need you to reach those who are not here and who will never hear this talk and who will never have the future they could otherwise have if not for something that you could do. The great challenge of your generation is to prove that every person here in this great land can live up to the fullest of their God-given capacity. If we do it, the 21st century will be the American century. The American dream will be kept alive if you will today answer the call to service.

Thank you, and God bless you all.

Source

Clinton, William J. *Public Papers of the Presidents of the United States: William J. Clinton, 1993*, vol. 1. Washington D.C., Government Printing Office, 1993: 224–229.

NATIONAL ASSOCIATION FOR THE ADVANCEMENT OF COLORED PEOPLE

The National Association for the Advancement of Colored People (NAACP) was founded in 1909, to challenge the culture of threats and violence surrounding blacks in southern states, and to challenge state and local segregation laws that kept blacks out of good schools, colleges, and jobs. The culture of violence and the segregation laws were causes of black poverty. According to Gilbert Jonas, "no private American organization has contributed as much to the realization of the American Dream during the twentieth century as the NAACP" (2005, 3).

The organization coalesced after black homes were burned and blacks were killed during a race riot in Springfield, Illinois, in 1908. The next year a group of white intellectuals, horrified at the violence, along with a few black leaders such as W. E. B. Du Bois, formed the NAACP to renew the struggle for equality for all people, regardless of race (Jonas 2005, 11).

Because state and local governments often did nothing to stop lynchings, one of the first and main goals of the NAACP was to call for a federal law against "lynchings" (murders of blacks by white supremacist groups such as the Ku Klux Klan). They also aimed to desegregate colleges and public schools, and to gain voting rights for blacks (Jonas 2005, 16, 25).

Although the NAACP founders realized that many blacks suffered from poverty, the organization did not focus specifically on poverty alleviation. According to Manfred Berg, at that time, many Americans believed that blacks had to progress economically first, before they could claim full citizenship rights. In fact, one prominent black leader of that time, Booker T. Washington, urged blacks to concentrate on education and economic progress, and to tolerate the segregation laws. The NAACP disagreed with

Washington. Instead, they believed that blacks should work toward both civil rights and economic progress—that even poor people deserved the rights of full citizenship (Berg 2005, 14–15).

To remove segregation laws, the NAACP recruited black and white lawyers who agreed to take cases for free. In 1915, the NAACP challenged an Oklahoma constitutional amendment that barred illiterate men from voting, with the exception of illiterate people whose ancestors had been allowed to vote before 1866. This amendment was a way to prevent blacks from voting (since many of them were poorly educated), but to allow uneducated whites to vote. The Supreme Court invalidated this amendment as being counter to the Fifteenth Amendment of the U.S. Constitution (which allowed black men to vote). In 1917, the NAACP took on the Louisville, Kentucky, law that barred blacks from living in certain areas of the city. The Supreme Court declared this law unconstitutional, because the Fourteenth Amendment guaranteed the same rights to all citizens (Jonas 2005, 34–35).

The NAACP attacked segregation in higher education in 1935 and 1936, gaining admission for black students to the law schools at the University of Maryland and the University of Missouri. While the NAACP lawyers were attacking segregation laws in court, the NAACP magazine and fundraising campaigns publicized these struggles around the country, making Americans aware of the problem of segregation in education (Jonas 2005, 43–45).

The NAACP's most famous legal victory is *Brown v. Board of Education of Topeka*. The NAACP began this campaign in 1950, by educating the black community about the need to desegregate all public schools. Instead of approaching the problem piecemeal, by suing individual schools one at a time, they aimed to desegregate all public schools at once. Lawsuits were initiated against school systems in several states. The cases reached the U.S. Supreme Court in 1952. In May 1954, the Court decided that, based on the Fourteenth Amendment, public schools could not be racially segregated (Jonas 2005, 56–64).

After the *Brown* victory, the NAACP's strategy of combining legal cases with citizen education inspired the formation of other groups who made use of the same strategies. Antiwar groups, women's groups, and organizations for other racial minorities were inspired by the NAACP's success (Jonas 2005, 33).

As of 2008, the NAACP continues to be one of the largest organizations dedicated to racial equality. According to the mission statement on their Web site, the organization works for the equality of all people: "The mission of the National Association for the Advancement of Colored People is to ensure the political, educational, social, and economic equality of rights of all persons and to eliminate racial hatred and racial discrimination" (NAACP, Mission Statement).

See also: Civil Rights Movement; Legal Services for the Poor; Segregation Laws

Sources

Berg, Manfred. *The Ticket to Freedom: The NAACP and the Struggle for Black Political Integration.* Gainesville, FL: University Press of Florida, 2005.

Jonas, Gilbert. *Freedom's Sword: The NAACP and the Struggle against Racism in America, 1909–1969.* New York: Routledge, 2005.

Web Sites

NAACP (National Association for the Advancement of Colored People). http://www.naacp.org (accessed July 2008).

NAACP (National Association for the Advancement of Colored People). Mission Statement. http://www.naacp.org/about/mission/index.htm (accessed July 2008).

NATIONAL CONSUMERS LEAGUE

The National Consumers League, founded in 1899, was one of the first organizations to bring the power of consumers to bear on the problem of poverty, low wages, and inhumane working conditions. Many other activists had looked to governments, private charities, and labor unions to solve the problem of poverty. The National Consumers League saw that consumers could also exert pressure in this area.

The National Consumers League was a coalition of several state consumers leagues. The first of these, in New York, grew out of the Working Women's Society of New York. A former department-store worker, Alice Woodbridge, compiled evidence from saleswomen with the help of Josephine Shaw Lowell, a prominent social reformer. This evidence of long hours, low wages, and sexual harassment was presented at a public meeting of philanthropists and clergymen. In 1891, Lowell and others formed the Consumers' League of the City of New York to help consumers make ethical purchasing decisions. The league published a list of department stores that paid their workers more and treated them better, and encouraged consumers to patronize only these stores. The league also sought to have department-store workers covered by the same maximum-hour laws that applied to factory workers (Waugh 1997, 197–202).

Similar leagues were started in other cities. In 1899, a national league was formed. Its first leader was Florence Kelley, who had been the chief factory inspector of Illinois, working to abolish child labor and to enforce maximum-hour laws for women (Goldmark 1953, 51–57).

Kelley traveled the country, encouraging activists to form local and state consumers leagues. From 1903 to 1905, the League focused on pushing for state child labor laws. After 1907 or so, the national and state-level consumers leagues were absorbed with pushing for passage of state laws that would restrict women's working hours (Skocpol 1992, 386–387).

Kelley realized that, although states might pass such laws, the Supreme Court could very well overrule them. So in 1907, she asked a lawyer friend, Louis Brandeis, to prepare a brief in defense of an Oregon law limiting women's work to ten hours per day. This Oregon law was heading toward the Supreme Court, and Kelley feared that the Court would decide that the law interfered with a woman's right to make any kind of work contract she wanted. Fortunately, the Supreme Court upheld the Oregon law in 1908. After this success, the National Consumers League continued to defend such laws in the face of court challenges (Skocpol 1992, 394–395).

The National Consumers League also decided that they wanted to award a special label to factories that paid their employees a living wage and limited working hours, and that did not

---

SALESCLERK'S MISERY

Maud Nathan, vice president of the National Consumers League, eloquently portrayed the lot of the young women who worked as salesclerks in the late 1800s and early 1900s:

From seven forty-five in the morning until eleven after night, with only a short time allowed for meals, they were expected to stand behind counters, smile on would-be customers, and cajole them into buying what they didn't want, if the article they asked for didn't happen to be in stock.... Clerks were not permitted even to bring up boxes from basements to sit upon. If they did this surreptitiously, the boxes were removed the following day. If they pulled out a drawer at the back of the counter, and sat on its edge, they were rebuked by the floor-walker; if they leaned on the front counter, they were told it looked unbusinesslike and that a straight posture was required. Girls were known to faint occasionally; when this happened they were stretched out on the concrete floor of the retiring room, and if they did not recover rapidly, they were sent home and their pay envelopes suffered in consequence.... There was no special duration of time accorded for the luncheon hour; twenty minutes was *supposed* to be the rule, but during the rush season saleswomen were *advised* to take but ten minutes for their frugal repast, in order that they might return as quickly as possible to wait on customers.... Floor-walkers ... were veritable tsars; they often ruled with a rod of iron. Only the girls who were "free-and-easy" with them, who consented to lunch or dine with them, who permitted certain liberties, were allowed any freedom of action, or felt secure in their positions. Rules in regard to leaving the counter were in some instances so rigid that the health of the saleswomen was apt to be impaired. Sometimes, rather than ask permission of the floor-walker to retire, they would use repression which involved physical suffering. In some instances permission to leave the counter was denied. A complaint lodged against a floor-walker or against the head of a department—superior officers—was almost invariably followed by dismissal of the one who had made the complaint. So little trust was placed in the ethical behavior of saleswomen that, in some of the large department stores, no privacy was accorded them in their retiring rooms. Doors were taken down from the toilets, and not even a curtain was put up to replace it.

Source: Nathan, Maud. *The Story of an Epoch-Making Movement.* Garden City, NY: Doubleday, Page and Company, 1926, 2–8.

---

employ child labor. This "White Label" would allow consumers to choose to buy goods that were produced in a fair manner. The League had to educate the public to ask for articles with such a label, and had to persuade factories to allow themselves to be inspected, and, if they passed the

inspection, to use the National Consumers League label.

The League first started inspecting factories that made women's underwear. To earn the White Label, the factories had to adhere standards of safety and cleanliness, and they were not allowed to employ young women under the age of sixteen. Women were to work no longer than fifty-four hours per week and were not allowed to work at night. The League's investigators were to have access, at any time, to the factory premises, and were also to have access to records of hours and wages. By 1914, sixty-eight companies had met the standards for the White Label (Nathan 1926, 72, 226–227).

The Consumers League, along with their local affiliates, helped launch campaigns in other sectors of the economy. In an effort to ensure a clean supply of milk, labels were awarded to dairies that met standards of sanitation. The New York Consumers' League investigated the working hours and wages of waitresses and demanded legislation to better their working conditions. The National Consumers League also investigated and publicized their findings relating to the canning industry (which used child labor and required long hours), the artificial flower industry (which employed children working in their own homes), and public laundries (which required long hours of work). The National Consumers League supported state campaigns for minimum wages for women, and pushed for the creation of the U.S. Children's Bureau (Nathan 1926, 74, 77–81; National Consumers League Web site).

Many of the women and men who worked at the Consumers League later went on to become government administrators during President Franklin Roosevelt's New Deal program to lift the country out of the Great Depression. First Lady Eleanor Roosevelt worked with the New York Consumers' League before she was married. Frances Perkins, secretary of the Department of Labor under Roosevelt, was head of the New York Consumers' League before starting her government career. Many years later, Perkins gave a speech in which she revealed that, when she was appointed secretary of labor, she felt "that it was the Consumers League who was appointed, and that I was merely the symbol who happened to be at hand, able and willing to serve at the moment" (Ware 1981, 36).

In the 1930s, during the Great Depression, the National Consumers League lobbied on behalf of the Fair Labor Standards Act, a national law passed in 1938 that outlaws child labor in most sectors of the economy and includes minimum-wage regulations.

Since then, the National Consumers League has worked for equal pay for equal work, fair labor laws for migratory workers, workplace compensation, disability insurance, Medicaid (health care for the poor), and Medicare (health care for the elderly).

Gradually, the League began to focus more on consumer safety issues and less on fair labor issues. As of 2009, the National Consumers League is still in operation, with headquarters in Washington, D.C. Although the League focuses more on consumer protection issues such as insurance fraud, health education for the layperson, and safe food, the organization continues to be interested in fair labor practices: one of their current projects is a campaign against child labor in agriculture.

See also: Children's Bureau; Child Labor Laws; Fair Labor Standards Act of 1938; Kelley, Florence; Lowell, Josephine Shaw; Minimum-Wage Laws; New Deal Women's Network; Perkins, Frances; Progressive Era; Roosevelt, Eleanor

Sources

Goldmark, Josephine. *Impatient Crusader: Florence Kelley's Life Story.* Urbana, IL: University of Illinois Press, 1953.

Nathan, Maud. *The Story of an Epoch-Making Movement.* Garden City, NY: Doubleday, Page and Company, 1926.

Skocpol, Theda. *Protecting Soldiers and Mothers: The Political Origins of Social Policy in the United States.* Cambridge, MA: Harvard University Press, 1992.

Ware, Susan. *Beyond Suffrage: Women in the New Deal.* Cambridge, MA: Harvard University Press, 1981.

Waugh, Joan. *Unsentimental Reformer: The Life of Josephine Shaw Lowell.* Cambridge, MA: Harvard University Press, 1997.

Web Site

National Consumers League. http://www.nclnet.org/ (accessed February 2008).

NATIONAL HEALTH INSURANCE

National health insurance is a government program of health insurance for all. This idea has been proposed many times in the United States, but as of 2008, no program for the general public has passed. Most Americans rely on private health insurance, usually offered through employers, but as of 2005, about 16 percent of the American public had no health insurance (National Coalition on Health Care Web site).

However, health clinics for poor women and children have been funded by the national government from 1921 to 1929, as part of the Sheppard-Towner Maternity and Infancy Act, and from 1935 to the early twenty-first century under Title V of the Social Security Act. National health insurance plans for the elderly (Medicare) and the poor (Medicaid) have been in place since the 1960s. A general national health insurance plan would especially help nonelderly people whose incomes are too high for Medicaid, and those who do not have access to affordable private health insurance through an employer.

Private health insurance began in the late 1920s and early 1930s, a time when health care began to improve, and at the same time to become too expensive for the normal American. Hospitals could not cover their costs because patients could not afford to pay. In 1929, Baylor Hospital in Dallas, Texas, came up with its own insurance plan for Dallas public school teachers: for $0.50 per month, teachers would have insurance coverage for up to twenty days of hospitalization. Similar plans were implemented at hospitals around the country, and the private insurance industry was born. Many of these plans were marketed through employers, and so health insurance became linked to employment. Although some people did not have access to health insurance, this system worked fairly well until the 1980s, when medical costs and health insurance costs increased rapidly. Many businesses stopped offering health insurance coverage for their employees (Cohn 2007, 6–10).

As part of President Franklin Roosevelt's New Deal of the 1930s, he wanted to include some sort of national health insurance in the Social Security legislation. This proved difficult, however, as related by Frances Perkins, head of the committee that drew up the Social Security law: "Powerful elements of the medical profession were up in arms over the idea of any kind of government-endorsed system" (1946, 289). The Social Security Act passed in 1935 but had no health insurance provisions for the general public.

President Harry Truman also tried to address unequal access to health care. He wanted every American, regardless of income, to be able to have access to modern medical care, and in 1945, he proposed a universal health insurance plan. Truman's plan would have funded more doctors and hospitals in rural and low-income areas, and would have created a national health insurance program. The plan would have provided cash to replace wages when someone was sick and unable to work. Despite the fact that Truman explained that his plan was not "socialized medicine," because doctors would not work for the government, the American Medical Association implied that the Truman administration was following Socialist or Communist ideas, and lobbied heavily against it. The Korean War, which started in 1950, diverted the country's attention away from health care (Harry S. Truman Library and Museum Web site).

In the 1960s, President Lyndon Johnson introduced a bill into Congress that would provide health insurance to the elderly and the poor. The Medicare bill that passed in 1965 included a mandatory plan that provided hospital coverage for everyone over age sixty-five, and a voluntary plan to pay doctors' bills. Medicare is financed through payroll taxes paid by employees and employers. A section of this bill created Medicaid, which was for low-income people. Although the American Medical Association again lobbied heavily against this bill, it passed Congress by a wide margin. Johnson arranged to sign the bill at

President Truman's hometown of Independence, Missouri, in honor of Truman's efforts on behalf of health care. One problem with Medicare was that at first it did not include any price controls on doctor and hospital fees, so the costs of the programs grew quickly. One initial problem with Medicaid was that it left out a lot of needy people because its eligibility requirements were so stringent (Andrew 1998, 97–101).

In the 1990s, President Bill Clinton and his wife, Hillary Clinton, led an effort to bring universal health insurance to all Americans. They consulted with almost 500 health policy experts, economists, and other professionals. Clinton's plan, the Health Security Act of 1993, would have required employers to provide health insurance to workers, and would have created a network of new "health insurance purchasing cooperatives." The plan included price controls on medical fees and an expansion of measures to address public health issues. Unfortunately, the Clinton plan ended up being complicated. According to Jonathan Engel, Clinton's health care task force "produced a twelve-hundred-page bill so byzantine that few lawmakers (or their staffers) actually managed to read it." The health insurance industry ran television ads against the plan, and many Americans at that time were wary of the idea of creating an entirely new, government-run health care bureaucracy. The Clinton bill was defeated in 1994 (Engel 2006, 230–231).

Many health care advocacy groups call for a "single-payer" style of health insurance, such as other industrial countries use. For example, a nonprofit organization called Physicians for a National Health Program promotes the

First Lady Hillary Rodham Clinton speaks at a health care rally at the University of Colorado. Her husband appointed her to head the Task Force on National Health Care Reform in 1993, though the Clintons abandoned the effort within a year because of intense opposition. (The White House)

idea of a single government or non-profit agency that would pay for, or organize the payment for, all health care costs. Health care still would be provided mostly by private doctors and hospitals. They describe their plan as an "expanded and improved version of Medicare" for all Americans. Their Web site points out that the government already funds more than 60 percent of U.S. health spending, including Medicare, Medicaid, tax subsidies for private insurance, and government purchases of private insurance for government employees such as teachers and police officers (Physicians for a National Health Program Web site).

See also: Johnson, Lyndon; Maternal and Child Health Services; Medicaid; Medicare; Roosevelt, Franklin Delano; Sheppard-Towner Maternity and Infancy Act of 1921; Social Security Act

Sources

Andrew, John A. III. *Lyndon Johnson and the Great Society.* Chicago, IL: Ivan R. Dee, 1998.

Cohn, Jonathan. *Sick: The Untold Story of America's Health Care Crisis—and the People Who Pay the Price.* New York: HarperCollins, 2007.

Engel, Jonathan. *Poor People's Medicine: Medicaid and American Charity Since 1965.* Durham, NC: Duke University Press, 2006.

Perkins, Frances. *The Roosevelt I Knew.* New York: Viking Press, 1946.

Web Sites

Harry S. Truman Library and Museum. http://www.trumanlibrary.org/anniversaries/health program.htm (accessed July 2008).

National Coalition on Health Care. http://www.nchc.org/facts/coverage.shtml (accessed July 2008).

Physicians for a National Health Program. http://www.pnhp.org/ (accessed July 2008).

PRIMARY DOCUMENT 20

Excerpt from a Special Message to the Congress Recommending a Comprehensive Health Program, President Harry S. Truman, November 9, 1945

President Truman is careful to repeat that his plan is not "socialized medicine," a label that has been used for years to tarnish any kind of national health insurance plan. Truman gave this speech shortly after the end of World War II, which is why he emphasizes the fact that many young men and women were not found healthy enough for the Armed Services.

To the Congress of the United States:

In my message to the Congress of September 6, 1945, there were enumerated in a proposed Economic Bill of Rights certain rights which ought to be assured to every American citizen.

One of them was: "The right to adequate medical care and the opportunity to achieve and enjoy good health." Another was the "right to adequate protection from the economic fears of ... sickness...."

Millions of our citizens do not now have a full measure of opportunity to achieve and enjoy good health. Millions do not now have protection or security against the economic effects of sickness. The time has arrived for action to help them attain that opportunity and that protection.

The people of the United States received a shock when the medical examinations conducted by the Selective Service System revealed the widespread physical and mental incapacity among the young people of our nation. We had had prior warnings from eminent medical authorities and from investigating committees. The statistics of the last war had shown the same condition. But the Selective Service System has brought it forcibly to our attention recently—in terms which all of us can understand.

As of April 1, 1945, nearly 5,000,000 male registrants between the ages of 18 and 37 had been examined and classified as unfit for military service. The number of those rejected for military service was about 30 percent of all those examined.

The percentage of rejection was lower in the younger age groups, and higher in the higher age groups, reaching as high as 49 percent for registrants between the ages of 34 and 37.

In addition, after actual induction, about a million and a half men had to be discharged from the Army and Navy for physical or mental disability, exclusive of wounds; and an equal number had to be treated in the Armed Forces for diseases or defects which existed before induction.

Among the young women who applied for admission to the Women's Army Corps there was similar disability. Over one-third of those examined were rejected for physical or mental reasons.

These men and women who were rejected for military service are not necessarily incapable of civilian work. It is plain, however, that they have illnesses and defects that handicap them, reduce their working capacity, or shorten their lives.

It is not so important to search the past in order to fix the blame for these conditions. It is more important to resolve now that no American child shall come to adult life with diseases or defects which can be prevented or corrected at an early age.

Medicine has made great strides in this generation—especially during the last four years. We owe much to the skill and devotion of the medical profession. In spite of great scientific progress, however, each year we lose many more persons from preventable and premature deaths than we lost in battle or from war injuries during the entire war.

We are proud of past reductions in our death rates. But these reductions have come principally from public health and other community services. We have been less effective in making available to all of our people the benefits of medical progress in the care and treatment of individuals.

In the past, the benefits of modern medical science have not been enjoyed by our citizens with any degree of equality. Nor are they today. Nor will they be in the future—unless government is bold enough to do something about it.

People with low or moderate incomes do not get the same medical attention as those with high incomes. The poor have more sickness, but they get less medical care. People who live in rural areas do not get the same amount or quality of medical attention as those who live in our cities.

Our new Economic Bill of Rights should mean health security for all, regardless of residence, station, or race—everywhere in the United States.

We should resolve now that the health of this Nation is a national concern; that financial barriers in the way of attaining health shall be removed; that the health of all its citizens deserves the help of all the Nation.. . .

FIRST: CONSTRUCTION OF HOSPITALS AND RELATED FACILITIES

The Federal Government should provide financial and other assistance for the construction of needed hospitals, health centers and other medical, health, and rehabilitation facilities. With the help of Federal funds, it should be possible to meet deficiencies in hospital and health facilities so that modern services—for both prevention and cure—can be accessible to all the people. Federal financial aid should be available not only to build new facilities where needed, but also to enlarge or modernize those we now have.. . .

SECOND: EXPANSION OF PUBLIC HEALTH, MATERNAL AND CHILD HEALTH SERVICES

Our programs for public health and related services should be enlarged and strengthened. The present Federal-State cooperative health programs deal with general public health work, tuberculosis and venereal disease control, maternal and child health services, and services for crippled children.

These programs were especially developed in the ten years before the war, and have been extended in some areas during the war. They have already made important contributions to national health, but they have not yet reached a large proportion of our rural areas, and, in many cities, they are only partially developed.

No area in the Nation should continue to be without the services of a full-time health officer and other essential personnel. No area should be without essential public health services or sanitation facilities. No area should be without community health services such as maternal and child health care.

Hospitals, clinics and health centers must be built to meet the needs of the total population, and must make adequate provision for the safe birth of every baby, and for the health protection of infants and children.. . .

THIRD: MEDICAL EDUCATION AND RESEARCH

The Federal Government should undertake a broad program to strengthen professional education in medical and related fields, and to encourage and support medical research.

Professional education should be strengthened where necessary through Federal grants-in-aid to public and to non-profit private institutions. Medical research, also, should be encouraged and supported in the Federal agencies and by grants-in-aid to public and non-profit private agencies.. . .

FOURTH: PREPAYMENT OF MEDICAL COSTS

Everyone should have ready access to all necessary medical, hospital and related services.

I recommend solving the basic problem by distributing the costs through expansion of our existing compulsory social insurance system. This is not socialized medicine.

Everyone who carries fire insurance knows how the law of averages is made to work so as to spread the risk, and to benefit the insured who actually suffers the loss. If instead of the costs of sickness being paid only by those who get sick, all the people—sick and well—were required to pay premiums into an insurance fund, the pool of funds thus created would enable all who do fall sick to be adequately served without overburdening anyone. That is the principle upon which all forms of insurance are based.

During the past fifteen years, hospital insurance plans have taught many Americans this magic of averages. Voluntary health insurance plans have been expanding during recent years; but their rate of growth does not justify the belief that they will meet more than a fraction of our people's needs. Only about 3% or 4% of our population now have insurance providing comprehensive medical care.

A system of required prepayment would not only spread the costs of medical care, it would also prevent much serious disease. Since medical bills would be paid by the insurance fund, doctors would more often be consulted when the first signs of disease occur instead of when the disease has become serious. Modern hospital, specialist and laboratory services, as needed, would also become available to all, and would improve the quality and adequacy of care. Prepayment of medical care would go a long way toward furnishing insurance against disease itself, as well as against medical bills.

Such a system of prepayment should cover medical, hospital, nursing and laboratory services. It should also cover dental care—as fully and for as many of the population as the available professional personnel and the financial resources of the system permit.

The ability of our people to pay for adequate medical care will be increased if, while they are well, they pay regularly into a common health fund, instead of paying sporadically and unevenly when they are sick. This health fund should be built up nationally, in order to establish the broadest and most stable basis for spreading the costs of illness, and to assure adequate financial support for doctors and hospitals everywhere. If we were to rely on state-by-state action only, many years would elapse before we had any general coverage. Meanwhile health service would continue to be grossly uneven, and disease would continue to cross state boundary lines.

Medical services are personal. Therefore the nation-wide system must be highly decentralized in administration. The local administrative unit must be the keystone of the system so as to provide for local services and adaptation to local needs and conditions. Locally as well as nationally, policy and administration should be guided by advisory committees in which the public and the medical professions are represented.

Subject to national standards, methods and rates of paying doctors and hospitals should be adjusted locally. All such rates for doctors should be adequate, and should be appropriately adjusted upward for those who are qualified specialists.

People should remain free to choose their own physicians and hospitals. The removal of financial barriers between patient and doctor would enlarge the present freedom of choice. The legal requirement on the population to contribute involves no compulsion over the doctor's freedom to decide what services his patient needs. People will remain free to obtain and pay for medical service outside of the health insurance system if they desire, even though they are members of the system; just as they are free to send their children to private instead of to public schools, although they must pay taxes for public schools.

Likewise physicians should remain free to accept or reject patients. They must be allowed to decide for themselves whether they wish to participate in the health insurance system full time, part time, or not at all. A physician may have some patients who are in the system and some who are not. Physicians must be permitted to be represented through organizations of their own choosing, and to decide whether to carry on in individual practice or to join with other doctors in group practice in hospitals or in clinics.

Our voluntary hospitals and our city, county and state general hospitals, in the same way, must be free to participate in the system to whatever extent they wish. In any case they must continue to retain their administrative independence.

Voluntary organizations which provide health services that meet reasonable standards of quality should be entitled to furnish services under the insurance system and to be reimbursed for them. Voluntary cooperative organizations concerned with paying doctors, hospitals or others for health services, but not providing services directly, should be entitled to participate if they can contribute to the efficiency and economy of the system.

None of this is really new. The American people are the most insurance-minded people in the world. They will not be frightened off from health insurance because some people have misnamed it "socialized medicine".

I repeat—what I am recommending is not socialized medicine.

Socialized medicine means that all doctors work as employees of government. The American people want no such system. No such system is here proposed.

Under the plan I suggest, our people would continue to get medical and hospital services just as they do now—on the basis of their own voluntary decisions and choices. Our doctors and hospitals would continue to deal with disease with the same professional freedom as now. There would, however, be this all-important difference: whether or not patients get the services they need would not depend on how much they can afford to pay at the time.

I am in favor of the broadest possible coverage for this insurance system. I believe that all persons who work for a living and their dependents should be covered under such an insurance plan. This would include wage and salary earners, those in business for themselves, professional persons, farmers, agricultural labor, domestic employees, government employees and employees of non-profit institutions and their families.

In addition, needy persons and other groups should be covered through appropriate premiums paid for them by public agencies. Increased Federal funds should also be made available by the Congress under the public assistance programs to reimburse the States for part of such premiums, as well as for direct expenditures made by the States in paying for medical services provided by doctors, hospitals and other agencies to needy persons....

FIFTH: PROTECTION AGAINST LOSS OF WAGES FROM SICKNESS AND DISABILITY

What I have discussed heretofore has been a program for improving and spreading the health services and facilities of the Nation, and providing an efficient and less burdensome system of paying for them.

But no matter what we do, sickness will of course come to many. Sickness brings with it loss of wages.

Therefore, as a fifth element of a comprehensive health program, the workers of the Nation and their families should be protected against loss of earnings because of illness. A comprehensive health program must include the payment of benefits to replace at least part of the earnings that are lost during the period of sickness and long-term disability. This protection can be readily and conveniently provided through expansion of our present social insurance system, with appropriate adjustment of premiums.

Insurance against loss of wages from sickness and disability deals with cash benefits, rather than with services. It has to be coordinated with the other cash benefits under existing social insurance systems. Such coordination should be effected when other social security measures are reexamined. I shall bring this subject again to the attention of the Congress in a separate message on social security.

I strongly urge that the Congress give careful consideration to this program of health legislation now.

Source

Truman, Harry S. Special Message to the Congress Recommending a Comprehensive Health Program, November 19, 1945. Harry S. Truman Library and Museum. http://www.trumanlibrary.org/publicpapers/index.php?pid=483&st=&st1= (accessed on February 13, 2009).

NATIONAL LABOR RELATIONS ACT

Passed in 1935 as part of President Franklin Roosevelt's New Deal to lift the country out of the Great Depression, the National Labor Relations Act (NLRA) made it easier for workers to organize into unions and bargain with employers as a group (collective bargaining), and led to a dramatic rise in the membership of labor unions. Because of the NLRA, workers gained higher wages, shorter working hours, and other benefits. The NLRA, also called the Wagner Act after its Senate sponsor Robert Wagner, is today one of the nation's most important labor laws. According to historian Roger Biles, "overall, collective bargaining became the New Deal's greatest bequest to labor" (1991, 171). Historian Melvyn Dubofsky goes even farther, noting that many scholars "consider the Wagner Act perhaps the most radical piece of New Deal legislation.... Clearly, never before had the sanction and weight of federal power been arrayed so fully behind the claims of trade unionism and industrial democracy" (1994, 129, 131).

Roosevelt's administration first tried to help workers organize through section 7(a) of the National Industrial Recovery Act, which was passed in 1933. Section 7(a) guaranteed the right to bargain collectively. However, it was not strongly enforced. Senator Robert Wagner of New York drafted a new bill that would give the government more power to help workers organize into unions. The NLRA passed Congress and was signed by Roosevelt in June of 1935. At that time many employers believed that the law might be struck down by the U.S. Supreme Court (which had been busy striking down other federal laws and agencies relating to labor, such as the first part of the National Industrial Recover Act). So businesses did not pay much attention to the new law until it was upheld by the U.S. Supreme Court in 1937, in the case *National Labor Relations Board v. Jones & Laughlin Steel Corporation.* The Supreme Court declared that Congress did have the power to regulate employers whose businesses affected interstate commerce, even if that particular business was not directly engaged in interstate commerce.

The NLRA created a National Labor Relations Board (NLRB) with the authority to help workers unionize and to certify unions as the legitimate elected representatives of workers. It also prohibits certain antiunion activities on the part of employers (such as interfering with union organizing or refusing to hire union members). With the support of the NLRB, union membership grew from 3.8 million to 6.6 million by 1939, and to 8.4 million by 1941. In the 1950s, union membership reached 15 million, or about a third of nonagricultural workers (agricultural workers are not covered under the law) (Biles 1991, 161, 167).

In addition to helping unions organize workers, the NLRA also clearly states that union organizing was good for the nation's economy: "the act also declared trade unionism to be the single best instrument for establishing industrial democracy, spreading wealth and income more widely, and averting future depressions" (Dubofsky 1994, 130).

The NLRA has been amended several times. The Taft-Hartley Act (also called the Labor Management Relations Act), passed in 1947, prohibited unions from coercing employees to join or from imposing excessively high membership fees. Certain kinds of strikes were also banned. In 1959,

amendments were passed to regulate the internal business operations of unions, because government investigation had uncovered evidence of corruption, bribery, and mismanagement in some unions. The NRLA's jurisdiction has been expanded to cover nonprofit hospitals and nursing homes; private, nonprofit colleges and universities; and professional baseball and soccer.

At the request of employees, employers, or unions, the NLRB will help employees hold elections to determine by which union, if any, the employees wish to be represented. The NRLB also investigates allegations of unfair labor practices. Employees, unions, and employers may submit such complaints to the NLRB. After investigation, if the NRLB finds a violation of the law, they will ask the employer or union to make changes. If changes are not made, the NRLB can take the employer or union to court. The NRLA does not cover agricultural workers, domestic workers, independent contractors, or government employees.

The ability to organize and bargain collectively has been extremely important in providing higher wages and more benefits to working people. According to historian Michael Katz, the NRLA has also allowed workers to bargain with employers for health care and other benefits that the government did not provide. "Here, more than in social security or public assistance, was the New Deal's great legacy to the American worker" (1996, 251–252).

Especially at the beginning of the National Labor Relations Act, however, unions often helped men more than women, who tended not to belong to a union. Union leaders tended to be male.

PRIMARY DOCUMENT 21

Excerpt from the National Labor Relations Act

It is interesting that, in Section I, the law is deemed important not for humanitarian reasons, but because it protects the free flow of commerce by ensuring workers' rights to organize and bargain collectively (as a group) with their employers. The law is designed to prevent strikes and "other forms of industrial strife or unrest" that would obstruct commerce. Although one purpose of the law is to prevent the need for strikes, strikes still are legal under this law. The law points out that when workers do not have equal bargaining power with employers, wages are low and purchasing power is low, which is not good for the economy.

Sec. 1. [§151.] The denial by some employers of the right of employees to organize and the refusal by some employers to accept the procedure of collective bargaining lead to strikes and other forms of industrial strife or unrest, which have the intent or the necessary effect of burdening or obstructing commerce by (a) impairing the efficiency, safety, or operation of the instrumentalities of commerce; (b) occurring in the current of commerce; (c) materially affecting, restraining, or controlling the flow of raw materials or manufactured or processed goods from or into the channels of commerce, or the prices of such materials or goods in commerce; or (d) causing diminution of employment and wages in such volume as substantially to impair or disrupt the market for goods flowing from or into the channels of commerce.

The inequality of bargaining power between employees who do not possess full freedom of association or actual liberty of contract and employers who are organized in the corporate or other forms of ownership association substantially burdens and affects the flow of commerce, and tends to aggravate recurrent business depressions, by depressing wage rates and the purchasing power of wage earners in industry and by preventing the stabilization of competitive wage rates and working conditions within and between industries.

Experience has proved that protection by law of the right of employees to organize and bargain collectively safeguards commerce from injury, impairment, or interruption, and promotes the flow of commerce by removing certain recognized sources of industrial strife and unrest, by encouraging practices fundamental to the friendly adjustment of industrial disputes arising out of differences as to wages, hours, or other working conditions, and by restoring equality of bargaining power between employers and employees.

Experience has further demonstrated that certain practices by some labor organizations, their officers, and members have the intent or the necessary effect of burdening or obstructing commerce by preventing the free flow of goods in such commerce through strikes and other forms of industrial unrest or through concerted activities which impair the interest of the public in the free flow of such commerce. The elimination of such practices is a necessary condition to the assurance of the rights herein guaranteed

It is declared to be the policy of the United States to eliminate the causes of certain substantial obstructions to the free flow of commerce and to mitigate and eliminate these obstructions when they have occurred by encouraging the practice and procedure of collective bargaining and by protecting the exercise by workers of full freedom of association, self-organization, and designation of representatives of their own choosing, for the purpose of negotiating the terms and conditions of their employment or other mutual aid or protection.. . .

RIGHTS OF EMPLOYEES

Sec. 7. [§ 157.] Employees shall have the right to self-organization, to form, join, or assist labor organizations, to bargain collectively through representatives of their own choosing, and to engage in other concerted activities for the purpose of collective bargaining or other mutual aid or protection, and shall also have the right to refrain from any or all such activities except to the extent that such right may be affected by an agreement requiring membership in a labor organization as a condition of employment as authorized in section 8(a)(3) [section 158(a)(3) of this title].

UNFAIR LABOR PRACTICES

Sec. 8. [§ 158.] (a) [Unfair labor practices by employer] It shall be an unfair labor practice for an employer—

(1) to interfere with, restrain, or coerce employees in the exercise of the rights guaranteed in section 7 [section 157 of this title];

(2) to dominate or interfere with the formation or administration of any labor organization or contribute financial or other support to it: *Provided*, That subject to rules and regulations made and published by the Board pursuant to section 6 [section 156 of this title], an employer shall not be prohibited from permitting employees to confer with him during working hours without loss of time or pay;

(3) by discrimination in regard to hire or tenure of employment or any term or condition of employment to encourage or discourage membership in any labor organization: *Provided*, That nothing in this Act [subchapter], or in any other statute of the United States, shall preclude an employer from making an agreement with a labor organization (not established, maintained, or assisted by any action defined in section 8(a) of this Act [in this subsection] as an unfair labor practice) to require as a condition of employment membership therein on or after the thirtieth day following the beginning of such employment or the effective date of such agreement, whichever is the later, (i) if such labor organization is the representative of the employees as provided in section 9(a) [section 159(a) of this title], in the appropriate collective-bargaining unit covered by such agreement when made, and (ii) unless following an election held as provided in section 9(e) [section 159(e) of this title] within one year preceding the effective date of such agreement, the Board shall have certified that at least a majority of the employees eligible to vote in such election have voted to rescind the authority of such labor organization to make such an agreement: *Provided further*, That no employer shall justify any discrimination against an employee for non-membership in a labor organization (A) if he has reasonable grounds for believing that such membership was not available to the employee on the same terms and conditions generally applicable to other members, or (B) if he has reasonable grounds for believing that membership was denied or terminated for reasons other than the failure of the employee to tender the periodic dues and the initiation fees uniformly required as a condition of acquiring or retaining membership;

(4) to discharge or otherwise discriminate against an employee because he has filed charges or given testimony under this Act [subchapter];

(5) to refuse to bargain collectively with the representatives of his employees, subject to the provisions of section 9(a) [section 159(a) of this title]. . . .

Source

National Labor Relations Board. http://www.nlrb.gov/about_us/overview/national_labor_relations_act.aspx (accessed May 2008).

Even unions of predominantly women workers, such as the International Ladies Garment Workers Union, had male leadership (Biles 1991, 203–204).

See also: Great Depression; Labor Unions; National Recovery Administration; New Deal; Roosevelt, Franklin Delano; Supreme Court and Poverty

Sources

Biles, Roger. *A New Deal for the American People*. DeKalb, IL: Northern Illinois University Press, 1991.

Dubofsky, Melvyn. *The State and Labor in Modern America*. Chapel Hill, NC: University of North Carolina Press, 1994.

Katz, Michael. *In the Shadow of the Poorhouse: A Social History of Welfare in America*. New York: Basic Books, 1996.

National Labor Relations Board. "The First Sixty Years: The National Labor Relations Board, 1935–1995." http://www.nlrb.gov/publications/history/thhe_first_60_years.aspx (accessed May 2008).

National Labor Relations Board. "The National Labor Relations Board and You: Unfair Labor Practices." http://www.nlrb.gov/nlrb/shared_files/brochures/engulp.pdf (accessed May 2008).

Web Site

National Labor Relations Board. http://www.nlrb.gov (accessed May 2008).

NATIONAL RECOVERY ADMINISTRATION

The National Recovery Administration (NRA) was a federal agency created in 1933, at the beginning of the New Deal, to administer the first part of the National Industrial Recovery Act (NIRA). The second part of NIRA was carried out by the Public Works Administration.

Although the NRA was not successful at improving wages and decreasing unemployment, and although it was ruled unconstitutional by the U.S. Supreme Court in 1935, because it gave too much power to the president, still the NRA laid the groundwork for future New Deal programs. According to Frances Perkins, Roosevelt's Secretary of Labor, "The NRA was a seed bed out of which many other activities and experiments grew" (1946, 213).

The NRA was designed to cure the American economy of its ills through "codes of fair labor," including minimum wages and maximum hours, which every business within a given industry had to abide by. Instead of the government imposing rules on businesses, each industry was to get together and come up with ways of doing business that were fair to both workers and employers. The idea was to keep wages high enough so that workers could buy what they needed, which in turn would stimulate the economy. Although industries had some freedom in creating the codes, they were required to include provisions allowing workers to organize and unionize; and they had to include a maximum number

A Pomo Indian, Chief Little John, with his great grandson Little Eagle Feather, work side by side with the Blue Eagle, September 1933. Businesses that operated according to a National Recovery Administration code of operation could display a poster bearing the blue eagle insignia. (Bettmann/Corbis)

of hours of labor and a minimum rate of pay.

The president would then approve of these codes. Every business within a given industry was required to abide by the codes to prevent a "race to the bottom," in which businesses lowered wages and prices in an effort to compete with each other. Businesses that did not abide by the approved codes could be fined $500 for every day they continued to be in violation of the law. Furthermore, if the president found evidence of wage and price cutting in an industry, he could require all businesses in that field to be licensed. This law gave the president "unprecedented peace-time powers" (Lyon et al. 1935, 12, 14, 893, 896).

President Franklin Roosevelt had high hopes for NIRA. Upon signing the law in June of 1933, he said,

History probably will record the National Industrial Recovery Act as the most important and far-reaching legislation ever enacted by the American Congress. It represents a supreme effort to stabilize for all time the many factors which make for the prosperity of the nation and the preservation of the American standards. Its goal is the assurance of a reasonable profit to industry and living wages for labor, with the elimination of the piratical methods and practices which have not only harassed honest business but also contributed to the ills of labor. (Lyon et al. 1935, 3)

"NRA IS NOT AT ALL POPULAR"

Lorena Hickok, a government worker charged with interviewing Americans during the Great Depression and reporting on their experiences, discusses reactions to the National Recovery Administration (NRA) in Iowa in 1933:

The NRA is not at all popular, to be sure. Well, how *could* it be? Their prices *did* go up faster than their incomes. And businessmen in smaller cities—just above 2,500 for instance—that are trading centers wholly dependent on agriculture, and as a matter of fact practically every city and town in Iowa, from Des Moines on down, is almost wholly dependent on agriculture, must have been having a tough time if they tried to live up to NRA. The truth is—they haven't. Hotels, for instance. You see the same crew on all day and far into the night. Clerks—some hotels apparently have only one. Waitresses. Dick and I had dinner at 8 o'clock in the coffee shop at the Warrior in Sioux City one night last week, and at breakfast at 6:30 the next morning the same waitress served us. I doubt if the Warrior could take on any more help and remain solvent. There couldn't have been more than a dozen guests in the place while we were there, and it's practically new, not over 3 years old, and a very good hotel. ... Walk up to the desk in any of these hotels and look over the mail boxes. Certainly 80 percent of them will be empty, with the keys lying in them. Many of them—the Warrior, for instance—keep only one elevator running. Take situations like that, combined with—let us say the rather brusque—tactics of General Johnson, and NRA isn't going to be very popular. You know a lot of these small businessmen really are *for* the President. Among them there seems to be no organized attack as there is in so-called "Big Business." I think most of them, perhaps, would like to comply. But they can't and stay in business.

Source: Hickok, Lorena, Richard Lowitt, and Maurine Beasley. *One Third of a Nation: Lorena Hickok Reports on the Great Depression.* Urbana, IL: University of Illinois Press, 1981, 117.

Unfortunately, the NRA did not live up to Roosevelt's hopes. NRA administrator Hugh Johnson was a stubborn, alcoholic man who favored big business and alienated labor leaders, small businesses, and other leaders within the Roosevelt administration. By mid-July he had only managed the creation of one code, for the cotton textile industry. At this point Roosevelt proposed the creation of a voluntary code for all businesses, who were asked to eliminate child labor, pay at least $12 per week, and limit working hours to thirty-five in industry and forty-four for white-collar workers. Businesses who agreed to abide by this code were awarded a "blue eagle," and consumers were urged to support only businesses displaying the blue eagle (Biles 1991, 80–84).

Many of the larger industries, such as the steel, iron, and auto industries, resisted raising wages, reducing working hours, and allowing workers to unionize. The codes that were created tended to favor big business. Labor leaders criticized the codes. Nevertheless, according to historian Roger Biles, "Roosevelt stopped short of truly empowering labor for fear of the negative impact on the NRA" (1991, 85). This favoritism toward big business resulted in higher prices and lower wages. Consumers had less purchasing power, instead of more.

Eventually, codes were created in hundreds of industries. However, businesses that violated the codes were rarely fined. Weekly wages often did not increase, and even the lower working hours did not end up providing more work to the unemployed. Consumers often sought out stores without the blue eagle, assuming that the prices would be lower. Roosevelt tried to fix the NRA by creating all sorts of boards to study the NRA and to negotiate with labor leaders. But by January 1935, it became clear that real wages had not increased during the previous year. Still, Roosevelt asked Congress for a two-year extension of the NRA (it was set to expire in June) (Bellush 1975, 57; Biles 1991, 85–92).

Before Congress could act, however, the U.S. Supreme Court did. In October 1934, a Brooklyn, New York, business, Schechter Poultry, had been accused of violating the NRA wage and hour regulations. A federal district court and a circuit court both found the company guilty. The business appealed the case to the U.S. Supreme Court; and in May 1935, the court ruled unanimously that Title I of the NIRA was unconstitutional, because in effect it gave the president power to make laws (approval of the codes), and this power belonged to Congress. According to the Court, "Extraordinary conditions do not create or enlarge constitutional power"

(Bellush 1975, 169–170). The NRA was dead.

Despite its failure, the NRA did succeed in discouraging the use of child labor and also helped clear the way for future federal legislation on minimum wages and maximum hours. Nevertheless, as Biles notes, "its immediate impact on the economy was, at best, negligible, and, at worst, damaging" (Biles 1991, 79, 90).

See also: Fair Labor Standards Act of 1938; Great Depression; Minimum-Wage Laws—Supreme Court Cases; National Labor Relations Act; New Deal; Public Works Administration; Roosevelt, Franklin Delano

Sources

Bellush, Bernard. *The Failure of the NRA.* New York: W.W. Norton, 1975.

Biles, Roger. *A New Deal for the American People.* DeKalb, IL: Northern Illinois University Press, 1991.

Davis, Kenneth S. *FDR: The New Deal Years, 1933–1937.* New York: Random House, 1986.

Lyon, Leverett S., Paul T. Homan, Lewis L. Lorwin, George Terborgh, Charles L. Dearing, and Leon C. Marshall. *The National Recovery Administration: An Analysis and Appraisal.* Washington, DC: Brookings Institution, 1935.

Perkins, Frances. *The Roosevelt I Knew.* New York: Viking Press, 1946.

NATIONAL SCHOOL LUNCH ACT

The National School Lunch Act was passed in 1946 to ensure that poor children had some nutritious food. The law provides federal and state money to schools so they can buy food and feed schoolchildren.

Before the 1930s, schools did not routinely provide lunch to students.

Starting in the late nineteenth century, private charities often raised money to provide a school lunch to poor children. In the 1920s, some school districts began to spend government funds for school lunches (Levine 2008, 33–37).

Governments got involved with providing food to schoolchildren during the Great Depression of the 1930s. Doctors and nutritionists were concerned that malnourished children would not be able to learn in school. By the mid-1930s, states passed laws to allow local school boards to use tax money to pay for school meals. At the same time, farmers were suffering because people did not have enough money to buy all the food the farms were producing, and prices were falling for farm products. The solution to this was the Surplus Marketing Administration: the federal government purchased extra farm products to keep prices high for such products. Starting in about 1936, these extra farm products were then donated to schools and welfare offices. Because the program started as a way to use up excess agricultural products, the program was and continues to be housed at the U.S. Department of Agriculture (Levine 2008, 41–47).

By March 1937, more than 300,000 children were being served through the school lunch program. By the early 1940s, almost 80,000 schools and more than 5 million children benefited from this program. One problem with using donated food was that the schools never knew what kind of food they would have to work with, so it was difficult to plan meals. Schools complained of receiving grapefruit, which the students would not eat, or so many eggs that they had to serve eggs for days in a row (Levine 2008, 48–49; USDA,

National School Lunch Program History).

With U.S. entry into World War II at the end of 1941, surplus farm products were no longer available for schoolchildren. From 1942 to 1946, Congress provided money year by year to schools to purchase food. The National School Lunch Act of 1946 made this program permanent (Carleton 2002, 90–91).

The National School Lunch Act required states to partially fund the program: up to $3 of state money had to be provided for every $1 of federal money. Many states simply counted the students' payment for lunch as the state contribution to the program. Surplus agricultural products were also donated to schools. The law required schools to serve lunches that met a minimum nutritional requirement. It also required schools to provide free or reduced-cost meals to poor children, and not to discriminate against children. By 1960, 14 million children were being fed through this program. However, this was only one-third of all American schoolchildren. The federal government did not oversee states and local school districts to make sure they did not discriminate against black children. Teachers, principals, or social workers decided which children received free lunches—there were no national guidelines (Levine 2008, 89–91; USDA, National School Lunch Program History).

A 1962 survey commissioned by the U.S. Department of Agriculture found that very few poor children were receiving free school lunches. In 1962, Congress passed amendments to the National School Lunch Act that required the Department of Agriculture to enforce the provisions for free

SCHOOL LUNCH IN 1946

The National School Lunch Act included guidelines for the kinds of foods children should be served. The Type A lunch below was designed to meet one-third to one-half of the nutritional requirements of children ages ten to twelve. Schools could make adjustments to feed children of different ages. The Type B lunch was for schools that did not have the facilities to prepare a Type A lunch.

Table 1. National School Lunch Act Type A and Type B Lunches

	Type A	Type B
Milk, whole	0.5 pint	2 pints
Protein-rich food consisting of any of the following or a combination thereof:		
— Fresh or processed meat, poultry meat, cheese, cooked, or canned fish	2 oz.	1 oz.
— Dry peas or beans or soy beans, cooked	0.5 cup	0.25 cup
— Peanut butter	4 tbsp.	2 tbsp.
— Eggs	1 portion	0.5 portion
Raw, cooked, or canned vegetables or fruits, or both	0.75 cup	0.5 cup
Bread, muffins, or hot bread made of whole grain cereal or enriched flour	1 portion	1 portion
Butter or fortified margarine	2 tsp.	1 tsp.

Source: National School Lunch Program History, http://www.fns.usda.gov/cnd/Lunch/About Lunch/ProgramHistory_5.htm (accessed August 2008).

meals—although no funds were appropriated for this new enforcement function until 1966, with the passage of the Child Nutrition Act. This law provided funds specifically for free lunches, and was, according to history professor Susan Levine, "a milestone in the transformation of school lunches from farm subsidy to welfare" (2008, 113).

Nevertheless, even under the amended National School Lunch Act, states and school districts could make their own decisions as to which schools and which students received free meals. For example, Alabama and Georgia gave no money for free lunches to poor black counties. Some states concentrated their school lunch money in just a few schools. The federal government still had not established standards as to which students should receive free lunches. In addition, in many schools, children who received free lunches were required to perform chores in exchange for the lunch, or to stand in a separate line (Levine 2008, 115–119).

Middle-class Americans believed that all poor children were receiving a free lunch, but this was far from true. In the late 1960s, national women's organizations started a campaign to make sure poor children received free lunches. These women's groups were the National Council of Catholic Women, the National Council of Jewish Women, the National Council of Negro Women, Church Women United, and the Young Women's Christian Association. They studied the situation for eighteen months and came out with a report, *Their Daily Bread,* which revealed that because many states relied heavily on children's fees to fund the program, very little money was left to provide free lunches for the needy. Of the estimated 6 million poor school-children, less than 2 million received a free lunch. The women's groups recommended that the federal government provide a uniform federal standard as to which children should receive a free lunch; that states reduce the price of the lunch so more children could afford to pay; and that state and local governments contribute more funding (Levine 2008, 128–136; Robin n.d., 13, 122–125).

As a result of the national pressure brought by these women's groups, as well as by civil rights groups such as the Black Panther Party, Congress increased the amount of money for school lunches in 1969. Congress also set the standard that all children who lived at or below 125 percent of the federal "poverty line" should receive a free lunch. The federal poverty line—the level of income below which a family would be considered poor—had been established in 1963. School districts had to increase the number of free lunches to continue receiving federal funds, and schools were not allowed to simply increase lunch fees.

Antipoverty groups also held demonstrations and filed lawsuits to force states to provide more money for the cost of the program. States complied, and the number of free lunches increased dramatically (Levine 2008, 140–143).

As a result, the National School Lunch Program has become one of the country's most important welfare programs. In 2007, more than 30.5 million children participated in the program. Almost 49 percent received free lunches, and another 9 percent paid a reduced price (USDA, National School Lunch Program Annual Summary).

The School Breakfast Program first started as a pilot program in 1966, and became permanent in 1975. Students who are eligible for a free or reduced-price lunch are also eligible for a free or reduced-price breakfast. As of the 2006–2007 school year, 9.9 million children participated in this program. The federal government also provides funding for summer meals programs for poor children, and funding for meals and snacks at child care centers and after-school programs (Food Research and Action Center, Federal Food Programs).

See also: Black Panther Party; Great Depression; Hunger and Food Insecurity; Poverty Line; Public Schools; Special Supplemental Nutrition Program for Women, Infants and Children

Sources

Carleton, David. *Landmark Congressional Laws on Education.* Westport, CT: Greenwood Press, 2002.

Levine, Susan. *School Lunch Politics: The Surprising History of America's Favorite Welfare Program.* Princeton, NJ: Princeton University Press, 2008.

Robin, Florence, director, Committee on School Lunch Participation. *Their Daily Bread.* Atlanta, GA: McNelley-Rudd Printing Service, n.d. (probably 1968).

PRIMARY DOCUMENT 22

Excerpt from Their Daily Bread, Committee on School Lunch Participation

This report published by a coalition of six women's groups in the late 1960s aimed to shatter the myth that every poor child in the country received a free school lunch. The women's groups conducted extensive interviews with state school lunch directors and others within forty cities, towns, and rural communities. This study was influential in boosting funding for the school lunch program and ensuring that virtually all poor children had access to a free lunch. The following excerpt includes samples from interviews, showing the plight of poor, hungry children at lunchtime.

PHILADELPHIA, PENNSYLVANIA

(From an interview with a junior high school principal): "If a child does not have the money for lunch and is not bringing lunch from home, in other words is not eating, he is required to go to the lunchroom and sit with the other children who are eating."

LEE COUNTY, SOUTH CAROLINA

(From interviews at a school where 519 free lunches are rotated among 800 eligible children): "The desperately hungry usually eat at least several times a week." ... "Sometimes a child becomes ill in the morning from lack of food."

(From an interview with an elementary school principal): "Nothing can be done for these children who cannot buy lunch and are not eligible that day for free lunch, except that those who ask to eat because they are hungry are allowed to do so if there is enough food left over when the others finish eating. The teachers try to rotate the lunches among the pupils."

GREEN BAY, WISCONSIN

(From an interview with a teacher of low income high school students): "In one of my classes, five out of six children are getting no lunch or bringing inadequate food. In most of my other classes, 20% to 25% are getting no lunch or an inadequate one. There is only one girl in my classes who gets a free lunch and she works for it in the kitchen. Since getting a free lunch she

has shown a marked improvement in attitude. Last year she was a major discipline problem."

(From an interview with the mother of eight children who used to be on welfare): "All my children pay regular price. I can afford to pay this about three months of the year. I can't afford it during the cold months, when they need it most, because of extra fuel bills, the need for warm clothing, and so on. During the winter I try to fix them oleo [margarine] sandwiches or sometimes peanut butter. At one time my husband had major surgery and was laid up for a long time. I went to school and asked for free lunch and was told the children could eat daily but I must repay the total amount after my husband got back to work. I did repay this."

DONNA, TEXAS (A community with large percentage of migrant workers)

(From a school principal interview):"We have a specific allocation of free lunches. There are always more children to feed than funds allow. We have a policy that no child goes hungry. If they can't get a lunch, they get milk and crackers."

LA CONNER, WASHINGTON

(From the interview with the Local School Lunch Director): This community has a high proportion of needy children. Of 459 children in the two schools here, 24 get free or reduced price lunches. "The children are given the

opportunity to work one day for a free lunch the next day. Older children can do the work for the younger ones."

(From a parent interview): "I know of several families who ought to be getting a free lunch. Some families keep their children out of school when they don't have lunch to give them or money for them to buy it."

TALLAHASSEE, FLORIDA

(From an interview with a teacher in a slum junior-senior high school with 1,264 Negro students): Of 250 children in the lunch program, there are six reduced price lunches and one free lunch. "Seventeen out of my 36 children are either not getting any lunch or an inadequate one. I see definite personality changes when a child doesn't get lunch."

(From an interview with an elementary school teacher): "I give up most of my lunch each day. I want food for all the children, but I can't afford to buy tickets for all of them. You can't teach a hungry child."

MOBILE, ALABAMA

(From an elementary school principal interview): "The child with nothing to eat plays outdoors during the lunch hour. Lunches are rotated among the needy on a weekly basis. One thousand children need free lunches, but only 15 get them."

(From an elementary school principal interview): "We choose the children for free lunches at the beginning of the year. There is no rotation of free lunches. If you have to go hungry, you might as well get used to it."

Source

Robin, Florence, director, Committee on School Lunch Participation. *Their Daily Bread.* Atlanta, GA: McNelley-Rudd Printing Service, n.d. (probably 1968), 15–20.

Web Sites

Food Research and Action Center. Federal Food Programs. http://www.frac.org/html/federal_food_programs/federal_index.html (accessed August 2008).

USDA (U.S. Department of Agriculture). National School Lunch Program. http://www.fns.usda.gov/cnd/Lunch/ (accessed August 2008).

NATIONAL SERVICE

National service is the idea that the government should help people to engage in volunteer work, or work that carries only a small monetary stipend, and that benefits the community or the country. National service is also called "civic service," "community service," and "citizen service." Since the 1930s, the federal government has created programs to get people involved in national service. Some of these national service projects provide services to the poor. In addition, national service programs—because they often come with stipends or other incentives—can be a way for low-income people to participate in community service, learn job skills, and gain work experience.

The first national service programs were created during the New Deal of the 1930s, as a response to the poverty and unemployment of the Great Depression. These programs were designed both to create jobs for the unemployed and to provide useful services to the community and the country. For example, the young men who participated in the Civilian Conservation Corps planted trees, built campgrounds, and improved parks. They received good food and some payment

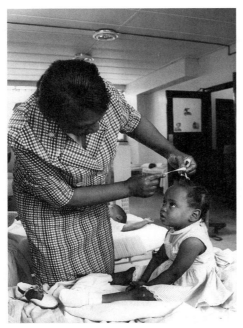

A foster grandmother dresses a child at McMahon Memorial shelter. "Foster Grand-parents," a volunteer organization, gives the elderly a chance to care for small children while their mothers are working, New York City, May 1967. (National Archives)

for their work. The Works Progress Administration (WPA) was responsible for hiring the unemployed to build and renovate schools, parks, playgrounds, libraries, swimming pools, and hospitals. WPA workers also prepared and served lunches to low-income school-children, and staffed nursery schools.

The New Deal national service programs were seen as temporary measures, necessary only until the economy got back on its feet. However, in the 1960s, the federal government created some permanent national service programs. These programs were not created in response to economic distress—in fact, the country at that time was doing well economically. Instead, when President John F. Kennedy established

the Peace Corps in 1961, he challenged Americans to use their skills to help poor people in other countries.

Also in the 1960s, President Lyndon Johnson established several national service programs to serve the United States, including Volunteers in Service to America (VISTA), the Foster Grand-parent Program, and Teacher Corps. These were all part of Johnson's Great Society initiative to address the nation's social problems, such as poverty. VISTA, created through the Economic Opportunity Act of 1964, provided funds to place volunteers in government agencies to help fight poverty. The Foster Grandparent Program aimed to encourage low-income elderly people to get involved in community service as "foster grandparents"—they were to establish one-on-one relationships with disabled children and other children with special needs. Foster grandparents are eligible for tax-free stipends. Teacher Corps was designed to train teachers to serve in low-income areas of the country. It was in existence until 1982.

In 1970, the federal government created the Youth Conservation Corps (YCC), patterned after the Civilian Conservation Corps. The YCC was a summer work program for teenagers. It evolved into a year-round program, Young Adult Conservation Corps, which lasted until 1982, when the administration of President Ronald Reagan cut funding for it. California then created a similar program just for that state—the California Conservation Corps (Perry and Thomson 2004, 11–14).

The phrase "service-learning" was coined in the 1960s to describe students who learn while volunteering. This concept grew in popularity until in

1981, the National Center for Service Learning for Early Adolescents was founded. In 1990, President George H. W. Bush signed the National and Community Service Act, which provided federal grants to schools for service-learning projects (Eniclerico 2006, 172–173).

When President Bill Clinton took office in 1993, one of his goals was to expand national service programs. He introduced the National and Community Service Trust Act of 1993, which passed in that year, and which created the Corporation for National and Community Service to manage all federally funded civic service programs. VISTA became part of this, as did the Foster Grandparent Program, other senior volunteer programs, and the service-learning program. In addition, the law created a new program, AmeriCorps, which provides stipends, health insurance, and education awards to people who volunteer for a year in education, public safety, environmental programs, or human welfare programs. In 1994, 20,000 people served in AmeriCorps. By 2004, AmeriCorps had enough funding to grow the program to 75,000 participants per year (AmeriCorps, Timeline).

Research on national service programs has shown positive results. Participants in service programs learn new skills, develop civic responsibility, and gain education opportunities. They report satisfaction with their work. As a result of service programs, communities gained more and improved services (Perry and Thomson 2004, 120–121).

See also: Civilian Conservation Corps; Economic Opportunity Act of 1964; Great Depression; Great Society; National and Community Service Trust Act of 1993; New Deal; Works Progress Administration

Sources
Eniclerico, Ronald, ed. *National Service.* New York: H.W. Wilson Company, 2006.
Perry, James L., and Ann Marie Thomson. *Civic Service: What Difference Does It Make?* Armonk, NY: M.E. Sharpe, 2004.

Web Sites
AmeriCorps. Timeline. http://www.americorps.org/about/ac/history_timeline.asp (accessed October 2008).
California Conservation Corps. http://www.ccc.ca.gov/ (accessed October 2008).
Foster Grandparents. http://www.seniorcorps.gov/about/programs/fg.asp (accessed October 2008).
Peace Corps. History. http://www.peacecorps.gov/index.cfm?shell=learn.whatispc.history (accessed October 2008).

NATIONAL VOTER REGISTRATION ACT OF 1963

The National Voter Registration Act (NVRA) aims to make it easier for poor people to register to vote. The law requires states to allow voter registration at agencies that serve the poor and the disabled, as well as through the mail. The NVRA also prohibits states from removing the names of people who had not voted in the last several years. The law is also called the "motor voter" law, because it allows voter registration at drivers' license agencies.

As a result of this law, 73 percent of eligible voters were registered by 1996—the highest percentage of voter registration since 1960, when records were first kept. The law may also account for the fact that voter turnout increased from about 52 percent of eligible voters in the 1992 presidential election, to 60 percent in 2004 ("Executive Summary" 1997; U.S. Election Project Web site).

Before the passage of this law, states could decide when and where people could register to vote, and what documentation they had to provide to register. Some states had a policy of "purging" the names of people who were registered but who had not voted in the past two to four years. These people would then have to reregister to be eligible to vote.

During the 1970s and 1980s, some states made their voter registration processes easier, but many states did not. The federal government grew concerned that voter registration procedures were keeping people from voting. In 1974, federal courts struck down a Texas law that permitted registration only for four months of the year. In the 1970s, Congress considered bills that would have required states to allow mail-in registration, but these bills were defeated. President Jimmy Carter proposed the National Uniform Registration Act in 1977, to require that people be allowed to register on election day, but this bill was also defeated.

In 1983, a coalition of organizations began pushing for a law to allow voter registration at agencies that served the poor as well as at other government agencies, and mail-in voter registration. Making it easier for poor people to vote would benefit the Democratic Party, so Republicans were opposed to this bill. They argued that the federal government ought not to get involved in voter registration, which was the responsibility of the states. In 1988 and 1991, the bill was defeated in the Senate. In 1992, the bill passed, but President George H. W. Bush (a Republican) vetoed it. The bill passed again in 1993, and was signed by President Bill Clinton (a Democrat) (Keyssar 2000, 312–315).

According to Alexander Keyssar, a history professor at Harvard University, the NVRA was the culmination of a forty-year struggle (since the 1960s civil rights movement) to broaden voting rights and nationalize voting laws. "By the end of the twentieth century, what had been a long historical swing toward contraction of the franchise had been decisively reversed," says Keyssar (2000, 315).

The law took effect in 1995, and applies to forty-four states plus the District of Columbia. Six states are exempt from the requirements of the NVRA because they have no voter registration requirements, or because they allow election-day registration at the polls (National Voter Registration Act, Civil Rights Division).

See also: Civil Rights Movement; Voting Rights; Voting Rights Act of 1965

Sources

Keyssar, Alexander. *The Right to Vote: The Contested History of Democracy in the United States.* New York: Basic Books, 2000.

"Executive Summary of the Federal Election Commission's Report to the Congress on the Impact of the National Voter Registration Act of 1993 on the Administration of Federal Elections." June 1997. http://www.fec.gov/votregis/nvrasum.htm (accessed October 2008).

Web Sites

National Voter Registration Act. United States Department of Justice, Civil Rights Division. http://www.usdoj.gov/crt/voting/nvra/activ_nvra.php (accessed October 2008).

U.S. Elections Project. Voter Turnout. http://elections.gmu.edu/voter_turnout.htm (accessed October 2008).

NATIONAL YOUTH ADMINISTRATION

The National Youth Administration (NYA) was a federal government program that operated from 1935 to 1943. It was created as part of President Franklin Roosevelt's New Deal to lift the country out of the Great Depression. The NYA was one of two major New Deal programs targeting youth. The other was the Civilian Conservation Corps. President Roosevelt created the agency by executive order in June of 1935. It was part of the Works Progress Administration, the largest New Deal agency.

First Lady Eleanor Roosevelt was a strong force behind the formation of the NYA. She noted that many New Deal programs ignored youth: the Works Progress Administration, for example, hired only those over twenty-four years of age. The Civilian Conservation Corps discriminated against black men and did not hire any women. Starting in 1933, she began prodding her husband to create something for young people (Cook 1999, 268–270).

One goal of the NYA was to provide part-time jobs within their own schools and colleges to needy teens and young adults, so they could continue their education. The other goal was to provide work training and experience to unemployed young people who were no longer in school. Some of the work training was offered at vocational boarding schools.

Students performed clerical, construction, and other work for their own schools, and they received maximum monthly payment of $6 for high school students, $15 for college students, and $30 for graduate students. At its height in 1936 and 1937, more than 400,000 students participated in this program. For students who were out of school, under the NYA, they could work a maximum of seventy hours per month and earn wages of up to $21 per month, depending on the region of the country. Needy young people between the ages of eighteen and twenty-five were eligible. About 90 percent of these youth lived at home, while about 10 percent lived away from home. The program started with about 180,000 young people, and in 1941, increased to more

Young men work on telephone poles in Maine as participants in vocational training under the National Youth Administration program, ca. 1935–1943. (Library of Congress)

than 400,000 when military training was expanded (Meriam 1946, 446–453).

The NYA was one of the most inclusive of the New Deal agencies. Women and men both benefited from NYA work projects, although women continued to be paid less than men. Blacks were included in the NYA programs in proportion to their presence in the general population. More than 120 traditional black colleges participated in the program. Mary McLeod Bethune, a black educator, served as its director of negro affairs. Eleanor Roosevelt continued to be heavily involved with the NYA: she talked daily with the NYA administrator, suggested projects (such as a survey of occupations for women), and protested when women were discriminated against in certain communities (Lindley and Lindley 1938, 18; Biles 1991, 108; Cook 1999, 270–271).

Male NYA workers planted trees and built picnic tables and other amenities in public parks; repaired school buildings and playgrounds; and built school bus shelters, tennis courts, tuberculosis isolation huts, and community centers. They helped maintain and repair automobiles, fire trucks, and short-wave radios for police cars; repaired furniture; and worked in city print shops. Young men and women worked in libraries and performed clerical work. Women worked as nursery school aides and hospital nursing aides, worked in sewing rooms, canned vegetables, and prepared school lunches. The NYA workers also built community youth centers in every state, where young people could gather for workshops and recreation (Lindley and Lindley 1938, 25–61).

The NYA operated a vocational guidance program for all unemployed young people ages sixteen to twenty-four—not just those who worked at NYA jobs. With the goal of helping young people find jobs or return to school, this program conducted classes, provided individual career counseling, and prepared brochures and information about occupations (Johnson and Harvey 1974, 79–81).

Over its eight years of existence, the NYA helped more than 2 million young people and was one of the most popular of the New Deal programs (Biles 1991, 108).

A future U.S. president was involved with the NYA: Lyndon Johnson, a former high school teacher, served as head of the Texas NYA in the 1930s. Johnson, who launched his War on Poverty program in the 1960s, credited his experience with the NYA for giving him the ideas for some of his administration's programs to alleviate poverty (Reiman 1992, 194).

See also: Bethune, Mary McLeod; Civilian Conservation Corps; Great Depression; Johnson, Lyndon; New Deal; Roosevelt, Eleanor; Works Progress Administration

Sources

Biles, Roger. *A New Deal for the American People.* DeKalb, IL: Northern Illinois University Press, 1991.

Cook, Blanche Wiesen. *Eleanor Roosevelt, Volume Two: 1933–1939.* New York: Viking Press, 1999.

Johnson, Palmer O., and Oswald L. Harvey. *The National Youth Administration.* New York: Arno Press, 1974 (reprint of 1938 edition).

Lindley, Betty, and Ernest K. Lindley. *A New Deal for Youth.* New York: Viking Press, 1938.

Meriam, Lewis. *Relief and Social Security.* Washington, DC: Brookings Institution, 1946.

Reiman, Richard A. *The New Deal and American Youth: Ideas and Ideals in a Depression Decade.* Athens, GA: University of Georgia Press, 1992.

NEW DEAL

The New Deal is the name given to the many varied programs of poverty relief, social insurance, and economic planning that were started during the Great Depression by the federal government under President Franklin Roosevelt. Roosevelt first used the words "new deal" in 1932, in a speech accepting the Democratic presidential nomination. The New Deal marks the first time the federal government got involved significantly with poverty relief.

During the New Deal, the president and Congress created dozens of new laws, agencies, and programs in an attempt to figure out how to solve the economic crisis. From March 9 to June 16, 1933, Roosevelt sent Congress numerous bills and Congress passed fifteen major laws to combat the poverty, unemployment, and business failures of the Great Depression. This session of Congress is known as the "Hundred Days."

Roosevelt did not necessarily have all the answers as to how to solve the country's economic problems, but he was willing to experiment with a broad range of tactics. He first tackled the banking crisis—when he took office, banks around the country were on the verge of failing. To restore confidence in the American banking system, Roosevelt and Congress passed the Emergency Banking Act in March of 1933, which closed all banks temporarily and directed the secretary of the treasury to examine banks and reopen those that were financially sound. After two months, most banks had reopened. In June, Congress created the Federal Deposit Insurance Corporation to insure bank accounts up to $2,500. This further helped people to feel confident that their money was safe in a bank (Biles 1991, 34–35, 45).

Roosevelt believed it would be good for unemployed young men to perform conservation work in nature. In March 1933, at his request, Congress created the Civilian Conservation Corps (CCC), which hired unmarried men between the ages of eighteen and twenty-five to perform work such as constructing buildings and trails in parks, installing telephone and power lines, constructing logging and fire roads, and planting trees. The program continued until 1942.

Another major poverty-relief effort of the Hundred Days was the Federal Emergency Relief Administration (FERA), created in May 1933, which gave $500 million to states for use on work-relief projects and direct aid to the poor. Roosevelt ended the FERA in 1935, because he believed these kinds of relief projects had to be temporary. However, because the problems of poverty and unemployment continued, Roosevelt and Congress started that same year the Works Progress Administration (WPA), which was the largest New Deal agency. The WPA provided jobs for people across the country in a variety of fields, from construction to arts to media to education. The project provided food, clothing, and housing to the needy. The WPA continued until 1943.

Roosevelt also addressed the crisis in agriculture. Although farmers made up 30 percent of the labor force in 1933, their share of the national income had fallen from 25 percent in 1919, to just 10.4 percent by 1929; and during the early 1930s, the situation grew even worse. Farmers were heavily in debt, and many of them lost their farms because they could not afford to pay the mortgage. The Agricultural Adjustment Act (AAA), passed in May of 1933, set minimum prices for farm products, and paid farmers *not* to grow or raise certain crops and animals (because one reason for the decrease in farm income was the oversupply of things like cotton and pigs). The AAA was declared unconstitutional by the U.S. Supreme Court in 1936, because it sought to control an area (farm production) that was, according to the Court, the province of the state governments. In 1938, Congress passed another AAA, which allowed farmers to voluntarily choose to reduce their production and receive payments if they did so. As a result of these laws, farm income did rise (Biles 1991, 37, 69–70).

Roosevelt was interested in experimenting with government control of the production of electricity and with government economic planning on a regional scale. He found an appropriate project in the Tennessee River area. This area had been plundered of its trees, soil, and natural resources, resulting in a barren, poverty-stricken landscape. Most farms and houses had no electricity, because the private power companies did not consider it profitable to run power lines to this poor region. Roosevelt wondered whether the government could transform this area into a prosperous, self-sufficient region. The

law creating the Tennessee Valley Authority (TVA) was passed in May 1933. The TVA built dams on the Tennessee River and ran power lines to homes, businesses, and farms in the region. The TVA developed fertilizers to improve the soil and replanted forests. As of 2009, the TVA is the nation's largest public power company (Davis 1986, 90–94; TVA Web site).

One problem with the economy was that wages in many jobs were too low to allow people to buy what they needed, let alone what they wanted. Many people were unemployed and had little or no money to spend. As a result, products did not sell, businesses lost money, and employers laid off workers, which caused more unemployment, meaning that people had even less money to spend. Roosevelt wanted to work with businesses and industry to raise wages and reduce unemployment. He and Congress passed the National Industrial Recovery Act in June 1933, the first part of which created the National Recovery Administration (NRA). The NRA encouraged businesses to work together and come up with codes of fair competition, including minimum wages, maximum hours, and limits on child labor. These codes were to be approved by the president. The NRA was ruled unconstitutional in 1935 by the U.S. Supreme Court because it gave too much power to the executive branch of the government. Although it was only operational for a few years, the ideas behind the NRA were later incorporated into other New Deal legislation.

Roosevelt and his advisers could see that millions of people would starve during the winter of 1933–1934, if something was not done fast. The

Public Works Administration (created by the second part of the National Industrial Recovery Act) was not coming up with work projects fast enough, and the FERA gave money to states for their own work projects. Roosevelt wanted a federally controlled, massive but temporary public works project that would carry people through the winter. He created the Civil Works Administration in November 1933, with the goal of putting 4 million unemployed people to work from December to February. This sounded like an impossible proposal on such short notice, but the administrator of the program, Harry Hopkins, had 800,000 people working in ten days, and 2 million within two weeks. By mid-January, the program was employing more than 4 million (Davis 1986, 306–310).

One of the most significant of the New Deal programs was the Social Security Act of 1935. Employers and employees were to make contributions into the program, and employees would receive pensions when they retired. The government made no contributions. This was the first time that the federal government had instituted any kind of broad-based "social insurance" program not dependent upon veteran status. The Social Security Act also contained provisions for unemployment insurance and gave federal grants to states for aid to mothers with dependent children, and to the blind. In his statement on signing the Social Security Act, Roosevelt pointed out that, in addition to helping individuals, the act was meant to temper the effects of future depressions by ensuring that the needy had at least some money to spend, which would not only meet their own basic needs, but also would keep the economy going.

In addition to helping individuals and families, a few small New Deal programs created cooperative communities as a way of helping the poor survive the Great Depression. The federal government created about 100 communities of "subsistence homesteads" in which families were provided with basic homes, some land for growing food, and a few animals. The federal government also created three cooperative "greenbelt" towns. These were some of the most innovative of the New Deal programs.

The New Deal for Women and Minorities

Women went to work in increasing numbers during the Great Depression to help support families in which husbands or fathers were unemployed. Some people felt it was wrong for women to work when men were unemployed. The CCC specifically excluded women from being hired. Work relief projects through the FERA, the Civil Works Administration, and the WPA would not hire women for the higher-paid construction work, but only for lower-paid jobs such as domestic work, sewing, and canning. The Fair Labor Standards Act of 1938 allowed a lower minimum wage to be set for women. While the Social Security Act provided money for poor mothers and their children, it excluded domestic workers, most of whom were women, from coverage (Biles 1991, 199–202).

Although many New Deal programs discriminated against women who were poor, at the same time, Roosevelt promoted many women to high positions within the federal government, such as Secretary of Labor Frances Perkins.

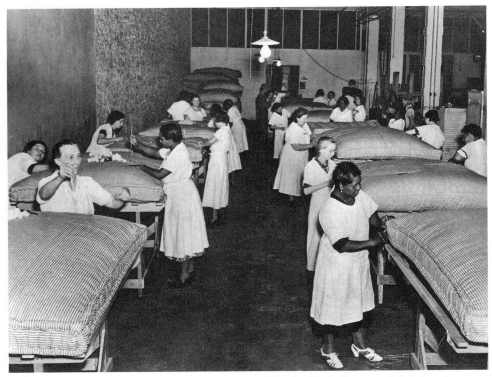

Women sew mattresses as part of a project sponsored by the Works Progress Administration (WPA), Topeka, Kansas, ca. 1936. (National Archives)

Women also headed some New Deal agencies, such as the Federal Theater Project, the WPA Workers Education Project, and the WPA Women's and Professional Project. Women reformers were so important and influential during the New Deal that they were known as the "Women's Network," led by First Lady Eleanor Roosevelt (Biles 1991, 195–198; Katz 1996, 229–230).

During the Great Depression, African Americans went from poor to poorer. A much higher percentage of blacks were unemployed compared with whites, and those blacks who were able to find work were often harassed by unemployed whites. Southern states (where most blacks lived) gave smaller relief payments to needy black families, compared with what was given to white families. Some private charities completely refused aid to blacks (Biles 1991, 172–174).

Although the New Deal programs did not specifically exclude blacks, in practice, African Americans often did not benefit because of widespread racial discrimination. For example, the director of the CCC was a southern man who believed in racial segregation. Most CCC camps were segregated, and because fewer camps were available for African Americans, blacks had a longer waiting list. The TVA tended to hire black workers only for the lowest-paid jobs. The local officials in charge of distributing the FERA money often

APPLYING FOR WORK AT THE CWA

Nine million people applied for jobs with the Civil Works Administration. To process these applications, temporary employment centers were set up in schools and other public buildings around the country. Bonnie Fox Schwartz describes the scene at some of these places:

After midnight, November 28, when offices opened in New York City, about 500 people formed a thin line outside the Manhattan USES, 124 East 28th Street, but by dawn long files extended to Fourth Avenue below 27th Street. Approximately 5,000 crowded the sidewalk and spread onto the street by the Brooklyn station, while mounted police had to keep 2,000 behind barriers near the Long Island City center. In all, 15,000 jammed offices throughout the five boroughs that first day. In Chicago, a reported 70,000 assembled before sunrise on November 23, when the city opened forty-one park field houses and the Eighth Regiment Armory to register CWA applicants. By evening over 32,000 had filled out forms. An estimated 150,000 flocked to sign up the first week in North Carolina.

Source: Schwartz, Bonnie Fox. *The Civil Works Administration, 1933–1934*. Princeton, NJ: Princeton University Press, 1984, 43.

would give blacks less relief per month than was awarded to whites, and would hire blacks last. While two-thirds of blacks worked as agricultural or domestic workers, the Social Security program excluded these two occupational categories (Biles 1991, 177–178, 191).

However, some New Deal programs tried to ensure that blacks would benefit. The Public Works Administration set up a quota system to reserve a percentage of jobs for blacks. The administrator of the Farm Security Administration, created in 1937 to help poor farmers, insisted that black farmers receive a fair number of loans. The WPA also had a good record of hiring blacks (Biles 1991, 182–185).

Native Americans fared better during the New Deal because of John Collier, commissioner of Indian Affairs, who made sure that American Indians had specific New Deal programs developed just for them.

Although the New Deal did not end the Great Depression—in 1938, the unemployment rate was still about 19 percent—it was somewhat successful in easing the pain of the Great Depression. Unemployment did decrease from 13 million in 1933 to 9 million in 1936, and wages also rose (Biles 1991, 226–227).

The New Deal ended with the U.S. entry into World War II in 1941. Government spending on the war effort virtually wiped out unemployment. As Robert McElvaine explains,

The New Deal was highly successful in its first objective of easing the pain of the depression. But it never quite managed to bring about the full recovery it sought, largely because Roosevelt declined to be sufficiently bold in calling for the sort of massive government spending in peacetime that would be readily accepted in war. As a result, the depression did not end until 1941, when U.S. entry into World War II necessitated the level of spending needed to stimulate the economy. (2000, 15)

Since the New Deal, the federal government has continued to be heavily involved with regulating the economy and providing funding for social insurance and poor relief. Many New Deal laws and programs have continued to this day and are among the country's most influential mandates, including the Fair Labor Standards Act, the Federal Deposit Insurance Corporation, the National Labor Relations Act, the Securities and Exchange Commission, and Social Security.

See also: Agricultural Adjustment Act; Civilian Conservation Corps; Civil Works Administration; Fair Labor Standards Act of 1938; Federal Emergency Relief Act; Great Depression; Hopkins, Harry; Indian New Deal; National Labor Relations Act; National Recovery Administration; National Youth Administration; New Deal Cooperative Communities; New Deal Women's Network; Perkins, Frances; Public Works Administration; Roosevelt, Eleanor; Roosevelt, Franklin Delano; Social Security Act; Tennessee Valley Authority; Unemployment Insurance; Works Progress Administration

Sources

Biles, Robert. *A New Deal for the American People*. DeKalb, IL: Northern Illinois University Press, 1991.

Davis, Kenneth. *FDR: The New Deal Years, 1933–1937: A History*. New York: Random House, 1986.

Katz, Michael. *In the Shadow of the Poorhouse: A Social History of Welfare in America*. New York: Basic Books 1996.

McElvaine, Robert. *The Great Depression: America, 1929–1941*. New York: Times Books, 1984.

McElvaine, Robert. *The Depression and New Deal: A History in Documents*. New York: Oxford University Press, 2000.

Roosevelt, Eleanor. *The Autobiography of Eleanor Roosevelt*. New York: Harper and Brothers, 1961.

Roosevelt, Franklin. "Franklin Roosevelt's Statement on Signing the Social Security Act." August 14, 1935. http://www.fdrli brary.marist.edu/odssast.html (accessed March 2008).

Web Sites

National New Deal Preservation Association. http://newdeallegacy.org/index.html (accessed March 2008).

New Deal Network. http://newdeal.feri.org/ (accessed March 2008).

Tennessee Valley Authority. http://www.tva. gov/ (accessed March 2008).

NEW DEAL COOPERATIVE COMMUNITIES

In addition to helping poor individuals and families during the Great Depression, the New Deal programs of President Franklin Roosevelt also helped create a number of cooperative communities. These communities enabled needy but employable families to work together to create a higher standard of living for all. This was the first time the federal government had attempted to create cooperative communities. While the communities programs were a fairly small part of the New Deal, they were important philosophically, because, as Paul Conkin observes, "their development reflected one of the most open breaks with the individualistic tradition in American history" (1959, 6).

The New Deal communities programs can be divided into two classes:

subsistence homestead communities for farmers, miners, and other unemployed workers, and "greenbelt" suburbs that were designed to provide an alternative to inner-city slums. A total of ninety-nine different communities were funded, providing housing and employment for about 10,000 families.

The New Deal communities were created and managed by a confusing mix of different New Deal agencies. The first federally funded subsistence homesteads were a project of the Public Works Administration, which started in 1933. At the same time another agency, the Federal Emergency Relief Administration, gave money to states to set up their own subsistence homesteads programs. In 1935, the subsistence housing work of both these agencies was taken over by the newly created Resettlement Administration, except for three communities, which were taken over by the Works Progress Administration. The Resettlement Administration then started the "greenbelt" towns program. In 1937, the Resettlement Administration became the Farm Security Administration (Conkin 1959, 7, 93).

A subsistence homestead meant a home and land on which the family could grow or raise most of the food they would require. The settlers were supposed to eventually own their land, and they would share some land and amenities with the other settlers in their community. Ideally, the communities would be located near industrial areas, so part-time industrial work would be possible. The idea was to create communities that

A woman and child cultivate a garden at the El Monte Subsistence Homesteads, February 1936. Each home in the federally sponsored community had three-quarters of an acre of land on which occupants could raise most of their food. Photograph by Dorothea Lange. (Library of Congress)

had the best of the rural and urban environments: the fresh air and sunshine of rural life, and the social, cultural, and money-making advantages of the city (Leighninger 2007, 138–139).

At the urging of First Lady Eleanor Roosevelt, the subsistence houses were not merely shacks, but durable homes with at least four rooms, plumbing, and electricity. In addition to homes and land, education was seen as extremely important to fostering an economically successful community. The subsistence homesteaders benefited from the presence of experts to teach them better techniques for farming, canning, and food processing, as well as study groups to teach adults how to operate a cooperative business.

While the poor and unemployed were eager for subsistence homesteads, the program was not welcomed by everyone. Established farmers were afraid that the government-supported subsistence farmers would cut into their market. Businesses were afraid that any government-sponsored industry in the communities would threaten their business. Some members of Congress were opposed to the cooperative, communal aspect of these communities, labeling them "Communist."

The subsistence homestead communities succeeded in lifting people out of poverty and in providing them with decent housing, education, and other necessities. However, most of the communities were not able to make enough income to pay the government back and to become self-sufficient, as had been envisioned. Because of this failure, they were criticized as being a waste of money.

Many of the communities involved part-time subsistence farming and part-time employment in industry. Arthurdale

in West Virginia was one of the first and most publicized of these. The government bought 1,200 acres of land to start the community in 1933. Eventually, 165 homes were built, along with several school buildings, an administration building, gas station, forge, cooperative store, furniture factory, flour mill, barbershop, weaving room, health clinic, and other community buildings.

Arthurdale never managed to make enough money to justify the federal government's investment in it. The government was never able to find a suitable industry that could provide cash income to supplement the subsistence farms and community businesses, and that would allow the settlers to pay an adequate amount of rent.

When Arthurdale and similar subsistence homesteads were criticized for costing too much money, Eleanor Roosevelt replied, "I have always felt that many human beings who might have cost us thousands of dollars in tuberculosis sanitariums, insane asylums, and jails were restored to usefulness and given confidence in themselves" (Roosevelt 1961, 180).

The Resettlement Administration originally envisioned twenty-five greenbelt towns, but ultimately only three such towns were constructed under the New Deal: Greenbelt, Maryland; Greenhills, Ohio; and Greendale, Wisconsin. These were the largest of the New Deal communities, together containing more than 2,000 family units. "Based on world-wide influence, the greenbelt cities, next to the Tennessee Valley Authority, were probably the most influential creations of the New Deal," says Paul Conkin. "They represented ... the most daring, original and ambitious experiments in public housing in the

MEETINGS GALORE

David Granahan was an early settler in Greenbelt. He recalls his experiences:

The joke in those days was that you couldn't live in Greenbelt for more than a week before you became a member of a committee. And that was about it. We never received wages. We ran the theater, the gas station, the grocery store. We had meetings galore about the price of theater tickets, what films should be shown, whether the service station was giving good service, etc. In Greenbelt, we became very much influenced by interesting people. It helps a lot if you are around people who are creative in their own selves, and I am not talking about the artists. I mean people who have creative thoughts about how a town should be governed.

Source: Virtual Greenbelt Web Site. http://www.otal.umd.edu/%7Evg/ (accessed April 2008).

history of the United States" (Conkin 1959, 167, 305; Leighninger 2007, 157).

Greenbelt, Maryland, was the first town to be completed, in 1937. It grouped houses into five neighborhoods, each containing a central park. The houses were connected with pedestrian walkways—no roads were within the neighborhoods. The town also contained a lake, school, restaurant, movie theater, swimming pool, community-controlled retail stores, and community gardens. Greenhills, created in 1938, near Cincinnati, Ohio, was planned more for the automobile and less for pedestrian traffic. Like Greenbelt, it featured parks, stores, and so forth, but the town was bisected by a main highway. Greendale, near Milwaukee, Wisconsin, also started in 1938, and was surrounded by farms. It was designed to resemble a normal country village, with houses arranged in city blocks.

The cooperative stores, credit unions, and health care services within each community were financially successful. In fact, residents were so enthusiastic about cooperatives that in Greenbelt, Maryland, the schoolchildren operated their own cooperative store to sell candy, pencils, and other childhood necessities.

The major criticism of the greenbelt towns was their cost. They ended up being quite expensive to build, and the rent had to be subsidized because the low-income settlers could not afford to pay for the full cost of the housing and community services. Other critics felt it was inappropriate for the federal government to compete with private business in building housing.

Town planners from around the world were fascinated by the greenbelt towns experiment. The towns were radical in that they gave low-income residents living in government-subsidized housing control over their local government, and in that they planned for a system of cooperative institutions to serve the residents. All three towns are still thriving today. Greenbelt, Maryland, is a National Historic Landmark.

The New Deal communities programs came under attack by Congress and other critics as being a waste of money, and as being antithetical to the American values of individualism and free enterprise. Robert Leighninger, a sociologist at Arizona State University, asks whether these programs were simply real-estate ventures, or something more.

> What would it have cost to have these families on relief for six or eight years? If the thousands of relief workers who built the greenbelt cities had not had those jobs, they would have absorbed public relief funds without tangible return. Without improved nutrition, what kind of health problems would the resettled farm families have had in later years, and what would they have cost? (2007, 168).

The government began selling the communities starting in 1944. The subsistence farmstead units were sold at market value to low-income families, and the greenbelt homes were also sold to low-income settlers when possible. Greenbelt residents formed a housing cooperative that bought the homes.

See also: Federal Emergency Relief Act; Great Depression; Housing, Low-Income; Indian New Deal; National Recovery Administration; New Deal; Public Works Administration; Roosevelt, Eleanor

Sources

Arnold, Joseph. *The New Deal in the Suburbs: A History of the Greenbelt Town Program, 1935—1954.* Columbus, OH: Ohio State University Press, 1971.

Conkin, Paul. *Tomorrow a New World: The New Deal Community Program.* Ithaca, NY: Cornell University Press, 1959.

Davis, Kenneth. *FDR, The New Deal Years, 1933–1937: A History.* New York: Random House, 1986.

Leighninger, Robert D., Jr. *Long-Range Public Investment: The Forgotten Legacy of the New Deal.* Columbia, SC: University of South Carolina, 2007.

Roosevelt, Eleanor. *The Autobiography of Eleanor Roosevelt.* New York: Harper and Brothers, 1961.

Web Site

Greenbelt, MD. http://www.greenbeltmd.gov/ (accessed April 2008).

NEW DEAL WOMEN'S NETWORK

President Franklin Roosevelt's New Deal of the 1930s was designed to lift the country out of the Great Depression. During that time, First Lady Eleanor Roosevelt worked with a number of other women leaders within the federal government, as well as women leaders of reform organizations, to ensure that the needs of the poor were met, especially the needs of poor women and children. At the urging of his wife, Franklin Roosevelt appointed an unprecedented number of women to high positions within the administration. According to women's history expert Susan Ware,

> the New Deal offered greatly expanded roles for women in public life in the 1930s, a record not matched until the 1960s.... The outstanding characteristic of women's participation in the New Deal was the development of a "network" of friendship and cooperation among the women, which maximized their influence in politics and government. (1987, 1–2)

Women who participated in this New Deal women's social reform network saw themselves as a second generation of women reformers, following in the footsteps of early-twentieth-century reformers such as Jane Addams, Florence Kelley, and Julia Lathrop. While the New Deal women were conscious of their pioneering role as women in public life, and realized their responsibility to help other women, they also wanted to help the needy regardless of gender.

Before the New Deal, many of these women had been involved with the movement for women's suffrage. Many of them were also active in reform organizations like the National Consumers League, the settlement-house movement, the Women's Trade Union League, and the National Child Labor Committee. According to Eleanor Roosevelt's biographer Blanche Wiesen Cook, during the 1920s, the women's social reformer network's organizations "grew in strength and purpose—and became during the Depression America's most vital institutions of resistance to despair" (1999, 60).

In addition to Eleanor Roosevelt, another important member of the New Deal "women's network" was Molly Dewson, head of the women's division of the Democratic National Committee. She worked with Eleanor Roosevelt to persuade President Roosevelt to appoint women to leadership positions within the federal government, and by 1935, more than fifty women had been appointed to top federal jobs, in addition to hundreds of women hired for leadership positions in state and local governments. Eleanor Roosevelt believed that women in power would address the needs of poor women, whereas men in

power tended to overlook women's needs (Cook 1999, 67, 69).

One of Dewson's major successes was the appointment of Frances Perkins as secretary of labor—the first woman ever to serve as a member of a U.S. president's cabinet. Dewson wanted Perkins to have the job because she believed Perkins had solutions to the country's problems. Perkins had ideas for unemployment insurance, minimum wages, maximum hours, and the abolition of child labor. To prepare the public for the appointment of a women in such a high position, even before President Roosevelt had asked Perkins to take the job, Dewson released reports to the newspapers that Roosevelt was considering her. She also worked to convince Perkins to accept the position, if Roosevelt offered it to her—which he did (Martin 1976, 235–239; Ware 1987, 176–179).

Another important appointee was Ellen Sullivan Woodward, who headed women's divisions within the Federal Emergency Relief Administration and the Works Progress Administration, and was a member of the Social Security Board. At a time when single women's needs were overlooked and many people believed that married women should not work, Woodward pushed to open up public works jobs to all women, and to increase their pay. In all, Susan Ware identifies twenty-eight women in top government positions who had strong influences on New Deal legislation: "in many cases the network of women in the New Deal played a crucial role in developing and implementing the New Deal's social welfare policy" (1981, 11–12, 87).

In their attempts to make sure that government laws and programs treated poor women fairly, the women in government often worked closely with women's reform organizations, including the National Consumers League, Women's Trade Union League, Federation of Business and Professional Women, Young Women's Christian Association, National League of Women Voters, and General Federation of Women's Clubs. For example, these organizations and the women's network protested when the industrial codes of the National Recovery Administration (NRA) allowed industries to pay women less than men for performing the same work. However, the discriminatory codes remained during the short lifetime of the NRA.

Other efforts of the women's network were more successful. The Department of Labor under Frances Perkins contained many women workers, including those who staffed the Children's Bureau and the Women's Bureau. Under her leadership, the Department of Labor helped write and push for such legislation as the Social Security Act of 1935 and the Fair Labor Standards Act of 1938. For example, the Aid to Dependent Children section of the Social Security legislation was based on a report written by the women who headed the Children's Bureau. The child labor prohibition in the Fair Labor Standards Act was also added due to efforts by Perkins and the Children's Bureau. Congresswoman Mary Norton, chair of the House Labor Committee, helped shepherd the labor bill to passage. "Reforms such as social security, maternal and child welfare, health insurance, mothers' pensions, and minimum wage and maximum hour legislation had been top

priority for women in the network throughout their long careers," comments Susan Ware. "The New Deal finally gave them the opportunity to implement these goals" (Ware 1981, 97, 99, 103–104).

In addition to new laws, the New Deal also created federal relief programs to help the needy across the nation. Eleanor Roosevelt and others in the women's network wanted to make sure that needy women would also benefit from federal government help. In November 1933, they helped organize a White House Conference on the Emergency Needs of Women, which came up with ideas of work relief projects for women. They were somewhat successful over the years at ensuring that women were eligible for federal works projects: of the 4 million people hired under the Civil Works Administration, about 8 percent were women; about 12 percent of the workers hired through the Federal Emergency Relief Act were women; and women made up 12 percent to 19 percent of the Works Progress Administration workers (Ware 1981, 106–110).

Eleanor Roosevelt and the women of the network also prodded the government to set up camps for needy young women, similar to the popular Civilian Conservation Corps camps for young men. Some women's camps were set up, although the women stayed at them for only a month, and did not perform real work or receive wages (Ware 1981, 113).

During the late 1930s, the influence of the women's network waned, as Molly Dewson retired and Eleanor Roosevelt turned her attention to helping blacks and young people. And although many New Deal laws have continued to the present day, such as the Social Security Act and the Fair Labor Standards Act, the strength and influence in government that women achieved during the New Deal lapsed until the women's movement of the 1960s (Ware 1981, 135).

See also: Addams, Jane; Children's Bureau; Civilian Conservation Corps; Fair Labor Standards Act of 1938; Federal Emergency Relief Act; Kelley, Florence, Lathrop, Julia; National Consumers League; National Recovery Administration; New Deal; Perkins, Frances; Roosevelt, Eleanor; Settlement Houses; Social Security Act; Woodward, Ellen Sullivan; Works Progress Administration

Sources

Cook, Blanche Wiesen. *Eleanor Roosevelt, Volume Two: 1933–1938.* New York: Viking Press, 1999.

Martin, George. *Madame Secretary: Frances Perkins.* Boston, MA: Houghton Mifflin Company, 1976.

Swain, Martha H. *Ellen S. Woodward: New Deal Advocate for Women.* Jackson, MS: University Press of Mississippi, 1995.

Ware, Susan. *Beyond Suffrage: Women in the New Deal.* Cambridge, MA: Harvard University Press, 1981.

Ware, Susan. *Partner and I: Molly Dewson, Feminism, and New Deal Politics.* New Haven, CT: Yale University Press, 1987.

O

ORPHANAGES

During the nineteenth and early twentieth centuries, orphanages cared for not only children without parents, but also children whose parents were too poor to keep them at home. Poor parents had few other options at that time.

The word "orphanage" conjures up images of deprived and possibly abused children relegated to warehouse-like buildings. In fact, orphanages have often been useful institutions that provided good care for children who could not be raised by their parents. As journalism professor Marvin Olasky observes,

> The conventional history of American orphanages is a tale of sound and fury directed against the helpless, with the absence of close government oversight leading to unmitigated child abuse. The real story, however, is richer; it shows how good orphanages combated both material and spiritual poverty among children who would otherwise have been the truly wretched of the earth. (1999, 65)

The first American orphanage started in 1729, in New Orleans by the Ursuline Convent. Many of the early orphanages were started by religious institutions or religious groups. The first government-run orphanage was started in Charleston, South Carolina, in the 1790s, to care for poor children orphaned as a result of the Revolutionary War. However, orphanages were not widespread in early America. At that time, small children who were orphaned were generally cared for by relatives or neighbors, and older children were apprenticed to learn a trade. By 1800, the country had only a handful of orphanages (Hacsi 1997, 17–18; Olasky 1999, 65–66).

The number of orphanages grew during the 1800s, in response to several things: disease epidemics that left more children orphaned; more people moving to urban areas, far from relatives who could care for children if needed; and

Orphans on a sightseeing excursion, August 1923. (Library of Congress)

the increasing immigrant population, also far from relatives. By 1850, there were more than seventy orphanages in the country. Still, at this time, many poor children simply lived with their families in poorhouses.

After the Civil War, which ended in 1865, the number of orphanages increased greatly to care for children whose fathers had died or been disabled in the war. States began to provide more funding for private orphanages, and to set up their own county-run or state-run orphanages. By 1880, there were more than 600 orphanages in the country. Because poor parents had few other options, parents turned to orphanages when they could not afford to care for their children. With their children safe in an orphanage, single

mothers and fathers were free to work, or to go to the poorhouse if they could not find work (Dulberger 1996, 9–10; Olasky 1999, 67). According to historian Timothy Hacsi, "More than any other late-nineteenth-century institution, orphan asylums helped poor families by caring for their children, for months or years" (1997, 13, 16–17, 20–27).

Another reason for the growth of orphanages after the 1850s is that some states passed laws requiring poor children to be removed from poorhouses. Reformers believed that children would be harmed by living in poorhouses, which sometimes also housed petty criminals. Reformers believed that poor children would receive better care in institutions dedicated just to children.

ORPHANAGE CORRESPONDENCE

In 1884, three children of William and Jane Richardson were admitted to the Albany Orphan Asylum in Albany, New York, because their father was imprisoned and their mother was forced to take refuge at a poorhouse with an older daughter. The following is William Richardson's letter to his children on February 1, 1885. A few months later, one of the children died of illness at the orphanage. In this letter, Richardson blames his wife for separating the family. Later, Richardson reconciles with his wife and the children and parents were eventually reunited in June of that year.

My Dear Children Johnny Katie and Willie:

I now take the Pleasure of Riting to yous to let you know I am Well and in good health and I hope thoes lines Will find youes all Enjoying the Same With the help of God. Children, I would of Rote to youes Before only I did not know Whear to Rite to untill last Sunday. I Rote a letter tow months a go to the County house in Ballston to find out Whear you Ware and I did not Reseave any answer to my letter till last Sunday and they Enformed me Whear you Was. So now I though[t] i Would Rite to youes and let you Know I had not forgoten youes Children. . . . Now Children, I hope you are good Children [and] are obedent to your teacher and I Would like to hear of you loving your teacher and of her a loving you and When I get my Freedom I Will come and See you and I Will Be Verry glad to hear you are good children. I do Not Know What I Shall do When I get out But no matter What i do i Shall never forgit youes dear little ones. your mother has done Wrong to Both you and me So She can Not Blame me and you children must not Blame me. But When Ever I do get my freedom I Shall do all I can for you children as soon as I can get to Work to Erne any thing. Now Behave your Selfes and I Shall See you Soone. I Will look for an answer to this letter By next Sunday and I Will See you in Six Weeks time if god Spares us all till then and i hope he Will. I Pray for youes Every night and Every day and I aske god to Spare us all to meet a gane. Now I Will Bring my letter to a close for this time By a Bidding you all good Bye till We can meet a gane and god Bless you all and I hope you Will Pray for me. So good Bye. With a Kiss to you all, I Remane,

Your loving Father,
Mr. William Richardson

Source: Dulberger, Judith A. *"Mother Donit fore the Best": Correspondence of a Nineteenth-Century Orphan Asylum.* Syracuse, NY: Syracuse University Press, 1996, 102–103. Used with permission.

Of course, as states passed laws mandating the removal of children from poorhouses, this meant that poor parents were separated from their children (Hacsi 1997, 25, 30).

By the late 1800s, as orphanages were proliferating, some people had begun criticizing orphanages for their regimentation and lack of attention to a child's individuality. And it was true that orphanages often had strict routines, meager food, and sometimes harsh discipline. Still, many children in orphanages received better food and care, as well as access to better education and medical treatment, than they would have at home (Hacsi 1997, 149–158). Judith Dulberger suggests that "the late nineteenth century orphan asylum became the poor man's boarding school" (1996, 11).

Reformers increasingly assumed that care within a family was best. Charles Loring Brace was a vocal advocate of placing children in homes rather than in institutions. He and his New York City–based organization, the Children's Aid Society, came up with the idea of sending poor children to farmers where they would work part-time for room, board, and an education. Farming families in upstate New York and Midwestern states were enthusiastic about taking in orphans, and between 1853 and 1893, about 91,000 children were placed in homes. Local committees oversaw these placements, and the children generally received good care (Olasky 1999, 69–71).

By the early 1900s, criticism of orphanages had increased such that President Theodore Roosevelt, at the 1909 White House Conference on Dependent Children, was calling for "mothers' pensions" to allow poor widowed women to stay at home with their children, and many states began passing laws allowing poor single mothers to receive small pensions. Foster care also increased: the government paid families to take in children, so they could be raised in a home-like setting. As a result of the Great Depression, mothers' pensions generally disappeared as state budgets grew tighter.

The Social Security Act of 1935, however, included a kind of national mothers' pension——that is, Aid to Dependent Children (later called Aid to Families with Dependent Children). Unemployment insurance, workers' compensation, and Social Security became available to many workers after the Great Depression, further easing the need for poor parents to send their children to orphanages. After the 1930s, orphanages ceased to be places for poor children. Instead, some orphanages transformed into agencies to place abused and neglected children into foster care. Other orphanages began caring for children with special needs, such as emotional and behavioral problems (Hacsi 1997, 37–39, 42–43, 45–48).

See also: Aid to (Families with) Dependent Children; Great Depression; Mothers' Pensions; New Deal; Poorhouses; Social Security Act; Unemployment Insurance; Workers' Compensation

Sources

Dulberger, Judith A. *"Mother Donit fore the Best": Correspondence of a Nineteenth-Century Orphan Asylum.* Syracuse, NY: Syracuse University Press, 1996.

Hacsi, Timothy A. *Second Home: Orphan Asylums and Poor Families in America.* Cambridge, MA: Harvard University Press, 1997.

Olasky, Marvin. "The Rise and Fall of American Orphanages," in *Rethinking Orphanages for the 21st Century,* ed. Richard B. McKenzie. Thousand Oaks, CA: Sage Publications, 1999.

OUTDOOR RELIEF

"Outdoor relief" refers to the practice of providing aid to the needy in their homes. "Indoor relief" refers to helping the needy by housing and feeding them in poorhouses and almshouses. Although "outdoor relief" is the dominant way of helping the poor in the twenty-first century, that term is no longer used.

From colonial times, American governments have relied on outdoor relief as the main way of helping the needy. Until about the mid-1800s, most poor people were helped through food, fuel, clothing, and money given to them in their own homes. Sometimes, the poor were "boarded out" to other families. Until the mid-1800s, few institutions were available to house the poor. At this time, outdoor relief was considered to be the job of local governments. State and federal governments rarely got involved.

Local governments gave out only enough to keep people from freezing or starving. During the 1870s, in New York, for example, each family would receive either food or coal to last one week—but not both in the same week. Only flour, potatoes, or rice were provided in terms of food (Katz 1996, 49).

In the early 1800s, as poverty became a larger problem in eastern cities, states began investigating the problem. Reformers called for an end to outdoor relief and instead recommended building poorhouses for the needy. They believed that it would be cheaper to help the poor in an institutional setting. They believed that, by confining the poor to institutions, their behavior could be controlled, and they could be educated and reformed.

Starting in the late 1800s, the "scientific charity" movement also began criticizing outdoor relief. Reformers believed that when the government provided aid to people in their own homes, this encouraged laziness and deprived

the poor of their self-respect. The scientific charity reformers preached that outdoor relief should be given only by private charity—never by the government.

However, even as states and counties built more and more poorhouses, governments in most places continued to provide outdoor relief. Only about ten cities succeeded in temporarily ending the government provision of outdoor relief. The first of these was Brooklyn, New York, which ended outdoor aid in 1879. Unfortunately, private charity could not fill the government's shoes and help all the poor people in Brooklyn. Desperate parents were forced to break up their families, send the children to orphanages, and go to the poorhouse themselves (Katz 1996, 51–53).

Although critics of outdoor relief claimed that it was more expensive than institutions for the poor, in fact the opposite proved true. It was quite a bit more expensive to house and feed people in special institutions than it was to provide them with occasional food or fuel in their homes. For example, in 1880, New York State spent about $749,000 to help about 70,000 people with outdoor relief (about $11 per person), but spent more than $1.7 million to help just 90,000 people in poorhouses (about $19 per person) (Katz 1996, 38).

Nevertheless, poorhouses persisted in America until the 1930s. At the same time, governments started other forms of outdoor relief. For example, in the early 1900s, many states began offering "mothers' pensions"—payments that allowed widows and abandoned mothers to stay at home with their children, rather than go out to work. Missouri was the first state to pass a mothers' pension law, in 1911. By 1919, thirty-nine states offered mothers' pensions (Trattner 1989, 225; Katz 2001, 60).

During the 1930s, with the federal government's New Deal programs to provide help during the Great Depression, outdoor relief again became the dominant form of aid to the poor, and poorhouses were no longer needed. Instead, the elderly could rely on Social Security to provide for their needs; poor children and their mothers were helped with Aid to Dependent Children; and the unemployed benefited from unemployment insurance.

Since the Great Depression, governments in the United States have continued to rely on helping the poor in their own homes. In addition to federal help, many states continue to offer their own form of poor relief, which is called "general assistance." Despite the constant criticism of outdoor relief, University of Pennsylvania history professor Michael Katz points out that

outdoor relief has proved to be the bedrock of American welfare. Its persistence shows the crucial need for a government role in the care of needy people throughout America's past and undermines the claim that volunteerism and private charity suffice to meet the needs of people unable to survive on their own. (2001, 58)

See also: Aid to (Families with) Dependent Children; General Assistance; Mothers' Pensions; New Deal; Poorhouses; Poor Laws, Early American; Quincy Report; Scientific Charity; Social Security Act; Temporary Assistance for Needy Families; Unemployment Insurance

Sources

Katz, Michael B. *In the Shadow of the Poorhouse: A Social History of Welfare in America.* New York: Basic Books, 1996.

Katz, Michael B. *The Price of Citizenship: Redefining the American Welfare State.* New York: Henry Holt, 2001.

Trattner, Walter I. *From Poor Law to Welfare State: A History of Social Welfare in America.* New York: The Free Press, 1989.

P

PAINE, THOMAS
(1737–1809)

Thomas Paine was one of the most influential writers and activists in colonial America. Paine wrote many pamphlets in favor of equality and freedom, and against slavery and poverty. His most famous pamphlet, "Common Sense," called for freedom of the American colonies from Great Britain and was a major influence behind the American Revolution. "Common Sense" was the first widely circulated pamphlet that specifically called for the independence of the American colonies. It also was the first public writing that appealed to the common person—farmers and merchants—rather than only the educated upper class. Toward the end of his life Paine wrote "Agrarian Justice," which called for a kind of old-age insurance, such as was finally passed in 1935 as the Social Security Act.

Paine was born in England to a working-class family. His father made "stays" (the strips of material used to stiffen corsets). Paine left school at thirteen to work in his father's shop. He worked as a stay-maker until the age of twenty-seven, when he was appointed a customs officer (someone who collects dues for the king from exporters and importers).

The first pamphlet he wrote, in 1772, called for higher wages for customs officers. Paine organized other customs officers to pay a small fee to print 4,000 copies of the essay, which was given to every member of Parliament. Paine argued that the low pay of customs officers tempted them to dishonesty. "Poverty, in defiance of principle, begets a degree of meanness that will stoop to almost anything," he wrote. Unfortunately, the pamphlet had no effect on Parliament at all (Aldridge 1959, 21–22).

Paine was dismissed as a customs officer in the spring of 1774. At some point during the following months, he met Benjamin Franklin, who was in

*Thomas Paine, author of the extremely popular pamphlet **Common Sense**, probably did more to inspire Americans to seek their independence from Britain than any other writer. (Library of Congress)*

the American Revolution, but also was translated into French and Spanish, and helped to influence the French Revolution and the independence movements of Venezuela, Mexico, and Ecuador (Aldridge 1959, 43).

Paine enlisted in the army to fight against the British in the American Revolution. He also wrote a series of pamphlets called "The Crisis" to inspire the American soldiers.

In the late 1780s, Paine wrote another famous work, *The Rights of Man*, published in 1791. This was in support of the French Revolution. He went to France after the publication of this book and served in that country's National Convention (the revolutionaries' newly formed legislative assembly, which abolished the monarchy and took over the government). Some French members of the Convention eventually grew to mistrust him, and he was arrested and imprisoned in December 1793, under a law that prohibited foreigners from serving in the National Convention. He was released from prison ten months later by the efforts of the American minister in France.

Before he was imprisoned, Paine had begun to write *The Age of Reason,* which attacked Christianity and promoted something called "deism," or a religion based on reason, rather than on the supernatural. He wrote the second part of *The Age of Reason* after his release from prison. According to his biographer Alfred Owen Aldridge, "Paine was the first author to make the direct statement that the Bible is not the Word of God in clear, forthright language which the common man would understand and enjoy reading" (1959, 234). Because of this disapproval of mainstream Christianity, Paine was

England as an agent for Pennsylvania and other American colonies. Franklin was impressed with Paine and gave him a letter of introduction to his son-in-law in Philadelphia. Paine sailed for America toward the end of 1774. He soon became a newspaper editor in Pennsylvania.

Paine wrote "Common Sense" in 1775, and had it printed in January 1776. Thousands of copies were sold—Paine claimed 150,000 copies sold. However, Paine never made any money from the pamphlet, because the printers insisted there had been no profits. "Common Sense" not only influenced

PRIMARY DOCUMENT 23

Excerpt from "Agrarian Justice," by Thomas Paine, 1797

To preserve the benefits of what is called civilized life, and to remedy at the same time the evil which it has produced, ought to considered as one of the first objects of reformed legislation.

Whether that state that is proudly, perhaps erroneously, called civilization, has most promoted or most injured the general happiness of man is a question that may be strongly contested. On one side, the spectator is dazzled by splendid appearances; on the other, he is shocked by extremes of wretchedness; both of which it has erected. The most affluent and the most miserable of the human race are to be found in the countries that are called civilized.

To understand what the state of society ought to be, it is necessary to have some idea of the natural and primitive state of man; such as it is at this day among the Indians of North America. There is not, in that state, any of those spectacles of human misery which poverty and want present to our eyes in all the towns and streets in Europe.

Poverty, therefore, is a thing created by that which is called civilized life. It exists not in the natural state. On the other hand, the natural state is without those advantages which flow from agriculture, arts, science and manufactures.

The life of an Indian is a continual holiday, compared with the poor of Europe; and, on the other hand it appears to be abject when compared to the rich.

Civilization, therefore, or that which is so-called, has operated two ways: to make one part of society more affluent, and the other more wretched, than would have been the lot of either in a natural state.

It is always possible to go from the natural to the civilized state, but it is never possible to go from the civilized to the natural state. The reason is that man in a natural state, subsisting by hunting, requires ten times the quantity of land to range over to procure himself sustenance, than would support him in a civilized state, where the earth is cultivated.

When, therefore, a country becomes populous by the additional aids of cultivation, art and science, there is a necessity of preserving things in that state; because without it there cannot be sustenance for more, perhaps, than a tenth part of its inhabitants. The thing, therefore, now to be done is to remedy the evils and preserve the benefits that have arisen to society by passing from the natural to that which is called the civilized state.

In taking the matter upon this ground, the first principle of civilization ought to have been, and ought still to be, that the condition of every person born into the world, after a state of civilization commences, ought not to be worse than if he had been born before that period.

But the fact is that the condition of millions, in every country in Europe, is far worse than if they had been born before civilization begin, had been born among the Indians of North America at the present. I will show how this fact has happened.

It is a position not to be controverted that the earth, in its natural, uncultivated state was, and ever would have continued to be, *the common property of the human race*. In that state every man would have been born to property. He would have been a joint life proprietor with rest in the property of the soil, and in all its natural productions, vegetable and animal.

But the earth in its natural state, as before said, is capable of supporting but a small number of inhabitants compared with what it is capable of doing in a cultivated state. And as it is impossible to separate the improvement made by cultivation from the earth itself, upon which that improvement is made, the idea of landed property arose from that parable connection; but it is nevertheless true, that it is the value of the improvement, only, and not the earth itself, that is individual property.

Every proprietor, therefore, of cultivated lands, owes to the community *ground-rent* (for I know of no better term to express the idea) for the land which he holds; and it is from this ground-rent that the fund prod in this plan is to issue.

It is deducible, as well from the nature of the thing as from all the stories transmitted to us, that the idea of landed property commenced with cultivation, and that there was no such thing, as landed property before that time. It could not exist in the first state of man, that of hunters. It did not exist in the second state, that of shepherds: neither Abraham, Isaac, Jacob, nor Job, so far as the history of the Bible may credited in probable things, were owners of land.

Their property consisted, as is always enumerated in flocks and herds, they traveled with them from place to place. The frequent contentions at that time about the use of a well in the dry country of Arabia, where those people lived, also show that there was no landed property. It was not admitted that land could be claimed as property.

There could be no such thing as landed property originally. Man did not make the earth, and, though he had a natural right to *occupy* it, he had no right to *locate as his property* in perpetuity any part of it; neither did the Creator of the earth open a land-office, from whence the first title-deeds should issue. Whence then, arose the idea of landed property? I answer as before, that when cultivation began the idea of landed property began with it, from the

impossibility of separating the improvement made by cultivation from the earth itself, upon which that improvement was made.

The value of the improvement so far exceeded the value of the natural earth, at that time, as to absorb it; till, in the end, the common right of all became confounded into the cultivated right of the individual. But there are, nevertheless, distinct species of rights, and will continue to be, so long as the earth endures.

It is only by tracing things to their origin that we can gain rightful ideas of them, and it is by gaining such ideas that we, discover the boundary that divides right from wrong, and teaches every man to know his own. I have entitled this tract "Agrarian Justice" to distinguish it from "Agrarian Law."

Nothing could be more unjust than agrarian law in a country improved by cultivation; for though every man, as an inhabitant of the earth, is a joint proprietor of it in its natural state, it does not follow that he is a joint proprietor of cultivated earth. The additional value made by cultivation, after the system was admitted, became the property of those who did it, or who inherited it from them, or who purchased it. It had originally no owner. While, therefore, I advocate the right, and interest myself in the hard case of all those who have been thrown out of their natural inheritance by the introduction of the system of landed property, I equally defend the right of the possessor to the part which is his.

Cultivation is at least one of the greatest natural improvements ever made by human invention. It has given to created earth a tenfold value. But the landed monopoly that began with it has produced the greatest evil. It has dispossessed more than half the inhabitants of every nation of their natural inheritance, without providing for them, as ought to have been done, an indemnification for that loss, and has thereby created a species of poverty and wretchedness that did not exist before.

In advocating the case of the persons thus dispossessed, it is a right, and not a charity, that I am pleading for. But it is that kind of right which, being neglected at first, could not be brought forward afterwards till heaven had opened the way by a revolution in the system of government. Let us then do honor to revolutions by justice, and give currency to their principles by blessings.

Having thus in a few words, opened the merits of the case, I shall now proceed to the plan I have to propose, which is,

To create a national fund, out of which there shall be paid to every person, when arrived at the age of twenty-one years, the sum of fifteen pounds sterling, as a compensation in part, for the loss of his or her natural inheritance, by the introduction of the system of landed property:

And also, the sum of ten pounds per annum, during life, to every person now living, of the age of fifty years, and to all others as they shall arrive at that age. . . .

Source

Social Security Administration. http://www.ssa.gov/history/paine4.html.

---

criticized and the English monarchy charged him with blasphemy.

"Agrarian Justice," written in 1795, proposed solutions to economic inequality. At a time when poverty was accepted by most Americans as a normal part of life, Paine believed that poverty was an unfortunate by-product of civilization and that steps should be taken to alleviate economic inequality. His ideas come, in part, from observing the economic equality of the Native American Indians. Paine believed that, in a "natural," uncivilized state, all humans were originally equal, and that civilization introduced economic inequality. His solutions aimed to correct this "evil," as he called it, while maintaining a civilized society.

Although the ideas presented in "Agrarian Justice" were revolutionary at that time, and were not implemented within Paine's lifetime, they were taken up hundreds of years later. Paine's idea that land, in its uncultivated state, is the property of all humans, was later promoted by Henry George in his

"single-tax" theory, which became popular almost a century later, in the late 1800s. Paine's idea of a guaranteed minimum income for all American citizens fifty years and older has in a sense become a national policy: the Social Security program, enacted in the 1930s, provides a guaranteed minimum income to retired people.

See also: George, Henry; Poor Laws, Early American; Social Security Act

Sources

Aldridge, Alfred Owen. *Man of Reason: The Life of Thomas Paine*. Philadelphia, PA: J.B. Lippincott Company, 1959.

Myers-Lipton, Scott J. *Social Solutions to Poverty: America's Struggle to Build a Just Society*. Boulder, CO: Paradigm Publishers, 2006.

PERKINS, FRANCES (1880–1965)

Frances Perkins served as the secretary of labor of the United States from 1933 to 1945, under President Franklin Roosevelt. She was instrumental in creating important and enduring programs to address issues of poverty during the New Deal, such as the Fair Labor Standards Act of 1938 and Social Security. She was the first woman ever appointed as part of a U.S. president's "cabinet" (the heads of important departments).

She was born Fanny Coralie Perkins on April 10, 1880, in Boston, Massachusetts. Her family moved to Worcester, Massachusetts, when she was two. As a young woman, she changed her first name to "Frances." Her father was in the stationery business. Although her parents believed in helping the poor, they also believed (like many other people at that time) that poverty was caused by laziness or drinking alcohol.

Perkins attended Mount Holyoke College, where she majored in chemistry. She also took an economic history class, during which she was required to visit factories and write about the working conditions. After the experience of observing the dirty and dangerous working conditions in the factories, Perkins began to realize that poverty was not always caused by laziness or bad habits, but also might be caused by circumstances outside the control of the poor, such as industrial accidents.

While in college, Perkins and some classmates organized a local chapter of the National Consumers League, which aimed to educate consumers about low wages and bad working conditions. Florence Kelley, the head of the National Consumers League, came to speak at the campus, and this speech caused Perkins to realize that she might want to work on behalf of the poor.

After graduation in 1902, she tried to get a job with the New York Charity Organization Society, but the head of this organization advised Perkins to learn more about life by teaching and reading. She read *How the Other Half Lives* by Jacob Riis, which revealed through photos and text the lives of the poor in the slums of New York City. This book further convinced her that she wanted to work in the field of social justice.

Over the next several years, she taught science classes at a number of different high schools. While teaching in her hometown of Worcester, she worked in her spare time with a settlement house to run a club for working girls. While teaching in Chicago, she often visited and worked with two settlement houses, Chicago Commons and Hull House, during which time she changed her view of trade unions. Previously, she had thought trade unions were "an evil to be avoided, if possible. You did good to the poor with charitable relief, friendly visiting, . . . mother's clubs, and that sort of thing" (quoted in Pasachoff 1999, 18). However, at the settlement houses she encountered staff members who believed that trade unions were a key element to eliminating poverty.

In 1907, Perkins landed a job as the head of the Philadelphia Research and Protective Association, a new organization designed to research the situation of immigrant young women coming to Philadelphia for work, and to offer help to them. While in Philadelphia, she took economics and sociology classes at the University of Pennsylvania, and she was then offered a graduate-school fellowship at Columbia University in New York, where she moved in 1909.

After receiving her master's degree in June 1910, she became the head of the New York Consumers' League. During her two years at the League, she worked to pass a bill to limit the working hours of women and young people in factories to fifty-four hours per week (the law was passed in 1912), and she studied the sanitary conditions of bakeries and the fire-prevention techniques in factories.

In 1912, she became chief of the New York Committee on Safety, where she wrote and worked to pass laws to protect industrial workers. In 1913, she married Paul Wilson, an economist with a personal fortune. She chose not to change her last name after marriage. She eventually planned to ease out of paid work, have children, and concentrate on volunteer work. In 1916, she gave birth to a daughter, Susanna, and by 1918, she was trying to wind up her work with the Committee on Safety. At about this time, however, her husband lost his money through gambling, and he also exhibited symptoms of mental illness that caused him to be alternately depressed and excitable. Perkins realized that she would have to support the family.

In 1918, the new governor of New York, Al Smith, asked Perkins to be a member of the state's Industrial Commission, part of the state Department of Labor, and she agreed. This was her first government job. She served on the New York Industrial Commission in one capacity or another, first under Governor Smith and then under Governor Franklin Roosevelt, until 1933, when she was appointed U.S. secretary of labor.

In New York, she and her staff investigated factories and helped pass laws and codes for factory safety. At the beginning of the Great Depression, which started in 1929, when President Hoover's administration released figures showing that unemployment was down, she countered with her own figures from New York State, showing that unemployment was up. She became known as an expert on unemployment statistics. Reporters and state officials would call her for her data, whenever the national government released their figures. "She became the most prominent state labor official in the country," says her biographer, George Martin (1976, 214).

When Roosevelt won the U.S. presidency, Perkins somewhat reluctantly agreed to become his secretary of labor. In her biography of Roosevelt, Perkins describes how she worked with him. When she wanted his approval for a project, she would prepare not only a complete report, but also a one-page outline, which she would go over with him. She was careful to point out the opposition the program might face. She then checked with him several times as to whether he really wanted to go forward. In this way, she says, Roosevelt "never let me down," although others in the administration complained that he sometimes changed his mind about programs after giving the go-ahead. Perkins says that, by preparing Roosevelt sufficiently, she could ensure that he would continue to be supportive (Perkins 1946, 161–163).

In 1934, she became chair of the President's Committee on Economic Security, which wrote the Social Security legislation, passed in 1935. In 1935 and 1936, she helped create what became the Fair Labor Standards Act of 1938.

"HE SHOULD NOT APPOINT ME"

When Frances Perkins was asked to become the U.S. secretary of labor in February 1933, her first thought was to convince President Roosevelt that she was not the right person for the job:

I led off with my chief argument, that I was not a bona fide labor [union] person. I pointed out that labor had always had, and would expect to have, one of its own people as Secretary. Roosevelt's answer was that it was time to consider all working people, organized and unorganized.

I told him that it might be a good thing to have a woman in the cabinet if she were the best for the job, but I thought a woman Secretary of Labor ought to be a labor woman. He replied he had considered that and was going on my record as Industrial Commissioner of New York. He said he thought we could accomplish for the nation the things we had done for the state.

Since I seemed to be making little headway, I tried a new approach. I said that if I accepted the position of Secretary of Labor I should want to do a great deal. I outlined a program of labor legislation and economic improvement. None of it was radical. It had all been tried in certain states and foreign countries. But I thought Roosevelt might consider it too ambitious to be undertaken when the United States was deep in depression and unemployment.

In broad terms, I proposed immediate federal aid to the states for direct unemployment relief, an extensive program of public works, a study and an approach to the establishment by federal law of minimum wages, maximum hours, true unemployment and old-age insurance, abolition of child labor, and the creation of a federal employment service.

The program received Roosevelt's hearty endorsement, and he told me he wanted me to carry it out.

"But," I said, "have you considered that to launch such a program we must think out, frame, and develop labor and social legislation, which then might be considered unconstitutional?"

"Well, that's a problem," Mr. Roosevelt admitted, "but we can work out something when the time comes."

And so I agreed to become Secretary of Labor after a conversation that lasted but an hour.

Source: "A Mind in the Making," from *The Roosevelt I Knew* by Frances Perkins, copyright 1946 by France Perkins, © renewed 1974 by Susanna W. Coggeshall. Used by permission of Viking Penguin, a division of Penguin Group (USA) Inc.

After resigning from the Department of Labor, Perkins served on the U.S. civil service commission under President Harry Truman until 1952. She then devoted the rest of her career to teaching and lecturing. She died on May 14, 1965, in New York City.

See also: Fair Labor Standards Act of 1938; Great Depression; Kelley, Florence; National Consumers League; New Deal;

New Deal Women's Network; Riis, Jacob; Roosevelt, Franklin Delano; Settlement Houses; Social Security Act

Sources

Martin, George. *Madame Secretary: Frances Perkins.* Boston, MA: Houghton Mifflin Company, 1976.

Pasachoff, Naomi. *Frances Perkins: Champion of the New Deal.* New York: Oxford University Press, 1999.

Perkins, Frances. *The Roosevelt I Knew.* New York: Viking Press, 1946.

PERSONAL RESPONSIBILITY AND WORK OPPORTUNITY RECONCILIATION ACT OF 1996

The Personal Responsibility and Work Opportunity Reconciliation Act of 1996 (PRWORA) was the product of years of effort on the part of Republicans and Democrats to address problems in the Aid to Families with Dependent Children (AFDC) program, which provided cash benefits to poor families. The PRWORA ended AFDC (which was often called "welfare") and replaced it with Temporary Assistance for Needy Families (TANF). The PRWORA was "the most significant change in U.S. welfare policy since the passage of the Social Security Act," according to Steven Livingston (2002, 223).

The PRWORA had its roots in the late 1980s, when state governors pushed for more latitude and freedom in how they administered the AFDC programs in their states. They wanted to emphasize job training and job placement. The National Governors Association (NGA) was chaired by Governor Bill Clinton of Arkansas, who announced the NGA's welfare reform plan in 1987. However, the plan that ended up passing Congress, the Family Support Act of 1988, did not provide nearly enough money to help a large percentage of welfare recipients get jobs. Instead of shrinking, the AFDC program continued to grow (Livingston 2002, 210–211).

When Bill Clinton became president in 1992, he pledged to "end welfare as we know it." The first welfare plan he submitted to Congress in 1994 contained a time limit of two years on cash benefits; mandatory work requirements; and government help with health care and child care. Noncitizens were not eligible for cash benefits under Clinton's plan. Unfortunately, Democrats in Congress, and some within the Clinton administration, did not like this plan because of the time limit and work requirements, and the bill never made it out of committee.

After the elections in the fall of 1994, Republicans took over the U.S. Congress, and they had their own ideas about welfare reform. Their plan called for a lifetime limit of five years on cash benefits, and required work activities. Their bill also made noncitizens ineligible. Many poor children would be excluded, including children born to teenage unwed mothers; those whose fathers had not been identified; and children born to women who were already receiving cash aid. Under this bill, the federal government would provide a lump-sum payment to states in the form of "block grants," and states would be able to create their own programs. The Republicans plan also banned alcoholics, drug addicts, and children with behavioral disorders from Supplemental Security Income (federal

A family on welfare, Oregon, 1996. In order to continue receiving welfare benefits, the mother of nine must go to work. (David Butow/Corbis Saba)

cash assistance to the disabled). The bill that eventually passed Congress in 1995 also included cuts to food stamps, Medicaid, and supplemental food for children. Clinton vetoed this bill in early 1996, saying that it cut too much money from programs for the poor (Katz 2001, 323; Livingston 2002, 226–229).

Clinton requested that any future bill include benefits for legal immigrants; Medicaid coverage that continued even after the welfare time limit was reached; and more money for food stamps and other food aid. Congress accepted some of these suggestions and passed another bill that Clinton signed in August 1996. This law ended the "entitlement" aspect of AFDC—the federal guarantee that anyone with a low enough income would receive cash benefits with no time limits. The bill created a new program, TANF, which provided money to states in the form of a block grant.

Many Democrats in Congress, as well as within the Clinton administration, were horrified that Clinton had signed a bill that would end entitlements to cash benefits and that would impose strict time limits. They predicted that a million children would be thrown into poverty because of the new law. No one really knew what would be the result of the new law. Would it cause more hunger and poverty? Or would it encourage the poor to get jobs and be self-supporting?

Under the PRWORA, states have more latitude in how they structure their programs and spend their money. States are allowed to deny increased benefits to mothers who have another child while receiving TANF benefits.

PRIMARY DOCUMENT 24

Statement on Signing the Personal Responsibility and Work Opportunity Reconciliation Act of 1996, President Bill Clinton, August 22, 1996

Although President Clinton originally proposed a plan that would have made legal immigrants ineligible for cash benefits, in this speech, he criticized the Personal Responsibility and Work Opportunity Reconciliation Act of 1996 (PRWORA) for doing exactly that.

Today, I have signed into law H.R. 3734, the "Personal Responsibility and Work Opportunity Reconciliation Act of 1996." While far from perfect, this legislation provides an historic opportunity to end welfare as we know it and transform our broken welfare system by promoting the fundamental values of work, responsibility, and family.

This Act honors my basic principles of real welfare reform. It requires work of welfare recipients, limits the time they can stay on welfare, and provides child care and health care to help them make the move from welfare to work. It demands personal responsibility, and puts in place tough child support enforcement measures. It promotes family and protects children.

This bipartisan legislation is significantly better than the bills that I vetoed. The Congress has removed many of the worst provisions of the vetoed bills and has included many of the improvements that I sought. I am especially pleased that the Congress has preserved the guarantee of health care for the poor, the elderly, and the disabled.

Most important, this Act is tough on work. Not only does it include firm but fair work requirements, it provides $4 billion more in child care than the vetoed bills—so that parents can end their dependency on welfare and go to work—and maintains health and safety standards for day care providers. The bill also gives States positive incentives to move people into jobs and holds them accountable for maintaining spending on welfare reform. In addition, it gives States the ability to create subsidized jobs and to provide employers with incentives to hire people off welfare.

The Act also does much more to protect children than the vetoed bills. It cuts spending on childhood disability programs less deeply and does not unwisely change the child protection programs. It maintains the national nutritional safety net, by eliminating the Food Stamp annual spending cap and the Food Stamp and School Lunch block grants that the vetoed bills contained. In addition, it preserves the Federal guarantee of health care for individuals who are currently eligible for Medicaid through the AFDC program or are in transition from welfare to work.

Furthermore, this Act includes the tough personal responsibility and child support enforcement measures that I proposed 2 years ago. It requires minor mothers to live at home and stay in school as a condition of assistance. It cracks down on parents who fail to pay child support by garnishing their wages, suspending their driver's licenses, tracking them across State lines, and, if necessary, making them work off what they owe.

For these reasons, I am proud to have signed this legislation. The current welfare system is fundamentally broken, and this may be our last best chance to set it straight. I am doing so, however, with strong objections to certain provisions, which I am determined to correct.

First, while the Act preserves the national nutritional safety net, its cuts to the Food Stamp program are too deep. Among other things, the Act reinstates a maximum on the amount that can be deducted for shelter costs when determining a household's eligibility for Food Stamps. This provision will disproportionately affect low-income families with children and high housing costs.

Second, I am deeply disappointed that this legislation would deny Federal assistance to legal immigrants and their children, and give States the option of doing the same. My Administration supports holding sponsors who bring immigrants into this country more responsible for their well-being. Legal immigrants and their children, however, should not be penalized if they become disabled and require medical assistance through no fault of their own. Neither should they be deprived of food stamp assistance without proper procedures or due regard for individual circumstances. Therefore, I will direct the Immigration and Naturalization Service to accelerate its unprecedented progress in removing all bureaucratic obstacles that stand in the way of citizenship for legal immigrants who are eligible. In addition, I will take any possible executive actions to avoid inaccurate or inequitable decisions to cut off food stamp benefits—for example, to a legal immigrant who has performed military service for this country or to one who has applied for and satisfied all the requirements of citizenship, but is awaiting governmental approval of his or her application.

In addition to placing an undue hardship on affected individuals, denial of Federal assistance to legal immigrants will shift costs to States, localities, hospitals, and medical clinics that serve large immigrant populations. Furthermore, States electing to deny these individuals assistance could be faced with serious constitutional challenges and protracted legal battles.

I have concerns about other provisions of this legislation as well. It fails to provide sufficient contingency funding for States that experience a serious economic downturn, and it fails to provide Food Stamp support to childless adults who want to work, but cannot find a job or are not given the opportunity to participate in a work program. In addition, we must work to ensure that States provide in-kind vouchers to children whose parents reach the 5-year Federal time limit without finding work.

This Act gives States the responsibility that they have sought to reform the welfare system. This is a profound responsibility, and States must face it squarely. We will hold them accountable, insisting that they fulfill their duty to move people from welfare to work and to do right by our most vulnerable citizens, including children and battered women. I challenge each State to take advantage of its new flexibility to use money formerly available for welfare checks to encourage the private sector to provide jobs.

The best antipoverty program is still a job. Combined with the newly increased minimum wage and the Earned Income Tax Credit—which this legislation maintains—H.R. 3734 will make work pay for more Americans.

I am determined to work with the Congress in a bipartisan effort to correct the provisions of this legislation that go too far and have nothing to do with welfare reform. But, on balance, this bill is a real step forward for our country, for our values, and for people on welfare. It should represent not simply the ending of a system that too often hurts those it is supposed to help, but the beginning of a new era in which welfare will become what it was meant to be: a second chance, not a way of life. It is now up to all of us—States and cities, the Federal Government, businesses and ordinary citizens—to work together to make the promise of this new day real.

William J. Clinton
The White House,
August 22, 1996.

Source

Clinton, William J. *Public Papers of the Presidents of the United States: William J. Clinton, 1996*, vol. 2. Washington D.C., Government Printing Office, 1996: 1328–1330. Accessed at GPO Access http://frwebgate6.access.gpo.gov/cgi-bin/TEXTgate.cgi?WAISdocID=466126135968+3+1+0&WAISaction=retrieve on (accessed February 12, 2009).

States are also allowed to deny benefits to teenage unwed parents. States can also require that counties and towns take on the responsibility to plan and administer TANF programs. So the PRWORA has been a way to bring back state and local responsibility for poor relief (Katz 2001, 330).

The PRWORA also emphasized collecting child support payments from absent parents (mostly fathers). It created a Federal Parent Locator Service to help states track down noncustodial parents. Legal immigrants lost access to almost all poor relief. However, after signing the PRWORA, Clinton urged the U.S. Congress to reinstate eligibility for legal immigrants. Starting in 1997 and 1998, some legal immigrants were again eligible for Medicaid, Supplemental Security Income, and food stamps. Clinton urged private companies, and ordered federal agencies, to hire welfare recipients. In 1997, Congress passed the Welfare-to-Work Program, which provided additional money for child care, health insurance, and other supporting services for poor people entering the job market (Katz 2001, 327, 330).

The TANF program has proven to be effective at moving people off the welfare rolls and into jobs. Contrary to the worst fears of liberals, the law has not produced a large segment of poor and hungry children. However, former welfare recipients typically work in low-wage jobs.

See also: Aid to (Families with) Dependent Children; Child Support; Earned Income Tax Credit; Family Support Act of 1988; Food Stamp Program/Supplemental Nutrition Assistance Program; Medicaid; Social Security Act; Supplemental Security Income; Temporary Assistance for Needy Families

Sources

Katz, Michael. *The Price of Citizenship: Redefining the American Welfare State.* New York: Metropolitan Books, 2001.

Livingston, Steven G. *Student's Guide to Landmark Congressional Laws on Social Security and Welfare.* Westport, CT: Greenwood Press, 2002.

PLAYGROUNDS

Public playgrounds benefit all children, but they are especially useful for poor children who may not have any other safe space in which to play. Playgrounds and organized play activities were seen by many reformers as a way to improve the health of poor children, keep them safe from injury, and prevent juvenile crime and delinquency by giving poor children an outlet for their energy.

In the late 1800s and early 1900s, during the Progressive Era, social reformers pushed for the creation of playgrounds in slum areas. The settlement-house movement was active in creating playgrounds, as was photographer and journalist Jacob Riis, who wrote about and took some of the earliest photographs of the condition of poor people in the slums of New York.

In 1902, Riis described the lack of play areas for children in his book, *Children of the Poor.* Italian immigrant children who lived in a New York tenement had only a five-foot-wide "yard" to play in, "where it is always dark and damp as in a dungeon." Children played in the streets and used slanted cellar doors as slides. Riis believed that this lack of play space led to juvenile

Children play on a tenement playground in New York City, ca. 1888. Photograph by Jacob Riis. (Library of Congress)

delinquency: because ball playing and dancing were often prohibited in the streets, young people turned to other, more deviant activities (1973, 137, 165, 209).

In response to this lack of play space, starting in the 1880s, settlement-house workers and educators led a movement to create playgrounds and organized play activities for children and young people. At the request of a medical doctor, the city of Boston set up sandboxes in slum areas, to help keep children from playing in the dangerous streets. The sandboxes were often supervised by kindergarten teachers, since poor children frequently did not have any adult family member to watch over them. By 1895, sandboxes,

or "sandgardens," as they were called, were a common feature of schoolyards and settlement houses. In 1887, at the urging of settlement-house leader Charles Stover, New York City passed a law allowing the city to spend $1 million a year to establish playgrounds. However, the City Council refused to spend the money to create the playgrounds. In 1898, Stover and fellow settlement-house leader Lillian Wald, along with Jacob Riis and others, created the Outdoor Recreation League to open privately funded playgrounds and playing fields in New York City. In 1902, they finally persuaded the City Council to spend money to create and operate play areas. Settlement houses and other private organizations in

POVERTY GAP PLAYGROUND

In his book Children of the Poor, *published in 1902, Jacob Riis describes makeshift playgrounds established by private charities for poor children in New York City:*

These playgrounds do not take the place of small parks which the city has neglected to provide, but they show what a boon these will be some day. There are at present, as far as I know, three of them. . . . One of them, the largest, is in Ninety-second Street, on the East Side, another at the foot of West Fiftieth Street, and still another in West Twenty-eight Street, between Tenth and Eleventh Avenues, the block long since well named Poverty Gap. Two, three, or half a dozen vacant lots, borrowed or leased of the owner, have been leveled out, a few loads of sand dumped in them for the children to dig in; scups [swing seats], swings, and see-saws, built of rough timber; a hydrant in the corner; little wheelbarrows, toy spades and pails to go around, and the outfit is complete. Two at least of the three are sup-ported each by a single generous woman, who pays the salaries of a man janitor and two women "teachers" who join in the children's play, strike up "America" and the "Star Spangled Banner" when they tire of "Sally in the Alley" and "Ta-ra-ra-boom-de-ay," and by generally taking a hand in what goes on manage to steer it into safe and mannerly ways.

More than a hundred children were digging, swinging, seesawing, and cavort-ing about the Poverty Gap playground when I looked in on a hot Saturday after-noon last July. Long files of eager girls, whose shrill voices used to make the echoes of the Gap ring with angry clamor, awaited their turn at the scups, quiet as mice and without an ill word when they trod upon each other's toes. The street that used to swarm with mischevious imps was quiet as a church.

Source: Riis, Jacob. *The Children of the Poor.* Reprinted in *Jacob Riis Revisited: Poverty and the Slum in Another Era.* Clifton, NJ: Augustus M. Kelley Publishers, 1973, 226–227.

Chicago, Philadelphia, Rochester, and other cities also led the way to the creation of play spaces in slums. First these playgrounds were funded privately, and then the cities were persuaded to take over their funding and operation (Cavallo 1981, 23, 27–30).

Dominick Cavallo describes these playgrounds, which tended to lack grass, bushes, and greenery, due to limited funds:

[T]he typical urban playground was likely to be bounded on three sides by the drab, prison-like stone or wooden background provided by dilapidated tenements, and on the fourth side by a noisy, congested street. The largest portion of the facility was reserved for team games, particularly football and baseball. The remaining space was filled with paraphernalia for smaller children's games: slides, seesaws, . . . sand gardens, and perhaps horizontal bars. (1981, 27)

In 1906, a group of settlement-house leaders, child psychologists, and recreation educators joined to form a national organization, the Playground Association of America (PAA), to launch a national playground movement. According to the Association's Statement of Purpose, playgrounds and organized play would promote good citizenship, industrial efficiency, and even democracy: "Democracy rests on the most firm basis when a community has formed the habit of playing together" (Cavallo 1981, 32–37).

The PAA had a dramatic influence on the formation of playgrounds. The number of playgrounds in twenty-four cities grew from eighty-seven in 1905, to 169 in 1907. In 1911, a survey of 257 cities revealed 1,543 organized playgrounds with more than 4,000 full-time or part-time play directors. In 1917, 481 cities had almost 4,000 playgrounds and 8,700 play directors. About half of these were funded by the government, and the other half by private organizations (Cavallo 1981, 45).

The playground movement was part of the "child-saving" movement at that time, which called for reforms to help children, such as prevention of juvenile crime and better treatment for juvenile criminals. According to Dominick Cavallo, the playground movement was one of the better-funded campaigns of the child-saving movement: "Between 1880 and 1920, municipal governments spent over one hundred million dollars for the construction and staffing of organized playgrounds" (Cavallo 1981, 1–2).

After the United States entered World War I in 1917, the playground movement's funds and energies were directed toward the war effort, and after the war, public schools largely took over as centers for playgrounds and play activities (Cavallo 1981, 48).

See also: Juvenile Justice System; Progressive Era; Riis, Jacob; Settlement Houses; Wald, Lillian

Sources
Cavallo, Dominick. *Muscles and Morals: Organized Playgrounds and Urban Reform, 1880–1920*. Philadelphia, PA: University of Pennsylvania Press, 1981.
Riis, Jacob. *The Children of the Poor*. Reprinted in *Jacob Riis Revisited: Poverty and the Slum in Another Era*. Clifton, NJ: Augustus M. Kelley Publishers, 1973.

POORHOUSES

The word "poorhouse" evokes images of dreary, prison-like buildings in which poor people were virtually imprisoned and half-starved. While some poorhouses were inhumane places in which inmates experienced overcrowding, inadequate food, lack of medical care, and even beatings, others provided a real refuge for the poor and needy. Other names for the poorhouse include "almshouse" and "poor farm" (some poorhouses had farms attached, and residents were expected to work on the farm).

Poorhouses were used in the United States for more than 300 years, and as David Wagner emphasizes, their conditions and their role in society varied according to the time and place. Wagner researched poorhouses in New England and found that some of them evoked fond memories among former residents. Some poorhouses were cheerful, communal places in which single mothers, the unemployed, elderly, ill, and sometimes even petty criminals, all lived and worked together, ate the same food, enjoyed evening card games and other social activities, and more or less came and went as they pleased (2005, 19–38).

The first poorhouse in the United States was built in 1664, in Boston. During the 1700s, several other major cities also built poorhouses. However, until the mid-1800s, most places in the United States used "outdoor relief" to aid the poor—that is, they gave them food and fuel in their own homes, or paid another family in town to take them in (Katz 1996, 15).

As the problem of poverty grew, and as towns and cities began using more and more of their money on poverty relief, states began to investigate the problem. The Quincy Report of 1821, put out by the state of Massachusetts, and New York state's Yates Report of 1824 both recommended building more poorhouses. Other states wrote similar reports. The experts who studied the problem believed that it would be less expensive to care for the needy in one institution, than it would be to provide aid in individual homes. Many people also believed that poorhouses would be a way to reform the poor, by making them work for their aid, and by keeping them away from liquor and other vices. Furthermore, some charitable people believed that the poor would get better food and care in a government-run institution, because some needy people were mistreated by the families which took them in.

After the Quincy and Yates reports were published, more and more poorhouses were built throughout the country. At the beginning of the 1800s, there were just a handful of poorhouses in Massachusetts, for example. By the end of the Civil War in 1865, 80 percent of the poor in Massachusetts were housed in an institution. Other states soon followed this same pattern (Rothman 1971, 180–184).

As David Rothman emphasizes, poorhouses proliferated in an era in which reformers were eager to institutionalize and impose order and discipline on deviant populations, such as prisoners and the insane. "Almshouse organizers who agreed that the fact of poverty in the new republic pointed to a social as well as a personal disorganization looked to institutionalization as an effective antidote. A well-ordered environment would transform the poor, like the criminal and the mentally ill, into hardworking and responsible citizens" (1971, 193).

The goals of the poorhouse movement were contradictory, as University of Pennsylvania history professor Michael Katz points out. The poorhouses were to provide humane treatment for the poor, but at the same time not such good treatment that the needy actually wanted to go to the almshouse. Furthermore, the poorhouse was supposed to make their residents work—yet they also were supposed to discourage able-bodied people who could find work elsewhere from staying at the poorhouse. Therefore, often the poorhouse would find itself with mostly the elderly, ill, and children, who could not work; the able-bodied would often stay in the almshouse only during the winter, when they could not find work elsewhere, and when not much work could be done around the poorhouse. In fact, the idea that able-bodied residents had to work was so strong that sometimes poorhouses would create "make-work" for the residents, even when there was no real work to do: healthy men were required to dig holes and fill them up again, or to move a stack of wood and then move it back again (Katz 1996, 25; Wagner 2005, 55–56).

THE FEAR OF THE POORHOUSE

Jane Addams, the famous social reformer of the late 1800s and early 1900s, describes the following scene in Chicago, in which two men from the county agent's office were trying to remove an old woman from her home to the poorhouse:

> The poor creature had thrown herself bodily upon a small and battered chest of drawers and clung there, clutching it so firmly that it would have been impossible to remove her without also taking the piece of furniture. She did not weep nor moan nor indeed make any human sound, but between her broken gasps for breath she squealed shrilly like a frightened animal caught in a trap. The little group of women and children gathered at her door stood aghast at this realization of the black dread which always clouds the lives of the very poor when work is slack, but which constantly grows more imminent and threatening as old age approaches. The neighborhood women and I hastened to make all sorts of promises as to the support of the old woman and the county officials, only too glad to be rid of their unhappy duty, left her to our ministrations. (155)

Source: Addams, Jane. *Twenty Years at Hull-House.* New York: The Macmillan Company, 1911.

Unfortunately, poorhouses did not live up to the grand aims of their promoters. Many almshouses were badly run, because the job of superintendent was low paid and often did not attract educated or capable people. When members of the New York State Senate visited poorhouses in 1856, they wrote of crowded sleeping dormitories; inadequate medical care (often inmates cared for each other, because there were no professional nurses); and illegitimate births resulting from liaisons within the poorhouse. Furthermore, the superintendents of the poorhouses were often merchants or farmers who sold their own supplies to the poorhouses at high prices (Katz 1996, 26–27).

Nevertheless, some poorhouses were in fact pleasant places to live, and even productive institutions in their communities. This was especially the case in smaller towns. The Rockingham County Home in New Hampshire, which started in 1860, provided a library of classics to its residents. The Home was so inviting that it had a category of residents called "boarders"—people who paid their own way to stay there. Residents of most poorhouses performed much of the day-to-day work, such as cooking, cleaning, sewing, and nursing the ill. Some poor farms did manage to grow most or all of the food consumed in the home, and some provided garbage pickup services to the larger community (Rothman 1971, 200–201; Katz 1996, 29, 33; Wagner 2005, 31, 56).

Although many reformers believed that poorhouses were less expensive than "outdoor relief" (providing help in private homes), poorhouses did not in fact reduce the amount of money spent on poor relief. It turned out to be more expensive to keep someone in the poorhouse than to give them what they needed in their own home. Furthermore, the poorhouse did not achieve its goal of keeping the poor away from vices like liquor. Poorhouse doctors often prescribed large amounts of alcohol as medicine, and poorhouse residents did not find it difficult to indulge in liquor (Katz 1996, 29, 33).

Despite the fact that poorhouses did not meet the goals of the reformers who championed them, almshouses continued to serve large numbers of needy people through the Great Depression of the 1930s—mostly because the poor had nowhere else to go, and no other means of supporting themselves. With the advent in 1935 of Social Security payments to the elderly, unemployment insurance, and federal welfare programs for children and the disabled, there was less and less need for poorhouses. These institutions gradually transformed themselves into nursing homes, jails, or hospitals.

See also: Outdoor Relief; Poor Laws, Early American; Quincy Report, 1821; Scientific Charity

Sources

Katz, Michael. *In the Shadow of the Poorhouse: A Social History of Welfare in America.* New York: Basic Books, 1996.

Rothman, David. *The Discovery of the Asylum: Social Order and Disorder in the New Republic.* Boston, MA: Little, Brown and Company, 1971.

Trattner, Walter I. *From Poor Law to Welfare State: A History of Social Welfare in America.* New York: The Free Press, 1989.

Wagner, David. *The Poorhouse: America's Forgotten Institution.* Lanham, MD: Rowman and Littlefield, 2005.

POOR LAWS, EARLY AMERICAN

Early American "Poor Laws" were laws that spelled out how the poor were to be helped, and how to collect the money for their relief. At this time—from the founding of the American colonies in the seventeenth century, until about the mid-nineteenth century—poverty was seen as a permanent part of society, which had a duty to help the needy. Few people thought about preventing poverty or eliminating poverty. They simply accepted it as a normal part of life. The poor were seen as having a right to be helped.

For much of American history, until about the mid to late 1800s, caring for the poor was seen largely as a local concern. Even though states made the poor laws, and even though states and the federal government sometimes provided extra money to towns and cities in times of great need, poverty was not seen as a problem for the state or federal government to solve. The English Poor Law of 1601 was the model for the poor laws adopted by the various colonies and states in the United States.

The English Poor Law of 1601 was an effort to bring together a number of different laws and customs dealing with the poor. The goal was to create a stable society in which the truly needy were given food, shelter, and clothing, and in which aid was provided to those who could not find work. The Poor Law of 1601 ended up being the model for poor relief in England for almost 250 years, and was brought over to the American colonies.

This law stated that parents, as long as they were able, had the responsibility

PRIMARY DOCUMENT 25

Excerpt from *Rules and Regulations for the Government of the Portland Alms-House*, 1837

The almshouse in Portland, Maine, was in existence as early as 1803. In the 1930s, it changed its name to "Home and Hospital," although it continued to have poor inmates and to run a poor farm until the 1950s. According to David Rothman, many poorhouses aimed to conduct themselves along the strict and disciplined lines laid out below. Besides the rules for inmates printed below, the regulations also included instructions about how the managers were to handle the cooking and washing, and instructions about running the hospital and school associated with the almshouse. As David Wagner comments, "as one reads the rules, one does need to remind oneself that the almshouse was technically not a prison!" (Rothman 1971, 191; Wagner 2005, 16, 41).

Admission

Art. I: All persons admitted into the Alms-House, shall be examined, as to cleanliness from Vermin, or any infectious disease, and kept as separate as possible, until the difficulty is removed. Their clothes and furniture shall go with them unless ordered otherwise.

Rising and the Sabbath

Art. II: At the ringing of the morning Bell, every person, the sick and infirm excepted, shall rise, dress and wash themselves clean, after which if Sunday, put on their best apparel, and attend religious service, at the second ringing of the Bell.. . .

Meals

Art. III: The Bell will be run 10 minutes before each Meal, when every person shall cease from any occupation they may be engaged in, and be ready with clean hands and faces for the ringing of the second Bell, when they will repair to the Dining-Room, and take such seats as shall be assigned to them by the keeper, where they must strictly observe decency and good order. Half an hour each will be allowed for Breakfast and Supper, and one hour for Dinner, at the expiration of which times the Bell will be again rung, when every person shall immediately repair to the work assigned to them by the keeper. They shall not take any bread or other food with them; they shall not loiter on the way, but shall proceed with alacrity, and at once commence labor.. . .

Cleanliness

Art. V: Every tenanted room in the house, together with the entries and stairways, cells and cellars, must be swept clean every morning, and scoured once a week, or oftener if necessary, by such persons as the keeper shall appoint.. . . The whole inside of the house to be white-washed spring and fall.. . .

Rising in the Morning, and Retirement for the Night

Art. VII: At the first ringing of the bell in the morning, all the tenants of the house (the sick and infirm excepted) must immediately rise, dress, wash, and repair to their several appointments. At 9 o'clock PM in summer, and 8 o'clock PM in winter, on ringing the bell, every person in the house must repair to their apartments, extinguish the lights, secure the fires, and retire to bed. No person at any time allowed to stroll in to any room or entry, not leading directly to his Room unless by permission of the master.

Visitors

Art. VIII: No visitors allowed but by a written order from the overseers, and then only on Wednesdays, except friends of the sick, who may be admitted at any time by written permission. Visitors caught introducing spirits or any other improper articles, shall never be admitted again. No money to be received, or begging allowed in or out of the house by paupers.

Labour

Art. IX: Tasks shall be assigned by the keeper to all who are capable of labour, and those who perform them faithfully and cheerfully, shall be rewarded according to their merits by such indulgences as the Overseers may direct. No work whatever shall be performed by the inhabitants of this house, out of the same, for any citizen of the city except by permission.

Spirituous Liquors, Disorderly Conduct and Profane Language

Art. X: The severest punishment will be inflicted on all those who are guilty of drunkenness, disorderly conduct, profane or obscene language, theft, embezzlement, waste of food or manufacturing stock, or defacing these articles or any waste whatever; and no rum or other ardent spirits, on any occasion or under any pretence, whatever, will be permitted to be brought into the house, unless by written order of the physician, and then to be dealt out by the master. For bringing or assisting to bring into the house any spirituous liquors, for being intoxicated, or any other breach of these articles, the offender shall be punished with solitary confinement, and fed on bread and water, not exceeding two weeks, nor less than one day, and increased for the second offence.

Solitary Confinement

Art. XI: In all cases of solitary confinement for highly criminal conduct, the prisoner shall be debarred from seeing or conversing with any person, except by permission, and they shall in all these respects, be subject to the severest privations, fed on bread and water, and any tenant of the house, who shall without leave, have any communication with a person so counted, or who

shall refuse to assist the master when required to carry these rules into effect, shall suffer the same punishment. All persons confined to cells shall be previously searched and every instrument taken from them.. . .

Intercourse of the Sexes

Art. XII: No communication whatever, except in cases specially authorized by the keeper, shall be allowed between unmarried males and females belonging to the house; and all unlawful connexion between the sexes is strictly prohibited—any violation of this rule shall be subject to the severest punishment by solitary confinement and fed on bread and water not exceeding 20 days nor less than one day. . . .

Dismission and Leave of Absence

Art. XVI: Dismissions shall be made only by the Board, except when committed for short terms, the committee who committed, may discharge them. No inhabitant of the house will be permitted to go out on any pretence whatever, unless by permission of the keeper in writing, not more than once a month (extraordinary cases excepted) and every person so permitted, must return at or before sunset. For leaving without permission shall be punished by solitary confinement. For exceeding the granted permission, not to be allowed to go out again for three months.

Punishment

Art. XVII: The keeper will be vigilant in detecting every negligence of willful violation of these Rules, and will promptly inflict the most exemplary punishment—at the same time, those who conduct well, will receive the kindest treatment, and every reasonable indulgence.

Source

Wagner, David. *The Poorhouse: America's Forgotten Institution.* Lanham, MD: Rowman and Littlefield, 2005, 42–45.

to care for their own children and grand-children, and that adult children had the responsibility to care for their parents and grandparents. Able-bodied people who refused to work could be whipped, stoned, or even killed. Needy children were to be provided with apprentice-ships, so they could learn a trade; and those who were too old or sick to work were to be provided with help either in their own homes, or in institutions for the poor.

When white settlers began arriving in the New World in the early 1600s, they first helped each other. As towns and cities grew, governments began enacting poor laws based on the Eng-lish Poor Law of 1601. The Plymouth Colony in Massachusetts adopted a poor law in 1642, Connecticut adopted one in 1673, and Massachusetts in 1692. These laws directed local govern-ment officials to collect taxes for the purpose of aiding the poor.

One common way of helping the poor was for the government to pay families to take in poor people. Towns "auctioned" the needy: families could bid on how much they wanted to take in a poor person. The family who bid the lowest would get the poor person, plus the government payment. The poor people thus taken in were required to live with and work for the family that won the auction. The government also provided clothing and medical care for the needy person. See the accompany-ing sidebar from the 1819 Illinois Poor Law.

Sometimes poor people were treated cruelly by the families who bid for them. At other times, families of the poor would put in the lowest bid, to be able to keep their poor relatives at home with them (Katz 1996, 20).

Some of the larger cities built poor-houses—institutions where poor people could live and be fed. Boston built the first one in 1664, and in the 1700s, at least seven other cities built poor-houses. However, until the nineteenth century, most smaller towns relied on other means of helping the poor (Katz 1996, 15).

Since poverty relief was a local con-cern, one problem was that poor people sometimes would show up from other areas and require care. Towns and cities were reluctant to take on the care of needy strangers, and they often made laws to prevent poor people from moving to their area. For example, starting in 1636, strangers who wanted to stay in Boston for more than two weeks had to get official permission. Such permission was denied if the per-son was likely to need public aid. Poor relief in Plymouth Colony would be given only to people who had been liv-ing there for at least three months. In Rhode Island, needy people who were asked to leave, and then returned, were subject to fines and whipping. In port cities like Boston and New York, ship captains had to pay a bond for each poor person who might need public assistance.

After the American Revolution, when many people were displaced from their homes because of the war, it became difficult for cities, town, and counties to handle poverty relief on their own. States began to provide money for emergency relief for dis-placed people. However, the poor laws, and the general idea that poverty was a local concern, continued. As new states came into the union, they also adopted poor laws similar to those in the eastern states.

THE CARE OF MR. MOTT OF RHODE ISLAND

In 1644, the town of Portsmouth, Rhode Island, began to provide help to John Mott, an elderly man. For the first year of Mr. Mott's care, a fellow townsman was to provide food, lodging, and laundry services for a payment of nine pounds per year. In addition, the town was to buy the bedding for Mr. Mott. His son then offered a cow and five bushels of corn per year to the family who agreed to take him in. The town added thirty-five bushels of corn to this, and another townsman agreed to provide him with lodging, food, and laundry services. During the thirteen years of Mr. Mott's care by the town, he was taken in by at least five different families, and the fee paid to these families increased to more than thirteen pounds per year. The town also provided clothing to Mr. Mott when they had the money to do so. The cow contributed by Mr. Mott's son traveled with him to the family who was caring for him. Upon Mr. Mott's death, the townsman who last cared for him was allowed to keep the cow, in exchange for providing the town with a calf in the spring.

Source: Creech, Margaret. *Three Centuries of Poor Law Administration: A Study of Legislation in Rhode Island.* Chicago, IL: University of Chicago Press, 1936, 14–17.

By the early to mid 1800s, as western states continued to adopt a version of the English Poor Law of 1601, some people in the eastern cities were starting to question the idea that the poor had a right to aid. Reformers began to believe that poverty was caused by individual laziness or other moral failings, and that poor relief was one of the causes of poverty, by fostering laziness. In 1821, Massachusetts put out a report on poverty in the state, and in 1824, New York State did the same. The Quincy Report from Massachusetts concluded that, while society had a duty to care for poor children, the sick, and the elderly, society ought not to provide help to the able-bodied poor. The Yates Report from New York pointed out that the poor laws were ineffective in preventing poverty, because poor people were often treated badly by the families they were auctioned to; poor children were not educated; and able-bodied poor people were not always employed.

Other states prepared similar reports. Reformers called for an end to "outdoor aid"—in other words, helping poor people in their own homes or in the homes of those they were auctioned to—and demanded instead that more institutions be built to house the poor, so that their behavior could be controlled and they could be educated and reformed. This was basically the end of the early American poor law era, and the beginning of a new era of attempts to institutionalize and reform the poor.

See also: Outdoor Relief; Poorhouses; Quincy Report, 1821

Sources

Katz, Michael. *In the Shadow of the Poorhouse: A Social History of Welfare in America.* New York: Basic Books, 1996.

Trattner, Walter I. *From Poor Law to Welfare State: A History of Social Welfare in America.* New York: The Free Press, 1994.

PRIMARY DOCUMENT 26

Excerpt from the First Illinois Poor Law, 1819

The sections of the law below dealing with the auctioning, or "farming out," of the poor, and the section dealing with apprenticing orphan children illustrate what were common ways of dealing with the poor in early America. From a modern point of view, we would consider these unusual—even inhumane—ways of helping the poor. Parents, grandparents, and adult children were legally required to support their poor children, grandchildren, or parents, if they were financially able to do so.

Section 1. *Be it enacted by the people of the State of Illinois represented in the general assembly,* That the county commissioners in the several counties in this state, at every first session of their court, yearly and every year after the first day of January, shall nominate and appoint two substantial inhabitants of every township within their respective jurisdictions, to be overseers of the poor of such township.

Section 2. That if any overseer shall die, remove, or become insolvent, before the expiration of his office, two county commissioners on due proof being thereof made before them, shall appoint another in his stead. Every overseer so nominated and appointed, shall, before he enters upon the execution of his office, take an oath or affirmation respectively, according to law; which any commissioner or justice in the counties respectively, is hereby authorized and empowered to administer, that he will discharge the duties of the office of overseer of the poor, truly, faithfully and impartially, to the best of his knowledge and ability.

Section 3. That it shall be the duty of the overseers of the poor in each and every township, yearly and every year, to cause all poor persons who have, or shall become a public charge to be farmed out at public venue, or out cry, to wit: On the first Monday in May, yearly and every year, at some public place in each township in the several counties in this state, respectively to the person or persons, who shall appear to be the lowest bidder or bidders, having given ten days previous notice of such sale, in at least three of the most public places in their respective townships; which notices shall set forth the name and age as near as may be, of each person to be farmed out as aforesaid.

Section 4. That the overseers of the poor, shall make a return into the clerk's office of the county commissioners' court, of the sum or sums of money, for which the poor of their respective townships were sold, within fifteen days after every such sale shall have been made; and it shall be the duty of the county commissioners, to levy and cause to be collected in the same manner as other county rates are levied and collected, a sum of money equal to the amount of the several sums for which the poor of the several townships shall have been sold.

Section 5. That the farmers of the poor [i.e., the lowest bidders, who have agreed to take in the poor] shall be entitled to receive from the county treasury, half yearly on the order of the commissioners aforesaid, on the certificates of the overseers of the poor, stating the sum due, the compensation which shall have been stipulated as aforesaid, in full satisfaction for their trouble, and for all expenses in keeping and supporting the poor, for the term of one year as aforesaid; and if any person or persons shall become legally a town charge, after the poor of the township shall have been sold as aforesaid, or when by neglect any poor person shall not have been sold, or farmed out on said first Monday in May, it shall be the duty of the overseers to proceed, in the manner aforesaid, to dispose of such poor person or persons for the remainder of the year, giving the same notice of such farming out.

Section 6. That it shall be lawful for the farmers of the poor to keep all poor persons under their charge at moderate labor, and every person who shall refuse to be lodged, kept, maintained and employed in the house or houses of such farmers of the poor, he or she, shall not be entitled to receive relief from overseers during such refusal; and it shall be the duty of the overseers, on any complaint made to them, or on behalf of the poor, to examine into the grounds of such complaint and if in their opinion, the poor have not been sufficiently provided with the common necessities of life, or have been in any respect illy treated, by the farmers aforesaid, it shall be lawful for the overseers to withhold any part of the compensation aforesaid, not exceeding one half thereof.

Section 7. That it shall be lawful for the overseers of the poor of the townships aforesaid, by the approbation and consent of two justices of the peace of the county, to put out as apprentices, all such poor children, whose parents are dead, or shall be by the justices found unable to maintain them; males till the age of twenty-one and females till the age of eighteen years.. . .

[The deleted sections deal with how the overseer of the poor is to keep the accounts, and how to prevent poor people from moving into a township.]

Section 27. That the father and grandfather, and mother and grandmother, and the children of every poor, old, blind, lame and impotent person, or other poor person, not able to work, being of sufficient ability, shall at their own charge, relieve and maintain every such poor person, as the court . . . for the county where such persons reside, shall order and direct, on pain of forfeiting the sum of five dollars, for every month they shall fail therein.

Section 28. That whereas it sometimes happens that men separate themselves, without reasonable cause from their wives, and desert their children; and women also desert their children; leaving them a charge upon the said county or place, aforesaid, although such person may have estates which should contribute to the maintenance of such wives and children; it shall and may be lawful for the overseers of the poor of the said township or place, having first obtained a warrant or order from two justices of said county . . . to take and seize so much of the goods and chattels, and receive so much of the annual rents and profits of the lands and tenements of such husband, father or mother, as such two justices shall order and direct. . . .

Source

Breckinridge, Sophonisba P. *The Illinois Poor Law and Its Administration.* Chicago, IL: University of Illinois Press, 1939, 243–252.

POOR PEOPLE'S CAMPAIGN

The Poor People's Campaign was the last major campaign of the civil rights movement for African Americans. It was started in late 1967, and was led by Martin Luther King, Jr. and his organization, the Southern Christian Leadership Conference (SCLC). It was, according to Amy Nathan Wright, "the first national effort to unite poor people of all races to collectively protest for economic rights" (2007, 135).

Poor People's March in Washington, D.C., June 18, 1968. (Library of Congress)

Unfortunately, King was assassinated early in the campaign, and although the Poor People's Campaign continued for several months after his death, it did not survive past the end of 1968.

In his autobiographical writings, King states the goal of the campaign: jobs or income for all. The group planned a massive demonstration Washington, D.C., during the spring of 1968, to force Congress to take action on the issue. The campaign aimed to help not only poor blacks, but also poor people of all races (King 1998, 346–350).

History professor Gerald McKnight contends that the Poor People's Campaign was not just an extension of the civil rights movement, but a "radical transformation of the civil rights movement into a populist crusade calling for a redistribution of economic and political power" (1998, 21).

The idea for the Poor People's Campaign was born during the summer of 1966, when King visited a preschool in a poor region of Mississippi. He noticed that the children were all underweight, and after watching a teacher give each child a lunch consisting of a handful of crackers and a quarter of an apple, he started to cry. Later that night, he confessed to fellow SCLC leader Ralph Abernathy that

> I can't get those children out of my mind . . . We've got to do something for them . . . We can't let that kind of poverty exist in this country. I don't think people really know that little school children are slowly starving in the United States of America. I didn't know it. (Abernathy 1989)

King then suggested that the SCLC start a campaign against poverty (Abernathy 1989, 412–413).

In October of that year, King began calling for a guaranteed annual income of $4,000 for all citizens. In May 1967, the SCLC agreed to focus on the issue of economic human rights. In response to violent riots during the summer of 1967, which were prompted by poverty and unemployment, King called for nonviolent protest. Senator Robert Kennedy urged King to bring poor people to the nation's capital to publicize their plight. In December 1967, King announced that the SCLC would mobilize people from ten cities and five rural areas to camp out in Washington, D.C., until their demand for jobs or income was met (Wright 2007, 143, 150, 152–153, 156).

During the first part of 1968, while King and the SCLC were busy preparing for this descent onto Washington, sanitation workers were striking in Memphis, Tennessee. The workers invited King to help them, and in March, King agreed to go to Memphis, because he believed that the problems facing the black sanitation workers were similar to the problems of poor people all across the country. After leading a march of 6,000 sanitation workers and giving speeches, King was standing on the balcony of his hotel in Memphis on April 4, when he was shot and killed.

Despite this tragic loss, the SCLC decided to go ahead with the Poor People's Campaign. Ralph Abernathy took over the leadership of the SCLC, and on April 29, the SCLC brought 100 delegates from around the country to present government leaders with five basic demands, an "Economic Bill of Rights." These demands were as follows: a living-wage job for those who were able to work; a secure income for those who could not work; access to land; access to capital; and a significant role for poor people in the design of government programs (Wright 2007, 195–197).

In May, nine regional caravans began traveling to Washington, D.C. A total of 3,000 to 5,000 people of many races participated in these caravans. The Poor People's Campaign made arrangements for the participants to live in tents on the lawn between the Washington Monument and the Lincoln Memorial. This encampment was called "Resurrection City." The Poor People's Campaign provided tents, food, medical care, and other essential services. Although in reality the city was somewhat disorganized, and not everyone had what they needed, some poor people still felt they were better off than they had been at home (Wright 2007, 259, 351–373).

Resurrection City lasted for six weeks. During that time, participants staged daily protests at government agencies. The federal government did not react positively to the Poor People's Campaign. According to Gerald McKnight, "On the whole the Johnson administration reacted as though the campaigners were an invading horde from a strange land intent on the violent disruption of the government rather than fellow Americans, most of whom were underprivileged and powerless nonwhite citizens" (1998, 8).

Because they were not able to accomplish their political goals, many termed the Poor People's Campaign a failure. The Poor People's Campaign failed in part because the attention of Americans had turned toward the Vietnam War. In addition, President Johnson, who had been a friend of civil rights for many years, turned his back on the civil right movement when Martin Luther King, Jr., began speaking out publicly against the Vietnam War (McKnight 1998, 141).

In another sense, however, the Poor People's Campaign succeeded. "The caravans [to Resurrection City] connected activists from different regions and diverse political perspectives and helped forge national movements that still exist today," according to Amy Nathan Wright, who wrote her doctoral dissertation on the Poor People's Campaign. She also contends that although the Poor People's Campaign did not succeed in meeting its political goals, it was still a valuable experience for participants, who learned something about how to work within the political system. In addition, Native American and Chicano activists who participated in the Poor People's Campaign used the experience to launch their own movements (2007, 531–534, 536–537).

See also: Civil Rights Movement; Guaranteed Annual Income; Kerner Commission (National Advisory Commission on Civil Disorders); King, Martin Luther, Jr.; Welfare Rights Movement

Sources

Abernathy, Ralph David. *And the Walls Came Tumbling Down: An Autobiography.* New York: Harper and Row, 1989.

King, Martin Luther, Jr. *The Autobiography of Martin Luther King,* ed. Clayborne Carson. New York: Warner Books, 1998.

McKnight, Gerald D. *The Last Crusade: Martin Luther King, Jr., the FBI, and the Poor People's Campaign.* Boulder, CO: Westview Press, 1998.

Wright, Amy Nathan. *Civil Rights' Unfinished Business: Poverty, Race and the 1968 Poor People's Campaign.* Doctoral dissertation, University of Texas at Austin, 2007.

POVERTY LINE

To give aid to the poor, the government has to decide who is poor and who is not. How does one decide the bare minimum income required to live a decent life? Since the beginning of the 1900s, various governments and reformers have tried to estimate a minimum budget that would prevent malnutrition and suffering. This is called the "poverty line."

As the overall standard of living has risen in the United States, so too has the minimum standard of living specified by the poverty line. Diana Karter Appelbaum surveyed a number of poverty lines throughout the twentieth century. She found that the pre-1929 poverty-line budgets provided a less well-balanced diet, and allowed for smaller housing and fewer comforts, than the poverty-line budgets of the 1960s and after. For example, the pre-1929 poverty-line budgets provided less meat, milk, eggs, legumes, fruits, vegetables, and fats, than the budgets of 1964 and 1975. However, the pre-1929 budgets in general called for more flour and grain products, and more potatoes. The pre-1929 poverty-line budgets called for a dwelling with three rooms for a family of five (such as kitchen, living room, and one bedroom). Bathtubs were not considered essential. In contrast, the post-1960 poverty-line budget specified five rooms for a family of five, and a bathroom exclusively for the family's use, including flush toilets, bathing facilities, and hot water.

Appelbaum notes, however, that while the poverty line has risen to include a greater variety of food, more housing space, and more comforts, it has continued to be lower than the actual minimum income that a family needed. For example, when social service bureaus and labor organizers drew up estimates of minimum budgets for working-class families in the early 1900s, these budgets were about 150 percent more than the poverty-line budgets of that time. In 1975, the Bureau of Labor Statistics estimated that an urban family living an "austere" lifestyle would need to earn about 160 percent of the federal poverty line at that time. Appelbaum notes that "while the level of living provided by a poverty-line budget has improved, the status of these families relative to the rest of society has remained static. In this, the poverty lines reflect not what the poor need, but what those who determine such things believe they should have" (1977, 514).

In 1963, Mollie Orshansky, a staff economist at the Social Security Administration, came up with the federal government's official way of calculating the poverty line. She took an inexpensive food budget that was designed to meet basic dietary needs and multiplied by three to get the minimum income to meet basic needs. The assumption was that the typical low-income family spent about a third of their budget on food, which was true at that time. The poverty line is recalculated every year by the federal government, based on the Consumer Price Index (the price paid by consumers for common goods and services). Since 1967, the Census Bureau has used this measure of poverty to publish statistics on the number of people living in poverty in the country (Quigley 2003, 37).

Even the Census Bureau agrees that the federal poverty line may not adequately reflect whether a family can actually meet basic needs. According to their latest report on income and poverty, the poverty line "should be interpreted as a statistical yardstick rather than as a complete description of what people and families need to live" (DeNavas-Walt, Proctor, and Smith 2007, 43).

Government social service agencies also recognize that the federal poverty line is too low. The National School Lunch Program provides free or low-cost meals to families with incomes up to 185 percent of the poverty line, and the Earned Income Tax Credit is available to people with incomes of almost twice the federal poverty threshold (Quigley 2003, 41; USDA, Child Nutrition Programs 2007–2008).

How much does it really cost to cover basic expenses? An organization called the Family Economic Security Project has analyzed the basic cost of living in a number of states. They calculate minimum budgets by county, taking into consideration the cost of renting an apartment in that area, basic food, child care, transportation, health care, taxes (minus any tax credits the family is eligible for), and miscellaneous expenses, such as clothing and cleaning products. For example, their Pennsylvania report shows that in 2006 in Allegheny County (the site of Pittsburgh), a family of three (one adult, one preschooler, and one school-age child) would need an income of more than $39,000 to meet their basic needs. In contrast, for 2006, the federal poverty level for a family of three was $16,600. The report points out that food costs are a much smaller part of today's family's budget than they were in the 1960s, when the federal poverty line was developed. Food for a family of three in Allegheny County accounted for only 16 percent of the total budget in 2006—not one-third, as the federal government's poverty measure predicts. In reality, the largest chunks of income go to housing (24 percent) and child care (32 percent) (Pearce 2006, 13, 15).

Economic experts and activists for the poor have proposed a number of different ways to revise the poverty line, most of which would raise the poverty threshold. The poverty line might multiply food prices by five or six, since in the twenty-first century, people tend to spend a smaller percentage of their income on food. Or the poverty line could be based not on a multiplier of food prices, but on a multiplier of housing prices. Or poverty lines could be based on a number of different costs added together, such as food, housing, child care, transportation, health care, and other necessities. Poverty lines could be adjusted by state or region. The poverty line could fluctuate with the general well-being of the country: any family with an income of less than half of the median income of that family size might be considered poor. In other words, the poverty line is calculated by if charting all the incomes of a particular family size, taking the number in the middle (the median income), and dividing it by half. This last method is widely used in Europe to define poverty (Citro and Michael 1995, 47; Quigley 2003, 40).

Because more accurate methods of calculating what people really need, and thus the poverty threshold, would have the effect of raising the official poverty line, this would mean that the United States suddenly would have far more poor people, which is an uncomfortable idea for many government officials.

Sources

Appelbaum, Diana Karter. "The Level of the Poverty Line: A Historical Survey." *Social Service Review,* September 1977, 514–523.

Citro, Constance F., and Robert T. Michael, eds. *Measuring Poverty: A New Approach.* Washington, DC: National Academy Press, 1995.

DeNavas-Walt, Carmen, Bernadette D. Proctor, and Jessica Smith. U.S. Census Bureau, Current Population Reports, P60-233, *Income, Poverty, and Health Insurance Coverage in the United States: 2006,* U.S. Government Printing Office, Washington, DC, 2007. www.census.gov/prod/2007 pubs/p60-233.pdf (accessed April 2008).

Pearce, Diana. *The Self-Sufficiency Standard for Pennsylvania.* Prepared by the Family Economic Security Project for PathWays, PA, May 2006. http://www.sixstrategies. org/includes/productviewdetailsinclude. cfm?productID=503&strProductType= resource (accessed April 2008).

Quigley, William P. *Ending Poverty as We Know It.* Philadelphia, PA: Temple University Press, 2003.

Web Sites

Family Economic Security Project. http:// www.sixstrategies.org/ (accessed April 2008).

USDA (U.S. Department of Agriculture). Child Nutrition Programs. http:// www.fns.usda.gov/cnd/governance/notices/ iegs/iegs.htm (accessed April 2008).

PRIVATE CHARITY

An ongoing debate regarding helping the poor is whether the government should be involved with poverty relief at all. Shouldn't this task be left to private charities? In the nineteenth century, the "scientific charity" movement

believed that when government provided "outdoor relief"—food and fuel
to people in their own homes—this
encouraged laziness. The scientific
charity movement attempted to replace
government "outdoor relief" with private charity.

At the start of the Great Depression,
President Herbert Hoover believed that
the federal government ought not to get
involved with poverty relief because
that was more appropriately left to private philanthropy and local government. In the 1980s and 1990s,
President Ronald Reagan and President
George H. W. Bush both cut government funding for the poor, and instead
promoted private charity as an answer
to the problem of poverty. Bush coined
the phrase "thousand points of light"
to describe the many community organizations throughout the nation, which
he believed could and should solve
problems of poverty and homelessness.
Bush's son, President George W. Bush,
continued in this vein, pushing for federal funding of private religious charities. His speech extolling the work of
faith-based charities appears in the
accompanying sidebar.

From the beginning of the American
colonies, both private charity and government funds have been used to help
the poor. In the seventeenth century,
when the American colonies were just
beginning to form, neighbors at first
helped each other, and local governments, once they formed, taxed well-
off citizens to provide for the needy.
Although there were few wealthy individuals at this time, William Penn
(1644–1718), the Quaker governor of
Pennsylvania, encouraged his fellow
Quakers to be generous to the needy.
Also, the first immigrant aid society,

*The First private charity in New England was
the Scots' Charitable Society, formed in Boston in 1657. (Library of Congress)*

the Scots Charitable Society, was
founded in 1657, to provide help to fellow countrymen (Bremner 1988, 9–11;
Trattner 1994, 37).

In the eighteenth century, while
local governments were still responsible for helping the needy, private philanthropy became more popular among
the colonists. Several prominent colonists and speakers encouraged individuals to donate to those less fortunate.
Cotton Mather (1663–1728) encouraged individuals to form associations to
build churches for the poor and to help
needy clergymen. Benjamin Franklin
(1706–1790) believed in preventing
poverty by promoting self-help and by
improving social conditions. He raised
private and public money to improve
the streets of Philadelphia and set up a

police plan, a volunteer fire company, and a library. George Whitefield (1714–1770), an English preacher whose popular religious revivals are known as the "Great Awakening," raised money from his audiences for an orphanage in Georgia, for victims of disaster, and for the struggling colonial colleges (Bremner 1988, 12–22).

By the nineteenth century, as state governments were starting to get involved with poverty relief, private charities also flourished. According to Robert Bremner, "as early as 1820 the larger cities had an embarrassment of benevolent organizations" (1988, 44). Many of these organizations were concerned with spreading religion and morality, and they were involved with distributing Bibles, starting Sunday schools, and helping poor youths who wanted to become clergymen.

During the Civil War (1861–1865), private individuals and organizations became involved with tending wounded soldiers and raising money for the support of families of servicemen. Private charities sometimes appealed to the government for help when they realized that private efforts would fall short of their goal. For example, in early 1862, during the Civil War, about thirty private "freedmen's aid" societies sprung up to help the freed slaves. At the end of 1863, a joint committee representing these groups asked President Abraham Lincoln to establish a government bureau to provide help for the former slaves. In March 1865, the government created the Bureau of Refugees, Freedmen and Abandoned Lands, popularly referred to as the "Freedmen's Bureau" (Bremner 1988, 81–82).

Toward the end of the 1800s, a movement called "scientific charity" aimed to organize private charities in each city to provide efficient help to the needy, and to provide the moral guidance of well-off volunteers who would visit with the poor. Another private philanthropic movement of this time was the settlement-house movement, which allowed well-off, college-educated young women and men to live in poor neighborhoods, learn from the poor, and provide help to them. These movements eventually joined together and turned to the government to pass reforms to help the poor.

By 1889, there were an estimated 4,000 millionaires in the United States. One prominent philanthropist of this time was Andrew Carnegie. Born in Scotland in 1835, to a poor family, by 1889, Carnegie had become a millionaire thirty times over. His essay "Wealth," published in 1889, is "the most famous document in the history of American philanthropy," according to Robert Bremner. Carnegie encouraged millionaires to give away their wealth during their lifetimes for the betterment of humanity, instead of willing this wealth to their heirs. In the early 1900s, Carnegie and other wealthy Americans began establishing "foundations"—organizations to give money to worthy causes (Bremner 1988, 100, 111).

When the Great Depression began in the 1930s, President Herbert Hoover encouraged individuals and community charities to come to the aid of the needy. He did not believe the federal government should get involved with helping the poor, and he even praised the American Red Cross for turning down $25 million that Congress wanted to give it for drought relief activities. In 1931, Hoover and his administration conducted a nationwide campaign that succeeded in raising $100 million in private money for relief activities. However, this was not nearly enough to meet the needs of the poor and unemployed. The stock market crash of 1929 that had started the Great Depression had also dried up most private philanthropy (Bremner 1988, 137–140, 147).

Many people began to realize that private charity could not possibly meet the massive needs of the unemployed during the Great Depression. After President Franklin Delano Roosevelt took office in 1933, the federal government began a major series of programs to aid the unemployed, elderly, and poor. This New Deal was financed in part through higher taxes, and leaders of private charities were worried that businesses would no longer donate generously if they had to pay higher taxes. These leaders helped pass the Revenue Act of 1935, which allowed corporations to deduct charitable contributions from their taxable income. After World War II, more and more wealthy Americans began setting up foundations, which also offered tax advantages. Still, by the mid-1950s, about 75 percent of philanthropic donations came from individuals, and not foundations (Bremner 1988, 150–151, 164–165, 169).

In the 1960s, the tax laws allowed individuals to deduct charitable contributions from their income. Also at this time, the government began to make contracts with and provide funding to private agencies to carry out the work of helping the needy. This was in fact nothing new in American history: from colonial times, governments had provided money to private citizens and institutions to help care for the poor (Bremner 1988, 201–202).

Although the government now handles many important aspects of aid to the needy, such as old-age insurance, unemployment insurance, health care for the poor, and food security through food stamps and school lunches, private charity was alive and well at the end of the twentieth century. In 1984, a national survey reported that almost 90 percent of Americans contributed to charities. Emergency food programs, such as food banks and soup kitchens, are prominent modern examples of private charity.

See also: Emergency Food Programs; Freedmen's Bureau; New Deal; Outdoor Relief; Scientific Charity; Settlement Houses

Sources

Bremner, Robert H. *American Philanthropy.* Chicago, IL: University of Chicago Press, 1988.

Trattner, Walter I. *From Poor Law to Welfare State: A History of Social Welfare in America.* New York: The Free Press, 1994.

THE PROBLEM OF INDIAN ADMINISTRATION (1928)

This report was commissioned by the federal government as a scientific study of the economic conditions on American Indian reservations. The study was conducted by the Institute for Government Research (an independent organization that eventually became part of the Brookings Institute). The report was directed by Lewis Meriam and is often referred to as the "Meriam Report." Meriam and nine staff members spent

PRIMARY DOCUMENT 27

Excerpt from "President Bush Implements Key Elements of his Faith-Based Initiative," December 2002

This speech could have been delivered in the nineteenth century. With its emphasis on the importance of private charity and the importance of providing spiritual uplift to the poor, it is very much in line with the views of many nineteenth-century reformers, who saw moral failing as a major cause of poverty. However, unlike in the nineteenth century, President George W. Bush does not call for an end to government aid to the poor. In fact, he admits that faith-based charities can never replace government help. Instead, he wants the federal government to be able to provide funding to private faith-based charities on an equal basis with private secular charities. This speech was delivered at a White House Conference on Faith-Based and Community Initiatives. The reform of welfare he refers to is the Personal Responsibility and Work Opportunity Reconciliation Act, signed by President Bill Clinton in 1996.

We've reformed welfare in America to help many, yet welfare policy will not solve the deepest problems of the spirit. Our economy is growing, yet there are some needs that prosperity can never fill. We arrest and convict dangerous criminals; yet building more prisons is no substitute for responsibility and order in our souls.

No government policy can put hope in people's hearts or a sense of purpose in people's lives. That is done when someone, some good soul puts an arm around a neighbor and says, God loves you, and I love you, and you can count on us both.

And we find that powerful spirit of compassion in faith-based and community groups across our nation: People giving shelter to the homeless; providing safety for battered women; giving care and comfort to AIDS victims; bringing companionship to lonely seniors.

I saw that spirit of compassion earlier today when I visited adults and children involved in a program called Amachi at the Bright Hope Baptist Church right here in Philadelphia. In the Amachi program, good people from more than 50 churches in this area serve as mentors to the children of prisoners. They share their time and attention. They just serve as a friend.

Most of us find it difficult to imagine the life of a child who has to go through a prison gate to be hugged by their mom or dad. Yet this is the reality for almost a million-and-a-half American boys and girls. They face terrible challenges that no child deserves to face. Without guidance, they have a higher risk of failing in school and committing crimes themselves. The volunteers of Amachi, who are with us here today with the children they are loving, are such wonderful givers of guidance and love.. . .

Faith-based charities work daily miracles because they have idealistic volunteers. They're guided by moral principles. They know the problems of their own communities, and above all, they recognize the dignity of every citizen and the possibilities of every life. These groups and many good charities that are specifically religious have the heart to serve others. Yet many lack the resources they need to meet the needs around them.

They deserve the support of the rest of us. They deserve the support of foundations. They deserve the support of corporate America. They deserve the support of individual donors, of church congregations, of synagogues and mosques. And then deserve, when appropriate, the support of the federal government.

Faith-based groups will never replace government when it comes to helping those in need. Yet government must recognize the power and unique contribution of faith-based groups in every part of our country. And when the federal government gives contracts to private groups to provide social services, religious groups should have an equal chance to compete. When decisions are made on public funding, we should not focus on the religion you practice; we should focus on the results you deliver.

The Amachi program receives 38 percent of its funding from the federal government. My administration has been working for nearly two years to encourage this kind of support to good faith-based programs. And we're making some progress. . . .

Yet there's a lot to do. In government, we're still fighting old attitudes, habits and rules that discriminate against religious groups for no good purpose. In Iowa, for example, the Victory Center Rescue Mission was told to return grant money to the government because the mission's board of directors was not secular enough. The St. Francis House Homeless Shelter in South Dakota was denied a grant because voluntary prayers were offered before meals. A few years ago in New York, the Metropolitan Council on Jewish Poverty was discouraged from even applying for federal funds because it had the word "Jewish" in its name.

These are examples of a larger pattern, a pattern of discrimination. And this discrimination shows a fundamental misunderstanding of the law. I recognize that government has no business endorsing a religious creed, or directly funding religious worship or religious teaching. That is not the business of the government. Yet government can and should support social services provided by religious people, as long as those services go to anyone in need, regardless of their faith. And when government gives that support, charities and faith-based programs should not be forced to change their character or compromise their mission.

And I don't intend to compromise either. I have worked for a faith-based initiative to rally and encourage the armies of compassion. I will continue to work with Congress on this agenda. But the needs of our country are urgent and, as President, I have an authority I intend to use. Many acts of discrimination—many acts of discrimination against faith-based groups are committed by Executive Branch agencies. And, as the leader of the Executive Branch, I'm going to make some changes, effective today.. . . . I am going to sign an executive order directing all federal agencies to follow the principle of equal treatment in rewarding social service grants.

Every person in every government agency will know where the President stands. And every person will have the responsibility to ensure a level playing field for faith-based organizations in federal programs.. . .

Through all these actions, I hope that every faith-based group in America, the social entrepreneurs of America, understand that this government respects your work and we respect the motivation behind your work. We do not want you to become carbon copies of public programs. We want you to follow your heart. We want you to follow the word. We want you to do the works of kindness and mercy you are called upon to do.. . .

When government discriminates against religious groups, it is not the groups that suffer most. The loss comes to the hungry who don't get fed, to the addicts who don't get help, to the children who drift toward self-destruction. For the sake of so many brothers and sisters in needs, we must and we will support the armies of compassion in America.

Source

U.S. Department of Health and Human Services. http://innovationincompassion. hhs.gov/historical_docs/presidential.html (accessed January 2009).

seven months visiting ninety-five American Indian reservations, hospitals, and schools. Their goal was not to merely ascertain whether the Indian Service employees had done a good job with the money provided to them, but instead, the goal of the report was to measure the conditions of American Indians against the ideal. The goal was to "look to the future and insofar as possible to indicate what remains to be done to adjust the Indians to the prevailing civilization so that they may maintain themselves in the presence of that civilization according at least to a minimum standard of health and decency" (Meriam 1928).

The Meriam Report found widespread poverty on Native American reservations, despite the fact that the General Allotment Act of 1887 was supposed to have turned the American Indians into prosperous, landowning farmers. Many Americans were shocked to find out that American Indians were often destitute, and that they suffered from high infant mortality rates and epidemics of tuberculosis and other infectious diseases.

The report calls for respect for Native Americans, as well as better management and more funding by the U.S. government. In this sense, the report was trying to straddle two different points of view: the old view that American Indians needed help to become assimilated into American culture; and the emerging viewpoint, championed by John Collier and others, that American Indian traditions are valuable and must be respected and nurtured rather than stamped out. "Ideologically, the Meriam Report was a strange hybrid," reports James Wilson,

lurching uneasily between the assimilationist views of old-style reformers . . . and the very different vision of Collier and his supporters. On the one hand, it declared that "the fundamental requirement" of Indian policy was to enable Native Americans to be "absorbed into the prevailing civilization at least in accordance with a minimum standard of health and decency"; on the other, it urged "more understanding of and sympathy for the Indian point of view." (1999, 342)

The report blames the government for not appropriating enough money for Indian health care, education, and food. At government boarding schools for American Indian children, the report found that the children did not regularly have access to milk, fruits, and vegetables. Children above fourth grade were required to work half the day in the school laundry and other school facilities.

Also, the report found that the land allotted to the American Indians was often of poor quality; they were not taught proper farming techniques; and they were placed in remote areas without access to work for wages. Meriam and his colleagues urged that more money be appropriated to help Native Americans, and that the Indian Service become much more efficient.

The report also blamed the character of American Indians, claiming that the American Indians were not "industrious" in the same manner as white people; that the American Indians did not understand the value of money and were not capable of handling their own finances. Nevertheless, the report stated that Indians are entitled to unfailing courtesy and consideration from all government employees.. . . . Leadership will recognize the good in the economic and social life of the Indians in their religion and ethics and will seek to develop it and build on it rather than to crush out all that is Indian. The Indians have much to contribute to the dominant civilization, and the effort should be made to secure this contribution, in part because of the good it will do the Indians in stimulating a proper race pride and self respect. (Meriam 1928)

The accompanying document details the conditions of poverty that the report uncovered.

See also: Collier, John; General Allotment Act of 1887

Sources

Meriam, Lewis, Technical Director. *The Problems of Indian Administration.* Baltimore, MD: The Johns Hopkins University Press, 1928. http://www.alaskool.org/native_ed/research_reports/IndianAdmin/Indian_Admin_Problms.html (accessed November 2007).

Prucha, Francis Paul. *The Great Father: The United States Government and the American Indians.* Lincoln, NE: University of Nebraska Press, 1984.

Wilson, James. *The Earth Shall Weep: A History of Native America.* New York: Atlantic Monthly Press, 1999.

PROGRESSIVE ERA

The Progressive Era was a time of economic, political, and social reform in American history. It lasted from the 1890s to about 1917, when the United States entered World War I (although some reform efforts continued until 1920 and later). During the Progressive

Anti-Saloon League of America poster showing a menacing hand, signifying the legalized saloon, over a little girl. (Library of Congress)

Era, poverty was a major concern and strong private reform organizations, such as the settlement-house movement and the National Consumers League, pushed for new laws to provide for the poor, protect them from workplace dangers, remove children from the workplace, and require higher wages. State governments were active in passing these laws.

Reformers were also active in a national campaign to add an amendment to the Constitution prohibiting the sale of alcoholic beverages in the United States (the Eighteenth Amendment was ratified in 1919). The Prohibition movement was seen partly as a way to address poverty, because one

PRIMARY DOCUMENT 28

Excerpt from *The Problem of Indian Administration*

CHAPTER I
GENERAL SUMMARY OF FINDINGS AND RECOMMENDATIONS

The Conditions Among the Indians. An overwhelming majority of the Indians are poor, even extremely poor, and they are not adjusted to the economic and social system of the dominant white civilization. . . .

Health. The health of the Indians as compared with that of the general population is bad. Although accurate mortality and morbidity statistics are commonly lacking, the existing evidence warrants the statement that both the general death rate and the infant mortality rate are high. Tuberculosis is extremely prevalent. Trachoma, a communicable disease which produces blindness, is a major problem because of its great prevalence and the danger of its spreading among both the Indians and the whites.

Living Conditions. The prevailing living conditions among the great majority of the Indians are conducive to the development and spread of disease. With comparatively few exceptions, the diet of the Indians is bad. It is generally insufficient in quantity, lacking in variety, and poorly prepared. The two great preventive elements in diet, milk, and fruits and green vegetables, are notably absent. Most tribes use fruits and vegetables in season, but even then the supply is ordinarily insufficient. The use of milk is rare, and it is generally not available even for infants. Babies, when weaned, are ordinarily put on substantially the same diet as older children and adults, a diet consisting mainly of meats and starches.

The housing conditions are likewise conducive to bad health. Both in the primitive dwellings and in the majority of more or less permanent homes which in some cases have replaced them, there is great overcrowding, so that all members of the family are exposed to any disease that develops, and it is virtually impossible in any way even partially to isolate a person suffering from a communicable disease.. . .

Sanitary facilities are generally lacking. Except among the relatively few well-to-do Indians, the houses seldom have a private water supply or any toilet facilities whatever. Even privies are exceptional. Water is ordinarily carried considerable distances from natural springs or streams, or occasionally from wells.. . .

Economic Conditions. The income of the typical Indian family is low and the earned income extremely low. From the standpoint of the white man, the typical Indian is not industrious, nor is he an effective worker when he does work. Much of his activity is expended in lines which produce a relatively small return either in goods or money. He generally ekes out an existence through unearned income from leases of his land, the sale of land, per capita payments from tribal funds, or in exceptional cases through rations given him by the government. The number of Indians who are supporting themselves through their own efforts, according to what a white man would regard as the minimum standard of health and decency, is extremely small. What little they secure from their own efforts or from other sources is rarely effectively used.. . .

In justice to the Indians, it should be said that many of them are living on lands from which a trained and experienced white man could scarcely wrest a reasonable living. In some instances the land originally set apart for the Indians was of little value for agricultural operations other than grazing. In other instances part of the land was excellent but the Indians did not appreciate its value. Often when individual allotments were made, they chose for themselves the poorer parts, because those parts were near a domestic water supply or a source of firewood, or because they furnished some native product important to the Indians in their primitive life. Frequently the better sections of the land originally set apart for the Indians have fallen into the hands of the whites, and the Indians have retreated to the poorer lands remote from markets. . . .

The remoteness of their homes often prevents them from easily securing opportunities for wage earning, nor do they have many contacts with persons dwelling in urban communities where they might find employment. Even the boys and girls graduating from government schools have comparatively little vocational guidance or aid in finding profitable employment.

When all these factors are taken into consideration, it is not surprising to find low incomes: low standards of living, and poor health.. . .

When the government adopted the policy of individual ownership of the land on the reservations, the expectation was that the Indians would become farmers. Part of the plan was to instruct and aid them in agriculture, but this vital part was not pressed with vigor and intelligence. It almost seems as if the government assumed that some magic in individual ownership of property would in itself prove an educational civilizing factor, but unfortunately this policy has for the most part operated in the opposite direction. Individual ownership has in many instances permitted Indians to sell their allotments and to live for a time on the unearned income resulting from the sale. Individual ownership brought

promptly all the details of inheritance, and frequently the sale of the property of the deceased Indians to whites so that the estate could be divided among the heirs. To the heirs the sale brought further unearned income, thereby lessening the necessity for self support.. . .

Since the Indians were ignorant of money and its use, had little or no sense of values, and fell an easy victim to any white man who wanted to take away their property, the government, through its Indian Service employees, often took the easiest course of managing all the Indians' property for them. The government kept the Indians' money for them at the agency. When the Indians wanted something they would go to the government agent, as a child would go to his parents, and ask for it. The government agent would make all the decisions, and in many instances would either buy the thing requested or give the Indians a store order for it. Although money was sometimes given the Indians, the general belief was that the Indians could not be trusted to spend the money for the purpose agreed upon with the agent, and therefore they must not be given opportunity to misapply it. At some agencies this practice still exists, although it gives the Indians no education in the use of money, is irritating to them, and tends to decrease responsibility and increase the pauper attitude.

The typical Indian, however, has not yet advanced to the point where he has the knowledge of money and values, and of business methods that will permit him to control his own property without aid, advice, and some restrictions; nor is he ready to work consistently and regularly at more or less routine labor.

Source

Meriam, Lewis. "The Problem of Indian Administration: Report of a Survey Made at the Request of Honorable Hubert Work, Secretary of the Interior, and Submitted to Him," *Studies in administration*, Vol. 18 February 21, 1928.

cause of poverty was thought to be alcoholism.

The Progressive Era changed the government's role in the economy. Previously, the conventional wisdom was that government ought to stay out of the economy, and ought to allow industry free reign to grow as much as possible. Progressive reformers pushed for a government that regulated the economy for the benefit of workers. Some scholars see the Progressive Era as a precursor to the great expansion of government services to the poor that occurred during the 1930s, under President Franklin Roosevelt's New Deal program, as well as President Lyndon Johnson's War on Poverty in the 1960s (Gould 2001, ix–xi).

In addition to a concern with poverty, Progressive reformers were also interested in making government more democratic and ending corruption in politics. Interestingly, one Progressive Era reform has had a huge impact on the federal government's ability to address issues of poverty, even though at that time it was not seen as a way to deal with poverty. This was the Sixteenth Amendment to the U.S. Constitution, passed in 1913, which allows the federal government to collect income taxes. Supporters of this amendment saw it only as another way to raise federal revenue (in addition to tariffs—taxes on imported goods). However, over the years, the federal government's power to levy a tax on income has allowed it to provide for the widespread social programs of the twentieth century, such as Social Security and Medicare (health care for the elderly). "The enactment and adoption of the income tax amendment . . . proved to be one of the most important and long-lasting achievements of the reform period," says historian Lewis Gould. "The rise of the social welfare programs of the twentieth century would not have been possible without the funding mechanism of the income tax" (2001, 69).

Why did many people in the country want the government to get more involved in helping the poor at that time? What caused this shift in how people viewed the role of government in relation to the economy and to poverty? One reason is that at this time, more and more people were moving to urban areas for low-paid factory work, which caused crowding, poverty, crime, and health problems. Journalists and other writers began exposing these problems. They were called "muckrakers," a term given to them by President Theodore Roosevelt. He named them after a character who was condemned to rake muck in John Bunyan's book *Pilgrim's Progress*, and who never looked up from the filth even when offered a celestial crown. Roosevelt agreed that there were negative things about American life, but he wanted the muckraking journalists to also remember the positive. The magazines that printed the muckrakers' work had large circulations, reaching people across the country, so more and more people became aware of the problems (Gould 2001, 28–29; McGerr 2003, 175–176).

Two influential writers of the era were Jacob Riis and Upton Sinclair. Riis, a Danish-born journalist and photographer, wrote more than a dozen books to expose the living conditions of the poor, including *How the Other Half Lives,* about life in New York City's slums. This book influenced

---

PROHIBITION PARTY PLATFORM OF 1912

The "Prohibition Party" was formed in 1869, because antiliquor activists believed that neither of the major political parties was taking a strong enough stand on prohibition. The party worked not only for prohibition of alcoholic beverages, but also for women's suffrage, the abolition of child labor, and other issues. The party worked to pass the Eighteenth Amendment to the U.S. Constitution. Here is part of the party's platform (a statement of beliefs) from 1912. The Prohibition Party is still an active American political party as of 2009.

The Prohibition Party in National Convention at Atlantic City, N.J., July 10, 1912, recognizing God as the source of all governmental authority, makes the following declarations of principles and policies:

1. The alcoholic drink traffic is wrong; is the most serious drain on the wealth and resources of the nation; is detrimental to the general welfare and destructive of the inalienable rights of life, liberty and the pursuit of happiness. All laws taxing or licensing a traffic which produces crime, poverty and political corruption, and spreads disease and death should be repealed. To destroy such a traffic there must be elected to power a political party which will administer the government from the standpoint that the alcoholic drink traffic is a crime and not a business, and we pledge that the manufacture, importation, exportation, transportion and sale of alcoholic beverages shall be prohibited.

Source: Prohibition Party Background. http://www.prohibitionists.org/Background/background. html (accessed August 2008).

---

national political leaders, including Theodore Roosevelt and Frances Perkins, who was secretary of labor under President Franklin Roosevelt. Sinclair was a Socialist writer whose novel, *The Jungle,* revealed the true story of a filthy meat-packing plant that produced contaminated food. The novel became a bestseller and led to pure food laws.

According to historian Richard Hofstadter, "to an extraordinary degree the work of the Progressive movement rested upon its journalism" (1955, 185). The idea was that, if people knew about the problems, they would be motivated to solve them. And they were motivated. As historian Theda Skocpol notes, "the period witnessed an outpouring of voluntary civic efforts for purposes of social betterment: to make cities more livable; to help the working classes and the 'deserving' poor; to speed the assimilation of immigrants" (1992, 265). Progressives tried to provide help both through private organizations, as well as through influencing the government to pass new laws.

One movement of the era that hoped to transform the American economy was the Socialist movement. Socialism was a reaction to the widespread poverty caused by the Industrial Revolution. The Socialists believed that businesses should be cooperatively owned or publicly owned (such as by the government), so that wealth would be more evenly distributed. The Socialist Party of America, formed in 1901, gained members and strength during the Progressive Era by allying themselves with the labor union movement. Their most successful and inspirational leader, Eugene Debs, ran for U.S. president in 1904, 1908, 1912, and 1920. In 1912, he won 6 percent of the vote—a huge percentage for a minor-party candidate. The 1912 platform (set of beliefs) of the Socialist Party of America is excerpted in a primary document.

An alternative to socialism was the single-tax movement of Henry George, which was also popular during the Progressive Era. George and his supporters wanted to distribute wealth more equally. Their solution was that the government should tax only the increased value of land and that no other taxes should be imposed.

In addition to organizations and governments, the business world was also involved with reforms during the Progressive Era. To attract workers and promote their well-being, and also to blunt the importance of labor unions, more and more businesses began to offer services and benefits, such as company housing, preschools, libraries, playgrounds, medical care, sports fields, stock ownership, pensions, and profit sharing. These practices are called "welfare capitalism" (McGerr 2003, 126–127).

Racial equality was also a concern during the Progressive Era. In 1909, white intellectuals and black leaders formed the National Association for the Advancement of Colored People (NAACP). One of their main goals was to get rid of the segregation laws that kept blacks out of good schools, colleges, and jobs, and thus perpetuated the cycle of black poverty.

A few Progressive-Era reforms seem distasteful in the twenty-first century. For example, one reaction to the increase in poor immigrants in the cities was to try to pass laws to restrict immigration. Also at this time, people began trying to control the fertility of populations that were deemed "undesirable," such as the handicapped and criminals. This "eugenics" movement promoted the idea that certain people were genetically programmed to be inferior and thus to have difficulty supporting themselves, and so they should be sterilized to prevent them from reproducing (Katz 1996, 188–192; McGerr 2003, 214).

See also: Child Labor Laws; Children's Bureau; Debs, Eugene; Eugenics; George, Henry; Industrial Revolution; Johnson, Lyndon; Minimum-Wage Laws; Mothers' Pensions; National Association for the Advancement of Colored People; National Consumers League; New Deal; Perkins, Frances; Prohibition; Riis, Jacob; Segregation Laws; Settlement Houses; Sinclair, Upton; Socialism; Social Security Act; Welfare Capitalism; Workers' Compensation

Sources

Gould, Lewis L. *America in the Progressive Era, 1890–1914.* Harlow, England: Pearson Education, 2001.

Hofstadter, Richard. *The Age of Reform.* New York: Alfred A. Knopf, 1955.

Katz, Michael. *In the Shadow of the Poorhouse: A Social History of Welfare in America.* New York: Basic Books, 1996.

McGerr, Michael. *A Fierce Discontent: The Rise and Fall of the Progressive Movement in America, 1870–1920.* New York: Free Press, 2003.

Skocpol, Theda. *Protecting Soldiers and Mothers: The Political Origins of Social Policy in the United States.* Cambridge, MA: Harvard University Press, 1992.

PROHIBITION

Prohibition refers to the time period from 1920 to 1933 in U.S. history, when the making, selling, and importing of alcoholic beverages was banned by the Eighteenth Amendment to the U.S. Constitution. The supporters of Prohibition believed that excessive consumption of alcohol caused social problems such as poverty, crime, and abuse of women and children. They hoped that by banning alcoholic beverages, they could reduce these social ills. Prohibition ended in 1933, when the Eighteenth amendment was repealed by the Twenty-first Amendment.

From the time Europeans arrived on the shores of the New World, alcoholic beverages were a common and accepted part of American life. Beer, wine, and even hard liquor were considered health-giving drinks, especially since the water in early America was often dirty and contaminated. However, by the early 1800s, drinking had become a social problem. Instead of drinking moderately, more people started drinking until they were drunk. Between 1810 and 1830, the average American above the age of fourteen drank about seven gallons of pure alcohol per year, the highest alcohol consumption in the history of the United States. (In comparison, by the end of the twentieth century, alcohol consumption was 2.8 gallons a year per person on average.) One reason for this increase in alcohol consumption may have been the social and economic dislocation caused by the Industrial Revolution: tradition and communities were breaking down as people moved to cities for jobs, and existing laws to curb drinking were ignored as individual freedom became more important (Pegram 1998, 7–12).

In the 1820s, "temperance" (moderation in alcohol consumption) became a nationwide issue. Soon, reformers were calling not just for moderation, but for abstinence from hard liquor. Religious revivals of the early 1800s spread throughout the country, and revivalists preached that drinking hard liquor was sinful and should be abolished. According to prominent temperance reformer Theodore Dwight Weld, alcoholism accounted for half the nation's poor and 80 percent of imprisoned criminals. (He based these claims on statistics from one county). By 1835, about 1.5 million people were involved in the temperance movement (Pegram 1998, 21–23).

In the 1820s, chemists proved that beer and wine also contained alcohol, and from the 1830s onward, temperance reformers called for a total abstinence from all drinks containing alcohol. Temperance organizations began to get the government involved: New England towns were urged to stop awarding licenses to taverns and shops to sell liquor, and this no-license campaign spread to many states in the 1840s. However, government officials rarely cracked down on those who sold alcohol without a license, and so this campaign was not particularly effective.

In the 1840s, working-class Americans joined the middle class in the crusade. Working-class artisans in Baltimore started the "Washingtonian" movement, named after George Washington. This movement was secular and aimed to help unemployed workers see that they were only making thing worse by turning to drink. The Washingtonian society provided alcohol-free leisure activities as well as food, clothing, shelter, and sometimes jobs to alcoholics and their families who were struggling economically. Washingtonian clubs met several times a week. Each meeting featured a speech by a reformed drinker who detailed his battle with alcohol. By 1840, American drinking was down to 3.1 gallons of pure alcohol per person on average, and by 1845, this had dropped to 1.8 gallons (Pegram 1998, 31).

In 1851, Maine became the first state to pass a Prohibition law, banning the manufacture and sale of alcoholic beverages. By 1855, twelve more states had passed similar laws. After these successes, the temperance movement took a back stage to the Civil War until the late 1800s. In the 1870s, women took up the banner of temperance: the National Woman's Christian Temperance Union was founded in 1874. This was one of the first successful women's movements in the United States. They lobbied to require temperance education in schools. They urged states to pass laws to restrict liquor, and urged towns to prohibit liquor licenses. From 1883 to 1890, four states adopted constitutional amendments to ban the manufacture and sale of liquor (Pegram 1998, 79).

During the early 1900s, while immigrants from Germany and Ireland brought their drinking habits to the United States, doctors, scientists, and reformers publicized the harmful effects of alcohol. These professionals asserted that drinking contributed to poverty, crime, and child neglect. Alcohol fell out of favor for medicinal use, and the American Medical Association condemned its use. Prohibitionists began calling for a national constitutional amendment, which passed

Congress in 1917, just as the United States entered World War I. A national mood of sacrifice, order, and efficiency helped the amendment to receive enough state ratifications to become part of the Constitution in 1919.

Prohibition did succeed in reducing drinking. By 1934, alcohol consumption had fallen to less than one gallon per person fifteen years and above. During the first years of Prohibition, diseases caused by alcohol decreased. The death rate from alcohol in 1920 was one per 100,000—down from 5.8 per 100,000 in 1917. Grocery stores were doing better business—presumably people were buying food instead of liquor—and crime was down. Soon, however, a huge illegal liquor industry sprung up. Criminals grew rich because they could charge large amounts for illegal alcohol. Government agents hired to clamp down on the manufacture and sale of alcohol were bribed by these criminals. Alcohol-related deaths began to increase again (Behr 1996, 148–149; Pegram 1998, 164).

Anti-Prohibitionists argued that Prohibition had actually increased crime by providing a lucrative business to criminals. During the Prohibition Era, at the same time as alcohol consumption was decreasing, the United States was sliding into the Great Depression, the worst economic depression in the history of the country, which caused widespread poverty. Clearly, alcohol consumption and poverty were not as closely related as some reformers had assumed. By the early 1930s, the country had had enough of Prohibition. In 1933, Congress passed an amendment to repeal the Eighteenth Amendment, and the Twenty-first Amendment became part of the Constitution later that same year.

See also: Great Depression; Industrial Revolution; Progressive Era

Sources

Behr, Edward. *Prohibition: Thirteen Years that Changed America.* New York: Arcade Publishing, 1996.

Pegram, Thomas R. *Battling Demon Rum: The Struggle for a Dry America, 1800–1933.* Chicago, IL: Ivan R. Dee, 1998.

PUBLIC LIBRARIES

While public libraries benefit everyone, they are especially helpful to poor, low-income, and middle-income families who cannot afford to stock a personal library.

Before the American Revolution in the late 1700s, libraries were generally available only to wealthy colonists. Harvard's library, started in 1638, was the first library in the colonies. Some wealthy colonists collected thousands of books in private, home libraries. However, fairly early, some towns began setting up small libraries. The towns of Boston, Massachusetts, and New Haven, Connecticut had small public libraries as early as 1656, when books were donated to both towns for public use, but probably few members of the public actually used these libraries. In 1665, the town of Dorchester, Massachusetts, voted to buy some religious books for the town's use. In 1695, Reverend Thomas Bray became a prominent advocate of free lending libraries of religious books. Bray sent books to New York, South Carolina, Maryland, and North Carolina to establish such libraries. However, after his death in 1730, Bray's libraries declined (Predeek 1947, 85–86; Stone 1977, 126–128, 130).

In 1731, Benjamin Franklin founded the Library Company in Philadelphia, Pennsylvania. Franklin aimed to make his library accessible to skilled laborers and merchants. This was not a free library but a "subscription" library, in which members paid a small fee to be able to use the books. Unlike the libraries of the 1600s, the Library Company did not concentrate on religious books: in fact, its first book order was for dictionaries, an atlas, histories, and books on science and agriculture. Similar subscription libraries were started in many other cities and were called "social libraries," because they were often associated with social or literary clubs. By 1802, about 100 social libraries were opened just in the state of Massachusetts. These were the precursor to free public libraries (Stone 1977, 130, 139; Dickson 1986, 1–3).

During the early 1800s, libraries for apprentices and other skilled craftspeople opened in many cities. These libraries aimed to help apprentices gain an education, even if their parents could not afford to send them to school. Some of these libraries had tens of thousands of volumes, and a few had more than 100,000 books. While most libraries were for adults, some libraries catered to children. Starting in 1825, Sunday school libraries offered moral and religious books for children. In 1835, New York approved a law to levy taxes to support school libraries. By 1850, there were 8,000 school libraries in 11,000 school districts. By 1876, eighteen states had opened these school libraries to the general public (Predeek 1947, 91–92; Stone 1977, 142–143).

Boston became the first large city to establish a free public library. In 1848, the city passed a law allowing a tax to

Adult reading room in the Carnegie Library of Homestead, Munhall, Pennsylvania, ca. 1900. (Library of Congress)

be collected to support a public library. In 1852, the trustees of this future library wrote a report detailing why such a library was useful and necessary. They noted that the public school system "awakens a taste for reading, but it furnishes to the public nothing to be read." Furthermore, the trustees believed that the general public should have access to books to help them make informed decisions about their communities and the country. The trustees emphasized that the library must be designed primarily for people who would not otherwise have access to books. The Boston library opened in 1854. This is generally considered the first American public library of the kind we have now. In 1849 and 1851, New Hampshire and Massachusetts passed laws allowing towns and cities to raise money to establish public libraries. By 1880, all states had passed such laws, and by 1900, there were more than 5,300 public libraries. Still, cities provided only about half the money needed for public libraries—the rest of the funds came from private sources (Predeek 1947, 93–94, 107; Stone 1977, 158, 224–225).

The public library movement received a tremendous boost starting in the 1880s, when the wealthy owner of steel mills, Andrew Carnegie, began donating money to build libraries. Carnegie remembered how grateful he was that a wealthy man in his hometown of Allegheny City, Pennsylvania, had opened his personal library to the neighborhood working boys, including the young Carnegie. As a prosperous adult, Carnegie believed he could best help the poor by providing them the means to help themselves, through education. He funded the first Carnegie library in Allegheny City in 1886. By 1923, Carnegie had donated the money for almost 1,700 library buildings in the United States, as well as 830 libraries in other countries (Predeek 1947, 108; Van Slyck 1995, 8–11).

Starting in the 1920s, libraries began to make efforts to get books out to people in rural and remote areas, using branch libraries (sometimes housed in unconventional buildings, such as the fire station), and traveling libraries on buses and cars. Blacks were often prohibited from visiting libraries, although some segregated libraries were set up. During the Great Depression of the 1930s, the federal Works Progress Administration (WPA) provided funds to libraries. The WPA even hired women librarians in Kentucky to ride horses and mules to bring books to remote, mountainous areas. In the 1950s, blacks began demanding to be able to use the public libraries, and some libraries opened their doors to all races. After the passage of the federal Civil Rights Act of 1964, all public libraries were legally required to admit people of all races (Dickson 1986, 81–100, 174–187).

See also: Civil Rights Act of 1964; Public Schools; Works Progress Administration

Sources

Dickson, Paul. *The Library in America: A Celebration in Words and Pictures.* New York: Facts on File, 1986.

Predeek, Albert. *A History of Libraries in Great Britain and North America.* Chicago, IL: American Library Association, 1947.

Stone, Elizabeth W. *American Library Development, 1600–1899.* New York: The H.W. Wilson Company, 1977.

Van Slyck, Abigail A. *Free to All: Carnegie Libraries and American Culture, 1890–1920.* Chicago, IL: University of Chicago Press, 1995.

PRIMARY DOCUMENT 29

Excerpt from "Upon the Objects To Be Attained by the Establishment of a Public Library," Report of the Trustees of the Public Library of the City of Boston, 1852

The trustees believed that a public library would help citizens make informed decisions in a democracy. This is similar to the argument Thomas Jefferson put forward in 1779, for free public education. Compare the document below to Jefferson's document, "Bill 79 of 1779 for the 'More General Diffusion of Knowledge.'" Note that the trustees suggested requiring some members of the public to leave a monetary deposit for books they wanted to borrow.

The Trustees of the public library, in compliance with the order of the two branches of the City Council, submit the following report on the objects to be attained by the establishment of a public library and the best mode of effecting them:

Of all human arts that of writing, as it was one of the earliest invented, is also one of the most important. Perhaps it would be safe to pronounce it, without exception the most useful and important. It is the great medium of communication between mind and mind, as respects different individuals, countries, and periods of time. We know from history that only those portions of the human family have made any considerable and permanent progress in civilization, which have possessed and used this great instrument of improvement.

It is principally in the form of books that the art of writing, though useful in many other ways, has exerted its influence on human progress. It is almost exclusively by books that a permanent record has been made of word and deed, of thought and feeling; that history, philosophy and poetry, that literature and science in their full comprehension, have been called into being, by the co-operation of intellects acting in concert with each other, though living in different countries and at different periods, and often using different languages.. . .

Although the school and even the college and the university are, as all thoughtful persons are well aware, but the first stages in education, the public makes no provision for carrying on the great work. It imparts, with a noble equality of privilege, a knowledge of the elements of learning to all its children, but it affords them no aid in going beyond the elements. It awakens a taste for reading, but it furnishes to the public nothing to be read. It conducts our young men and women to that point, where they are qualified to acquire from books the various knowledge in the arts and sciences which books contain; but it does nothing to put those books within their reach. As matters now stand, and speaking with general reference to the mass of the community, the public makes no provision whatever, by which the hundreds of young persons annually educated, as far as the elements of learning are concerned, at the public expense, can carry on their education and bring it to practical results by private study.. . .

There is another point of view in which the subject may be regarded, a point of view, we mean, in which a free public library is not only seen to be demanded by the wants of the city at this time, but also seen to be the next natural step to be taken for the intellectual advancement of this whole community and for which this whole community is peculiarly fitted and prepared.

Libraries were originally intended for only a very small portion of the community in which they were established, because few persons could read, and fewer still desired to make inquires that involved the consultation of many books. Even for a long time after the invention of printing, they were anxiously shut up from general use; and, down to the present day, a large proportion of the best libraries in the world forbid anything like a free circulation of their books;—many of them forbidding any circulation at all.. . .

And yet there can be no doubt that such reading ought to be furnished to all, as a matter of public policy and duty, on the same principle that we furnish free education, and in fact, as a part, and a most important part, of the education of all. For it has been rightly judged that, under political, social and religious institutions like ours, it is of paramount importance that the means of general information should be so diffused that the largest possible number of persons should be induced to read and understand questions going down to the very foundations of social order, which are constantly presenting themselves, and which we, as a people, are constantly required to decide, and do decide, either ignorantly or wisely. That this *can* be done, that is, that such libraries can be collected, and that they will be used to a much wider extent than libraries have ever been used before, and with much more important results, there can be no doubt; and if it can be done *anywhere,* it can be done *here* in Boston; for no population of one hundred and fifty thousand souls, lying so compactly together as to be able, with tolerable convenience, to resort to one library, was ever before so well fitted to become a reading, self-cultivating population, as the population of our own city is at this moment.

To accomplish this object, however, which has never yet been attempted, we must use means which have never before been used; otherwise the library we propose to establish, will not be adjusted to its especial purposes. Above all, while the rightful claims of no class, however highly educated already, should be overlooked, the first regard should be shown, as in the case of our Free Schools, to the wants of those, who can, in no other way supply themselves with the interesting and healthy reading necessary for their farther education. What precise plan should be adopted for such a library, it is not, perhaps, possible to settle beforehand. It is a new thing, a new step forward in general education; and we must feel our way as we advance.. . .

As to the terms on which access should be had to a City Library, the Trustees can only say, that they would place no restrictions on its use, except such as the nature of individual books, or their safety may demand; regarding it as a great matter to carry as many of them as possible into the home of the young; into poor families; into cheap boarding houses; in short, wherever they will be most likely to affect life and raise personal character and condition. To many classes of persons the doors of such a library may, we conceive, be at once opened wide. All officers of the City Government, therefore, including the police, all clergymen settled among us, all city missionaries, all teachers of our public schools, all members of normal schools, all young persons who may have received medals or other honorary distinctions on leaving our Grammar and higher schools, and, in fact, as many classes, as can safely be entrusted with it *as classes,* might enjoy, on the mere names and personal responsibility of the individuals composing them, the right of taking out freely all books that are permitted to circulate, receiving one volume at a time. To all other persons, women as well as men—living in the City, the same privilege might be granted on depositing the value of the volume or of the set to which it may belong; believing that the pledge of a single dollar or even less, may thus insure pleasant and profitable reading to any family among us.. . .

Source

South Central Library System, Madison, Wisconsin. http://www.scls.lib.wi.us/ mcm/history/report_of_trustees.html.

PUBLIC SCHOOLS

Public schools benefit all children as well as the entire society. However, they are especially important for poor families, who cannot afford to pay the fees of private schools.

In colonial times, young people received much of their education through apprenticeships. Only children of wealthy families were exempt from learning a particular trade. Preteen boys and girls were bound to a master who would teach them a vocation or craft.

Masters were also supposed to teach the apprentices to read and write (Monroe 1971, 34–35).

During the 1600s, schooling in America was often only for the wealthy. Southern plantation owners hired tutors for their children, and sometimes children of plantation managers also attended these "plantation schools." Private schools, funded by students' fees, were founded in southern states on old, unproductive fields, and were thus called "old field schools." Sometimes poor children were allowed to attend these schools for free. Churches often started schools, and some of these were open to the poor. Quaker schools in Pennsylvania were open to the poor and to girls.

The New England states were the first to require towns to set up schools. In 1647, Massachusetts passed a law requiring every town to set up a school, or to pay a fee to a nearby town that had a school. Dedham, Massachusetts, instituted a property tax in 1648, which was used to fund the schools. Other towns also began collecting taxes for schools. Still, students were sometimes charged tuition to help fund the schools. Many of these schools focused on teaching religion (Pulliam 1968, 11–25).

In the 1700s, most colonial children from well-off families attended schools by paying a fee, and some towns also offered schooling to poor children. In 1779, Thomas Jefferson proposed a system of public schooling that would provide three years of free education to all boys and girls. Higher education would be available to all who could pay, and a few places would be reserved for talented poor boys. Jefferson believed that all citizens should have a minimum level of education, so that the nation could function as a democracy. Jefferson's idea of government-supported, free education was considered too radical at that time, and did not pass Congress (Pulliam 1968, 34–36).

Although schooling was and still is considered a local government function, the federal government became involved quite early in public education. The U.S. Congress passed the Land Ordinance of 1785, which called for the Northwest Territory (the area of the Midwestern states) to be surveyed into townships of six square miles, with thirty-six lots in each township. Lot number sixteen was to be set aside to support the town school: the land could be sold or leased to provide money for the school. This federal law ensured that every new town would have some sort of school (Carleton 2002, 13–18).

By the early 1800s, the idea of free, public schooling for all was becoming more popular. In the 1830s and 1840s, the New York City government took over the "charity schools" run by private organizations for the poor. These government-funded schools provided free education to anyone who wanted to attend. From 1837 to 1848, Horace Mann served as the nation's first state secretary of education (in Massachusetts). He rode on horseback to inspect the state's schools, and found them to be in sad condition. While wealthy children had access to good schools, poor children could attend only a short school term taught by an untrained teacher. Schools provided no books, so students had to bring whatever books they had at home, and learn from those. Mann and other reformers called for increased government spending on schools; standardized textbooks; and better teacher training, among other changes (Mondale and Patton 2001, 25–31; Reese 2005, 12, 26).

Supporters of free public education emphasized the social benefits of having all white children, wealthy and poor, educated together. This kind of common education would foster liberty and freedom, they asserted. Massachusetts increased taxation to better fund the schools. Other states followed the lead of Massachusetts. Starting in the 1850s, states began passing laws requiring young people to attend school. Massachusetts passed the first such law in 1852. By 1865, "common schools" (free public elementary schools for white children) were widespread, although their quality of instruction was often low. Slaves in the south were not educated, and African Americans in the northern states were generally relegated to a few schools. Massachusetts, in 1855, became the first state to pass a law to abolish segregated schools (Pulliam 1968, 54–58; Mondale and Patton 2001, 45; Reese 2005, 26).

After the slaves were emancipated in 1863, northern charities set up schools for the free blacks in the south. In 1865, the federal government set up the "Freedmen's Bureau" to provide help to the newly freed slaves. The Bureau created thousands of free schools for blacks and as well as several teacher-training schools, which have evolved into some of the country's most noteworthy historically black colleges (Carleton 2002, 41–49).

From the late 1800s to the early 1900s, public schooling grew enormously. In 1870, 57 percent of all young people ages five to eighteen were enrolled in school. By 1900, that percentage reached 72 percent. In the second part of the 1800s, it was not so common to use taxpayer money to fund high schools. When the town of Kalamazoo, Michigan, established a tax-supported high school in 1858, the school system was sued by three taxpayers who said that the high school was not part of the common school system. In 1874, the Supreme Court of Michigan ruled that high schools could be funded by taxes, and after that decision free public high schools were established across the country. By the beginning of World War I, in 1914, free public education encompassed eight years of elementary school and four years of high school (Pulliam 1968, 61–68; Reese 2005, 77).

The federal government did not get involved in providing funding to schools until the New Deal of the 1930s. Several New Deal jobs-creation programs were involved with building or renovating public school buildings. Surplus food was distributed to schools starting in 1935, and federal funding of school lunches became permanent with the National School Lunch Act of 1946. The 1954 Supreme Court decision, *Brown v. Board of Education,* outlawed segregated public schools. In 1965, Congress passed the Elementary and Secondary Education Act, which provided additional money to schools specifically for the education of disadvantaged children. Title IX of the Educational Amendments of 1972 prohibited sex discrimination in education.

See also: Apprenticeship; Elementary and Secondary Education Act of 1965; Freedmen's Bureau; Great Depression; Mann, Horace; National School Lunch Act; New Deal; Title IX of the 1972 Educational Amendments

Sources

Carleton, David. *Landmark Congressional Laws on Education.* Westport, CT: Greenwood Press, 2002.

Mondale, Sarah, and Sarah B. Patton, eds. *School: The Story of American Public Education.* Boston, MA: Beacon Press, 2001.

Monroe, Paul. *Founding of the American Public School System: A History of Education in the United States.* New York: Hafner Publishing Company, 1971.

Pulliam, John D. *History of Education in America.* Columbus, OH: Charles E. Merrill Publishing Company, 1968.

Reese, William J. *America's Public Schools: From the Common School to "No Child Left Behind."* Baltimore, MD: The Johns Hopkins University Press, 2005.

PRIMARY DOCUMENT 30

Bill 79 of 1779 for the "More General Diffusion of Knowledge," by Thomas Jefferson

Jefferson believed that an educated citizenship could prevent government from becoming "perverted into tyranny," and so he proposed three years of free education for all "free children" (not slaves). He also believed that poor, talented boys should be further educated at public expense, so that the country could have the advantage of their wisdom. The "grammar schools" mentioned in Section IX are schools of further education, beyond the county schools. Many of the poor boys selected for the grammar schools were to have been disqualified from receiving a free education after one year, and most after two years. And of the boys who were lucky enough to finish their grammar school education, only a very few would have been able to go on to college at public expense.

Sect. I. Whereas it appeareth that however certain forms of government are better calculated than others to protect individuals in the free exercise of their natural rights, and are at the same time themselves better guarded against degeneracy, yet experience hath shown, that even under the best forms, those entrusted with power have, in time, and by slow operations, perverted it into tyranny; and it is believed that the most effectual means of preventing this would be, to illuminate, as far as practicable, the minds of the people at large, and more especially to give them knowledge of those facts, which history exhibiteth, that, possessed thereby of the experience of other ages and countries, they may be enabled to know ambition under all its shapes, and prompt to exert their natural powers to defeat its purposes; And whereas it is generally true that that people will be happiest whose laws are best, and are best administered, and that laws will be wisely formed, and honestly administered, in proportion as those who form and administer them are wise and honest; whence it becomes expedient for promoting the publick happiness that those persons, whom nature hath endowed with genius and virtue, should be rendered by liberal education worthy to receive, and able to guard the sacred deposit of the rights and liberties of their fellow citizens, and that they should be called to that charge without regard to wealth, birth or other accidental condition or circumstance; but the indigence of the greater number disabling them from so educating, at their own expence, those of their children whom nature hath fitly formed and disposed to become useful instruments for the public, it is better that such should be sought for and educated at the common expence of all, than that the happiness of all should be confided to the weak or wicked:.. . .

[The deleted sections have to do with electing Aldermen, who will establish schools in each county.]

Sect. VI. At every of these schools shall be taught reading, writing, and common arithmetick, and the books which shall be used therein for instructing the children to read shall be such as will at the same time make them acquainted with Graecian, Roman, English, and American history. At these schools all the free children, male and female, resident within the respective hundred [school section], shall be intitled to receive tuition gratis, for the term of three years, and as much longer, at their private expence, as their parents, guardians or friends shall think proper.

Sect. VII. Over every ten of these schools (or such other number nearest thereto, as the number of hundreds in the county will admit, without fractional divisions) an overseer shall be appointed annually by the Aldermen at their first meeting, eminent for his learning, integrity, and fidelity to the commonwealth, whose business and duty it shall be, from time to time, to appoint a teacher to each school, who shall give assurance of fidelity to the commonwealth, and to remove him as he shall see cause; to visit every school once in every half year at the least; to examine the schollars; see that any general plan of reading and instruction recommended by the visiters of William and Mary College shall be observed; and to superintend the conduct of the teacher in every thing relative to his school.

Sect. VIII. Every teacher shall receive a salary of _____ by the year [this amount was left blank in the bill], which, with the expences of building and repairing the school-houses, shall be provided in such manner as other county expences are by law directed to be provided and shall also have his diet, lodging, and washing found him, to be levied in like manner, save only that such levy shall be on the inhabitants of each hundred for the board of their own teacher only.

Sect. IX. And in order that grammar schools may be rendered convenient to the youth in every part of the commonwealth, be it therefore enacted, that on the first Monday in November, after the first appointment of overseers for the hundred schools, if fair, and if not, then on the next fair day, excluding Sunday, after the hour of one in the afternoon, the said overseers appointed for the schools in the counties of Princess Ann, Norfolk, Nansemond and Isle-of-Wight, shall meet at Nansemond court house; those for the counties of Southampton, Sussex, Surry and Prince George, shall meet at Sussex court-house; those for the counties of Brunswick, Mecklenburg and Lunenburg, shall meet at Lunenburg

court-house; those for the counties of Dinwiddie, Amelia and Chesterfield, shall meet at Chesterfield court-house; those for the counties of Powhatan, Cumberland, Goochland, Henrico and Hanover, shall meet at Henrico court-house; those for the counties of Prince Edward, Charlotte and Halifax, shall meet at Charlotte court-house; those for the counties of Henry, Pittsylvania and Bedford, shall meet at Pittsylvania court-house; those for the counties of Buckingham, Amherst, Albemarle and Fluvanna, shall meet at Albemarle court-house; those for the counties of Botetourt, Rockbridge, Montgomery, Washington and Kentucky, shall meet at Botetourt court-house; those for the counties of Augusta, Rockingham and Greenbrier, shall meet at Augusta court-house; those for the counties of Accomack and Northampton, shall meet at Accomack court-house; those for the counties of Elizabeth City, Warwick, York, Gloucester, James City, Charles City and New-Kent, shall meet at James City court-house; those for the counties of Middlesex, Essex, King and Queen, King William and Caroline, shall meet at King and Queen court-house; those for the counties of Lancaster, Northumberland, Richmond and Westmoreland, shall meet at Richmond court-house; those for the counties of King George, Stafford, Spotsylvania, Prince William and Fairfax, shall meet at Spotsylvania court-house; those for the counties of Loudoun and Fauquier, shall meet at Loudoun court-house; those for the counties of Culpeper, Orange and Louisa, shall meet at Orange court-house; those for the counties of Shenandoah and Frederick, shall meet at Frederick court-house; those for the counties of Hampshire and Berkeley, shall meet at Berkeley court-house; and those for the counties of Yohogania, Monongalia and Ohio, shall meet at Monongalia court-house; and shall fix on such place in some one of the counties in their district as shall be most proper for situating a grammar school-house, endeavouring that the situation be as central as may be to the inhabitants of the said counties, that it be furnished with good water, convenient to plentiful supplies of provision and fuel, and more than all things that it be healthy.. . .

Sect. XIII. In these grammar schools shall be taught the Latin and Greek languages, English grammar, geography, and the higher part of numerical arithmetick, to wit, vulgar and decimal fractions, and the extraction of the square and cube roots.. . .

Sect. XVI. Every overseer of the hundred schools shall, in the month of September annually, after the most diligent and impartial examination and enquiry, appoint from among the boys who shall have been two years at the least at some one of the schools under his superintendance, and whose parents are too poor to give them farther education, some one of the best and most promising genius and disposition, to proceed to the grammar school of his district; . . .

Sect. XVII. Every boy so appointed shall be authorised to Proceed to the grammar school of his district, there to be educated and boarded during such time as is hereafter limited; and his quota of the expences of the house together with a compensation to the master or usher for his tuition, at the rate of twenty dollars by the year, shall be paid by the Treasurer quarterly on warrant from the Auditors.

Sect. XVIII. A visitation shall be held, for the purpose of probation, annually at the said grammar school on the last Monday in September, if fair, and if not, then on the next fair day, excluding Sunday, at which one third of the boys sent thither by appointment of the said overseers, and who shall have been there one year only, shall be discontinued as public foundationers, being those who, on the most diligent examination and enquiry, shall be thought to be of the least promising genius and disposition; and of those who shall have been there two years, all shall be discontinued, save one only the best in genius and disposition, who shall be at liberty to continue there four years longer on the public foundation, and shall thence forward be deemed a senior.

Sect. XIX. The visiters for the districts which, or any part of which, be southward and westward of James river, as known by that name, or by the names of Fluvanna and Jackson's river, in every other year, to wit, at the probation meetings held in the years, distinguished in the Christian computation by odd numbers, and the visiters for all the other districts at their said meetings to be held in those years, distinguished by even numbers, after diligent examination and enquiry as before directed, shall chuse one among the said seniors, of the best learning and most hopeful genius and disposition, who shall be authorised by them to proceed to William and Mary College, there to be educated, boarded, and clothed, three years; the expence of which annually shall be paid by the Treasurer on warrant from the Auditors.

Source

Conant, James. *Thomas Jefferson and the Development of American Public Education*. Berkeley, CA: University of California Press, 1963, 88–93.

PUBLIC WORKS ADMINISTRATION

The Public Works Administration (PWA) was a jobs-creation program set up in 1933, as the second part of the National Industrial Recovery Act (NIRA) of the federal government's New Deal program to lift the country out of the Great Depression. The first part of the NIRA was carried out by the National Recovery Administration. Even though the first part of the NIRA was ruled unconstitutional in 1935, the PWA was not affected by this ruling and continued on until 1942.

The PWA was slightly different from other New Deal jobs-creation projects such as the Civil Works Administration and the Works Progress Administration (WPA). Those agencies were designed to hire as many workers as quickly as possible, find jobs for them according to their skill level, and spend a comparatively small amount of money on materials. The PWA, in contrast, was to hire skilled workers for specific projects, and more money was available for materials. Therefore, while the PWA did not get involved with nearly as many projects as did the WPA, the PWA ended up constructing some of the most well-known and lasting pieces of architecture and infrastructure in the country. "More than any other New Deal agency . . . the Public Works Administration has left dramatic reminders of this age of public building," says Robert Leighninger, a sociologist at Arizona State University. PWA projects included the Triborough Bridge in New York City; the Bay Bridge and the Mint office building in San Francisco; the Alameda County Courthouse in Oakland, California; the ten-story City Hall in Houston; as well as university buildings, public libraries, post offices, hospitals, subway systems, streets, airports, sewer and water systems, and electrical power projects across the country (Leighninger 2007, 86–101).

The PWA was originally given a budget of more than $3 billion to hand out. The administrator, Harold Ickes, was a cautious man who wanted to make sure every project was built to high standards and without corruption. Perhaps he felt overwhelmed by the sum of money he was required to distribute, because in a book about the PWA he says,

> Few people can even encompass such a sum within their imaginations. It helped me to estimate its size by figuring that if we had it all in currency and should load it into trucks we could set out from Washington for the Pacific Coast, shovel off one million dollars at every milepost and still have enough left to build a fleet of battleships. (1935, 56)

The pace of PWA work has been termed "glacial," and it did get off to a very slow start. While some of the money was put immediately into federal projects such as building ships for the Navy, other projects had to be proposed by states and cities, and had to be approved. The PWA funded a certain percentage of each project (30 to 45 percent), and the rest was loaned and had to be paid back eventually. Ickes wanted to make sure that each project received thorough consideration before it was approved. He also set up an inspection division to make sure that workers were hired and paid according to federal guidelines, that the projects adhered to high building standards, and

Public Works Administration construction site in Washington, D.C., 1933. (Franklin D. Roosevelt Presidential Library)

that politicians were not diverting funds or materials for their own personal use (Leighninger 2007, 36–42, 80).

PWA workers could labor up to thirty hours per week. They were paid according to their skill level and the region of the country in which they were working. They had to be qualified for the job and had to be unemployed. Union workers, veterans, and local workers were given preference (Ickes 1935, 34–35, 48–49).

The PWA also had two small divisions devoted to housing: the Housing Division, which built fifty-five apartment buildings in thirty-nine cities for low-income families; and the Subsistence Homestead Division, which set up cooperative communities of homesteads.

The Housing Division created plans for low-income housing to help architects ensure that the apartments were safe and had adequate light and ventilation. Twenty-seven of the fifty-five projects were built on land that was first cleared of slums, and the rest were built on vacant land. Almost all were racially segregated—they were constructed for either white families or black families. All the buildings were sturdy, with bathtub, toilet, sink, and closets. Many had electric stoves and refrigerators—at a time when 85 percent of U.S. homes had neither. Some projects had outdoor playgrounds, indoor play spaces for children, community rooms with kitchens, and health clinics. Because they were built so well at the outset, most were still in use as of 2007, almost seventy-five years later. However, the cost of building these good-quality apartments meant that the rents were too high for families with the lowest incomes. But for working-class families who could afford the rent, "PWA housing was a godsend. It was clean, safe, solid, and in many cases had modern appliances that were the envy of many middle-class families" (Leighninger 2007, 125–129).

The PWA's Housing Division was ended in 1937, when federal funding for low-income housing was taken over by the U.S. Housing Authority (USHA), which was not allowed to spend nearly as much per unit as had the PWA. As a result, the USHA housing was of inferior quality, but they did manage to build many more units to house 120,000 families by 1942, when it, too, ended.

The Subsistence Homesteads Division of the PWA was one of several New Deal agencies that funded cooperative communities throughout the country. A "subsistence homestead" meant a home and land on which the family could grow or raise most of the food they would require. The settlers were supposed to eventually own their land, and would share some land and amenities with the other settlers in their community. Ideally, the communities would be located near industrial areas, so part-time industrial work would be possible. The idea was to create communities that had the best of the rural and urban environments: the fresh air and sunshine of rural life, and the social, cultural, and money-making advantages of the city (Leighninger 2007, 138–139).

The PWA built thirty-four communities of subsistence homesteads from 1933–1935, after which the subsistence homesteads program was taken over by a new agency, the Resettlement Administration. The subsistence homesteads succeeded in lifting people out of poverty and in providing them with decent housing, education, and other necessities. However, most of the communities were not able to make enough income to pay the government back and to become self-sufficient, as had been envisioned. Because of this failure, they were criticized as being a waste of money (Leighninger 2007, 140–143).

See also: Affirmative Action; Great Depression; National Recovery Administration; New Deal; New Deal Cooperative Communities; Public Works Projects; Roosevelt, Franklin Delano

Sources

Biles, Roger. *A New Deal for the American People.* DeKalb, IL: Northern Illinois University Press, 1991.

Ickes, Harold L. *Back to Work: The Story of the PWA.* New York: Macmillan Company, 1935.

Leighninger, Robert D., Jr. *Long-Range Public Investment: The Forgotten Legacy of the New Deal.* Columbia, SC: University of South Carolina Press, 2007.

PUBLIC WORKS PROJECTS

Since the beginning of the United States, most people have agreed that it is better to put needy, employable people to work, rather than to give them handouts of money and food. Sometimes this "work" has involved useless projects, such as moving rock piles from one place to another. However, at other times, particularly during the Great Depression, governments have tried to put unemployed people to work at socially useful projects.

State governments have, since the beginning of the country, used tax money or borrowed money to finance projects such as canals, roads, and railroads, which private business could not or would not undertake. Local governments have paid for clean water, sanitation, education, and police. However, until the late nineteenth century, few people linked these kinds of public works projects with the prevention of poverty and unemployment. Poverty and unemployment were still seen as being caused by laziness or individual failure, and not by economic forces beyond the control of the individual.

In the mid to late 1800s, some cities started hiring the unemployed for government-funded work. In the 1850s, those seeking aid in New York were asked to apply for jobs enlarging the Erie Canal, or were given jobs cleaning streets or quarrying stone. During the 1893 depression, public works projects were used by cities as a major method of poor relief. The needy and unemployed were put to work sweeping and paving streets, and constructing sewers and buildings. During the winter of 1914–1915, ninety-nine cities provided work for the needy and unemployed (Gayer 1935, 5; Katz 1996, 153).

The federal government organized a conference in 1921, to discuss using public works projects to stimulate the economy, but many participants concluded that these kinds of projects were more appropriate for state and local governments. It took the national crisis of the Great Depression to propel the federal government into the arena of using public works to provide jobs to the unemployed (Leighninger 2007, 4–7).

President Herbert Hoover, who was in office as the Great Depression

Drillers excavate for construction of the Hoover Dam in May 1933. (Library of Congress)

began, recognized the usefulness of public works projects during times of economic depression. However, he, like many others, believed this was a job for local and state governments. Unfortunately at that time, local and state governments were struggling under the burden of unemployment and need. Hoover did make available some federal loans at high interest rates to the states, but only for projects that could generate revenue, and thus pay back the loans. Very few projects were approved to receive these loans, although a few significant projects were started, including bridges in New York, San Francisco, and New Orleans; and in several other cities, a stadium, a planetarium, a sewer project, and waterworks (Leighninger 2007, 6–10).

When President Franklin Roosevelt took office in 1933, everyone knew that something had to be done, since businesses were failing, unemployment was rising, and people were starving. For the first time, the federal government pumped enormous amounts of money into public works projects throughout the country via several different agencies during the New Deal: the Civil Works Administration, Civilian Conservation Corps, Federal Emergency Relief Administration, Public Works Administration, Tennessee Valley Authority, and Works Progress Administration. Under these agencies, almost all of which lasted less than ten years, thousands of buildings and projects were completed, many of which have endured for decades, including roads, schools, courthouses, hospitals, parks, zoos, waterworks, golf courses, tennis courts, stadiums, auditoriums, museums, city halls, fire stations, and fairgrounds. "Few people, even historians, are aware of just how much was built and how much is still in use," comments Robert Leighninger (2007, xv).

One problem with creating useful work projects is that it is actually more expensive in the short term to employ people in useful work, than it is to simply give them money and food. Josephine Chapin Brown, who was involved in managing some of the federal government's New Deal public works projects during the Great Depression, explains:

> There were . . . conflicts between the desire to get work done efficiently and the desire to give a maximum of relief to the greatest number of people. Direct relief was undesirable, but it was the least expensive method of aiding the destitute. Hastily planned devices by which the unemployed could work for relief grants were less costly than socially useful projects which paid a regular security wage. (1940, 158)

Robert Leighninger, a sociologist at Arizona State University, points out that when people complain about the upfront cost of public works projects, they do not take into consideration the long-term benefits that society receives from those projects. "Public works are . . . attacked as wasteful, pork-barrel spending. The fact that they might last seventy years as community assets is not part of the calculation" (2007, xv).

Since the Great Depression ended with the U.S. entry into World War II, public works projects seem to have been largely forgotten as a way to provide jobs and money to the needy and unemployed. The federal, state, and local governments continue to fund public works projects such as highways, dams, and airports, but emphasis has shifted to efficiency and national security, and not the creation of jobs for those who have none. This was partly because unemployment was not such a huge national problem (Smith 2006, 232–233).

In terms of helping the unemployed, the emphasis shifted more to job training than job creation. In 1961, Congress passed the Area Redevelopment Act, which gave financial incentives and provided federally subsidized employee training to employers if they located their business in economically depressed rural areas. The Manpower Development and Training Act, passed in 1962, provided subsidies to employers who offered on-the-job training, and small monthly stipends to people in job-training programs. President

Lyndon Johnson's War on Poverty campaign during the 1960s created some job training programs for poor youths, such as the Neighborhood Youth Corps and the Job Corps. During the 1970s, several other youth employment and training programs were started as a result of the Comprehensive Employment and Training Act of 1973. Under President Bill Clinton, the AmeriCorps program started in 1993, to provide government funding for community service projects around the country (Rose 1995, 78–80; Leighninger 2007, 184–193).

Some of these twentieth-century jobs programs targeting the needy have been more effective than others, but none of them has been as large or as widespread as the New Deal public works projects. Leighninger points out that when unemployment is widespread and seen as everyone's problem, the solution is thought to be economic—providing jobs. When unemployment is confined to certain sections of the population, such as poor whites in Appalachia or poor blacks in the inner city, it is more difficult to drum up the political support and money to implement effective, useful public works projects (Leighninger 2007, 193).

Another view of the issue is that we now address the problem of unemployment in a different way. With the passage of the Social Security Act in 1935, states were required to set up unemployment insurance programs. Perhaps because of the availability of unemployment insurance, the government and the public is now less interested in jobs creation and work relief than it was during the New Deal, when no unemployment insurance was available: "federal and state outlays for unemployment insurance and transfer payments dwarf those outlays that are directed toward employment expansion and the creation of useful output" (Jerrett and Barocci 1979, 35).

See also: Civilian Conservation Corps; Civil Works Administration; Comprehensive Employment and Training Act; Economic Opportunity Act of 1964; Federal Emergency Relief Act; Great Depression; Hoover, Herbert; Job Corps; Johnson, Lyndon; National and Community Service Trust Act of 1993; National Service; Public Works Administration; Roosevelt, Franklin Delano; Social Security Act; Tennessee Valley Authority; Unemployment Insurance; Works Progress Administration

Sources

Brown, Josephine Chapin. *Public Relief 1929–1939.* New York: Henry Holt, 1940.

Gayer, Arthur. *Public Works in Prosperity and Depression.* New York: National Bureau of Economic Research, 1935.

Jerrett, Robert III, and Thomas Barocci. *Public Works, Government Spending, and Job Creation: The Job Opportunities Program.* New York: Praeger Publishers, 1979.

Katz, Michael B. *In the Shadow of the Poorhouse: A Social History of Welfare in America.* New York: Basic Books, 1996.

Leighninger, Robert D., Jr. *Long-Range Public Investment: The Forgotten Legacy of the New Deal.* Columbia, SC: University of South Carolina Press, 2007.

Rose, Nancy Ellen. *Workfare or Fair Work: Women, Welfare and Government Work Programs.* New Brunswick, NJ: Rutgers University Press, 1995.

Smith, Jason Scott. *Building New Deal Liberalism: The Political Economy of Public Works, 1933–1956.* New York: Cambridge University Press, 2006.

Q

QUINCY REPORT, 1821

The Quincy Report was put out by a Massachusetts state commission to study poverty in the state. The report was officially called the Report of the Committee on the Pauper Laws of This Commonwealth, but since the commission was chaired by Boston mayor Josiah Quincy, his name is often given to the report. While until this time poverty relief had been seen as a more or less local concern, the Quincy Report was one of the earliest instances of state interest in the causes of poverty, and one of the earliest statewide reports on poverty.

The Quincy Report was prompted by the fact that poverty was a growing problem, and that cities and towns were having a difficult time helping all the poor people in their area. The state legislature decided they needed to step in and investigate the problem. After requesting information from Massachusetts cities and towns as to the number of their poor and how they cared for them, the Quincy Report concluded that the poor law system was at least partly responsible for the increase in paupers: "your Committee do consider themselves justified . . . in concluding that the pernicious consequences of the existing system are palpable, that they are increasing, and that they imperiously call for the interference of the Legislature" (Quincy 1971, 3).

The report divided poor people into two classes: children, widows, the ill, and the elderly, who were considered worthy of aid; and able-bodied poor adults, who were not considered worthy of aid. The report declared that providing "outdoor relief"—money, food, and fuel to the poor in their own homes—destroyed their incentive to work and caused the poor to be lazy and to indulge in alcohol and other vices. According to the report, the fault was that the local "overseers of the poor" were well-off men who hated to see the poor suffer and would rather pamper them than see them in want of anything. Furthermore, the poor began to see aid as their right, and to depend on it.

PRIMARY DOCUMENT 31

Excerpt from the Report of the Committee on the Pauper Laws of This Commonwealth (Quincy Report), 1821

The poor are of two classes. 1. The impotent poor; in which denomination are included all, who are wholly incapable of work, through old age, infancy, sickness or corporeal debility. 2. The able poor; in which denomination are included all, who are capable of work, of some nature, or other; but differing in the degree of their capacity, and in the kind of work, of which they are capable.

With respect to the first class; that of poor, absolutely impotent, were there none other than this class, there would be little difficulty, either as to principle, or as to the mode of extending relief.

But another class exists; that of the able poor; in relation to which, and from the difficulty of discriminating between this class and the former, and of apportioning the degree of public provision to the degree of actual impotency, arise all the objections to the principle of the existing pauper system. The evils, also, which are attributed to this system, of diminishing the industry, destroying the economical habits and eradicating the providence of the labouring class of society may all be referred to the same source;—the difficulty of discriminating between the able poor and the impotent poor and of apportioning the degree of public provision to the degree of actual impotency.

This difficulty cannot, apparently, be removed by any legislative provision. There must be, in the nature of things, numerous and minute shades of difference between, the pauper, who, through impotency, can do absolutely nothing, and the pauper, who is able to do something, but that, very little. Nor does the difficulty of discrimination, proportionally, diminish as the ability, in any particular pauper, to do something,

increases. There always must exist, so many circumstances of age, sex, previous habits, muscular, or mental, strength, to be taken into the account, that society is absolutely incapable to fix any standard, or to prescribe any rule, by which the claim of right to the benefit of public provision shall be absolutely determined. The consequence of that admission, or rejection, of the claim to such relief is necessarily left to the discretion of the Overseers [local authorities who provide poor relief]; or to those, who are entrusted by law, with the distribution of the public charity.

The necessity of entrusting this discretion, the class of society to which it must be entrusted, and the circumstances and feelings, under which such distribution must be made, are the proximate causes of the evils, resulting from a public, or compulsory, provision for the poor.

From the nature of things, this discretion will always be entrusted to men in good, generally in easy, circumstances; that is, to the prosperous class of society. "The humanity natural to this class, will never see the poor, in any thing like want, when that want is palpably and visibly brought before it, without extending relief." Must less will this be the case, when they have means, placed in their hands by society itself, applicable to this very purpose. In executing the trust, they will, almost unavoidably, be guided by sentiments of pity and compassion, and be very little influenced by the consideration of the effect of the facility, or fullness, of provision, to encourage habits of idleness, dissipation, and extravagance among the class, which labor. "They first give necessaries, then comforts; and often, in the end, pamper, rather than relieve." [The quotation marks are in the original document].

If the means, placed under their control, are confined to provision for the poor, in public poor, or alms houses, the effect of these dispositions and feelings appears, in the ease, with which admission is obtained; the kindness with which the poor are treated, during their residence, and in the superiority of the food of the public table, to that, which they have been accustomed. If those means consist of funds, the same temper and feelings predominate, in their distribution.. . . . The poor begin to consider it as a right; next, they calculate upon it as income. The stimulus to industry and economy is annihilated, or weakened; temptations to extravagance and dissipation are increased, in proportion as public supply is likely, or certain, or desirable. The just pride of independence, so honorable to man, in every condition, is thus corrupted by the certainty of public provision; and is either weakened, or destroyed according to the facility of its attainment, or its amount.

. . . . Upon the whole, your Committee . . . concur in the five following results, which may be well adopted as principles, in relation to the whole subject.

1. That of all modes of providing for the poor, the most wasteful, the most expensive, and the most injurious to their morals and destructive of their industrious habits is that of supply in their own families.

2. That the most economical mode is that of Alms Houses; having the character of Work Houses, or Houses of Industry, in which work in provided for every degree of ability in the pauper; and thus the able poor made to provide, partially, at least for their own support; and also to the support, or at least the comfort of the impotent poor.

3. That of all modes of employing the labor of the pauper, agriculture affords the best, the most healthy, and the most certainly profitable; the poor being thus enabled, to raise, always, at least their own provisions.

4. That the success of these establishments depends upon their being placed under the superintendence of a Board of Overseers, constituted of the most substantial and intelligent inhabitants of the vicinity.

5. That of all causes of pauperism, intemperance, in the use of spirituous liquors, is the most powerful and universal.

Source
Quincy, Josiah. "Report of the Committee on the Pauper Laws of This Commonwealth." Reprinted in *The Almshouse Experience: Collected Pamphlets*. New York: Arno Press, 1971.

The solution was to build poorhouses, or almshouses, for the worthy poor, and workhouses for the able-bodied poor, so their behavior could be monitored.

After the Quincy Report came out, New York, Pennsylvania, and New Hampshire also published similar reports in the 1820s. New York's report, the Yates Report of 1824, has been called "one of the most influential documents in American social welfare history." The Yates Report advocated poorhouses not only because of the belief that the outdoor relief system destroyed the work incentive, but also because some of the common practices of helping the poor were often cruel. For example, auctioning the poor to the lowest bidder often resulted in inhumane treatment for the needy. The Yates Report believed that the poor would receive better care in poorhouses (Trattner 1994, 59).

This dividing of the poor into two groups or classes has persisted to the present day in the United States. In fact, University of Pennsylvania history professor Michael Katz suggests that "it is only a slight exaggeration to say that the core of most welfare reform in America since the early nineteenth century has been a war on the able-bodied poor: an attempt to define, locate, and purge them from the roles of relief" (1996, 19).

While the Quincy Report and other similar state reports were ultimately influential, and caused many more poorhouses to be built, not every American agreed with the conclusions of the state reports. One prominent Philadelphia printer and newspaper editor, Mathew Carey, printed at his own expense several editions of a pamphlet to refute the idea that aid to the poor caused dependency and laziness. Carey attempted to prove that poverty was caused by low wages and unemployment. Carey's pamphlet, "Plea for the Poor," is excerpted in a primary document accompanying Carey's encyclopedia entry.

See also: Carey, Mathew; Outdoor Relief; Poorhouses; Poor Laws, Early American

Sources

Katz, Michael. *In the Shadow of the Poorhouse: A Social History of Welfare in America.* New York: Basic Books, 1996.

Quincy, Josiah. "Report of the Committee on the Pauper Laws of This Commonwealth." Reprinted in *The Almshouse Experience: Collected Pamphlets.* New York: Arno Press, 1971.

Trattner, Walter I. *From Poor Law to Welfare State: A History of Social Welfare in America.* New York: The Free Press, 1994.

R

RECONSTRUCTION ERA

The "Reconstruction Era" was the period of time after the Civil War, during which the federal government worked to maintain the freedom of the former slaves, to help them gain political power and education, and to help them make economic progress. Reconstruction lasted from 1865 to 1877.

President Abraham Lincoln officially freed the slaves on January 1, 1863. The former slaves were desperately poor, uneducated, and powerless. Even before the Civil War ended in May 1865, Congress passed a law in March 1865 to create the Freedmen's Bureau. This was a federal agency to help the 4 million freed slaves. The Freedmen's Bureau's most important accomplishment was setting up thousands of schools for former slaves. Some of these schools have grown into respected traditional black colleges. The Freedmen's Bureau's work ended in 1872.

As soon as the war ended, southern governments began to pass laws to restrict the rights of blacks, and to return them to a state of virtual slavery. These laws were called "black codes." Some towns prohibited blacks from entering without their employer's permission. Other laws allowed the police to arrest blacks who were out in public after ten at night. Unemployed blacks could be jailed, and children of poor black parents could be taken away from them and apprenticed to their former owners. Blacks were required to pay high fees to go into business as a shopkeeper or peddler. Some laws stated that blacks who entered into contracts with employers and left before the contract ended would not be paid at all (Smith, 1982, 678–679).

The northerners were outraged that their hard work to free the slaves was being undone. Congress passed a series of Reconstruction Acts in 1867, abolishing southern state governments and stationing federal troops in the south. To be readmitted as part of the United States, the southern states were required to allow black males to vote.

African American women and children sell goods in the street in Charleston, South Carolina, 1879. (Library of Congress)

White males would be allowed to vote as long as they had not been disenfranchised for participating in the rebellion of the southern states. (Interestingly, at that time many northern states denied the vote to blacks). These voters would elect new state governments.

To be readmitted to the country, the southern states were also required to ratify a new constitutional amendment. The Fourteenth Amendment, which passed Congress in 1866, specified that all people born or naturalized in the United States are citizens; that no state could make laws to deprive citizens of their life, freedom, or property; and that all citizens are entitled to equal protection of the law. This amendment made it clear that former slaves are citizens. By 1868, the amendment had been ratified by enough states to become part of the Constitution.

One important issue of the time was "reparations"—payments owed to the former slaves to make up for the fact that they worked for hundreds of years for no pay. The Freedmen's Bureau was originally supposed to distribute land to the former slaves, but this plan was killed by President Andrew Johnson. Representative Thaddeus Stevens of Pennsylvania then proposed a bill in March 1867, that would have distributed all public lands in the southern states to the former slaves. This bill did not pass Congress. As a result, the former slaves continued to be largely landless and poor (Salzberger and Turck 2004, 63–65).

In 1869, Congress passed the Fifteenth Amendment, which extended the right to vote to all males, regardless of race. This amendment became part of the Constitution in 1870.

By 1870, all the southern states had been readmitted to the union. Black voters helped elect new state governments set up by the Reconstruction Acts. In South Carolina, blacks were a majority of the legislature at that time, and seventeen blacks were elected to the U.S. Congress from the southern states. Some blacks were elected as mayors, and many were elected to town councils. Blacks served as sheriffs, tax collectors, and school commissioners (Foner 1988, 355–364).

During the twelve years of the Reconstruction Era, black leadership helped the southern states became much more responsive to the needs of blacks and the poor. The "black codes" ended. Laws were passed to make sure laborers were paid for their work. Public schools, hospitals, and orphan asylums were started or expanded. Some state and local governments provided medical care for the poor. Alabama provided free legal help to poor people accused of crimes.

Some blacks attempted to create racially integrated schools, and although these attempts often failed, the schools in New Orleans were integrated by 1874. However, many black leaders went along with the idea of segregated schools, reasoning that it was better to have some schools for blacks than no schools. Black legislators introduced laws to ban racial segregation on trains and boats, and in hotels, restaurants, and other public places. Beginning in 1869, South Carolina, Texas, Mississippi, Louisiana, and Florida passed laws banning racial discrimination in public places. However, these laws were often not enforced.

Although blacks wanted to own land, few states passed laws to help with this goal. South Carolina, however, started a land distribution program to allow people to buy land on long-term credit. By 1876, about one-seventh of the state's black population owned homesteads (Foner 1988, 364–375).

The Reconstruction Era ended because the federal government and northerners grew tired of the issue. White supremacist groups such as the Ku Klux Klan began using violence to prevent blacks from voting, and starting in 1870, the former slaveholders began gaining control of governments in southern states. Federal troops were withdrawn from southern states starting in the mid-1870s, and more and more southern governments were taken over by whites who were not sympathetic to the rights of blacks. By 1877, President Rutherford Hayes withdrew all federal troops. After this time, southern governments began passing segregation laws to keep blacks out of schools, colleges, and public places. The southern states also passed laws to prevent blacks from voting. These segregation laws remained largely in place until the civil rights movement of the 1950s and 1960s.

See also: Civil Rights Movement; Freedmen's Bureau; Reparations for Slavery; Segregation Laws; Slavery

Sources

Foner, Eric. *Reconstruction: America's Unfinished Revolution.* New York: Harper and Row, 1988.

Franklin, John Hope. *Reconstruction after the Civil War.* Chicago, IL: University of Chicago Press, 1994.

Salzberger, Ronald P., and Mary C. Turck, eds. *Reparations for Slavery: A Reader.* Lanham, MD: Rowman and Littlefield, 2004.

Smith, Page. *Trial by Fire: A People's History of the Civil War and Reconstruction.* New York: McGraw Hill, 1982.

REPARATIONS FOR SLAVERY

The United States benefited from the free labor of slaves, whereas the slaves were completely impoverished by the institution. Even after the slaves were officially emancipated in 1863, another century of segregation laws caused free blacks to be discriminated against, and to remain disproportionately poor. Should the descendants of the slaves receive any compensation for the enslavement of their ancestors? Such compensation is called "reparations."

The question of reparations has been debated since the beginning of the Civil War in 1860, when abolitionists called on the government to confiscate the land of plantation owners who had kept slaves, and to give this land to the former slaves. In 1861, Congress enacted a plan to confiscate this land. In January 1865, Major General W. T. Sherman of the Union army issued Special Field Orders that gave land to the former slaves and about 40,000 blacks settled on land that they were told was theirs. When the federal government created the Freedmen's Bureau in March 1865, to help the newly freed slaves, the bureau originally promised to give land to each free black man. Later in 1865, however, President Andrew Johnson ended this land redistribution and ordered confiscated land to be returned to the original white owners.

The next reparations attempt was made by Representative Thaddeus Stevens of Pennsylvania. He introduced a bill into Congress in 1867, calling for the federal government to seize all public lands in the southern states, and redistribute these lands to the former slaves. His bill did not pass Congress.

From 1890 to 1917, more than 600,000 former slaves demanded pensions from the federal government to compensate for their unpaid labor during slavery. A white, racist southern man named Walter Vaughan drafted the bill asking for these pensions. He believed that if former slaves had some money to spend, this would boost the incomes of white southern business owners. The bill was first introduced into Congress in 1890. After Vaughan grew tired of the campaign, the movement was named the National Ex-Slave Mutual Relief, Bounty and Pension Association, and was led by a former slave named Callie House. She traveled the country, setting up local chapters and asking former slaves to sign petitions to the federal government. In

1899, the federal government barred House and her organization from using the postal system, based on charges of fraud—the government claimed that they were collecting money to fund an effort that had no hope of success (Winbush 2003, 27; Berry 2005, 6–82).

House continued her activities, using expensive private mail services. Next she decided to try the court system, since her organization was not making much progress with Congress. She asked Cornelius Jones, a prominent African American lawyer, to file a case against the U.S. Treasury Department, demanding that the federal tax collected on cotton from 1862 to 1868 be turned over to former slaves. The Treasury had an estimated $68 million in cotton taxes that had not been spent. House argued that this money was owed to the former slaves to make up for their hundreds of years of unpaid labor. Jones filed the suit in 1915. The federal government dismissed the case, saying the government could not be sued without its consent. In 1916, the federal government arrested House on charges of fraud. She was sentenced to one year in prison. Her movement ended with her imprisonment (Berry 2005, 171–212).

In the 1950s and 1960s, some civil rights activists again began publicizing the idea of reparations. By this time most former slaves had died, so the issue was not about payment to individuals, but payment to the black community as a whole, for the harms inflicted as a result of slavery and segregation laws. The Reparations Committee of Descendants of United States Slaves was founded in 1955. In 1969, James Forman presented a "black manifesto" that called for white Christian churches and Jewish synagogues to provide $500 million to blacks. This money would be used to set up a land fund, and to start publishing and media enterprises for blacks (Winbush 2003, xii, 103; Salzberger and Turck 2004, 70–72).

In 1987, a national organization of blacks was formed to seek reparations: the National Coalition of Blacks for Reparations in America (N'COBRA). In 1989, Representative John Conyers (D-MI) introduced a bill that would set up a federal commission to study the effects of slavery and propose a reparations plan. Conyers has introduced his bill in every Congress since then, but it has not passed.

In 2002, black activists began initiating lawsuits against corporations that had benefited from slavery, demanding apologies and reparations. Deadria Farmer-Paellmann filed a lawsuit in March 2002, on behalf of herself and all other descendants of slaves, against several major financial institutions, including Fleetboston Financial Corporation and Aetna Inc, on the charge that they "conspired with slave traders, with each other and other entities ... to commit and/or knowingly facilitate crimes against humanity, and to further illicitly profit from slave labor" (quoted in Winbush 2003, 357). The lawsuit alleges that the founder of Fleetboston owned ships that engaged in the slave trade, and that Aetna insured slaveholders against the loss of their slaves. The case was consolidated with eight other similar cases, and the Seventh Circuit Court of Appeals ruled that the companies were guilty of lying about their role in slavery, but said that former slaves should have filed the case themselves—that the descendants of slaves cannot file such a case. Farmer-Paellmann argues that none of the facts were even known until she started researching the issue in 2000. This case reached the U.S. Supreme Court in May of 2007. The Supreme Court had not issued a ruling as of press time (Winbush 2003, 354–358; Restitution Study Group Web site).

See also: Civil Rights Movement; Freedmen's Bureau; Reconstruction Era; Slavery

Sources

Berry, Mary Frances. *My Face Is Black Is True: Callie House and the Struggle for Ex-Slave Reparations.* New York: Alfred A. Knopf, 2005.

Salzberger, Ronald P., and Mary C. Turck, eds. *Reparations for Slavery: A Reader.* Lanham, MD: Bowman and Littlefield, 2004.

Winbush, Raymond A. *Should America Pay? Slavery and the Raging Debate on Reparations.* New York: HarperCollins, 2003.

Web Site

Restitution Study Group. http://www.rsgincorp.com/ (accessed August 2008).

PRIMARY DOCUMENT 32

Special Field Orders, No. 15, Issued by Major-General W.T. Sherman, January 16, 1865

I. The islands from Charleston, south, the abandoned rice-field along the rivers for thirty miles back from the sea, and the country bordering the St. Johns

River, Florida, are reserved and set apart for the settlement of the negroes now made free by the acts of war and the proclamation of the President of the United States.

II. At Beaufort, Hilton Head, Savannah, Fernandina, St. Augustine, and Jacksonville, the blacks may remain in their chosen or accustomed vocations; but on the islands, and in the settlements hereafter to be established, no white person whatever, unless military officers and soldiers detailed for duty, will be permitted to reside; and the sole and exclusive management of affairs will be left to the freed people themselves, subject only to the United States military authority, and the acts of Congress. By the laws of war, and orders of the President of the United States, the negro is free, and must be dealt with as such. He cannot be subjected to conscription or forced military service, save by the written orders of the highest military authority of the Department, under such regulations as the President or Congress may prescribe. Domestic servants, blacksmiths, carpenters, and other mechanics, will be free to select their own work and residence, but the young and able-bodied negroes must be encouraged to enlist as soldiers in the service of the United States, to contribute their share toward maintaining their own freedom, and securing their rights as citizens of the United States.

Negroes so enlisted will be organized into companies, battalions, and regiments, under the orders of the United States military authorities, and will be paid, fed, and clothed according to law. The bounties paid on enlistment may, with the consent of the recruit, go to assist his family and settlement in procuring agricultural implements, seed, tools, boots, clothing, and other articles necessary for their livelihood.

III. Whenever three respectable negroes, heads of families, shall desire to settle on land, and shall have selected for that purpose an island or a locality clearly defined within the limits above designated, the Inspector of Settlements and Plantations will himself, or by such subordinate officer as he may appoint, give them a license to settle such island or district and afford them such assistance as he can to enable them to establish a peaceable agricultural settlement. The three parties named will subdivide the land, under the supervision of the inspector, among themselves, and such others as may choose to settle near them, so that each family shall have a plot of not more than (40) forty acres of tillable ground, and when it borders on some water-channel, with not more than 800 feet water front, in the possession of which land the military authorities will afford them protection until such time as they can protect themselves, or until Congress shall regulate their title. The Quartermaster may, on the requisition of the Inspector of Settlements and Plantations, place at the disposal of the Inspector, one or more of the captured steamers, to ply between the settlements and one or more of the commercial points heretofore named, in order to afford the settlers the opportunity to supply their necessary wants, and to sell the products of their land and labor.

IV. Whenever a negro has enlisted in the military service of the United States, he may locate his family in any one of the settlements at pleasure, and acquire a homestead, and all other rights and privileges of a settler, as though present in person. In like manner, negroes may settle their families and engage on board the gunboats, or in fishing, or in the navigation of the inland waters, without losing any claim to land or other advantages derived from this system. But no one, unless an actual settler as above defined, or unless absent on Government service, will be entitled to claim any right to land or property in any settlement by virtue of these orders.

V. In order to carry out this system of settlement, a general officer will be detailed as Inspector of Settlements and plantations whose duty it shall be to visit the settlements, to regulate their police and general arrangement, and who will furnish personally to each head of a family, subject to the approval of the President of the United States, a possessory title in writing, giving as near as possible the description of boundaries; and who shall adjust all claims or conflicts that may arise under the same, subject to the like approval, treating such titles altogether as possessory. The same general officer will also be charged with the enlistment and organization of the negro recruits, and protecting their interests while absent from their settlements; and will be governed by the rules and regulations prescribed by the War Department for such purposes.

VI. Brigadier-General R. Saxton is hereby appointed Inspector of Settlements and Plantations, and will at once enter on the performance of his duties. No change is intended or desired in the settlement now on Beaufort Island, nor will any rights to property heretofore acquired be affected thereby.

By order of Major-General W. T. Sherman

Source

Reprinted in Winbush, Raymond A. *Should America Pay? Slavery and the Raging Debate on Reparations.* New York: HarperCollins, 2003. It can also be found in: William Tecumseh Sherman, *Memoirs of General William T. Sherman,* vol. 2. New York: D. Appleton, 1875, pages 730–732.

PRIMARY DOCUMENT 33

Statement by Representative John Conyers (D-MI), The Impact of Slavery on African Americans Today, April 5, 2005

In January of 1989, I first introduced the bill H.R. 40, *Commission to Study Reparation Proposals for African Americans Act.* I have re-introduced HR 40 every Congress since 1989, and will continue to do so until it's passed into law.

One of the biggest challenges in discussing the issue of reparations in a political context is deciding how to have a national discussion without allowing the issue to polarize our party or our nation. The approach that I have advocated for over a decade has been for the federal government to undertake an official study of the impact of slavery on the social, political and economic life of our nation.

Over 4 million Africans and their descendants were enslaved in the United States and its colonies from 1619 to 1865, and as a result, the United States was able to begin its grand place as the most prosperous country in the free world.

It is un-controverted that African slaves were not compensated for their labor. More unclear however, is what the effects and remnants of this relationship have had on African-Americans and our nation from the time of emancipation through today.

I chose the number of the bill, 40, as a symbol of the forty acres and a mule that the United States initially promised freed slaves. This unfulfilled promise and the serious devastation that slavery had on African-American lives has never been officially recognized by the United States Government.

My bill does four things:

1. It acknowledges the fundamental injustice and inhumanity of slavery;
2. It establishes a commission to study slavery, its subsequent racial and economic discrimination against freed slaves;
3. It studies the impact of those forces on today's living African Americans; and
4. The commission would then make recommendations to Congress on appropriate remedies to redress the harm inflicted on living African Americans.

The commission established would also shed light on the capture and procurement of slaves, the transport and sale of slaves, the treatment of slaves in the colonies and in the United States. It would examine the extent to which Federal and State governments in the U.S. supported the institution of slavery and examine federal and state laws that discriminated against freed African slaves from the end of the Civil War to the present.

Many of the most pressing issues, which have heretofore not been broached on any broad scale, would be addressed. Issues such as the lingering negative effects of the institution of slavery, whether an apology is owed, whether compensation is warranted and, if so, in what form and who should eligible would also be delved into.

H.R. 40 has strong grass roots support within the African American community, including major civil rights organizations, religious organizations, academic and civic groups from across the country. This support is very similar to the strong grassroots support that proceeded another legislative initiative: the Martin Luther King, Jr. Holiday bill. It took a full 15 years from the time I first introduced it on April 5, 1968 to its passage in the fall of 1983. Through most of those 15 years, the idea of a federal holiday honoring an African American civil rights leader was considered a radical idea.

Like the King Holiday bill, we have seen the support for this bill increase each year. Today we have over 40 co-sponsors, more than at any time in the past. What is also encouraging is the dramatic increase in the number of supporters for the bill among Members of Congress who are not members of the Congressional Black Caucus. Just this past month my Colleague Tony Hall, from Ohio introduced a bill calling for an apology as well as the creation of a reparations commission. So now, for the first time we now have two bills in Congress that call for the creation of a commission.

We are also encouraged by the support of city councils and other local jurisdiction that have supported our bill. Already the city councils in Detroit, Cleveland, Chicago and Atlanta have passed bills supporting H.R. 40. And just this past month a councilman in Los Angeles, the site of our 2000 convention has introduced a bill with the strong support of the Los Angeles community. Also, there are presently two bills in the Michigan State House of Representatives addressing the issue of reparations.

It is a fact that slavery flourished in the United States and constituted an immoral and inhumane deprivation of African slaves' lives, liberty and cultural heritage. As a result, millions of African Americans today continue to suffer great injustices.

But reparation is a national and a global issue, which should be addressed in America and in the world. It is not limited to Black Americans in the US but is an issue for the many countries and villages in Africa, which were pilfered, and the many countries, which participated in the institution of slavery.

Another reason that this bill has garnered so much resistance is because many people want to leave slavery in the past - they contend that slavery happened so long ago that it is hurtful and divisive to bring it up now. It's too painful. But the concept of reparations is not a foreign idea to either the U.S. government or governments throughout the world.

Though there is historical cognition for reparations and it is a term that is fairly well known in the international body politic, the question of reparations for African Americans remains unresolved. And so, just as we've discussed the Holocaust, and Japanese interment camps, and to some extent the devastation that the colonists inflicted upon the Indians, we must talk about slavery and its continued effects.

Source

Congressman John Conyers. http://www. house.gov/conyers/news_reparations. shtml (accessed August 2008).

RIIS, JACOB (1849–1914)

Jacob Riis was a journalist, photographer, and lecturer who documented and publicized the living conditions of poor people in New York City in the late 1800s and early 1900s. He was one of the "muckraking" journalists of the Progressive Era, who aimed to shine light on the facts of poverty in an effort to reform society and help the needy. Riis's photographs, writing, and lectures spurred changes in such areas as housing reform, child labor laws, the establishment of playgrounds and neighborhood parks, and clean drinking water.

Riis was born on May 3, 1849, in Ribe, the oldest town in Denmark. His father was a schoolteacher. After completing his education, Riis trained as a carpenter. Failing to get a job in Denmark, he emigrated to the United States in 1870. He worked as a carpenter, miner, farm hand, hunter, and salesman. At one job, where he was paid for every door he planed and finished, he found out that the faster he worked, the less his employer was willing to pay per door. His employer did not want to pay more than $10 per week, no matter how many doors Riis managed to finish (Alland 1974, 20).

Riis was sometimes out of work and out of money, and lived on the streets. Once he slept in a police station lodging (a common way of housing out-of-town homeless men at that time) and was horrified at his experience in that crowded, filthy place. Eventually Riis began getting jobs reporting for newspapers, and after returning to Denmark to get married and bringing his wife to America with him, in 1877, he found work as the police reporter for the *New York Tribune*. In the course of his work, he became familiar with New York City slums. In 1887, he saw an ad in the newspaper about flash photography. He hired some photographers to take pictures of the slums at night and indoors. Unhappy with the work of the hired photographers, Riis in 1888 bought his own camera and learned how to use it (Alland 1974, 26–27, 32–33).

Riis took his slum photographs to magazines, but no one was interested in publishing them. He then began showing slides and giving lectures at church meetings. An editor with *Scribner's* magazine heard a lecture and asked Riis

Jacob Riis' startling print and photographic exposés of conditions in New York City's slums in the late 19th century influenced a generation of investigative reporters, known as muckrakers, and set the standard for future photojournalists. (Library of Congress)

to write an article to go along with the photographs, which were published in December 1889. Riis was soon asked to expand the article into a book. *How the Other Half Lives: Studies among the Tenements of New York* was published in 1890. In addition to the shocking photographs, Riis included suggestions for reform, including building modern tenements and remodeling older ones. It was one of the first books ever published with photographs, and the first book about social conditions to be illustrated with photographs. It became a popular book, and publishers asked him for more. In all, Riis published fourteen books, including *The Children of the Poor* and *The Battle with the Slum.*

Riis's first book caught the attention of a young New York politician, Theodore Roosevelt. Riis and Roosevelt became friends, and Riis educated Roosevelt about the deplorable situation of the poor. In 1895, Roosevelt was appointed head of the city police board, and he closed all police station lodging rooms.

Although Riis stopped taking photographs in about 1898, he continued to use the ones he had already taken in his lectures and writings. He stopped being a reporter in 1901, and devoted his time to lecturing across the country. Ironically, Riis apparently did not consider himself to be a photographer. Years later, his grandson related that no one in the family ever spoke of him as a photographer. Riis did not seem to value his negatives, because after his death his children did not know where they were. Yet it was these photographs that revealed to the upper and middle classes, for the first time, the conditions of poverty of the lower classes in urban America. According to Alexander Alland, who rescued Riis's photographic negatives from obscurity in the 1940s, "Civic leaders everywhere regarded Riis as an expert who could give them encouragement and point the way to enactment of practical reforms in their cities and towns." Riis personally worked for more than nine years to raze the Mulberry Bend slums, where he had worked as a police reporter, and replace them with a park (Alland 1974, 35, 37, 43).

See also: Housing, Low-Income; Perkins, Frances; Playgrounds; Progressive Era

Source

Alland, Alexander Sr. *Jacob A. Riis: Photographer and Citizen.* New York: Aperture, 1974.

Web Site

Open Collections Program at Harvard University Library, Jacob Riis (includes links to online copies of many of his books). http://ocp.hul.harvard.edu/immigration/people_riis.html.

ROOSEVELT, ELEANOR (1884–1962)

Eleanor Roosevelt was First Lady of the United States during the Great Depression and the New Deal, during which time the federal government significantly entered the field of poverty relief for the first time. Her encouragement and help allowed her handicapped husband, Franklin Roosevelt, to remain in politics and win the presidency, and her empathy for the needy pushed President Roosevelt toward helping the downtrodden, especially poor women. She was a leader of the "Women's Network," a loose coalition of women who agitated for laws and government programs to help the poor and unemployed during the Roosevelt administration.

Eleanor was born in New York to a wealthy family. Her father was the younger brother of Theodore Roosevelt, who was President of the United States from 1901 to 1909. By the time she was ten, both her parents had died and she moved in with her maternal grandmother. At the age of fifteen she was sent to school in England, where she studied for three years. By 1902, she was again living in New York City and attending fashionable dinners and dances, but soon she became interested in helping the poor. She taught classes to children at the Rivington Street Settlement House, and investigated garment factories and department stores as part of the Consumers League. By this time she was also becoming acquainted with

a distant cousin, Franklin Roosevelt. They were married in March 1905.

From 1906 to 1916, Eleanor was busy giving birth to and caring for six babies, with the help of many servants. Of this period of her life, Roosevelt relates that "I was not developing any individual taste or initiative. I was simply absorbing the personalities of those about me and letting their tastes and interests dominate me" (1961, 61).

The family moved to Albany, New York, in 1910, when Franklin won a seat in the New York senate. Eleanor took little interest in politics at this point, and had lost her earlier "crusading spirit" about the poor, as she explains:

> I had been told I had no right to go into the slums or into the hospitals, for fear of bringing diseases home to my children, so I had fallen into the easier way of sitting on boards and giving small sums to this or that charity and thinking the whole of my duty to my neighbor was done. (1961, 68)

When her husband ran for vice president in 1920, his political adviser Louis Howe persuaded Eleanor to become involved in the campaign by asking for her advice on speeches and ideas. Howe helped Eleanor build up her confidence about political issues. After Franklin lost the election, Eleanor got involved with the League of Women Voters, the Women's Trade Union League, and the Democratic State Committee. Her biographer Blanche Wiesen Cook describes her transformation: "ER became a social feminist . . . , a political activist, a New Woman" (Roosevelt 1961, 91, 112; Cook 1992, 288).

Eleanor Roosevelt was the first wife of a president to use her unique position to fight for the rights of minorities, women, and the destitute. After her husband died, Roosevelt expanded her responsibilities, serving as U.S. delegate to the United Nations and chairing the committee that drafted the Universal Declaration of Human Rights. (Library of Congress)

While her husband was recovering from polio in the 1920s, Eleanor encouraged him to remain engaged in politics. She also continued her own political involvement, working in support of the Child Labor Amendment to the U.S. Constitution, and raising state funds for women's and children's health clinics under the Sheppard-Towner Act. Although she tried to downplay her own political activities, Cook asserts that "in 1928, ER was one of the best-known and highest-ranking Democrats in the United States" (Cook 1992, 362, 366).

In 1933, Eleanor became First Lady of the United States. According to Cook, during her husband's presidency, she was "running actually a parallel administration concerned with every aspect of national betterment.... FDR never credited ER with a job well done or publicly acknowledged her political influence. But little of significance was achieved without her input, and her vision shaped the best of his presidency" (Cook 1999, 30).

As First Lady, she wanted to ensure that the poor and needy women of the country were not forgotten—as in fact they often were. The Economy Act, passed in 1933, required a federally employed woman to be fired if her husband also worked for the federal government. Many people during the Great Depression believed that married women should not take jobs that ought to go to men. Some states passed laws to prevent married women from working. Eleanor was outraged. In November 1933, she helped organize a White House Conference on the Emergency Needs of Women. She encouraged her husband to appoint women to high government positions, providing him with names of qualified women. At the national level, more than fifty women were appointed by 1935 to leadership positions within the government, as well as hundreds more at the state and local levels. Eleanor believed that women leaders would address the needs of poor women, while men leaders often would not (Cook 1999, 67, 69, 70–73).

Eleanor worked with many women leaders within the federal government to encourage the government to remember the homeless, the unemployed, poor children, single women, and others in need. This group of women government leaders has come to be called the Women's Network of the New Deal.

They demanded—often in vain—that New Deal work programs pay women the same wages as men received. Eleanor insisted that women should be allowed to participate in the same kind of outdoor work camps that men benefited from through the Civilian Conservation Corps, and a few work camps just for women were set up (Cook 1999, 77, 87, 88–90).

Eleanor was especially interested in creating communities of "subsistence homesteads"—each family received basic housing, a few animals for milk, eggs, and meat, land for a garden, and industrial work opportunities, all within a cooperative community setting. She took personal interest in setting up the community of Arthurdale in a poor mining area of West Virginia, which opened in June 1934. She was instrumental in setting up the National Youth Administration, which started in 1935. Students in high school, college, and graduate school were given a stipend so they could continue their education, and work training was offered to those not in school. Women, men, and blacks were treated equally in this program (Cook 1999, 130–152; 269–270).

Franklin was open to his wife's suggestions, but tended to be more cautious politically and economically. As Franklin Roosevelt's biographer Frank Freidel explains, "Both Franklin and Eleanor Roosevelt fundamentally took a moral rather than an economic view of the great problems facing the nation, but Franklin Roosevelt tempered his moral fervor with political realism that sometimes to his wife seemed to be overcaution" (1990, 94).

Eleanor Roosevelt transformed the role of First Lady from White House hostess to political activist. She believed that every woman ought to be interested in politics and economics, because these issues affect everyone's lives (see her essay "In Defense of Curiosity," excerpted in the accompanying sidebar). After her husband's death in 1945, she continued to work on behalf of human rights and racial justice. In the late 1940s, she chaired the United Nations commission which drafted the Universal Declaration of Human Rights. She worked until the end of her life: in 1961, she began chairing President John F. Kennedy's Commission on the Status of Women.

See also: Child Labor Laws; Civilian Conservation Corps; National Consumers League; National Youth Administration; New Deal; New Deal Cooperative Communities; New Deal Women's Network; Perkins, Frances; Roosevelt, Franklin Delano; Settlement Houses; Sheppard-Towner Maternity and Infancy Act of 1921; Universal Declaration of Human Rights; Woodward, Ellen Sullivan

Sources

Cook, Blanche Wiesen. *Eleanor Roosevelt, Volume One 1884–1933*. New York: Viking Press, 1992.

Cook, Blanche Wiesen. *Eleanor Roosevelt, Volume Two 1933–1938*. New York: Viking Press, 1999.

Freidel, Frank. *Franklin D. Roosevelt: A Rendezvous with Destiny*. Boston, MA: Little, Brown and Company, 1990.

Roosevelt, Eleanor. *The Autobiography of Eleanor Roosevelt*. New York: Harper and Brothers, 1961.

Web Sites

The Eleanor Roosevelt Papers Project. http://www.gwu. edu/~erpapers/ (accessed March 2008).

Franklin D. Roosevelt Presidential Library and Museum. http://www.fdrlibrary.marist. edu/ (accessed March 2008).

PRIMARY DOCUMENT 34

Excerpt from "In Defense of Curiosity," by Eleanor Roosevelt, *Saturday Evening Post*, August 24, 1935

Starting in 1935, Eleanor Roosevelt visited coal mines, which prompted the cartoon referred to below. In this essay she encourages women to be curious about the outside world, and to get involved in bettering the lives of the poor, because of the interconnectedness of lives. Roosevelt does not deny the importance of women's role in the home—in fact, she emphasizes that because home is so important, and so interconnected with the rest of the world, women (who are the keepers of the home) must therefore take an interest in the rest of the world.

A short time ago a cartoon appeared depicting two miners looking up in surprise and saying with undisguised horror, "Here comes Mrs. Roosevelt!"

In strange and subtle ways, it was indicated to me that I should feel somewhat ashamed of that cartoon, and there certainly was something the matter with a woman who wanted to see so much and to know so much.

Somehow or other, most of the people who spoke to me, or wrote to me about it, seemed to feel that it was unbecoming in a woman to have a variety of interests. Perhaps that arose from the old inherent theory that woman's interests must lie only in her home. This is a kind of blindness which seems to make people feel that interest in the home stops within the four walls of the house in which you live. Few seem capable of realizing that the real reason that home is important is that it is so closely tied, by a million strings, to the rest of the world. That is what makes it an important factor in the life of every nation.

Whether we recognize it or not, no home is an isolated object. We may not recognize it, and we may try to narrow ourselves so that our interest only extends to our immediate home circle, but if we have any understanding at all of what goes on around us, we soon see how outside influences affect our own existence. Take, for example, the money we have to spend. The economic conditions of the country affect our income whether it is earned or whether it is an income which comes to us from invested capital. What we are able to do in our home depends on the cost of the various things which we buy. All of us buy food, and food costs vary with conditions throughout the country and world.

It took us some time to realize that there was a relationship between the farm situation and the situation of the rest of our country, but eventually wage earners in the East did feel the results of the lack of buying power on the farms in the Middle West. To keep an even balance between the industrial worker and the agricultural worker is an extremely difficult thing. Every housewife in this country should realize that if she lives in a city and has a husband who is either a wage earner or the owner of an industry, her wages or her profits will be dependent, not only on the buying power of people like herself but upon the buying power of the great mass of agricultural people throughout the country. The farm housewife must realize, too, that her interests are tied up with those of the wage earner and his employer throughout the nation, for her husband's products can only find a ready market when the city dweller is prosperous.

There is ever present, of course, the economic question of how to keep balanced the cost of living and the wages the man receives. The theory of low wages and low living costs has been held by many economists to be sound, for they contend what money one has will provide as much as high wages do in countries where living costs are also high.

We have gone, as a rule, on the theory, in this country, particularly in eras of prosperity, that high wages and high costs make for a higher standard of living, and that we really obtain more for our money, even though our prices are higher.

This question is argued back and forth, and the method by which one or the other theory shall be put into practice is an equally good field for arguments.

It may seem like an academic discussion, but any housewife should know that it is the first way in which her home brings her in touch with the public questions of the day.

The women of the country are discovering their deep concern as to the policies of government and of commercial agencies, largely because these policies are reflected in many ways in their daily lives. . . .

This correlation of interests is something that every woman would understand if she had the curiosity to find out the reason for certain conditions instead of merely accepting them, usually with rather bad grace. . . .

Therefore, anyone who fully appreciates the value of home life must, of necessity, reach out in many directions in an effort to protect the home, which we know is our most valuable asset. Even the primitive civilizations reached out from the home to the boundaries of their knowledge, and our own pioneer homes reached back into the countries from which they came and out into the new lands which they were discovering and subduing to their needs.

It is man's ceaseless urge to know more and to do more which makes the world move, and so, when people say woman's place is in the home, I say, with enthusiasm, it certainly is, but if she really cares about her home, that caring will take her far and wide. . . .

A few years ago, when I was conducting a class in the study of city government, we took up one of the functions of the government—namely, public health. This is closely allied to housing, so I suggested that our group visit some of the different types of tenements. There was considerable concern among some of the mothers, for fear some illness might be contracted. It apparently never occurred to them that hundreds of young people lived in these tenements all the time, nor that, very likely, there entered into their sheltered homes daily people who served as delivery boys, servants and workmen, who spent much of their time in tenements; so, even if the sheltered children did not visit them, the tenement home radiated out all that was good in it and all that was bad in it and touched the home on Park Avenue. No home is isolated, remember, so why should we not have a curiosity about all the homes that must in one way or another affect our own?

On visiting the various types of tenements, I found again that the lack of curiosity makes a poor background for real understanding. To these children of the rich, I had to explain what it meant to sleep in a room which had no window, what it meant to pant on fire escapes in hot July with people draped on fire escapes all around you, what it meant for a women with her husband and eight children to live in three rooms in a basement, and why a toilet with no outside ventilation could make a home unhealthy and malodorous.

Lack of curiosity in these young people meant lack of imagination and complete inability to visualize any life but their own, and, therefore, they could not recognize their responsibility to their less-fortunate brothers and sisters. . . .

It is curiosity which makes scientists willing to risk their lives in finding some new method of alleviating human suffering, often using themselves as the best medium of experimentation. It is curiosity which makes people go down under the water to study the life on the floor of the ocean, or up into the air and out and over new and untried trails to find new ways of drawing this old world closer together.

I often wonder, as I look at the stars at night, if someday we will find a way to communicate and travel from one to the other. I am told that the stars are millions and millions of miles away, though sometimes they look so near, but it seems to me, at times, to be almost as hard for people who have no curiosity to bridge the gap from one human being to another. Perhaps the day will come when our curiosity will not only carry us out of our homes and out of ourselves to a better understanding of material things, but will make us able to understand one another and to know what the Lord meant when He said, "He that hath ears to hear, let him hear." And we might well add: "He that hath eyes to see, let him see."

Source

Eleanor Roosevelt Papers. http://www.gwu.edu/~erpapers/documents/articles/indefenseofcuriosity.cfm (accessed March 2008). Used with permission.

ROOSEVELT, FRANKLIN DELANO (1882–1945)

The longest-serving president of the United States, Franklin Roosevelt presided over the federal government during the Great Depression and World War II. The policies of his administration launched the national government into large-scale efforts to eliminate poverty and regulate the economy that continue to this day, such as Social Security, the Fair Labor Standards Act, the National Labor Relations Act, and federal aid to poor families.

Franklin Roosevelt was born on January 30, 1882, into a wealthy family in Hyde Park, New York. He was educated by private tutors and governesses, and had visited Europe nine times by the time he was fourteen. He attended Groton, a prestigious private high school in Massachusetts, earned a degree from Harvard University, and attended law school at Columbia University. While still a law student, he married a distant cousin, Eleanor Roosevelt, in 1905. Eleanor was already interested in helping the poor, and during their courtship, she arranged to meet Franklin at tenement houses in New York, so he could see conditions of poverty (Freidel 1990, 12).

After he passed the bar examination in 1907, he worked as a clerk for a law firm in New York City. In 1910, he ran for the New York Senate and won a seat. At first he was not particularly interested in the fate of the working class or the poor, but as Frank Freidel says, "day-by-day politics transformed him into an energetic young progressive" (Freidel 1990, 21). As he learned more about the needs of the lower classes, he wanted to help them.

In 1913, he was appointed assistant secretary of the Navy by President

The only U.S. president ever to serve more than two terms, Franklin D. Roosevelt was elected to office in 1932 and was reelected three more times before he died near the end of World War II. (Library of Congress)

Woodrow Wilson. He ran for U.S. vice president in 1920, on a ticket with James Cox, and although they lost the election to Warren Harding, Roosevelt gained valuable political experience. He then took a job with a financial services company in New York City, but still maintained his involvement with the Democratic Party.

In August 1921, Roosevelt was struck with a severe case of polio that paralyzed his legs. Many people assumed he would give up his involvement in politics because of his handicap, but he continued to do what he could as he recuperated and began exercising to strengthen himself. Eleanor helped him to continue his political activities by making speeches for him, and his adviser Louis Howe wrote letters for him. By 1922, he started to

practice walking with the help of braces and crutches. In 1927, he used two-thirds of his personal fortune to buy Warm Springs in Georgia, where he and other polio victims found relief by swimming in the warm water. He transformed the springs into a national center to provide low-cost polio treatment (Freidel 1990, 47, 49–50).

Frances Perkins, who worked with Roosevelt politically both before and after his illness, says that Roosevelt

> underwent a spiritual transformation during the years of his illness. I noticed when he came back that the years of pain and suffering had purged the slightly arrogant attitude he had displayed on occasion before he was stricken. The man emerged completely warmhearted, with humility of spirit and with a deeper philosophy. Having been to the depths of trouble, he understood the problems of people in trouble. (Perkins 1946, 29)

By 1928, Roosevelt still could barely walk, even with crutches and braces. Nevertheless, he ran for governor of New York and won. When the stock market crashed in 1929, no one knew that this would be the beginning of a decade-long, nationwide economic depression—a period of massive unemployment and poverty. Just after the crash, Roosevelt said he thought the country's industry and trade were still healthy. Yet he was eager to learn about the extent of the problem. Perkins, who was his industrial commissioner, gave him weekly reports on unemployment in the state. Nevertheless, even in 1930, he was wary of spending public money on creating jobs.

As Roosevelt realized that the Depression was worsening, he threw

A CREATIVE ARTIST

Frances Perkins was the U.S. secretary of labor under President Roosevelt. In a biography she wrote of him, she describes how she believed his mind worked as he created laws and programs to help end the Great Depression:

In the use of his faculties Roosevelt had almost the quality of a creative artist. One would say that it is the quality of the modern artist as distinct from the classical artist. The name for it in the graphic arts is automatism. It describes an artist who begins his picture without a clear idea of what he intends to paint or how it shall be laid out upon the canvas, but begins anyhow, and then, as he paints, his plan evolves out of the material he is painting. So Roosevelt worked with the materials and problems at hand. As he worked one phase, the next evolved.

Roosevelt's plans were never thoroughly thought out. They were burgeoning plans; they were next steps; they were something to do next week or next year. One plan grew out of another. Gradually they fitted together and supplemented one another.

Source: Perkins, Frances. *The Roosevelt I Knew.* New York: Viking Press, 1946, 163.

aside his caution. In 1931, he pushed through legislation to establish the Temporary Emergency Relief Administration. The title of the law shows that he still believed that temporary measures would be enough to help people through the hard times. This program gave relief to about 10 percent of families in New York. The state scrambled to find the money to fund the program and eventually realized that the federal government had to help (Freidel 1990, 60–62).

Roosevelt ran for president in 1932, and won. In his speech accepting the Democratic presidential nomination, he first used the words "new deal," which would become attached to his administration's collection of federal laws and programs designed to bolster the economy and alleviate the suffering caused by poverty. However, although Roosevelt used the words "new deal," he did not know exactly what the country needed to rise out of the Depression.

According to Perkins, who was now his secretary of labor, "the New Deal was not a plan with form and content. It was a happy phrase he had coined during the campaign.... When he got to Washington, he had no fixed program" (Perkins 1946, 166). Roosevelt once explained his approach during the New Deal: "Take a method and try it. If it fails admit it frankly and try another. But above all, try something" (quoted in Biles 1991, 225).

To help him figure out how to end the Great Depression, Roosevelt called together a number of experts in politics and economics. These experts have come to be called the "Brain Trust." The most important members of the Brain Trust were Raymond Moley, Rexford Tugwell, and Adolf Berle, all of whom were professors at Columbia University in New York. Frances Perkins and Eleanor Roosevelt also advised him, pressing him to consider the needs of the poor and not just the needs of business (Fusfeld 1956, 208, 216; Cook 1999, 15, 70–71).

According to Perkins, although there was no overall plan behind the New Deal, the impetus was "Roosevelt's general attitude that *the people mattered*. Government programs designed to give reality to that attitude developed and fitted into one another out of the necessities of the times" (1946, 173, italics in original).

As soon as he took office in March 1933, Roosevelt called Congress into session and began sending drafts of bills for their approval. At this point, the economy was in shambles, and Congress and the public were desperate to try new things. "[Roosevelt] possessed for the moment power to innovate such as few presidents ever enjoy, and he made the most of it," notes his biographer Frank Freidel (1990, 92).

Congress passed the first bill he submitted, the Emergency Banking Act, within hours. From March 9 to June 16, Roosevelt sent bill after bill to Congress, which passed many of these laws with little debate, including the Agricultural Adjustment Act, the Federal Emergency Relief Act, the Civilian Conservation Corps, the Tennessee Valley Authority Act, and the National Industrial Recovery Act. This session of Congress has come to be known as the "Hundred Days." Roosevelt biographer Kenneth Davis notes that legislation was introduced into Congress "helter-skelter as fast as draft bills could be prepared" (1986, 77).

During the Hundred Days, Roosevelt also started the first of his nationwide radio addresses, called the "Fireside Chats," to explain his policies and ideas directly to the American people.

After the Hundred Days, the pace of legislation slowed down considerably. Some people began criticizing Roosevelt for not having gone far enough and for not having done enough to help the poor.

Several popular movements may have urged Roosevelt to enter into what is known as the "Second New Deal" and to propose strong laws in 1935 to help the poor. These movements included the Townsend Movement, which called for an old-age pension plan; the Share Our Wealth movement led by Senator Huey Long, which called for redistribution of wealth; the National Union of Social Justice led by Father Charles Coughlin, which called for changes in the country's fiscal policy; and the EPIC (End Poverty in California) movement, led by Upton Sinclair. Roosevelt realized these movements had broad popular appeal, and that may have pushed him into proposing stronger laws. The Works Progress Administration, the Social Security Act, and the National Labor Relations Act all passed in 1935; and the Fair Labor Standards Act was passed in 1938.

Although the New Deal did not actually end the Great Depression—the unemployment rate was still 17 percent in 1939—it did ease the suffering of many people. The New Deal did not so much end as it "simply faded away," according to historian Robert McElvaine. By the end of the 1930s, Roosevelt's and the country's attention shifted to the war that was beginning in Europe in 1939, which became World War II. The increased government spending on the war effort virtually wiped out unemployment (McElvaine 1984, 306–309).

PRIMARY DOCUMENT 35

Excerpt from the "Economic Bill of Rights," President Roosevelt's State of the Union message, January 11, 1944

During his State of the Union address in 1944, Roosevelt detailed an "economic bill of rights" that would continue the full employment and prosperity of the war years even after the war was over. He did not want the end of the war to usher in another period of economic depression. He equates economic security in the United States with peace and prosperity around the world. Unfortunately, this economic bill of rights has yet to be enacted in the United States.

This Nation in the past two years has become an active partner in the world's greatest war against human slavery.

We have joined with like-minded people in order to defend ourselves in a world that has been gravely threatened with gangster rule.

But I do not think that any of us Americans can be content with mere survival. Sacrifices that we and our allies are making impose upon us all a sacred obligation to see to it that out of this war we and our children will gain something better than mere survival.

We are united in determination that this war shall not be followed by another interim which leads to new disaster—that we shall not repeat the tragic errors of ostrich isolationism—that we shall not repeat the excesses of the wild twenties when this Nation went for a joy ride on a roller coaster which ended in a tragic crash. . . .

The one supreme objective for the future . . . can be summed up in one word: Security.

And that means not only physical security which provides safety from attacks by aggressors. It means also economic security, social security, moral security—in a family of Nations. . . .

All our allies want freedom to develop their lands and resources, to build up industry, to increase education and individual opportunity, and to raise standards of living.

All our allies have learned by bitter experience that real development will not be possible if they are to be diverted from their purpose by repeated wars—or even threats of war.

China and Russia are truly united with Britain and America in recognition of this essential fact:

The best interests of each Nation, large and small, demand that all freedom-loving Nations shall join together in a just and durable system of peace. In the present world situation, evidenced by the actions of Germany, Italy, and Japan, unquestioned military control over disturbers of the peace is as necessary among Nations as it is among citizens in a community. And an equally basic essential to peace is a decent standard of living for all individual men and women and children in all Nations. Freedom from fear is eternally linked with freedom from want.

There are people who burrow through our Nation like unseeing moles, and attempt to spread the suspicion that if other Nations are encouraged to raise their standards of living, our own American standard of living must of necessity be depressed.

The fact is the very contrary. It has been shown time and again that if the standard of living of any country goes up, so does its purchasing power- and that such a rise encourages a better standard of living in neighboring countries with whom it trades. . . .

In this war, we have been compelled to learn how interdependent upon each other are all groups and sections of the population of America.

Increased food costs, for example, will bring new demands for wage increases from all war workers, which will in turn raise all prices of all things including those things which the farmers themselves have to buy. Increased wages or prices will each in turn produce the same results. They all have a particularly disastrous result on all fixed income groups.

And I hope you will remember that all of us in this Government represent the fixed income group just as much as we represent business owners, workers, and farmers. This group of fixed income people includes: teachers, clergy, policemen, firemen, widows and minors on fixed incomes, wives and dependents of our soldiers and sailors, and old-age pensioners. They and their families add up to one-quarter of our one hundred and thirty million people. They have few or no high pressure representatives at the Capitol. In a period of gross inflation they would be the worst sufferers. . . .

It is our duty now to begin to lay the plans and determine the strategy for the winning of a lasting peace and the establishment of an American standard of living higher than ever before known. We cannot be content, no matter how high that general standard of living may be, if some fraction of our people—whether it be one-third or one-fifth or one-tenth- is ill-fed, ill-clothed, ill housed, and insecure.

This Republic had its beginning, and grew to its present strength, under the protection of certain inalienable political rights—among them the right of free speech, free press, free worship, trial by jury, freedom from unreasonable searches and seizures. They were our rights to life and liberty.

As our Nation has grown in size and stature, however—as our industrial economy expanded—these political rights proved inadequate to assure us equality in the pursuit of happiness.

We have come to a clear realization of the fact that true individual freedom cannot exist without economic security and independence. "Necessitous men are not free men." People who are hungry and out of a job are the stuff of which dictatorships are made.

In our day these economic truths have become accepted as self-evident. We have accepted, so to speak, a second Bill of Rights under which a new basis of security and prosperity can be established for all regardless of station, race, or creed.

Among these are:

The right to a useful and remunerative job in the industries or shops or farms or mines of the Nation;

The right to earn enough to provide adequate food and clothing and recreation;

The right of every farmer to raise and sell his products at a return which will give him and his family a decent living;

The right of every businessman, large and small, to trade in an atmosphere of freedom from unfair competition and domination by monopolies at home or abroad;

The right of every family to a decent home;

The right to adequate medical care and the opportunity to achieve and enjoy good health;

The right to adequate protection from the economic fears of old age, sickness, accident, and unemployment;

The right to a good education.

All of these rights spell security. And after this war is won we must be prepared to move forward, in the implementation of these rights, to new goals of human happiness and well-being.

America's own rightful place in the world depends in large part upon how fully these and similar rights have been carried into practice for our citizens. For unless there is security here at home there cannot be lasting peace in the world. . . .

I ask the Congress to explore the means for implementing this economic bill of rights—for it is definitely the responsibility of the Congress so to do. Many of these problems are already before committees of the Congress in the form of proposed legislation. I shall from time to time communicate with the Congress with respect to these and further proposals. In the event that no adequate program of progress is evolved, I am certain that the Nation will be conscious of the fact.

Source

Franklin Roosevelt. State of the Union Message to Congress, January 11, 1944. Franklin D. Roosevelt Presidential Library and Museum. http://www.fdrlibrary.marist.edu/011144.html (accessed on February 13, 2009).

Even during the war, however, Roosevelt continued to think about how poverty could be permanently ended in the United States. In his State of the Union speech to Congress in 1944 he detailed an "economic bill of rights." Roosevelt died in April 1945, and as of 2009, this economic bill of rights has not yet been put into place.

While Roosevelt was himself wealthy, he had immense sympathy for those who were struggling economically and wanted to help them. At the same time, he was economically fairly conservative. He had no thought of radically changing the economy of the United States to create a more equal distribution of wealth. Ultimately, his New Deal was, as Eleanor Roosevelt says in her autobiography, "an effort to preserve our economic system" (1961, 278).

See also: Coughlin, Charles; Great Depression; Hoover, Herbert; Hopkins, Harry; Long, Huey; New Deal; Roosevelt, Eleanor; Sinclair, Upton; Townsend Movement

Sources

Biles, Roger. *A New Deal for the American People.* DeKalb, IL: Northern Illinois University Press, 1991.

Cook, Blanche Wiesen. *Eleanor Roosevelt, Volume Two 1933–1938.* New York: Viking Press, 1999.

Davis, Kenneth. *FDR: The New Deal Years, 1933–1937: A History.* New York: Random House, 1986.

Freidel, Frank. *Franklin D. Roosevelt: A Rendezvous with Destiny.* Boston, MA: Little, Brown and Company, 1990.

Fusfeld, Daniel. *The Economic Thought of Franklin D. Roosevelt and the Origins of the New Deal.* New York: Columbia University Press, 1956.

McElvaine, Robert. *The Great Depression: America, 1929–1941.* New York: Times Books, 1984.

Perkins, Frances. *The Roosevelt I Knew.* New York: Viking Press, 1946.

Roosevelt, Eleanor. *The Autobiography of Eleanor Roosevelt.* New York: Harper and Brothers, 1961.

Web Site

Franklin D. Roosevelt Presidential Library and Museum. http://www.fdrlibrary.marist.edu/ (accessed March 2008).

S

SANGER, MARGARET (1879–1966)

Margaret Sanger was a leader of the birth control movement in the United States. At a time when it was illegal to disseminate birth control devices and information, she aimed to help poor women limit their families and gain control of their lives. She founded Planned Parenthood, which has become one of the world's largest networks of family planning providers.

Margaret Louisa Higgins was born in Corning, New York, on September 14, 1879, the sixth child of eleven. Her father sculpted angels and saints for tombstones. As a child, she noticed that the well-off families who lived on the nearby hills had small families, while the poor had large families. "Very early in my childhood I associated poverty, toil, unemployment, drunkenness, cruelty, quarreling, fighting, debts, jails, with large families," she wrote (Sanger 1931, 5).

Because she did not get along with a high school teacher in Corning, her two older sisters pooled their earnings to send Sanger to a boarding school. However, there was not enough money for her to complete her education there. She came home to care for her ill mother, and she read books about nursing during this time. After her mother's death, she enrolled as a nursing student in a Westchester County hospital. While there she met William Sanger, an architect, and they married in 1902.

After giving birth to two sons and a daughter, Sanger and her family moved to New York City in 1910, where Margaret found part-time work with the Visiting Nurse Service in the poor, immigrant Lower East Side. She encountered suffering brought about by unwanted pregnancies. In particular, she was affected by the plight of "Mrs. Sacks," who had three young children, and had attempted a home abortion. Sanger was called in to care for her. After two weeks of round-the-clock nursing, Sanger managed to save the

Margaret Sanger dedicated her life to the birth-control movement in the United States, of which she was the founder and controversial leader. (Library of Congress)

woman's life. Mrs. Sacks then asked Sanger for birth control advice. Sanger knew about only two methods: withdrawal and condoms, both of which relied on the man. Three months later, Mrs. Sacks died of another unsafe abortion. After this experience, Sanger recalled that "I resolved that women should have knowledge of contraception. They have every right to know their own bodies. I would strike out—I would scream from the housetops. I would tell the world what was going on in the lives of these poor women" (Sanger 1931, 51–56).

Over the next several years she researched the subject of birth control in medical books, and traveled to Europe to learn how women dealt with the problem there. In 1914, she started a magazine called *The Woman Rebel* to challenge the "Comstock Act," the federal law that prohibited contraception. The Post Office prevented her from mailing the first issue, and she was arrested on criminal charges that could have led to forty-five years in prison. Before her trial, Sanger wrote a sixteen-page pamphlet called "Family Limitation," giving detailed advice about the contraceptives she had learned about by that time: withdrawal, douches, condoms, pessaries (a kind of cervical cap), and sponges soaked in vinegar or antiseptic solution. She also provided recipes for making vaginal suppositories.

Sanger believed that birth control was important not just for an individual woman's well-being or a family's economic status. It was also important in terms of reforming the economy as a whole. As she explained in "Family Limitation," "The working woman can use direct action by refusing to supply the market with children to be exploited, by refusing to populate the earth with slaves" (1931, 3).

Sanger arranged for this pamphlet to be distributed widely through a Socialist labor union, the Industrial Workers of the World. She then fled to Europe to avoid imprisonment. She returned to the United States in 1915. She stood trial in 1916, and by this time, society had come to be more accepting of publications on the subject of birth control, so all charges were dropped (Chesler 1992, 140).

Sanger was arrested again in 1916, for operating a birth control clinic in Brooklyn, New York—the first birth control clinic in the country. She spent thirty days in jail. In 1917, she launched a magazine, *Birth Control Review,* and in 1922, Sanger and others formed the American Birth Control

THE PLIGHT OF MRS. SACKS

After Sanger had saved Mrs. Sacks from death as a result of a home abortion, Mrs. Sacks asked Sanger for help with birth control. Sanger describes the scene:

But as the hour of my departure came nearer, her anxiety increased, and finally with trembling voice she said: "Another baby will finish me, I suppose."

"It's too early to talk about that," I said, and resolved that I would turn the question over to the doctor for his advice. When he came I said: "Mrs. Sacks is worried about having another baby."

"She might well be," replied the doctor, and then he stood before her and said: "Any more such capers, young woman, and there will be no need to call me."

"Yes, yes—I know, Doctor," said the patient with trembling voice, "but," and she hesitated as if it took all of her courage to say it, "*what* can I do to prevent getting that way again?"

"Oh, ho!" laughed the doctor good naturedly, "You want your cake while you eat it too, do you? Well, it can't be done." Then, familiarly slapping her on the back and picking up his hat and bag to depart, he said, "I'll tell you the only sure thing to do. Tell Jake to sleep on the roof!"

With those words he closed the door and went down the stairs, leaving both of us petrified and stunned.

Tears sprang to my eyes, and a lump came in my throat as I looked at that face before me. It was stamped with sheer horror. I thought for a moment she might have gone insane, but she conquered her feelings, whatever they may have been, and turning to me in desperation said: "He can't understand, can he?—he's a man after all—but you do, don't you? You're a woman and you'll tell me the secret and I'll never tell it to a soul."

She clasped her hands as if in prayer, she leaned over and looked straight into my eyes and beseechingly implored me to tell her something—*something I really did not know.*

Source: Sanger, Margaret. *My Fight for Birth Control.* New York: Farrar & Rinehart, 1931, 52–53.

League. This organization aimed to influence the U.S. Congress to repeal the Comstock Act. Although the Comstock Act remained on the books, over the next several years birth control gained popularity: even the Sears catalog advertised contraceptives. Birth control was being distributed with little interference from the government (Chesler 1992, 371–372).

Still, Sanger wanted birth control to be clearly legal. She decided to try the courts. In 1932, she arranged for a package of pessaries to be mailed from Japan to a gynecologist friend. After customs officers seized the package, the courts eventually declared in 1936 that doctors had the right to import contraceptives, and that furthermore, the importation and sale of contraceptives was not obscene or immoral under the Comstock Act. Although this ruling lifted the federal ban on birth control, poor women were still generally left out since they often could not afford to visit a doctor (Chesler 1992, 371–377).

Even though this was the time of the Great Depression, when poor families desperately needed a way to limit births, the federal and state governments did almost nothing to provide free or low-cost contraceptives to people. President and Mrs. Roosevelt were wary of getting involved in an issue that was opposed by Catholics, who were strong supporters of the Democratic Party. In 1941, Eleanor Roosevelt finally convened a White House meeting on birth control, which Sanger attended, but little came of this (Chesler 1992, 339, 387–391).

In 1942, the American Birth Control League changed its name to Planned Parenthood Federation of America. Sanger arranged for grants to be given to Dr. Gregory Pincus, who was researching hormonal methods of contraception. This research eventually resulted in the birth control pill, approved in 1960 by the U.S. Food and Drug Administration (Chesler 1992, 430–432).

See also: Contraception and Abortion; Eugenics; Great Depression; Roosevelt, Eleanor; Wald, Lillian

Sources

Chesler, Ellen. *Woman of Valor: Margaret Sanger and the Birth Control Movement in America.* New York: Simon and Schuster, 1992.

Sanger, Margaret. "Family Limitation," 6th ed., 1917. http://onlinebooks.library.upenn.edu/webbin/book/lookupid?key=olbp27718 (accessed June 2008).

Sanger, Margaret. *My Fight for Birth Control.* New York: Farrar and Rinehart, 1931.

SCIENTIFIC CHARITY

"Scientific charity" was a phrase that became popular in the late 1800s. It referred to a coordinated, private effort to help the poor—a rational, orderly system that would make sure that the poor were provided with the bare necessities, and also that the poor would benefit from the moral and practical influence of well-off volunteers who visited them in their homes. The movement originated in England, with the founding in 1869 of the first Charity Organization Society in London (Waugh 1997, 102).

Scientific charity aimed to reduce government help to the poor by coordinating the efforts of private charities. Supporters of scientific charity especially wanted to do away with "outdoor relief"—the government provision of food, fuel, and money to people in their own homes. Such relief should be provided only by private charity organizations, and government help should be limited to poorhouses, they believed. Scientific charity proponents aimed to reduce poverty itself through the moral example of the home visitors.

Scientific charity was a response to the economic depression of the 1870s, when millions of people became unemployed. Private charities sprang up to serve soup and bread, to distribute coal and clothing, and to provide free housing. The provision of relief was chaotic, and often corrupt as well: politicians sometimes handed out aid indiscriminately in the hopes of garnering votes. Many charity workers saw a need for organization and a need to provide the poor with guidance along with food and fuel (Waugh 1997, 105–106).

One important voice for scientific charity was Josephine Shaw Lowell, who was born into a family of social reformers in New York. She helped found and run organizations of private charities in New York State. In 1884, she published a book about the theoretical basis of scientific charity called *Public Relief and Private Charity*. Lowell believed that the poor had no inherent right to aid, and that the provision of relief was a cause of poverty by encouraging idleness. She also believed that charity should raise the morals and character of the beneficiary. Furthermore, she stressed that private charity organizations should not only help the poor, but also should study the poor and collect data, which would help inform future aid to the poor.

Another important proponent of scientific charity was S. Humphreys Gurteen, a New York pastor. In 1877, Gurteen spearheaded the founding of the Charity Organization Society in Buffalo, New York. The goal of the organization was to help all private charities in the city—regardless of their religious, political, or national bent—to cooperate with each other and with government relief agencies. The city was to be divided into districts. An agent would investigate all the poor people in that district and report back to district headquarters. Then, if the poor person or family was deemed worthy of help, they were to be directed to the appropriate private charity. This system was designed to prevent the poor person from receiving relief from a number of different charities, and thus getting more than they absolutely

needed. Furthermore, the Charity Organization Society would appoint a volunteer to visit with the family and help them live an upright life: to work hard, to send their children to school, and to keep their houses clean. The central office of the Charity Organization Society was to set up savings banks and nursery schools for the poor, and help the unemployed to find work.

Other cities wanted to start Charity Organization Societies of their own, and Gurteen wrote a handbook to guide the formation of such societies. A portion of this handbook is excerpted below.

Based on Gurteen's model, cities around the country began to set up Charity Organization Societies. By the time Gurteen published his guidebook, he lists nineteen Charity Organization Societies in the eastern and Midwestern parts of the country. In ten cities, these societies did succeed in ending outdoor relief by the government. However, most societies were not able to find enough volunteers to visit with the poor. They were not able to reduce poverty or even help all the needy in their city, especially when economic depressions struck. Still, the movement spread in the early twentieth century to smaller cities (Gurteen 1882, 19; Katz 1996, 84).

For many years, scientific charity and the Charity Organization Societies were at odds with the settlement-house movement, another private-charity movement that started in the late 1800s. The settlement-house movement set up communal households for educated, well-off young people to experience life in poor neighborhoods. Since they lived in the midst of the poor, settlement-house workers saw early on

PRIMARY DOCUMENT 36

Excerpt from "Charity Organization and the Buffalo Plan," by S. Humphreys Gurteen, 1882

We would call attention to two important facts:

First. In every one of our large cities, we see poverty, distress and want in a hundred different forms, from the temporary distress of the honest *poor* who prefer to work than to beg, to the chronic indigence of the *pauper* who prefers to beg rather than to work; and so down to the criminal who has qualified by dissipation and lawlessness for the reformatory or prison.

Second. At the same time we see in these same cities various agencies, official and private, for the relief of this wide-spread suffering and destitution— asylums, benevolent societies, hospitals and reformatories for the giving of food, clothing or medicine, or for the reclaiming of the erring.

Yet, in spite of all that is being done in the way of charitable relief, it is found on all hands:

1. That pauperism is steadily on the increase in almost every city in the land.
2. That the most truly deserving are those who do not seek, and, therefore, very often do not get relief.
3. That the pauper, the imposter and the fraud of every description carry off at least one-half of all charity, public and private, and hence there is a constant and deplorable waste in the alms-fund of every large city.
4. That by far the larger part of all that is given, even to the honest poor, in the name of charity, is doing positive harm by teaching them to be idle, shiftless and improvident.
5. That but little effort is made, as a rule, to inculcate provident habits among the poor, or to establish provident schemes based on sound business principles, so as to aid the poor to be self-supporting.
6. That little, if anything, is being done to check the evils arising from overcrowded and unhealthy tenements, or to suppress the curses of bastardy ... and other evils peculiar to the individual city.

Now, we say, without fear of contradiction, that no single parish, no single church, no single benevolent society, no single association ever has or ever can accomplish any permanent reform in this matter of pauperism, with all its attendant evils; and that so long at least as a community divided up, as every community is, into opposing creeds and parties, refuses to work on some common principles which all can adopt, no reform can be expected. On the contrary, the very fact of the existence of various conflicting interests preventing band-work, preventing union, preventing harmonious co-operation, can but tend to aggravate the evils which it is the object of each to eradicate.. . .

Now, Charity Organization means the banding together of all the various interests of the city for mutual protection against imposition; for effective working in the matter of relief; for the economic disbursement of the alms-fund of the city; for the improvement of the condition of the poor, and for the reform of abuses which at present are known, perhaps, only to the few. . . .

Now, the principles which the Society lays down in order to effect the full and complete co-operation of which we have spoken, and apart from which no lasting co-operation is possible, are the following:

1. There must be no exclusion of any person or body of persons on account of religious creed, politics or nationality. . . .
2. There must be no attempt at proselytism on the part of Agents or others employed by the Organization. . . .
3. There must be no interference with any existing benevolent societies; each society must retain its autonomy intact; its rules, funds, modes of operation and everything which gives it individuality. . . .
4. There must be no relief given by the Organization itself, except in very urgent cases. . . .
5. There must be no sentiment in the matter. It must be treated as a business scheme, if success is to attend its operations. . . .

These are the cardinal principles of successful Organization. Let any one of these "five points" be disregarded, and, sooner or later, Organization will end in total failure. . . .

But the further question remains, how are we to interest the citizens at large?

The first thing to be done is to show the community, in very plain language, the following facts:

1. That Organization renders most efficient aid to the clergy, benevolent societies, institutions, benevolent individuals and the city almoner, by investigating, *free of charge,* all cases applying for relief; thus removing a great burden and a great expense from the shoulders of the benevolent, who desire to give and to give wisely; also by instituting a method of *thorough* investigation, which it is utterly impossible for any single person or society to carry out; and, finally, by supplementing the Poormaster's investigations, by information which even he could not otherwise obtain.
2. That, wherever Organization has been started, it has, without a single exception, either abolished out-door city relief altogether or has reduced the amount, hitherto annually expended, within comparatively reasonable limits. . . .
3. That beggars and cripples are removed from the streets, and, if able to work, are compelled to do so; if not, they are provided for in some less degrading way. . . .
4. That the poor are gradually but surely led from a state often bordering on pauperization to love self-dependence; while in many cases, actual paupers are reclaimed, and brought to acknowledge the true kindness of the Society's plan, as it rekindles their all but extinct sense of independence.

Source
Gurteen, Rev. S. Humphreys. *A Handbook of Charity Organization.* Buffalo, NY: Published by the Author, 1882, 118–130.

that the causes of poverty were often beyond an individual's control. Settlement houses became involved in supporting labor unions and in trying to change public policy.

Eventually the scientific charity movement also realized that poverty was not caused primarily by moral failings. As they visited with the poor and collected data about the poor, they began to realize that poverty was often caused by such circumstances as low wages, illness, unemployment, or death of a breadwinner. One of the founders of the scientific charity movement, Josephine Shaw Lowell, realized that a major cause of poverty was low wages and began to help organize the labor movement.

By the late 1800s and the turn of the century, the scientific charity movement began working closely with the settlement-house movement. They invited prominent settlement-house workers to speak at their national conference, and in 1909, Jane Addams, one of the most well-known of the settlement-house founders, was elected president of the scientific charity movement's National Conference of Charities and Correction (Davis 1967, 21).

Because of its emphasis on home visits and gathering data, the scientific charity movement led to the field of "social science" and the beginning of a new profession: social work. Gathering unbiased data required trained workers, and this need led to training schools and paid professionals.

See also: Addams, Jane; Lowell, Josephine Shaw; Outdoor Relief; Poorhouses; Private Charity; Settlement Houses

Sources

Davis, Allen F. *Spearheads for Reform: The Social Settlements and the Progressive Movement, 1890–1914.* New York: Oxford University Press, 1967.

Gurteen, Reverend S. Humphreys. *A Handbook of Charity Organization.* Buffalo, NY: Published by the Author, 1882.

Katz, Michael. *In the Shadow of the Poorhouse: A Social History of Welfare in America.* New York: Basic Books, 1996.

Myers-Lipton, Scott. *Social Solutions to Poverty: America's Struggle to Build a Just Society.* Boulder, CO: Paradigm Publishing, 2006.

Waugh, Joan. *Unsentimental Reformer: The Life of Josephine Shaw Lowell.* Cambridge, MA: Harvard University Press, 1997.

SEATTLE/DENVER INCOME MAINTENANCE EXPERIMENTS

During the 1960s and 1970s, there was enormous interest in one particular solution to poverty: the guaranteed annual income. The idea was that the government should ensure that everyone had a certain basic level of income, and should provide the money for that income if an individual was not earning enough. Such a system would replace the current patchwork of government programs for the poor, such as unemployment insurance, welfare payments, and Supplemental Security Income. Economists, business leaders, and advocates for the poor all called for some sort of guaranteed annual income or "negative income tax," as the concept is also called.

To test the feasibility of such a system, the federal government funded several studies on the effects of a negative income tax. The initial, smaller studies were conducted in New Jersey, Indiana, and North Carolina. Subsequently, two larger-scale experiments were conducted from 1970 to 1976, in Seattle, Washington, and Denver, Colorado. Economic experts predicted that a negative income tax might cause a disincentive to work, so researchers were interested in studying the effects on working hours of various kinds of negative income tax structures. They were interested in finding out whether the negative income tax had any effect on marital stability. Would it encourage marriage? At that time, families with two parents were generally not eligible for welfare payments (Aid to Families with Dependent Children), even if the man of the house was unemployed or was paid a very low income. Thus, many experts feared that welfare had the effect of discouraging marriage and two-parent families. The hope was that a negative income tax that was provided to any low-income family, regardless of whether a man was present in the house, would encourage couples to stay together.

About 4,800 families were recruited to participate in this study. Families were eligible if the head of the family was between eighteen and fifty-eight years old, and was physically capable of work. Families had to have total earnings of less than $9,000 per year (or less than $11,000 if both the husband and wife were working). Single-parent families were included, as were childless couples. Three ethnic groups were included: black, Chicano, and white. Participants were assigned to either a three-year experiment or a five-year experiment. Some of the participants were part of a "control group" and received no benefits at all during the duration of the experiment. Other participants were assigned to one of eleven different negative income tax plans. The plans had three different levels of guaranteed income combined with either three or four different tax situations (the percentage at which earnings above the guaranteed minimum would be taxed).

The lowest level of support was set at $3,800 per year for a family of four,

because this would ensure that the family's income never fell below the official federal poverty line. The experiment also tested support levels of $4,800 and $5,600 per year. These amounts were raised every year of the study to account for cost-of-living increases. The tax rate on earned income was set at either flat rates of 50 percent and 70 percent, or "declining" tax rates that started at 70 percent and 80 percent, and declined by 5 percent for each extra $1,000 earned. The researchers wanted to see whether the declining tax rate would encourage people to work more, because their tax rate would go down the more they earned. Families who earned too much to receive any government benefit were assured that, if their income were to fall below the level of the negative income tax (NIT) grant to which they were assigned, they would receive benefits.

All participants (except those in the control group) received free career counseling throughout the experiment. Some groups also received reimbursements for education and training programs: either a 50 percent reimbursement of costs, or a 100 percent reimbursement of costs. The idea was to counteract the disincentive to work with an incentive to find a more satisfying, better-paid job. Participants (including those in the control group) were interviewed three times per year, and asked about their job history, earnings, and marital status, among other questions. Data on each family was also collected from the Internal Revenue Service and the Social Security office (*Overview of the Final Report* 1983; Robins et al. 1980, 6–12).

The results of the experiment showed that members of families who received the negative income tax did have more money to spend: they received about $1,000 more per year than families in the control group. The recipients of the negative income tax worked somewhat fewer hours per year than members of families assigned to the control group, but they did not generally drop out of the labor market entirely, as some had feared. Larger NIT benefits were in general associated with fewer hours worked. For example, male heads of families receiving the lowest NIT benefit worked 6 percent to 9 percent less than male heads of families in the control group. Those receiving the highest NIT benefit worked 9 percent to 12 percent less than those in the control group. The variations in tax rates did not seem to have any clear effect on working hours (*Overview of the Final Report* 1983).

Oddly, the career counseling and education subsidies did not help participants earn more money, even a year after the experiment ended. For almost all groups, the counseling and education had the effect of slightly reducing earnings, although for the single mothers, counseling alone (with no reimbursement for education) did help them to earn about 10 percent more on average than single mothers in the control group. The researchers were puzzled over this finding. They speculated that perhaps the counseling encouraged participants to be overly ambitious in their career goals, and maybe the program did not offer enough training to achieve those goals. In addition, often participants took classes that were not work related. The experimenters suggest that

[e]vidently, the SIME/DIME counseling/training subsidy program induced short-run reductions in earnings without supporting the type of training or education that would enable participants to secure better paying jobs, at least during the one- to three-year follow-up period.... Perhaps the counseling and training experiences of those with ambitious upward mobility goals actually made it more difficult to pursue a career consisting of a series of relatively low-paying jobs. (*Overview of the Final Report* 1983)

For many government officials, the most disturbing findings of the experiment were its effects on marital stability. Among the families that received the negative income tax, black families experienced 61 percent more marital dissolution than families in the control group, and the white families experienced 58 percent more. Chicano families that received NIT benefits had slightly fewer divorces on average. Interestingly, as the negative income tax level of support rose, fewer marriages ended. For those families that received the highest level of guaranteed income, there was basically no difference in marriage dissolution compared with the control group. Researchers explained this by noting that, for families that already were experiencing marital distress before the experiment started, the support of a small negative income tax, without the stigma attached to food stamps and welfare benefits, could help them decide to leave the marriage. In contrast, families that received larger benefits perhaps experienced a lower level of stress and decided to stay in their marriages (Robins et al. 1980, 167–171).

What if a negative income tax were instituted nationwide, permanently? Would the results be similar to the limited-time experiments in SIME/DIME? While it is difficult to extrapolate from a limited-time experiment to a permanent system, researchers felt that the SIME/DIME experiment provided valuable information about how best to structure a negative income tax to provide an adequate level of support for everyone, and to reduce the disincentive to work. However, people in government who previously had been supporters of the guaranteed annual income idea turned against it because of its negative effects on marriage (*Overview of the Final Report* 1983; Steensland 2008, 214–215).

See also: Guaranteed Annual Income

Sources

Overview of the Final Report of the Seattle-Denver Income Maintenance Experiment. U.S. Department of Health and Human Services, May 1983. http://aspe.hhs.gov/HSP/SIME-DIME83/index.htm (accessed July 2008).

Robins, Philip K., Robert G. Spiegelman, Samuel Weiner, and Joseph G. Bell, eds. *A Guaranteed Annual Income: Evidence from a Social Experiment.* New York: Academic Press, 1980.

Steensland, Brian. *The Failed Welfare Revolution: America's Struggle over Guaranteed Income Policy.* Princeton, NJ: Princeton University Press, 2008.

SEGREGATION LAWS

Segregation laws were state and local laws that kept blacks poorly paid, badly educated, and politically powerless. These laws prohibited blacks from attending the same schools and colleges as whites; restricted them to the lowest-paid jobs; made it difficult or impossible for them to vote; and kept them out of many public facilities. These laws were also called Jim Crow laws, after a black character—played by a white man—in a minstrel show of the 1830s. The segregation laws remained largely in place until the civil rights movement of the 1950s and 1960s.

The first segregation laws were passed by northern states in the 1800s, while blacks were still enslaved in the southern states. Free blacks in the North were denied the right to vote in many states. They were denied access to white schools. They had to live in only certain poor areas of town and had to take the lowest-paid jobs. Some states—Illinois and Oregon—even prevented blacks from entering the state. After the Civil War, which ended in 1865, some of the segregation laws in northern states were repealed, although schools often remained segregated (Wormser 2003, xi).

Southern states began passing laws to restrict the rights of free blacks almost as soon as the Civil War ended. Early laws prohibited blacks from owning land and allowed unemployed blacks to be imprisoned. Black children could be taken away from their parents and forced to work as apprentices. The laws permitted the whipping of black workers by employers. Some laws stated that blacks could work only in agriculture or as domestic servants. Some states passed laws prohibiting blacks from voting. Blacks were often barred from trains, parks, theaters, hotels, and other public places. These early segregation laws were called "black codes" (Wormser 2003, 8–9; Packard 2002, 42–43).

In response to the discrimination against free blacks, the Fourteenth and Fifteenth Amendments were added to

Group of African American students in a crowded school room, seated three to a seat, Pleasant Grove, South Carolina, 1934. (Library of Congress)

the U.S. Constitution. These amendments declared that blacks were citizens of the United States, and allowed black men to vote. During the first dozen years after the Civil War, federal government provided money and resources to maintain the freedom of the blacks in the southern states, and to help them get started economically. This is called the Reconstruction Era. The federal government also passed civil rights laws soon after the Civil War. The Civil Rights Act of 1866 gave full citizenship to African Americans. The Civil Rights Act of 1875 guaranteed equal treatment in public accommodations, regardless of race. This law was ruled unconstitutional by the U.S. Supreme Court in 1883, because it regulated the actions of private companies.

By 1877, the federal government had gotten tired of helping the South. Federal troops were withdrawn. Southern states began passing more segregation laws, and creating separate schools and public facilities for blacks and whites. The facilities for blacks were invariably inferior to those for whites. These Jim Crow laws were upheld by the U.S. Supreme Court in 1896, which declared in *Plessy v. Ferguson* that states could make laws requiring separate facilities for blacks and whites. During this time, says Jerrold Packard, "Jim Crow spread like pestilence.... Jim Crow became what it meant to be Southern" (2002, 65).

After the *Plessy* decision, more states began segregating everything from water fountains, waiting rooms, elevators, and building entrances, to hospitals and prisons—even cemeteries. Blacks were barred entirely from certain parks, swimming pools, beaches, neighborhoods, and entire towns. Blacks who attempted to flout these laws—by trying to register a black child at a "white" school, or by drinking from a "white" drinking fountain—could be arrested and fined or even imprisoned (Packard 2002, 163; Wormser 2003, 105).

In addition to official government laws and punishments, blacks in southern states also had to contend with unofficial punishment meted out by white supremacist groups such as the Ku Klux Klan. Blacks who were thought to have violated a segregation law or custom were threatened, harassed, and even killed (this kind of murder was called "lynching"). State and local law enforcement often looked the other way or even participated in these kinds of actions.

BLACK JOBS AND WHITE JOBS

Ralph Thompson discusses the segregation at his job in Memphis, Tennessee, in 1959:

After being discharged from the military, I just had little haphazard jobs and finally got a job at International Harvester which was one of the bigger manufacturing companies here in the city. . . . When I went in, they hired about 50 people that day. I was the only black person in the crowd and I can remember that guy coming into the conference room and he looked over and saw me in that crowd and he said, "Did I call your name?" And I said, "Yeah." He asked me my name and I told him, and he went and looked at his list to make sure I was on that list. And I guess out of a 100–150 [applicants] they only hired about five blacks. . . . And naturally, I had some business college, but I had graduated from high school, so I ended up working in the foundry for most of my time there, because it was segregated, and when you went into jobs they were basically "white jobs" and "black jobs." And black jobs were basically in the foundry. You went anywhere else, you were either disqualified or you were given such a hard time that you had to leave.

Source: Chafe, William H., Raymond Gavins, and Robert Korstad, eds. *Remembering Jim Crow: African Americans Tell About Life in the Segregated South.* New York: The New Press, 2001, 257.

Blacks began organizing and demanding their rights. In 1909, W. E. B. Du Bois and other activists founded the National Association for the Advancement of Colored People (NAACP). They publicized lynchings and brought legal cases to court to strike down segregation laws. In 1917, they won a case to enable black men to be commissioned as officers during World War I, and in 1946, they won a case that desegregated interstate bus and train travel. In 1954, they won an important case: *Brown v. Board of Education,* which overturned the *Plessy* decision. The U.S. Supreme Court declared that segregation in education was unconstitutional (NAACP Timeline).

This ruling was an inspiration for the mass demonstrations during the 1950s and 1960s of the civil rights movement, which resulted in the Civil Rights Act of 1964. This law made it illegal to deny someone education or employment on the basis of race, and made it illegal to keep blacks and other racial minorities out of public places. The Voting Rights Act of 1965 helped overcome the century of laws aimed at preventing blacks from voting.

The civil rights movement succeeded in wiping out all state and local segregation laws. Today, blacks and whites can attend the same schools and colleges, apply for the same jobs, and use the same public facilities. Because blacks suffer disproportionately from poverty, and because blacks and whites often live in different neighborhoods, blacks and whites often do attend different schools, and blacks tend to be lower-paid than whites.

See also: Civil Rights Act of 1964; Civil Rights Movement; Freedmen's Bureau; Great Depression; King, Martin Luther, Jr.; National Association for the Advancement of Colored People; Reconstruction Era; Reparations for Slavery; Slavery; Voting Rights Act of 1965

Sources

Packard, Jerrold M. *American Nightmare: The History of Jim Crow.* New York: St. Martin's Press, 2002.

Wormser, Richard. *The Rise and Fall of Jim Crow.* New York: St. Martin's Press, 2003.

Web Site

NAACP (National Association for the Advancement of Colored People) Timeline. http://www.naacp.org/about/history/timeline/index.htm (accessed July 2008).

SETTLEMENT HOUSES

In the late 1800s and early 1900s, settlement houses flourished in many cities of the United States. These were communal living arrangements, like college dorms, which allowed upper-class college graduates to live among the poor and experience life in a poor area. More than 400 such houses existed by 1910. Although the settlement-house movement was a private movement, its members often sought to influence the government to pass laws to help the poor.

While individual settlement houses may not have had much impact on reducing poverty in their neighborhoods, the settlement-house movement was influential on the national level: some people who lived or worked in settlement houses went on to become important leaders in the government during the New Deal, President Franklin Roosevelt's set of programs to combat poverty during the Great Depression

of the 1930s. These included Harry Hopkins, Frances Perkins, and even First Lady Eleanor Roosevelt (who worked briefly at a settlement house in New York City). Because of their experiences living and working among the poor, these former settlement-house workers were often able to create effective government policies to combat poverty. In addition, some of the larger settlement houses were able to reform laws and policies within their neighborhoods, cities, and states.

At first, settlement house residents were involved with providing cultural and artistic outlets for the poor—such as book clubs and art shows—and running nursery schools for poor working mothers. They also provided English and American history classes for poor immigrants, set up playgrounds for children, and agitated for amenities like cleaner streets and public bathhouses. Later, some settlement house residents began working to change local, state, and national laws to help the poor.

The settlement-house movement started first in England: Toynbee Hall was founded in 1884, by an Anglican clergyman, Samuel Barnett, and Oxford University students in the slums of East London. The goal was to bring together the rich and the poor, and to offer more than charity. In Barnett's views, "the poor need more than food; they need also the knowledge, the character, the happiness which are the gifts of God to this Age." Barnett hoped that not only would the poor be educated through the settlement movement, but also that the upper-class settlement residents would experience an education or transformation through their interactions with the poor (Davis 1967, 7).

Immigrant girls learn to knit at the Henry Street Settlement in New York, 1910. Photo attributed to Lewis Hine. (Library of Congress)

Some educated Americans visited Toynbee Hall, were inspired, and returned to the United States to set up similar houses. The first American house, Neighborhood Guild (later renamed University Settlement), was started in 1886, in the Lower East Side of New York City by several young men who were intellectuals, ministers, and Socialists. In 1889, seven college-educated young women started College Settlement nearby. The most famous and one of the longest-lived of the American settlement houses, Hull House in Chicago, was started in 1889 by Jane Addams and Ellen Starr, two college graduates. By 1897, there were seventy-four settlement houses in the United States, by 1900, more than 100, and by 1910, 400. While some of these settlements had a religious basis, most were nonsectarian. Most of the settlement houses were located in Chicago, Boston, New York, and Philadelphia. The southern and western United States had few settlement houses (Davis 1967, 12, 15–16, 23).

Most of the well-off young women and men who lived in settlement houses stayed only for a few years, and most were from old American families of English, Scotch, or Irish descent. After 1900, many children of immigrants who had benefited from settlement houses in their neighborhoods as they were growing up, returned to live for a time in a settlement house (Davis 1967, 33–34).

In addition to providing classes and playgrounds, the settlement houses soon became involved in political and labor activities. The residents came to see that the causes of poverty included low wages, unsafe working conditions that caused disabling injuries, and other factors beyond the control of the poor. Labor unions often met at settlement houses, and some houses tried to bring workers and employers together for lectures or discussions.

Settlement houses also worked to change laws and influence the government. Florence Kelley, a resident of Hull House, was appointed by the Illinois State Bureau of Labor to investigate child labor in the state. After completing her report in the early 1890s, she and Hull House worked to pass laws to limit and eventually outlaw child labor. Following this example, settlement houses in other states also pushed for child labor laws. The settlement-house movement was instrumental in pushing for the formation of the U.S. Children's Bureau, the first government agency in the world dedicated solely to the welfare of children (Skocpol 1992, 482–483).

In the early 1900s, the settlement movement joined with the "scientific charity" movement to conduct studies of poverty. They put together a committee and, with financial support from a private foundation, studied the city of Pittsburgh for several years, publishing their results in six volumes. The Pittsburgh Survey, which investigated low pay, diseases, industrial accidents, and unsuitable housing, was discussed across the country and led to other surveys and a movement to reform laws.

The settlement-house movement dwindled during and after World War I, which began in 1914. Many settlement workers became involved with peace activities during the war. After the war, in the 1920s, the country as a whole experienced prosperity, and fewer people were concerned about poverty. There were fewer donations and fewer young people interested in living in a settlement house. In addition, it sometimes seemed to settlement residents that their work was finished. As Allen Davis puts it,

> part of the settlement workers' problem in the 1920s resulted from their own success. College Settlement in New York was typical. A Carnegie library two blocks away had made the settlement library unnecessary; a public bath had replaced the settlement bath; two public parks had made the settlement playground obsolete. (1967, 234)

Many of the young people who did choose to live in a settlement house in the 1920s were trained social workers; and over the years, while a number of settlement houses closed, others evolved into neighborhood centers staffed by professionals who often did not live in the house. As late as 1980, 110 neighborhood centers were identified as being part of the settlement-house tradition (Trolander 1987, 4).

According to the Jane Addams Hull House Association Web site, for example, Hull House continues today as a neighborhood center, providing services such as child care, domestic violence counseling and prevention, job training, literacy training, and housing assistance to 60,000 people in and around Chicago.

See also: Addams, Jane; Child Labor Laws; Children's Bureau; Hopkins, Harry; Kelley, Florence; Lathrop, Julia; New Deal Women's Network; Perkins, Frances; Playgrounds; Progressive Era; Roosevelt, Eleanor; Scientific Charity; Wald, Lillian

Sources

Davis, Allen F. *Spearheads for Reform: The Social Settlements and the Progressive Movement, 1890–1914.* New York: Oxford University Press, 1967.

Skocpol, Theda. *Protecting Soldiers and Mothers: The Political Origins of Social Policy in the United States.* Cambridge, MA: Harvard University Press, 1992.

Trolander, Judith Ann. *Professionalism and Social Change: From the Settlement House Movement to Neighborhood Centers, 1886 to the Present.* New York: Columbia University Press, 1987.

Web Site

Jane Addams Hull House Association. http://www.hullhouse.org/ (accessed December 2007).

SHEPPARD-TOWNER MATERNITY AND INFANCY ACT OF 1921

The Sheppard-Towner Act, also called the "Act for the Promotion of the Welfare and Hygiene of Maternity and Infancy," was one of the first major welfare programs run by the federal government. Although this law existed for only eight years, it funded almost 3,000 child and maternal health centers in forty-five states, mostly in rural areas, and set the stage for future federal help to poor women and children through the New Deal programs during the Great Depression. It also spurred private medical doctors to begin offering preventive health care services, instead of only treating those who were already ill.

This maternal and child health law was first proposed by the first head of the U.S. Children's Bureau, Julia Lathrop. Using statistics collected by the Children's Bureau, Lathrop pointed out that the maternal mortality and infant mortality rates in the United States were higher than those in other wealthy countries. Although Children's Bureau statistics showed a link between poverty and the deaths of infants and mothers, Lathrop wanted her program to apply to all women and children—not just the poor—because she wanted to avoid the stigma of a charity program.

At that time, medical doctors—when they were available—treated only sick people. They did not provide help and counseling to healthy pregnant women or healthy children to prevent them from falling sick. In addition, medical care was often not available in rural or poor areas of the country. The Children's Bureau wanted to educate pregnant women and new mothers so they could keep themselves and their children healthy, and to offer health services to those women who did not have access to private medical care (Skocpol 1992, 516).

This bill was opposed by powerful groups, such as the American Medical Association (AMA), and was criticized for introducing government control into health care. Nevertheless the bill passed in 1921, largely due to the active support of women's organizations across the country, who urged their members of Congress to vote for the bill. These organizations included the General Federation of Women's Clubs and the National Congress of Mothers. Women's magazines such as *Good Housekeeping* urged their readers to write to their members of Congress in support of the bill. Theda Skocpol points out that women had just won the vote in 1920. Many members of Congress were fearful that the women's vote would cost them their seat, and so they voted for the Sheppard-Towner Act (1992, 500–505).

The Sheppard-Towner Act provided for $1 million to be given to states to establish programs for women's and children's health. To receive the money, each state had to provide an equal amount of state dollars and establish a state agency to coordinate the health programs. By the end of 1922, forty-two out of the forty-eight states had accepted the federal money, and eventually three more states also joined. Again, women's organizations within each state were active in persuading the states to set up programs. While each state could set up its own programs, the Children's Bureau provided information pamphlets to hand out to mothers and also encouraged the states to work toward decreasing infant mortality (Skocpol 1992, 481, 506–509).

The Sheppard-Towner Act was successful in reaching women in remote areas far from private medical services. In addition to the health clinics set up by the Sheppard-Towner Act, doctors and public health nurses also held conferences for pregnant women and mothers in churches, schools, and homes. The Children's Bureau sometimes provided a special truck set up as a child health center, to travel to remote areas, and states set up similar buses. Spanish-speaking nurses worked with the Hispanic population in New Mexico, Arizona, and Texas. Minnesota and Nebraska made special efforts to reach their Native American populations. African Americans in southern states benefited from expanded health services as well (Skocpol 1992, 509–510).

In addition to employing mostly female doctors and nurses, the Sheppard-Towner Act and the Children's Bureau sought to make use of midwives who already were providing help to pregnant women. Since no one knew how many midwives were working at that time, the Children's Bureau distributed a questionnaire and then estimated about 45,000 midwives were practicing across the country. At that time, midwives generally were considered to be working outside of standard medical practice. In fact, Grace Abbot, then head of the Children's Bureau, believed that care by a medical doctor was superior to that of a midwife. Nevertheless, because there simple were not enough medical doctors to serve all women, the Children's Bureau sought to educate and license midwives, rather than to outlaw them (Bradbury 1974, 24; Lindenmeyer 1997, 96).

About 4 million infants and children, and 700,000 pregnant women, were helped through this law. This work may have contributed to the decline in infant mortality. In 1921, among the states that kept statistics, about seventy-six babies died for every 1,000 live births. By 1929, this had decreased to sixty-eight per 1,000 (Lindenmeyer 1997, 97, 104).

The Sheppard-Towner Act was so successful and so well established that, in 1926, its supporters thought it would be easy to pass an extension of its funding, which was scheduled to run out in 1927. However, in 1926, the AMA—made up of male doctors—launched a strong campaign against the law. The AMA opposed the Sheppard-Towner Act, saying that it was government intrusion into health care. By this time, influenced by the preventive health clinics set up by the Sheppard-Towner Act, private medical doctors had also started preventive care to help people to stay healthy. Because of pressure from the AMA and others opposed to the law, the Sheppard-Towner Act was funded only until 1929, after which time the entire program would end (Skocpol, 1992, 514–516).

Despite this setback, the Children's Bureau staff believed they could win more funding from the next session of Congress. However, they were not successful in this quest. Some states continued to fund their health clinics even after federal funding stopped, but the Great Depression, which started in 1929, meant that much less money was available for maternal and child health, and many states dropped the program (Skocpol 1992, 514–515).

After the death of the Sheppard-Towner Act, the Children's Bureau was able to introduce, during the 1930s New Deal, new federal funding to help poor women and children: Title V of the Social Security Act, passed in 1935, included funding for maternal and child health clinics.

See also: Children's Bureau; Lathrop, Julia; Maternal and Child Health Services; New Deal; Social Security Act

Sources

Bradbury, Dorothy E. "Five Decades of Action for Children: A History of the Children's Bureau." Reprinted in *The United States Children's Bureau, 1912–1972,* ed. Robert H. Bremner. New York: Arno Press, 1974.

Lindenmeyer, Kriste. *A Right to Childhood: The U.S. Children's Bureau and Child Welfare, 1912–1946.* Urbana, IL: University of Illinois Press, 1997.

Skocpol, Theda. *Protecting Soldiers and Mothers: The Political Origins of Social Policy in the United States.* Cambridge, MA: Harvard University Press, 1992.

SINCLAIR, UPTON
(1878–1968)

Upton Sinclair was one of the most prominent "muckraking" journalists of the Progressive Era. He aimed to reveal the horrors of urban poverty and slum life through his writing. His novel *The Jungle,* published in 1906, exposed the unsanitary conditions of the meat-processing industry, and led to pure food laws and meat inspection laws. In 1934, during the Great Depression, Sinclair was successful at gaining the Democratic nomination for governor of California on a platform that emphasized ending poverty. His plan was called Ending Poverty in California (EPIC). Sinclair lost the election, but candidates running on his EPIC

Upton Sinclair enjoyed a long career as a prolific author of novels and nonfiction works attacking the country's economic and social ills in the name of social justice. Abroad, he was one of the best-known American authors of the time. (Library of Congress)

platform won thirty seats in the California legislature (Biles 1991, 120).

Upton Beall Sinclair, Jr. was born on September 20, 1878, in Baltimore, Maryland, and moved to New York City at the age of ten. His ancestors were wealthy southerners, and his maternal grandfather was secretary-treasurer of a railroad company and kept a "fashionable home," in Sinclair's words (1962, 9). His father was a traveling salesman, and although he earned good money, he tended to spend it on drink. The family often lived in boardinghouses, although Sinclair also spent months living with his wealthy grandfather and other relatives. In this way, he says, he became familiar with a variety of social classes (Mattson 2006, 23).

As a teenager, Sinclair began writing stories and selling them to magazines. He soon found he could make decent money through writing, and during his teenage and college years, he continued to sell jokes, stories, and juvenile novels to support himself and his mother. He sometimes produced as much as 8,000 words per day. At the age of twenty-two, after attending the College of the City of New York and Columbia University, Sinclair decided to abandon this kind of hack writing and devote his life to literary writing (Arthur 2006, 6–11).

His first attempts at literary novels did not interest publishers, however, and, even after Sinclair published them himself, they did not sell well. He found it extremely difficult to support himself, his wife, and their new baby. His wife's father helped them out financially. At the age of twenty-four, he was introduced to the ideas of socialism, and he attempted a new novel that included Socialist ideas, but

again he was not able to interest publishers (Arthur 2006, 21–22).

In 1904, his luck began to change. He asked for and received a year's living expenses from a Socialist weekly newspaper, *Appeal to Reason,* to research and write a novel about "wage slavery"—the exploitation of low-income workers—which Sinclair thought was similar to black slavery. The work was to be serialized in the newspaper. He also received an advance from a publishing company. He chose the Chicago stockyards as his theme, and spent seven weeks in Chicago, touring the stockyards and interviewing workers (Arthur 2006, 41–42). He was overwhelmed by the poverty and squalor that he found: "I went about, white-faced and thin, partly from undernourishment, partly from horror. It seemed to me I was confronting a veritable fortress of oppression," he writes in his autobiography (Sinclair 1962, 109).

The Jungle, the novel that emerged from his research, became a bestseller. It tells the story of a family of Lithuanian immigrants working in the Chicago meat-processing industry, and struggling to live in the slums of Chicago. Sinclair sent a copy to President Theodore Roosevelt, who was also receiving about 100 letters a day from readers of *The Jungle,* demanding that he do something about the dangerous and filthy situation of the meat-packing industry. Roosevelt invited Sinclair to meet with him, and Sinclair recommended a secret investigation of the industry. The commission that Roosevelt sent to Chicago confirmed the facts Sinclair had recorded in his novel. A Pure Food and Drug bill was introduced into Congress and, after some publicity work by Sinclair, passed in June 1906. The law called for federal inspections of meat-

"LIBERALS WERE HORRIFIED"

Frances Perkins, who was secretary of labor in President Franklin Roosevelt's administration, relates how people, including the president, reacted to Upton Sinclair's End Poverty in California (EPIC) plan:

I remember coming back from a trip to California when Upton Sinclair was running for Governor in a hot campaign, and his program, known as EPIC (End Poverty in California), was gaining adherence. Sober liberals in California were horrified. They begged me to tell the President that help would be needed from him to stem the tide of votes for Sinclair.

I went to see [Roosevelt] and told him the program was fanatic. I said there was danger that Sinclair might be elected and EPIC imposed, and that it would ruin the California banking system, according to the judgment of our friends in California.

He thought a minute. "Well, they might be elected in California. Perhaps they'll get EPIC in California. What difference, I ask you, would that make in Dutchess County, New York, or Lincoln County, Maine? The beauty of our state-federal system is that the people can experiment. If it has fatal consequences in one place, it has little effect upon the rest of the country. If a new, apparently fanatical, program works well, it will be copied. If it doesn't, you won't hear of it again."

Source: Perkins, Frances. *The Roosevelt I Knew.* New York: Viking Press, 1946, 124.

packing plants (Sinclair 1962, 118–121; Arthur 2006, 81–82).

With the money he earned from *The Jungle,* Sinclair set up a Socialist, cooperative community in a former boys' school in Englewood, New Jersey. The community, named Helicon Hall, started in November 1906 with twenty-four members, many of whom were writers and academics. The goal of the community was to share the housework and child care, and to cut living expenses, to allow the adults the freedom to pursue their writing, art, or research. The community ended six months later when a fire destroyed their building. Sinclair then lived for a time in two other cooperative communities, Fairhope in Alabama, and Arden in Delaware, all the while continuing to write books. However, none of his subsequent books achieved the fame or sales of *The Jungle* (Arthur 2006, 84–105, 122–128).

In 1916, he moved to southern California. "A friend had told me about the wonders of southern California, where there were no mosquitoes," he writes in his autobiography (1962, 211). He wanted to live in a warm place and play tennis. He made friends with Socialists, continued writing, and got involved with a new organization, the southern California chapter of the American Civil Liberties Union, which supported freedom of speech (Mattson 2006, 132–133).

In 1929, the Great Depression started with the crash of the stock market. Sinclair and other Socialists

PRIMARY DOCUMENT 37

Excerpt from Immediate EPIC: The Final Statement of the Plan, by Upton Sinclair

The answer to the question "What will you do first?" is "We will get production started. We will do it by any lawful method we can devise. We will get the unemployed factory workers into the factories and start the wheels turning. We will get access to the land for the unemployed land-workers, and each of these groups will produce as rapidly as possible, and will exchange their products among themselves, and thus enable them to become self-supporting, and put an end to that drain which is ruining the tax-payers."

In the little book, "I, Governor of California" I have drawn a picture of land colonies, in which great tracts of land are worked by modern machinery under the direction of agricultural experts, and in which the workers are comfortably housed in modern dwellings, with the use of social halls, community kitchens and dining-rooms, theaters, schools, churches, etc. I have imagined great factories placed near the sources of raw material, and with model villages erected for the housing of the workers. All that is within the scope of the Plan, and all that will be done; but it cannot be done at once, and we are discussing here the emergency steps to get production going; the method whereby the people of California, who have not forgotten how to work and are still willing to work, are to get the opportunity to work....

I have to make sure the reader understands the basic point, that we shall be turning out goods FOR USE. At the present time the private owner of the factory cannot turn out dresses, because he cannot find anybody to buy them at a profit; therefore his factory stands idle. But if the State puts the unemployed at producing for themselves, the problem vanishes; because every woman in our EPIC setup will proceed without hesitation to wear four new dresses per year. If we drive ahead too fast and make ten dresses a year, the sensible ones among the women will ask that we reduce the hours of the workers in the dress-factory, and let them have more time in which to show off the dresses already made....

Let us now examine another method of getting immediate production. Of the 10,121 factories in California, more than 1,600 are wholly out of use. Some of these have been dismantled and are out of repair. The owners are holding their property with difficulty, many being in arrears with their taxes. If the State should make an offer to rent these factories, giving certificates receivable for taxes, the owners would jump at the chance.

How can such factories be reconditioned and started up? The people have provided their answer in the form of co-operative, barter, and self-help groups all over California....

For two generations or more, the American people have been victimized by a propaganda which identifies Americanism with capitalism. For my part, I assert that these self-help and barter groups represent Americanism more truly than any other phenomenon of our time. They embody all our true pioneer virtues—self-reliance, initiative, frugality, equality, neighborliness. They are the most precious products of the depression; and what have we done with them? The answer is that we have done everything to handicap them, to humiliate them, to buy their leaders away from them, to corrupt and finally to exterminate them.

Why have we done this? Partly because they are believed to threaten "big business," but mainly because they threaten the "relief racket", which has become the mainstay of the politicians in these difficult times....

One of the declared purposes of EPIC is to put the credit power of the State behind the co-operatives and enable them to grow. All they ask is the use of the idle factories, with any old machinery they can find. They will put it into running order and start it up, and having got hold of one product, they will exchange it until they have all other products....

Let us next consider the question of food production within our EPIC system....

Every city and town in California today is ringed round with tracts of good land which the speculators are holding "for a rise." These speculators are most of them in trouble. Their taxes are in arrears and much of the land has reverted to the State. If the State offers to rent the land for even a portion of the taxes, the owners will eagerly agree, and if the State furnishes seed and tools and competent direction, we shall soon have thriving gardens surrounding our cities—a much pleasanter spectacle than the burned-over weeds we now gaze upon. By this method I believe that any Governor of California who is really thinking about the welfare of the people, instead of about his own political machine and the profits of his campaign contributors, can have an army of men at work within one or two months after the time he takes office....

THE EPIC PLAN

1. A legislative enactment for the establishment of State land colonies whereby the unemployed may become self-sustaining and cease to be a burden upon the taxpayers. A public body, the California Authority for Land (the CAL) will take the idle land, and land sold for taxes and at foreclosure sales, and erect dormitories, kitchens, cafeterias, and social rooms, and cultivate the land using modern machinery under the guidance of experts.

2. A public body entitled the California Authority for Production (the CAP), will be authorized to acquire factories and production plants whereby the unemployed may produce the basic necessities required for themselves and for the land colonies, and to operate these factories and house and feed and care for the workers. CAL and CAP will maintain a distribution system for the exchange of each other's products. The industries will include laundries, bakeries, canneries, clothing and shoe factories, cement-plants, brick-yards, lumber yards, thus constituting a complete industrial system, a new and self-sustaining world for those our present system cannot employ.

3. A public body entitled the California Authority for Money (the CAM) will handle the financing of CAL and CAP. This body will issue scrip to be paid to the workers and used in the exchanging of products within the system. It will also issue bonds to cover the purchase of land and factories, the erection of buildings and the purchase of machinery.

4. An act of the legislature repealing the present sales tax, and substituting a tax on stock transfers at the rate of 4 cents per share.

5. An act of the legislature providing for a State income tax, beginning with incomes of $5000 and steeply graduated until incomes of $50,000 would pay 30% tax.

6. An increase in the State inheritance tax, steeply graduated and applying to all property in the State regardless of where the owner may reside. This law would take 50% of sums above $50,000 bequeathed to any individual and 50% of sums above $250,000 bequeathed by any individual.

7. A law increasing the taxes on privately owned public utility corporations and banks.

8. A constitutional amendment revising the tax code of the State, providing that cities and counties shall exempt from taxation all homes occupied by the owners and ranches cultivated by the owners, wherever the assessed value of such homes and ranches is less than $3000. Upon properties assessed at more than $5000 there will be a tax increase of one-half of one per cent for each $5000 of additional assessed valuation.

9. A constitutional amendment providing for a State land tax upon unimproved building land and agricultural land which is not under cultivation. The first $1000 of assessed valuation to be exempt, and the tax to be graduated according to the value of land held by the individual. Provision to be made for a state building loan fund for those who wish to erect homes.

10. A law providing for the payment of a pension of $50 per month to every needy person over sixty years of age who has lived in the State of California three years prior to the date of the coming into effect of the law.

11. A law providing for the payment of $50 per month to all persons who are blind, or who by medical examination are proved to be physically unable to earn a living; these persons also having been residents of the State for three years.

12. A pension of $50 per month to all widowed women who have dependent children; if the children are more than two in number, the pension to be increased by $25 per month for each additional child. These also to have been residents three years in the State.

Source

Upton Sinclair. "Immediate EPIC: The Final Statement of the Plan." Social Security Administration History Archives. http://www.ssa.gov/history/epic.html (accessed February 13, 2009).

believed they had the answer to the widespread poverty and unemployment of the Depression: the government needed to provide the money to put people back to work. Sinclair had already tried running for office as a Socialist Party member several times, with little success. In 1934, he decided to run for governor of California as a Democrat. Sinclair started the EPIC movement and ran his campaign based on this movement. The movement would result in "a gigantic statewide cooperative," in the words of Sinclair biographer Anthony Arthur, and would be financed by high taxes on the very rich (Arthur 2006, 258).

Although he had gained few votes as a Socialist candidate, he was popular as a Democrat, and won that party's nomination for governor. Sinclair's goal was larger than winning the governorship of California: "We might not win," he wrote in his autobiography, "but if we cast a big vote we would force the Roosevelt administration to take relief measures" (1962, 271). Sinclair did not win the governorship, in part because Democratic President Franklin Roosevelt did not support him. Still, he made a good showing, winning more than 37 percent of the vote (Arthur 2006, 276–277).

The campaign had brought national attention to the ideas of the EPIC movement. Sinclair was getting ten pounds of mail a day. Sinclair's popularity perhaps encouraged President Roosevelt to move left politically, and to pass the Social Security Act and the National Labor Relations Act (Mattson 2006, 185–186).

See also: Great Depression; National Labor Relations Act; Progressive Era; Roosevelt, Franklin Delano; Socialism; Social Security Act

Sources

Arthur, Anthony. *Radical Innocent: Upton Sinclair.* New York: Random House, 2006.

Biles, Roger. *A New Deal for the American People.* DeKalb, IL: Northern Illinois University Press, 1991.

Mattson, Kevin. *Upton Sinclair and the Other American Century.* Hoboken, NJ: John Wiley and Sons, 2006.

Sinclair, Upton. *The Autobiography of Upton Sinclair.* New York: Harcourt Brace and World, 1962.

SLAVERY

Black slavery in the United States started during the colonial era. Slavery was written into state laws starting in the late 1600s, and the institution was accepted by the U.S. Constitution in 1787. Slave traders earned a profit by capturing and enslaving other humans, and slaveholders believed that they profited economically from the labor of slaves. In other words, black people were legally impoverished to provide wealth and prosperity for whites.

The first Africans were brought to the colonies in 1619 aboard a Dutch ship that had captured Africans in the Caribbean. In Jamestown, the Dutch shipowner traded the slaves for food. The Jamestown colonists were glad to have these workers for their tobacco farms. These first Africans were considered to be "indentured servants," bound to work for a period of years for their masters, after which they received their freedom. Indentured servitude was common in colonial America, and most indentured servants were poor white Europeans.

Soon, however, African servants began to be treated differently from whites. Africans were assumed to be barbarous, wild, and savage, and in need of the "civilizing" effects of slavery in a Christian country. As early as the 1640s, some Africans were enslaved for life. The colonists began passing laws to codify the slaves' legal status. In 1662, Virginia passed a law that children of slave mothers and free white masters would be slaves. In 1664, Maryland passed a law stating that a white woman who married a black slave would become a slave herself, as would her children. The first "slave code"—a law defining who was a slave—was passed in 1691, by Maryland. Other states passed similar slave codes.

By the time of the American Revolution in the late 1700s, all colonies had slave codes, stating that slaves were of African descent, served for life, inherited their slave status from their mother, and could be bought and sold. Most slaves lived in the southern colonies—the population of South Carolina, for example, was majority African. Slaves in the south worked on tobacco and cotton plantations, which depended on their labor. However, northern colonists also kept slaves. In 1750, New York slaves made up 15 percent of the population, and in Rhode Island, slaves accounted for 10 percent of the population. By 1770, almost 40 percent of the colonial population was made up of slaves (Horton and Horton 2005, 27–34, 41).

In the 1700s, some colonists began protesting the institution of slavery. Quakers were among the first. In 1758, a group of Philadelphia Quakers condemned slavery and removed any slaveholder leaders of their church. Quakers published antislavery pamphlets, and some Quaker meetings provided support to freed slaves. In 1773, Quaker meetings began to disown slaveholders who refused to free their slaves. As white Americans began pressing for freedom from British rule, black slaves wrote petitions and letters to government leaders, asking for freedom. Even some slaveholders began wondering about the morality of slavery. Instead of assuming that Africans were savage and fit only for slavery—a common belief in the past—more

people in the late 1700s began questioning these stereotypes (Kolchin 1993, 64–67; Horton and Horton 2005, 50–52, 55).

During the Revolutionary War, which began in 1775, many slaves fought on the side of the British, because some British leaders promised them freedom if the British won. During the confusion of the war, a large number of slaves also escaped from their owners and some found refuge with the British. South Carolina, for example, lost an estimated 30 percent of its slaves due to escape and death during the war. After the war, which ended in 1783, states revised their laws on slavery. New laws in Virginia, Maryland, and Delaware made it easier for slaveholders to free their slaves. Some northern states freed their slaves even before the war ended: Vermont was first, in 1777, followed by Massachusetts. Other northern states passed laws allowing the gradual emancipation of slaves. Northern and some southern states also began banning the importation of slaves from Africa. By 1810, 75 percent of blacks in the north were free.

The U.S. Constitution was adopted in 1787, and although it does not use the word "slavery," it accepted the fact of slavery. Because some southern states still demanded to be able to import slaves from Africa, the Constitution contained a provision that the Congress could not outlaw the slave trade until 1808, which it did in legislation passed in 1807. The Constitution also specified that slaves fleeing to non-slave-holding states would not be free, but had to be returned to their owners.

In addition to prohibiting the slave trade from Africa, the U.S. Congress took action to restrict the spread of

PRIMARY DOCUMENT 38

Slave Code—Virginia, 1705

This is one of the first American colonial laws to specify who is a slave and who is not. This law specifies that those who were not Christian before being brought into the colonies would be slaves. Even if a slave converts to Christianity after entering the colonies, that person is still a slave.

October 1705-CHAP. XLIX. An act concerning Servants and Slaves.

IV. And also be it enacted, by the authority aforesaid, and it is hereby enacted, That all servants imported and brought into this country, by sea or land, who were not christians in their native country, (except Turks and Moors in amity with her majesty, and others that can make due proof their being free in England, or any other christian country, before they were shipped, in order to transportation hither) shall be accounted and be slaves, and as such be here bought and sold notwithstanding a conversion to christianity afterwards.

V. And be it enacted, by the authority aforesaid, and it is hereby enacted, That if any person or persons shall hereafter import into this colony, and here sell as a slave, any person or persons that shall have been a freeman in any christian country, island, or plantation, such importer and seller as aforesaid, shall forfeit and pay, to the party from who the said freeman shall recover his freedom, double the sum for which the said freeman was sold. To be recovered, in any court of record within this colony, according to the course of the common law, wherein the defendant shall not be admitted to plead in bar, any act or statute for limitation of actions.

VI. Provided always, That a slave's being in England, shall not be sufficient to discharge him of his slavery, without other proof of his being manumitted there.

XI. And for a further christian care and usage of all christian servants, Be it

also enacted, by the authority aforesaid, and it is hereby enacted, That no negros, mulattos, or Indians, although christians, or Jews, Moors, Mahometans, or other infidels, shall, at any time, purchase any christian servant, nor any other, except of their own complexion, or such as are declared slaves by this act: And if any negro, mulatto, or Indian, Jew, Moor, Mahometan, or other infidel, or such as are declared slaves by this act, shall, notwithstanding, purchase any christian white servant, the said servant shall, ipso facto, become free and acquit from any service then due, and shall be so held, deemed, and taken: And if any person, having such christian servant, shall intermarry with any such negro, mulatto, or Indian, Jew, Moor, Mahometan, or other infidel, every christian white servant of every such person so intermarrying, shall, ipso facto, become free and acquit from any service then due to such master or mistress so intermarrying, as aforesaid.

XV. And also be it enacted, by the authority aforesaid, and it is hereby enacted, That no person whatsoever shall, buy, sell, or receive of, to, or from, any servant, or slave, any coin or commodity whatsoever, without the leave, licence, or consent of the master or owner of the said servant, or slave: And if any person shall, contrary hereunto, without the leave or licence aforesaid, deal with any servant, or slave, he or she so offending, shall be imprisoned one calender month, without bail or main-prize; and then, also continue in prison, until he or she shall find good security, in the sum of ten pounds current money of Virginia, for the good behaviour for one year following; wherein, a second offence shall be a breach of the bond; and moreover shall forfeit and pay four times the value of the things so bought, sold, or received, to the master or owner of such servant, or slave: To be recovered, with costs, by action upon the case, in any court of record in this her majesty's colony and dominion, wherein no essoin, protection, or wager of law, or other than one imparlance, shall be allowed.

XVI. Provided always, and be it enacted, That when any person or persons convict for dealing with a servant, or slave, contrary to this act, shall not immediately give good and sufficient security for his or her good behaviour, as aforesaid: then in such case, the court shall order thirty-nine lashes, well laid on, upon the bare back of such offender, at the common whipping-post of the county, and the said offender to be thence discharged of giving such bond and security.

XVIII. And if any woman servant shall have a bastard child by a negro, or mulatto, over and above the years service due to her master or owner, she shall immediately, upon the expiration of her time to her then present master or owner, pay down to the church-wardens of the parish wherein such child shall be born, for the use of the said parish, fifteen pounds current money of Virginia, or be by them sold for five years, to the use aforesaid: And if a free christian white woman shall have such bastard child, by a negro, or mulatto, for every such offence, she shall, within one month after her delivery of such bastard child, pay to the church-wardens for the time being, of the parish wherein such child shall be born, for the use of the said parish fifteen pounds current money of Virginia, or be by them sold for five

years to the use aforesaid: And in both the said cases, the church-wardens shall bind the said child to be a servant, until it shall be of thirty one years of age.

XIX. And for a further prevention of that abominable mixture and spurious issue, which hereafter may increase in this her majesty's colony and dominion, as well by English, and other white men and women intermarrying with negroes or mulattos, as by their unlawful coition with them, Be it enacted, by the authority aforesaid, and it is hereby enacted, That whatsoever English, or other white man or woman, being free, shall intermarry with a negro or mulatto man or woman, bond or free, shall, by judgment of the county court, be committed to prison, and there remain, during the space of six months, without bail or mainprize; and shall forfeit and pay ten pounds current money of Virginia, to the use of the parish, as aforesaid.

XX. And be it further enacted, That no minister of the church of England, or other minister, or person whatsoever, within this colony and dominion, shall hereafter wittingly presume to marry a white man with a negro or mulatto woman; or to marry a white woman with a negro or mulatto man, upon pain of forfeiting and paying, for every such marriage the sum of ten thousand pounds of tobacco; one half to our sovereign lady the Queen, her heirs and successors, for and towards the support of the government, and the contingent charges thereof; and the other half to the informer; To be recovered, with costs, by action of debt, bill, plaint, or information, in any court of record within this her majesty's colony and dominion, wherein no essoin, protection, or wager of law, shall be allowed.

XXIII. And for encouragement of all persons to take up runaways, Be it enacted, by the authority aforesaid, and it is hereby enacted, That for the taking up of every servant, or slave, if ten miles, or above, from the house or quarter where such servant, or slave was kept, there shall be allowed by the public, as a reward to the taker-up, two hundred pounds of tobacco; and if above five miles, and under ten, one hundred pounds of tobacco: Which said several rewards of two hundred, and one hundred pounds of tobacco, shall also be paid in the county where such taker-up shall reside, and shall be again levied by the public upon the master or owner of such runaway, for re-imbursement of the public, every justice of the peace before whom such runaway shall be brought, upon the taking up, shall mention the proper-name and sur-name of the taker-up, and the county of his or her residence, together with the time and place of taking up the said runaway; and shall also mention the name of the said runaway, and the proper-name and sur-name of the master or owner of such runaway, and the county of his or her residence, together with the distance of miles, in the said justice's judgment, from the place of taking up the said runaway, to the house or quarter where such runaway was kept.

XXIV. Provided, That when any negro, or other runaway, that doth not speak English, and cannot, or through obstinacy will not, declare the name of his or her masters or owner, that then it shall be sufficient for the said justice to certify the same, instead of the name of such runaway, and the proper name and sur-name of his or her master or owner, and the county of his or her residence and distance of miles, as aforesaid; and in such case, shall, by his warrant, order the said runaway to be conveyed to the public gaol, of this country, there to be continued prisoner until the master or owner shall be known; who, upon paying the charges of the imprisonment, or giving caution to the prison-keeper for

the same, together with the reward of two hundred or one hundred pounds of tobacco, as the case shall be, shall have the said runaway restored.

XXV. And further, the said justice of the peace, when such runaway shall be brought before him, shall, by his warrant commit the said runaway to the next constable, and therein also order him to give the said runaway so many lashes as the said justice shall think fit, not exceeding the number of thirty-nine; and then to be conveyed from constable to constable, until the said runaway shall be carried home, or to the country gaol, as aforesaid, every constable through whose hands the said runaway shall pass, giving a receipt at the delivery; and every constable failing to execute such warrant according to the tenor thereof, or refusing to give such receipt, shall forefeit and pay two hundred pounds of tobacco to the church-wardens of the parish wherein such failure shall be, for the use of the poor of the said parish: To be recovered, with costs, by action of debt, in any court of record in this her majesty's colony and dominion, wherein no essoin, protection or wager of law, shall be allowed. And such corporal punishment shall not deprive the master or owner of such runaway of the other satisfaction here in this act appointed to be made upon such servant's running away.

XXIX. And be it enacted, by the authority aforesaid, and it is hereby enacted, That if any constable, or sheriff, into whose hands a runaway servant or slave shall be committed, by virtue of this act, shall suffer such runaway to escape, the said constable or sheriff shall be liable to the action of the party agrieved, for recovery of his damages, at the common law with costs.

XXXII. And also be it enacted, by the authority aforesaid, and it is hereby enacted, That no master, mistress, or overseer of a family, shall knowingly permit any slave, not belonging to him or her, to be and remain upon his or her plantation, above four hours at any one time, without the leave of such slave's master, mistress, or overseer, on penalty of one hundred and fifty pounds of tobacco to the informer; cognizable by a justice of the peace of the county wherein such offence shall be committed.

XXXIV. And if any slave resist his master, or owner, or other person, by his or her order, correcting such slave, and shall happen to be killed in such correction, it shall not be accounted felony; but the master, owner, and every such other person so giving correction, shall be free and acquit of all punishment and accusation for the same, as if such incident had never happened: And also, if any negro, mulatto, or Indian, bond or free, shall at any time, lift his or her hand, in opposition against any christian, not being negro, mulatto, or Indian, he or she so offending shall, for every such offence, proved by the oath of the party, receive on his or her bare back, thirty lashes, well laid on; cognizable by a justice of the peace for that county wherein such offence shall be committed.

XXXV. And also be it enacted, by the authority aforesaid, and it is hereby enacted, That no slave go armed with gun, sword, club, staff, or other weapon, nor go from off the plantation and seat of land where such slave shall be appointed to live, without a certificate of leave in writing, for so doing, from his or her master, mistress, or overseer: And if any slave shall be found offending herein, it shall be lawful for any person or persons to apprehend and deliver such slave to the next constable or head-borough, who is hereby enjoined and required, without further order or warrant, to give such slave twenty lashes on his or her bare back well laid on, and so

send him or her home: And all horses, cattle, and hogs, now belonging, or that hereafter shall belong to any slave, or of any slaves mark in this her majesty's colony and dominion, shall be seised and sold by the church-wardens of the parish, wherein such horses, cattle, or hogs shall be, and the profit thereof applied to the use of the poor of the said parish: And also, if any damage shall be hereafter committed by any slave living at a quarter where there is no christian overseer, the master or owner of such slave shall be liable to action for the trespass and damage, as if the same had been done by him or herself.

XXXVI. And also it is hereby enacted and declared, That baptism of slaves doth not exempt them from bondage; and that all children shall be bond or free, according to the condition of their mothers, and the particular direction of this act.

XXXVII. And whereas, many times, slaves run away and lie out, hid or lurking in swamps, woods, and other obscure places, killing hogs, and committing other injuries to the inhabitants of this her majesty's colony and dominion, Be it therefore enacted, by the authority aforesaid, and it is hereby enacted, That in all such cases, upon intelligence given of any slaves lying out, as aforesaid, any two justices (Quorum unus) of the peace of the county wherein such slave is supposed to lurk or do mischief, shall be and are impowered and required to issue proclamation against all such slaves, reciting their names, and owners names, if they are known, and thereby requiring them, and every of them, forthwith to surrender themselves; and also impowering the sheriff of the said county, to take such power with him, as he shall think fit and necessary, for the effectual apprehending such out-lying slave or slaves, and go in search of them: Which proclamation shall be published on a Sabbath day, at the door of every church and chapel, in the said county, by the parish clerk, or reader, of the church, immediately after divine worship: And in case any slave, against whom proclamation hath been thus issued, and once published at any church or chapel, as aforesaid, stay out, and do not immediately return home, it shall be lawful for any person or persons whatsoever, to kill and destroy such slaves by such ways and means as he, she, or they shall think fit, without accusation or impeachment of any crime for the same: And if any slave, that hath run away and lain out as aforesaid, shall be apprehended by the sheriff, or any other person, upon the application of the owner of the said slave, it shall and may be lawful for the county court, to order such punishment to the said slave, either by dismembring, or any other way, not touching his life, as they in their discretion shall think fit, for the reclaiming any such incorrigible slave, and terrifying others from the like practices.

XXXVIII. Provided Always, and it is further enacted, That for every slave killed, in pursuance of this act, or put to death by law, the master or owner of such slave shall be paid by the public:

XXXIX. And to the end, the true value of every slave killed, or put to death, as aforesaid, may be the better known; and by that means, the assembly the better enabled to make a suitable allowance thereupon, Be it enacted, That upon application of the master or owner of any such slave, to the court appointed for proof of public claims, the said court shall value the slave in money, and the clerk of the court shall return a certificate thereof to the assembly, with the rest of the public claims.

XL. And for the better putting this act in due execution, and that no servants or slaves may have pretense of ignorance hereof, Be it also enacted, That

the church-wardens of each parish in this her majesty's colony and dominion, at the charge of the parish, shall provide a true copy of this act, and cause entry thereof to be made in the register book of each parish respectively; and that the parish clerk, or reader of each parish, shall, on the first sermon Sundays in September and March, annually, after sermon or divine service is ended, at the door of every church and chapel in their parish, publish the same; and the sheriff of each county shall, at the next court held for the county, after the last day of February, yearly, publish this act, at the door of the court-house: And every sheriff making default herein, shall forfeit and pay six hundred pounds of tobacco; one half to her majesty, her heirs, and successors, for and towards the support of the government; and the other half to the informer. And every parish clerk, or reader, making default herein, shall, for each time so offending, forfeit and pay six hundred pounds of tobacco; one half whereof to be to the informer; and the other half to the poor of the parish, wherein such omission shall be: To be recovered, with costs, by action of debt, bill, plaint, or information, in any court of record in this her majesty's colony and dominion, wherein no essoin, protection, or wager of law, shall be allowed.

XLI. And be it further enacted, That all and every other act and acts, and every clause and article thereof, heretofore made, for so much thereof as relates to servants and slaves, or to any other matter or thing whatsoever, within the purview of this act, is and are hereby repealed, and made void, to all intents and purposes, as if the same had never been made.

Source

Virtual Jamestown. http://www.virtualja mestown.org/laws1.html#51 (accessed June 2008). Used with permission.

slavery. In 1787, the Northwest Ordinance prohibited slavery in the Northwest Territories (present-day Ohio, Indiana, Illinois, Michigan, and Wisconsin). Nevertheless, slavery expanded in the new United States. By 1860, there were almost 4 million slaves in the country, compared with less than 700,000 in 1790 (Kolchin 1993, 70–73, 77–80, 93).

Tensions grew between northern states that opposed slavery, and southern states that believed slavery to be essential to their economy. When Missouri applied to be a state, the slave states wanted Missouri to be admitted as a slaveholding state, and the free states wanted Congress to ban slavery in Missouri. In 1820, Congress issued the "Missouri Compromise," which admitted Missouri as a slave state and Maine as a free state. This issue came up again and again as more territories asked to be admitted as states. In 1850, California was admitted as a free state, and many territories had the right to decide for themselves whether or not to accept slavery.

When Abraham Lincoln was elected president in 1860, the southern slaveholding states believed that he would end slavery, and they withdrew themselves from the country. The Civil War was fought to force the southern states to surrender and rejoin the country. During the war, Lincoln issued the Emancipation Proclamation in 1863, which freed the slaves. After the war, the Thirteenth Amendment to the U.S. Constitution was adopted in 1865, which officially ended slavery in the entire country.

Even after slavery ended legally, the freed blacks received little help from the government to get started on their new life. During the Reconstruction Era, the federal government helped blacks to gain political power in the southern states, and the government started schools for blacks. This period ended in 1877, however, after which time blacks continued to be discriminated against in both southern and northern states. The passage of segregation laws meant that blacks could be legally denied access to schooling, employment, political power, and public facilities.

See also: Freedmen's Bureau; Indentured Servitude; Reconstruction Era; Reparations for Slavery; Segregation Laws

Sources
Horton, James Oliver, and Lois E. Horton. *Slavery and the Making of America.* New York: Oxford University Press, 2005.
Kolchin, Peter. *American Slavery, 1619–1877.* New York: Hill and Wang, 1993.

SOCIALISM

Socialism is the idea that the public, or the community, should own productive property, such as land and factories. At the basis of socialism is the idea that every human is equal to every other human and that everyone's basic needs should be met. Socialists disagree with the idea that some individuals can accumulate great wealth while the vast majority of people remained poor.

While cooperative communities have probably existed since the dawn of civilization, modern Socialist ideas arose in response to the poverty created by the Industrial Revolution, during which time a few business owners became wealthy while many workers were desperately poor. Socialism is a contrast to capitalism, and especially to British philosopher Adam Smith's idea that markets should not be controlled or regulated by the government, but rather should be allowed to operate freely. Adam Smith, who wrote his influential book *Wealth of Nations* in 1776, before the start of the Industrial Revolution, provided a rationale for government to stay out of business operations. Smith felt that the natural market forces of supply and demand would automatically ensure that workers received fair wages and that consumers had access to the goods and services they wanted. However, the Industrial Revolution created factory owners who were so powerful that they could pay workers next to nothing and force them to work in dangerous, unsanitary conditions.

The word "socialism" was first used in the 1830s, in Europe, and became common in the 1840s. One of the most famous and influential Socialists was German-born Karl Marx (1818–1883). With German journalist Friedrich Engels he wrote *The Communist Manifesto* in 1848. He called his brand of socialism "scientific socialism." He looked down on many earlier Socialists who called for the formation of cooperative communities. Marx called them "utopian socialists." He said that his views were based not just on the wish to create a more just, equitable society, but on a scientific study of history.

Based on his study of history, Marx predicted that the oppressed workers of the Industrial Revolution would stage a violent revolt against the factory owners, take over the factories, and then rule as a "dictatorship of the proletariat." Eventually, Marx predicted, there would be no need for government at all and it would wither away. Marx and other Socialists later wrote that violent revolution was not the only way for workers to take charge; countries might also follow a peaceful path toward socialism.

Marx's brand of socialism was popular in Europe, and eventually, through the interpretation of Russian political activist Vladimir Lenin, led to the Communist governments of the Union of Soviet Socialist Republics (USSR—a federation of Russia and a number of nearby countries), some Eastern European countries, China, Cuba, North Korea, and Vietnam. This form of socialism relied on government ownership and control of factories, land, and other means of production. While the Communist governments often did achieve a more equitable distribution of wealth, they also suppressed individual freedom, imprisoning people who disagreed with the Communist Party. Instead of withering away, as Marx predicted, these Communist governments were all-powerful, controlling many aspects of people's lives. Most Communist governments ended in the 1990s.

Marx's form of socialism was never popular in the United States. Instead, the "utopian socialists" were active in forming cooperative communities during the 1800s and early 1900s. A popular book of the time was Edward Bellamy's *Looking Backwards: 2000 to 1887*, published in 1888. The novel is about a man, Julian West, who is transported from Boston in 1887, to Boston in the year 2000, where he encounters a utopian city. The pressing issue of Julian's era had been labor unrest. His host in 2000 explains that the labor problem was solved when all industries were taken over by the government.

PRIMARY DOCUMENT 39

Socialist Party Platform, 1912

Although the Socialist Party was seen as a radical political party in the United States, a number of the goals in this platform have been enacted in the United States, such as regulation ending child labor, public works projects to provide jobs to the unemployed, laws specifying maximum hours and minimum wages, an old-age pension system, workers' compensation, women's right to vote, federal departments of labor and education, and a graduated income tax.

One major goal of the Socialist Party of America was the public, collective (government) ownership of land, transportation systems, communications systems, forests, energy sources (such as mines and oil wells), food storage facilities, banking, and other necessities of life. This goal has not been achieved in the United States. As a country, we have preferred to emphasize private ownership over government ownership.

The Socialist party declares that the capitalist system has outgrown its historical function, and has become utterly incapable of meeting the problems now confronting society. We denounce this outgrown system as incompetent and corrupt and the source of unspeakable misery and suffering to the whole working class.

Under this system the industrial equipment of the nation has passed into the absolute control of a plutocracy which exacts an annual tribute of hundreds of millions of dollars from the producers. Unafraid of any organized resistance, it stretches out its greedy hands over the still undeveloped resources of the nation—the land, the mines, the forests and the water powers of every State of the Union.

In spite of the multiplication of laborsaving machines and improved methods in industry which cheapen the cost of production, the share of the producers grows ever less, and the prices of all the necessities of life steadily increase. The boasted prosperity of this nation is for the owning class alone. To the rest it means only greater hardship and misery. The high cost of living is felt in every home. Millions of wage-workers have seen the purchasing power of their wages decrease until life has become a desperate battle for mere existence.

Multitudes of unemployed walk the streets of our cities or trudge from State to State awaiting the will of the masters to move the wheels of industry. The farmers in every state are plundered by the increasing prices exacted for tools and machinery and by extortionate rents, freight rates and storage charges.

Capitalist concentration is mercilessly crushing the class of small business men and driving its members into the ranks of propertyless wage-workers. The overwhelming majority of the people of America are being forced under a yoke of bondage by this soulless industrial despotism.

It is this capitalist system that is responsible for the increasing burden of armaments, the poverty, slums, child labor, most of the insanity, crime and prostitution, and much of the disease that afflicts mankind.

Under this system the working class is exposed to poisonous conditions, to frightful and needless perils to life and limb, is walled around with court decisions, injunctions and unjust laws, and is preyed upon incessantly for the benefit of the controlling oligarchy of wealth. Under it also, the children of the working class are doomed to ignorance, drudging toil and darkened lives.

In the face of these evils, so manifest that all thoughtful observers are appalled at them, the legislative representatives of the Republican and Democratic parties remain the faithful servants of the oppressors. Measures designed to secure to the wage-earners of this Nation as humane and just treatment as is already enjoyed by the wage-earners of all other civilized nations have been smothered in committee without debate, the laws ostensibly designed to bring relief to the farmers and general consumers are juggled and transformed into instruments for the exaction of further tribute. The growing unrest under oppression has driven these two old parties to the enactment of a variety of regulative measures, none of which has limited in any appreciable degree the power of the plutocracy, and some of which have been perverted into means of increasing that power. Anti-trust laws, railroad restrictions and regulations, with the prosecutions, indictments and investigations based upon such legislation, have proved to be utterly futile and ridiculous.

Nor has this plutocracy been seriously restrained or even threatened by any Republican or Democratic executive. It has continued to grow in power and insolence alike under the administration of Cleveland, McKinley, Roosevelt and Taft.

We declare, therefore, that the longer sufferance of these conditions is impossible, and we purpose to end them all. We declare them to be the product of the present system in which industry is carried on for private greed, instead of for the welfare of society. We declare, furthermore, that for these evils there will be and can be no remedy and no substantial relief except through Socialism under which industry will be carried on for the common good and every worker receive the full social value of the wealth he creates.

Society is divided into warring groups and classes, based upon material interests. Fundamentally, this struggle is a conflict between the two main classes, one of which, the capitalist class, owns the means of production, and the other, the working class, must use these means of production, on terms dictated by the owners.

The capitalist class, though few in numbers, absolutely controls the government, legislative, executive and judicial. This class owns the machinery of gathering and disseminating news through its organized press. It subsidizes seats of learning—the colleges and schools—and even religious and moral agencies. It has also the added prestige which established customs give to any order of society, right or wrong.

The working class, which includes all those who are forced to work for a living whether by hand or brain, in shop, mine or on the soil, vastly outnumbers the capitalist class. Lacking effective organization and class solidarity, this class is unable to enforce its will. Given such a class solidarity and effective organization, the workers will have the power to make all laws and control all industry in their own interest. All political parties are the expression of economic class interests. All other parties than the Socialist party represent one or another group of the ruling capitalist class. Their political conflicts reflect merely superficial rivalries between competing capitalist groups. However they result, these conflicts have no issue of real value to the workers. Whether the Democrats or Republicans win politically, it is the capitalist class that is victorious economically.

The Socialist party is the political expression of the economic interests of the workers. Its defeats have been their defeats and its victories their victories. It is a party founded on the science and laws of social development. It proposes that, since all social necessities to-day are socially produced, the means of their production and distribution shall be socially owned and democratically controlled.

In the face of the economic and political aggressions of the capitalist class the only reliance left the workers is that of their economic organizations and their political power. By the intelligent and class conscious use of these, they may resist successfully the capitalist class, break the fetters of wage slavery, and fit themselves for the future society, which is to displace the capitalist system. The Socialist party appreciates the full significance of class organization and urges the wage-earners, the working farmers and all other useful workers to organize for economic and political action, and we pledge ourselves to support the toilers of the fields as well as those in the shops, factories and mines of the nation in their struggles for economic justice.

In the defeat or victory of the working class party in this new struggle for freedom lies the defeat or triumph of the common people of all economic groups, as well as the failure or triumph of popular government. Thus the Socialist party is the party of the present day revolution which makes the transition from economic individualism to socialism, from wage slavery to free co-operation, from capitalist oligarchy to industrial democracy.

Working Program

As measures calculated to strengthen the working class in its fight for the realization of its ultimate aim, the co-operative commonwealth, and to increase its power against capitalist oppression, we advocate and pledge ourselves and our elected officers to the following program:

Collective Ownership

1. The collective ownership and democratic management of railroads, wire and wireless telegraphs and telephones, express service, steamboat lines, and all other social means of transportation and communication and of all large scale industries.
2. The immediate acquirement by the municipalities, the states or the federal government of all grain elevators, stock yards, storage warehouses, and other distributing agencies, in order to reduce the present extortionate cost of living.
3. The extension of the public domain to include mines, quarries, oil wells, forests and water power.
4. The further conservation and development of natural resources for the use and benefit of all the people:
   a. By scientific forestation and timber protection.
   b. By the reclamation of arid and swamp tracts.
   c. By the storage of flood waters and the utilization of water power.
   d. By the stoppage of the present extravagant waste of the soil and of the products of mines and oil wells.
   e. By the development of highway and waterway systems.
5. The collective ownership of land wherever practicable, and in cases where such ownership is impracticable, the appropriation by taxation of the annual rental value of all the land held for speculation and exploitation.
6. The collective ownership and democratic management of the banking and currency system.

Unemployment

The immediate government relief of the unemployed by the extension of all useful public works. All persons employed on such works to be engaged directly by the government under a work day of not more than eight hours and at not less than the prevailing union wages. The government also to establish employment bureaus; to lend money to states and municipalities without interest for the purpose of carrying on public works, and to take such other measures within its power as will lessen the widespread misery of the workers caused by the misrule of the capitalist class.

Industrial Demands

The conservation of human resources, particularly of the lives and well-being of the workers and their families:

1. By shortening the work day in keeping with the increased productiveness of machinery.
2. By securing for every worker a rest period of not less than a day and a half in each week.
3. By securing a more effective inspection of workshops, factories and mines.
4. By the forbidding the employment of children under sixteen years of age.
5. By the co-operative organization of the industries in the federal penitentiaries for the benefit of the convicts and their dependents.
6. By forbidding the interstate transportation of the products of child labor, of convict labor and of all uninspected factories and mines.
7. By abolishing the profit system in government work and substituting either the direct hire of labor or the awarding of contracts to co-operative groups of workers.
8. By establishing minimum wage scales.
9. By abolishing official charity and substituting a non-contributary system of old age pensions, a general system of insurance by the State of all its members against unemployment and invalidism and a system of compulsory insurance by employers of their workers, without cost to the latter, against industrial diseases, accidents and death.

Political Demands

1. The absolute freedom of press, speech and assemblage.
2. The adoption of a graduated income tax and the extension of inheritance taxes, graduated in proportion to the value of the estate and to nearness of kin-the proceeds of these taxes to be employed in the socialization of industry.
3. The abolition of the monopoly ownership of patents and the substitution of collective ownership, with direct rewards to inventors by premiums or royalties.
4. Unrestricted and equal suffrage for men and women.
5. The adoption of the initiative, referendum and recall and of proportional representation, nationally as well as locally.
6. The abolition of the Senate and of the veto power of the President.
7. The election of the President and Vice-President by direct vote of the people.
8. The abolition of the power usurped by the Supreme Court of the United States to pass upon the constitutionality of the legislation enacted by Congress. National laws to be repealed only by act of Congress or by a referendum vote of the whole people.
9. Abolition of the present restrictions upon the amendment of the constitution, so that instrument may be made amendable by a majority of the voters in a majority of the States.
10. The granting of the right of suffrage in the District of Columbia with representation in Congress and a democratic form of municipal government for purely local affairs.
11. The extension of democratic government to all United States territory.
12. The enactment of further measures for the conservation of health. The creation of an independent bureau of health, with

such restrictions as will secure full liberty to all schools of practice.

13. The enactment of further measures for general education and particularly for vocational education in useful pursuits. The Bureau of Education to be made a department.

14. The separation of the present Bureau of Labor from the Department of Commerce and Labor and its elevation to the rank of a department.

15. Abolition of all federal districts courts and the United States circuit court of appeals. State courts to have jurisdiction in all cases arising between citizens of several states and foreign corporations. The election of all judges for short terms.

16. The immediate curbing of the power of the courts to issue injunctions.

17. The free administration of the law.

18. The calling of a convention for the revision of the constitution of the U. S.

Such measures of relief as we may be able to force from capitalism are but a preparation of the workers to seize the whole powers of government, in order that they may thereby lay hold of the whole system of socialized industry and thus come to their rightful inheritance.

Sources

Morgan, Wayne, ed. *American Socialism, 1900–1960*. Englewood Cliffs, NJ: Prentice-Hall, 1964, 55–60.

Sage History Web site. http://www.sage-history.net/progressive/SocialistPlat 1912.htm (accessed May 2008).

Bellamy's novel inspired the formation of 150 "Nationalist Clubs" across the country, calling for government ownership of industry. The novel also inspired the formation of a few cooperative Socialist communities, including the Llano communities of California and Louisiana (in existence from 1914 to 1937).

Some Socialists in the United States formed the Brotherhood of the Cooperative Commonwealths in 1895, with the idea of solving unemployment by starting cooperative colonies in western states. However, this idea was dismissed at a Socialist Party convention in 1898, because many Socialists believed that starting communities would hinder them from their political work of transforming the entire culture (Oved 1988, 12–13).

The Socialist Party of America was formed in 1901, and gained some power in the United States during the Progressive Era, especially under the leadership of Eugene V. Debs, who ran for U.S. president numerous times. In 1912, he gained 6 percent of the vote, which was a remarkable showing for a minor-party candidate. During that election year, more than 1,000 Socialists were elected to public office, including members of state legislatures; a U.S. congressman from Wisconsin; and mayors in Butte, Montana; Berkeley, California; and Flint, Michigan (Howe 1985, 3). The 1912 Socialist Party platform (set of beliefs) is excerpted in the accompanying primary document.

The Socialist Party continued to be strong through the 1917 elections. In fact, according to historian James Weinstein, by this time "many of [socialism's] ideas and much of its program had already been assimilated by progressives of both major parties" (2003, xvi). In turn, members of the Socialist party were active in

Progressive Era reform movements, such as the founding of the National Association for the Advancement of Colored People (NAACP), women's suffrage, and the labor union movement (Weinstein 2003, 115).

However, because of the Socialist Party's stance against the war in Europe (which would become World War I), the U.S. government began banning Socialist Party publications from being mailed. The Socialists did not believe in going to war against fellow laborers. They believed lasting world peace could be achieved by replacing the national capitalist system with an "international industrial democracy," as Debs put it. The government accused Socialist Party leaders of sedition (refusing to obey the government, and plotting to overthrow the government), and many of them were imprisoned, including Debs. Socialism was never again as popular in America (Howe 1985, 41–44; Debs 1916).

In addition to the U.S. government's persecution of Socialists, the Russian Revolution also harmed the cause of Socialists in the United States. Starting in 1917, Russia was implementing its own form of socialism. From this example, many Americans came to believe that socialism meant "a lower standard of living minus democracy" (Weinstein 2003, xvi–xvii).

One might assume that the collapse of the U.S. economy during the Great Depression would have been an ideal time for the rebirth of socialism in the United States. Instead, during the Great Depression, only one major Socialist political campaign was waged—that for governor of California in 1934—and the candidate, long-time Socialist Party member Upton Sinclair, ran as a

Democrat. As James Weinstein notes, by 1936, the Socialist political parties were essentially defunct. Still, during the Great Depression, many of socialism's goals were incorporated into the New Deal programs of President Franklin Roosevelt, such as child labor and minimum-wage laws, the eight-hour workday, and laws providing help for those in need (such as Social Security, unemployment insurance, and Medicaid) (Weinstein 2003, 169).

See also: Debs, Eugene; Great Depression; Industrial Revolution; Progressive Era; Sinclair, Upton

Sources

Bellamy, Edward. *Looking Backward, 2000–1887*. New York: Grosset and Dunlap, 1888.

Debs, Eugene V. "The Prospect for Peace." *American Socialist* February 19, 1916. http://www.marxists.org/archive/debs/works/1916/peace.htm (accessed May 2008).

Ebenstein, William, and Edwin Fogelman. *Today's Isms: Communism, Fascism, Capitalism, Socialism.* Englewood Cliffs, NJ: Prentice-Hall, 1980.

Howe, Irving. *Socialism and America.* San Diego, CA: Harcourt Brace Jovanovich, 1985.

Jarnow, Jesse. *Socialism: A Primary Source Analysis.* New York: Rosen Publishing Group, 2005.

Oved, Yaacov. *Two-Hundred Years of American Communes.* New Brunswick, NJ: Transaction Books, 1988.

Weinstein, James. *The Long Detour: The History and Future of the American Left.* Boulder, CO: Westview Press, 2003.

SOCIAL SECURITY ACT

The Social Security Act, passed by Congress and signed by President

Roosevelt in August of 1935, provides income to those who are retired from work. The law also provides federal payments to states for unemployment insurance, and aid to dependent children, as well as aid to the blind, and money for health clinics for pregnant women and children. The Social Security Act was part of Roosevelt's New Deal to lift the country out of the Great Depression. It has since been amended to include disability insurance and health insurance for the elderly and the poor. The Social Security program has become one of the most important government programs to provide for the needy and to prevent poverty.

The idea of social insurance for the aged in the United States was first publicized in 1795, when popular American author Thomas Paine wrote an essay, "Agrarian Justice," calling for a social insurance program for those over fifty years of age, and a lump-sum payment to young people when they reached the age of twenty-one. During the 1800s and early 1900s, some European countries began enacting laws for national health insurance, accident compensation, and old-age insurance. After the U.S. Civil War (which ended in 1865), the United States set up a pension program for disabled soldiers, and the widows and children of men who had died in battle. In 1923, Montana became the first state to enact an old-age pension law. Pennsylvania and Nevada followed suit, although their laws were later declared unconstitutional. By 1929, almost all states had some sort of workmen's compensation law to provide payments to workers injured on the job (Social Security Administration, History).

During the early 1930s, a private citizen, Dr. Francis Townsend, was publicizing his plan for old-age insurance, which became popular. By the mid-thirties, almost all states offered some form of social security to the blind, elderly, and dependent children, but the programs offered little money to a small number of people, because during the Great Depression states had little money to spare. "All states awaited magic from Washington," says historian James Patterson (1969, 85–86).

Even before his inauguration as president of the United States in 1933, Franklin Roosevelt had agreed to work on some sort of old-age insurance. The elderly were hit hard by the poverty of the Great Depression. According to the Social Security Administration Web site, in 1934, more than half of the elderly people in America could not support themselves. Roosevelt wanted to set up an old-age insurance program, especially since the Townsend Plan had made the idea so widely accepted. He also wanted to add unemployment insurance to this idea.

In June 1934, Roosevelt created the Committee on Economic Security to study the idea and create a bill. The chair of the committee was Secretary of Labor Frances Perkins. She was puzzled about how to create a law that would not be ruled unconstitutional by the Supreme Court, which had previously struck down federal laws mandating minimum wages and prohibiting child labor. One day she happened to be at a tea party at the home of a Supreme Court Justice, Harlan Fiske Stone. She expressed to him her difficulties with figuring out how to craft a law that would agree with the U.S. Constitution. Stone whispered to her that she should rely on the federal

PRIMARY DOCUMENT 40

Excerpt from President Roosevelt's Message to Congress on Social Security, January 17, 1935

When the Social Security bill was sent to Congress, President Roosevelt gave this speech to educate the members of Congress about the bill and encourage them pass it. He stresses that such social insurance programs have already been implemented successfully in other "advanced countries," and that it is therefore not an experimental program. He also emphasized that workers themselves would contribute to fund the program, and that states would manage part of the program—it would not be a completely federal initiative.

In addressing you on June eighth, 1934, I summarized the main objectives of our American program. Among these was, and is, the security of the men, women, and children of the Nation against certain hazards and vicissitudes of life. This purpose is an essential part of our task. In my annual message to you I promised to submit a definite program of action. This I do in the form of a report to me by a Committee on Economic Security, appointed by me for the purpose of surveying the field and of recommending the basis of legislation.. . .

The detailed report of the Committee sets forth a series of proposals that will appeal to the sound sense of the American people. It has not attempted the impossible, nor has it failed to exercise sound caution and consideration of all of the factors concerned: the national credit, the rights and responsibilities of States, the capacity of industry to assume financial responsibilities and the fundamental necessity of proceeding in a manner that will merit the enthusiastic support of citizens of all sorts.

It is overwhelmingly important to avoid any danger of permanently discrediting the sound and necessary policy of Federal legislation for economic security by attempting to apply it on too ambitious a scale before actual experience has provided guidance for the permanently safe direction of such efforts. The place of such a fundamental in our future civilization is too precious to be jeopardized now by extravagant action. It is a sound idea—a sound ideal. Most of the other advanced countries of the world have already adopted it and their experience affords the knowledge that social insurance can be made a sound and workable project.

Three principles should be observed in legislation on this subject. First, the system adopted, except for the money necessary to initiate it, should be self-sustaining in the sense that funds for the payment of insurance benefits should not come from the proceeds of general taxation. Second, excepting in old-age insurance, actual management should be left to the States subject to standards established by the Federal Government. Third, sound financial management of the funds and the reserves, and protection of the credit structure of the Nation should be assured by retaining Federal control over all funds through trustees in the Treasury of the United States.

At this time, I recommend the following types of legislation looking to economic security:

1. Unemployment compensation.
2. Old-age benefits, including compulsory and voluntary annuities.
3. Federal aid to dependent children through grants to States for the support of existing mothers' pension systems and for services for the protection and care of homeless, neglected, dependent, and crippled children.
4. Additional Federal aid to State and local public health agencies and the strengthening of the

Federal Public Health Service. I am not at this time recommending the adoption of so called "health insurance," although groups representing the medical profession are cooperating with the Federal Government in the further study of the subject and definite progress is being made.

With respect to unemployment compensation, I have concluded that the most practical proposal is the levy of a uniform Federal payroll tax, ninety per cent of which should be allowed as an offset to employers contributing under a compulsory State unemployment compensation act. The purpose of this is to afford a requirement of a reasonably uniform character for all States cooperating with the Federal Government and to promote and encourage the passage of unemployment compensation laws in the States. The ten per cent not thus offset should be used to cover the costs of Federal and State administration of this broad system. Thus, States will largely administer unemployment compensation, assisted and guided by the Federal Government. An unemployment compensation system should be constructed in such a way as to afford every practicable aid and incentive toward the larger purpose of employment stabilization. This can be helped by the intelligent planning of both public and private employment. It also can be helped by correlating the system with public employment so that a person who has exhausted his benefits may be eligible for some form of public work as is recommended in this report. Moreover, in order to encourage the stabilization of private employment, Federal legislation should not foreclose the States from establishing means for inducing industries to afford an even greater stabilization of employment.

In the important field of security for our old people, it seems necessary to adopt three principles: First, non-contributory old-age pensions for those who are now too old to build up their own insurance. It is, of course, clear that for perhaps thirty years to come funds will have to be provided by the States and the Federal Government to meet these pensions. Second, compulsory contributory annuities which in time will establish a self-supporting system for those now young and for future generations. Third, voluntary contributory annuities by which individual initiative can increase the annual amounts received in old age. It is proposed that the Federal Government assume one-half of the cost of the old-age pension plan, which ought ultimately to be supplanted by self-supporting annuity plans.

The amount necessary at this time for the initiation of unemployment compensation, old-age security, children's aid, and the promotion of public health, as outlined in the report of the Committee on Economic Security, is approximately one hundred million dollars.

The establishment of sound means toward a greater future economic security of the American people is dictated by a prudent consideration of the hazards involved in our national life. No one can guarantee this country against the dangers of future depressions but we can reduce these dangers. We can eliminate many of the factors that cause economic depressions, and we can provide the means of mitigating their results. This plan for economic security is at once a measure of prevention and a method of alleviation.

We pay now for the dreadful consequence of economic insecurity—and dearly. This plan presents a more equitable and infinitely less expensive means of meeting these costs. We cannot afford to neglect the plain duty before us. I strongly recommend action to attain the objectives sought in this report.

Source

Social Security History Online. http://www.ssa.gov/history/fdrstmts.html#message1 (accessed May 2008).

New York City postal workers wave Social Security applications as they begin to deliver the forms in November 1936. More than 3 million forms were distributed in New York City alone. (Library of Congress)

government's taxing power (Perkins 1946, 286; Pasachoff 1999, 90–91).

Perkins went back to her committee and insisted that the law had to use the government's taxing power as a way to build up the funds for the pension and insurance program. Payroll taxes are used to fund the programs: employers and employees both pay a portion. Because the workers themselves pay into the system for their own future benefits, these programs do not have the negative connotations of handouts or relief for the poor. In 1937, the U.S. Supreme Court upheld the law.

Roosevelt saw the law as not just a way to help the elderly and needy, but also a way to prevent future economic depressions by making sure most people would always have some money to spend. Upon signing the bill, Roosevelt described the law as

a structure intended to lessen the force of possible future depressions. It will act as a protection to future Administrations against the necessity of going deeply into debt to furnish relief to the needy. The law will flatten out the peaks and valleys of deflation and of inflation. It is, in short, a law that will take care of human needs and at the same time provide the United States an economic structure of vastly greater soundness. (Social Security Administration, History)

According to Perkins, Roosevelt believed that the Social Security Act was among his most important achievements: "He always regarded the Social

---

"INCOME I CAN COUNT ON"

In her autobiography, First Lady Eleanor Roosevelt relates this story of how Social Security provided confidence and comfort after a tragic incident in West Virginia:

> There was a mine accident in which several men were killed, and my husband asked me to go down and find out what the people were saying. One man received the Carnegie medal posthumously because he had gone back into the mine to help rescue other men. His widow had several children, so her social security benefits would make her comfortable. In talking to another widow who had three children and a fourth about to be born, I asked her how she was going to manage. She seemed quite confident and told me: "My sister and her two children will come to live with us. I am going to get social security benefits of nearly sixty-five dollars a month. I pay fifteen dollars a month on my house and land, and I shall raise vegetables and have chickens and with the money from the government I will get along very well. In the past probably the mine company might have given me a small check and often the other miners took up a collection if they could afford it, but this income from the government I can count on until my children are grown."

Source: Roosevelt, Eleanor. *The Autobiography of Eleanor Roosevelt.* New York: Harper and Brothers, 1961, 180.

Security Act as the cornerstone of his administration and, I think, took greater satisfaction from it than from anything else he achieved on the domestic front" (1946, 301).

The Social Security Act of 1935 "heralded a revolution in American social welfare," according to social welfare historian Roy Lubove. "It resulted in a decisive transfer of responsibility for income maintenance to the public sector and the federal government" (1986, 179). No longer would the federal government argue, as it had in the past, that poverty relief was solely the responsibility of the states, cities, or private agencies. With the Social Security Act, the federal government entered permanently into the business of offering relief to the poor.

Although the Social Security Act includes funds for unemployment and for aid to dependent children, in the twenty-first century, the term "Social Security" now refers only to old-age and disability insurance payments. The Social Security Act has been amended many times since 1935. In 1939, old-age insurance benefits were extended to the dependents (wives and children) of workers. In 1950, Social Security coverage was extended to 10 million more people. In 1952, Social Security old-age insurance benefits were increased to keep up with the cost of living. Until that time, the dollar amount of Social Security checks had remained the same as when the program first started. In 1954, disability insurance was added. In 1965, health care insurance plans for the elderly (Medicare) and for the poor (Medicaid) were added. In 1972, Social Security payments began to increase every year based on the increased cost of living. This provision took effect in 1975. No longer would beneficiaries have to wait until Congress passed a benefits increase—the increase would happen automatically every year.

Social Security payments have been important in lifting the elderly out of poverty. Surprisingly, payments to the elderly and disabled have also been important in lifting children out of poverty. According to the Center on Budget and Policy Priorities, a nonprofit organization that studies government programs for the poor, as of 2003, about 1 million children were not living below the poverty line because they or someone in their family received Social Security payments. Children might receive such payments directly if they are the dependent of a recipient who has died. Figure 1 illustrates how Social Security payments have helped a large percentage of the elderly to stay above the poverty line. The data are an average from the years 2000 to 2002.

In 1996, President Bill Clinton ended the "entitlement" part of Aid to Families with Dependent Children, which was part of the Social Security Act. In other words, no longer would any poor family be entitled to receive cash benefits year after year. A time limit was placed on cash benefits and a work requirement was put into place. The new program is called Temporary Assistance for Needy Families.

See also: Aid to (Families with) Dependent Children; Civil War Pensions; Great Depression; Maternal and Child Health Services; Medicaid; Medicare; New Deal; Paine, Thomas; Perkins, Frances; Personal Responsibility and Work Opportunity Reconciliation Act of 1996; Roosevelt, Franklin Delano; Supplemental Security Income; Temporary Assistance for Needy Families; Townsend Movement; Unemployment Insurance

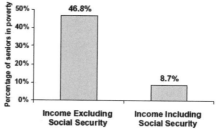

Source: Center on Budget and Policy Priorities

FIGURE 1. Social Security Reduces Number of Seniors in Poverty. Source: Center on Budget and Policy Priorities.

Sources

Lubove, Roy. *The Struggle for Social Security, 1900–1935.* Pittsburgh, PA: University of Pittsburgh Press, 1986.

Pasachoff, Naomi. *Frances Perkins: Champion of the New Deal.* New York: Oxford University Press, 1999.

Patterson, James T. *The New Deal and the States: Federalism in Transition.* Princeton, NJ: Princeton University Press, 1969.

Perkins, Frances. *The Roosevelt I Knew.* New York: Viking Press, 1946.

Web Sites

Center on Budget and Policy Priorities. Social Security. http://www.cbpp.org/pubs/socsec.htm.

Social Security Administration. History. http://www.ssa.gov/history (accessed May 2008).

SPECIAL SUPPLEMENTAL NUTRITION PROGRAM FOR WOMEN, INFANTS AND CHILDREN

The Special Supplemental Nutrition Program for Women, Infants and Children

(WIC) program, which provides nutritious food to low-income pregnant women and young children, is one of the largest federal food programs, along with food stamps and the school lunch program. The WIC program started in 1972.

Although the school lunch program started in the 1940s, and the food stamp program had been revived in 1961, by the late 1960s, the country discovered that many people were still hungry and even starving. Senators, doctors, women's organizations, and prominent citizens filed reports of hunger and malnutrition across the country. Food stamps at that time had to be purchased at a discount, and the poorest people could not afford to buy them. At that time the school lunch program did not have enough funding to provide lunches to all poor children.

As a result of these investigations into hunger, the food stamp and school lunch programs were expanded. In the late 1960s, some members of Congress wanted to add a new program just for pregnant women and young children. However, because of political opposition, this program did not pass until 1972.

This first program was a temporary one lasting for two years. It provided federal money to states, which then were to distribute these funds to local health and welfare agencies and non-profit health organizations. This money was to be used to provide extra food to pregnant women and children under four years of age who, in the opinion of the local welfare professionals, were malnourished or at risk of becoming so. Federal guidelines do not mandate who can receive the extra food. The law leaves this decision up to "competent professional authority" (quoted in Livingston 2002, 184).

The WIC program was made permanent in 1975. Pregnant women, nursing mothers, and young children with incomes of up to 185 percent of the federal poverty line, and who are anemic or have other nutritional risks, are eligible to receive vouchers or coupons with which they can purchase nutritious food at stores. Unlike the food stamp program, the WIC vouchers can be used only to purchase certain foods. Some states deliver the foods to the homes of pregnant women and children. These foods include iron-fortified infant formula, iron-fortified breakfast cereal, juice with a high vitamin C content, eggs, milk, cheese, peanut butter, dried beans, tuna fish, and carrots.

In the mid-1970s, concerns were raised about the amount of sugar in the cereal and flavored milk that WIC participants were allowed to buy, since sugar is associated with cavities and obesity. In 1977, the U.S. Department of Agriculture (USDA) noted that states could choose not to provide cereal or milk with a high sugar content. In 1982, the USDA eliminated flavored milk as an option, and instituted a rule that cereals should have no more than six grams of sugar per ounce (Richardson, Porter, and Jones 2004, 33–41).

As of 2008, WIC was available at 2,200 local agencies and 9,000 clinics across the country. In 2007, more than 8 million people participated in the program. They received about $39 worth of food per month. The WIC is not an "entitlement" program—in other words, every eligible person does not necessarily receive benefits. The federal government provides a finite amount of money to the program. WIC agencies are encouraged to provide benefits first to pregnant and lactating women, infants, and children who have a nutrition-related medical condition (such as anemia or underweight). If money is still available, the WIC program next provides benefits to pregnant women and children whose nutrition could be at risk because of an inadequate diet. Last served are any individuals in the community who might be at nutritional risk (WIC Web site).

In 1992, Congress added the Farmers' Market Nutrition Program to the WIC program, and as of 2008, forty-six states participate in this program. Women and children who are eligible for WIC are also eligible for this program. They receive additional coupons or vouchers with which to purchase fresh fruits and vegetables at local farmers' markets. The federal government provides up to $30 per year per person of benefits under this program, but states can provide additional funds to increase this amount. During 2006, about 2.5 million people participated in this program (WIC Web site).

The WIC program has been found to be effective at alleviating malnutrition and health problems related to an inadequate diet. Participation in WIC has been associated with fewer premature births, fewer infant deaths, less anemia, and improved cognitive development of children. A 1990 USDA study showed that for every dollar spent on WIC for pregnant women, health care costs through Medicaid (which provides health care for the poor) are reduced by $1.77 to $3.13 during the first sixty days after birth. For newborns alone, the cost-savings was $2.84 to $3.90. A 2006 USDA study showed that participation in WIC and the food stamp program reduced childhood anemia and nutritional deficiency. WIC also helped reduce child abuse and neglect, possibly because parents whose children are healthier experience less stress (Richardson, Porter, and Jones 2004, 8; Lee, Mackey-Bilaver, and Chin 2006, 20–21; WIC Web site).

See also: Child Abuse and Poverty; Food Stamp Program//Supplemental Nutrition Assistance Program; Hunger and Food Insecurity; Medicaid; Medicare; National School Lunch Act; Vouchers

Sources

Lee, Bong Joo, Lucy Mackey-Bilaver, and Meejung Chin. "Effects of WIC and Food Stamp Program Participation on Child Outcomes." Washington, DC: U.S. Department of Agriculture, December 2006.

Livingston, Steven G. *Student's Guide to Landmark Congressional Laws on Social Security and Welfare.* Westport, CT: Greenwood Press, 2002.

Richardson, Joe, Donna V. Porter, and Jean Yavis Jones. *Child Nutrition and WIC Programs: Background and Funding.* New York: Nova Science Publishers, 2004.

Web Site

WIC (Special Supplemental Nutrition Program for Women, Infants and Children). http://www.fns.usda.gov/wic/ (accessed October 2008).

SUPPLEMENTAL SECURITY INCOME

Supplemental Security Income (SSI) is a federal aid program created in 1972, for poor people who are elderly, or who are blind or have other disabilities. This replaced state-run programs for the disabled. The federal government provides a guaranteed minimum

Mothers and children follow along as they read through a nutrition booklet while attending a nutrition education class at the Dallas County Nutrition Program for Women, Infants and Children (WIC) office in Dallas, September 2006. (AP/Wide World Photos)

income that the states can then supplement as they wish. This was the first time that the federal government mandated and funded a guaranteed level of income for any segment of the population.

The federal government was considering the SSI provisions in the early 1970s, at about the same time as it was considering enacting a plan to provide a "guaranteed annual income" or "negative income tax" to every family in need. President Richard Nixon supported one particular guaranteed annual income plan called the Family Assistance Plan. These kinds of guaranteed income plans would have provided a certain basic level of income to all people in need and would have included work incentives. The Family Assistance

Plan would have replaced Aid to Families with Dependent Children, the welfare program that had been in place since 1935, to provide aid to poor single-mother families. The Family Assistance Plan generated much controversy and opposition, and never passed Congress although three different versions were introduced in 1970, 1971, and 1972.

While Congress was in the midst of considering the Family Assistance Plan, a few members of Congress had the idea to provide a guaranteed minimum income to only some of the needy, instead of to all of the needy. This new program would replace a number of previous programs that had provided aid to poor people who were elderly, or who were blind or otherwise disabled.

The older programs had been run by the states, and each state set different levels of payment and eligibility. Payments varied by more than 300 percent from state to state. The new federal program was to replace all the state programs, was to be funded and operated by the federal government, and was to create one minimum national standard that the states could supplement (Grimaldi 1980, 1–2; Livingston 2002, 169; Social Security History).

The SSI provisions were passed as part of amendments to the Social Security Act. President Nixon signed this into law on October 30, 1972. SSI payments are automatically adjusted each year based on cost-of-living increases. SSI is different from the disability payments offered since the 1950s through the Social Security Act. Social Security Disability Insurance is provided to anyone who has paid social security taxes into the system, and who happens to become disabled. SSI, in contrast, does not depend on anyone having paid into the system, and it is given based on economic need. Some people receive both SSI and Social Security disability insurance payments. SSI beneficiaries are generally eligible for Medicaid (federal health insurance for the poor) and may be eligible for food stamps (Social Security Disability Programs).

As of July 2008, more than 7 million people received SSI payments. The average monthly payment was $475 per month. While this is not enough by itself to lift anyone out of poverty, SSI can still help lift people above the poverty line when combined with other sources of income such as food stamps or earnings from other family members. For example in 2003, more than 2.4 million people saw their incomes rise above the poverty line because of SSI payments. This includes SSI recipients as well as other members of their family (Sweeney and Fremstad 2005; Social Security Administration, SSI Monthly Statistics).

See also: Aid to (Families with) Dependent Children; Food Stamp Program/Supplemental Nutrition Assistance Program; Guaranteed Annual Income; Medicaid; Medicare; Poverty Line; Social Security Act

Sources

Grimaldi, Paul L. *Supplemental Security Income: The New Federal Program for the Aged, Blind, and Disabled.* Washington, DC: American Enterprise Institute for Public Policy Research, 1980.

Livingston, Steven G. *Students' Guide to Landmark Congressional Laws on Social Security and Welfare.* Westport, CT: Greenwood Press, 2002.

Sweeney, Eileen P., and Shawn Fremstad. "Supplemental Security Income: Supporting People with Disabilities and the Elderly Poor." Washington, DC: Center on Budget and Policy Priorities, August 17, 2005. http://www.cbpp.org/7-19-05imm.htm (accessed September 2008).

Web Sites

Social Security Administration. Supplemental Security Income. http://www.ssa.gov/ssi/ (accessed September 2008).

Social Security Administration. SSI Monthly Statistics, July 2008. http://www.ssa.gov/policy/docs/statcomps/ssi_monthly/2008-07/table01.html (accessed September 2008).

Social Security Disability Programs. http://www.socialsecurity.gov/redbook/eng/overview-disability.htm (accessed September 2008).

Social Security History. http://www.socialsecurity.gov/history/history.html (accessed September 2008).

SUPREME COURT AND POVERTY

Traditionally in America, poverty alleviation was the job of local governments. In addition, since the founding of the United States and the drafting of the U.S. Constitution, the principle of individual liberty was considered to be extremely important. At the end of the 1800s and the beginning of the 1900s, when state and federal governments began to make laws to help the poor, the U.S. Supreme Court often struck down these laws as an infringement on individual freedom, or as an unconstitutional expansion of government power.

Child labor laws and minimum-wage laws were among the first and most important laws dealing with the federal government's involvement with poverty that the Supreme Court overruled. The first federal law against child labor was the Keating-Owen Child Labor Act of 1916, which banned goods produced by child workers from being transported and sold across state lines. In 1918, by a vote of five to four, the Court ruled the law unconstitutional, on the grounds that child labor was a matter for state governments to deal with (Jost 2003, 80).

In 1919, the federal government tried again to eliminate child labor with the Child Labor Tax Act, which imposed a 10 percent tax on the net profits of companies that employed young people. Again, state rights were invoked: in 1922, the U.S. Supreme Court invalidated the law, saying that the federal government could not use its taxing powers to regulate a matter that was the responsibility of state governments (Jost 2003, 80).

Minimum-wage laws had a similar fate. The Court took a narrow view of the federal government's role in regulating business, believing that the national government could get involved only in aspects of business that directly related to interstate commerce—shipping goods between states. In 1918, Congress had created a board to set minimum wages for women and children in the District of Columbia to protect them from poverty, which could lead to ill health and immoral behavior. In 1923, the Supreme Court declared that freedom of contract took precedence: a woman's freedom of contract should not be limited any more than a man's (Hall 1992, 9; Lewis and Wilson 2001, 11).

In 1933, the federal government tried again to deal with child labor and minimum wages with Title I of the National Industrial Recovery Act (NIRA), which pressured industries to come up with codes of fair competition, including prohibiting child labor, and setting minimum wages and maximum hours. The president was in charge of approving these industry codes. In 1935, the Supreme Court declared that Title I of the NIRA was invalid because the NIRA gave too much power to the president (Hall 1992, 757; Lewis and Wilson 2001, 832–833).

Toward the latter part of the 1930s, the Supreme Court began changing its views. The National Labor Relations Act passed in 1935, which gave the federal government more power to help workers organize into unions. Legal unions would help workers gain higher wages, which would be good for the economy. If workers could organize legally, there would be less need to hold strikes, which disrupted the economy. In 1937, this law was upheld by the Supreme Court, which declared that

Congress did have the power to regulate employers whose businesses affected interstate commerce, even if that particular business was not directly engaged in interstate commerce.

In 1938, Congress passed the Fair Labor Standards Act, which set nationwide minimum wages and maximum hours, and prohibited child labor. In 1941, the Court unanimously upheld the Fair Labor Standards Act and officially allowed the federal government to regulate such matters as child labor and minimum wages. This time, the court decided that these matters did affect interstate commerce, and therefore the federal government did have the right to regulate them (Jost 2003, 80).

During the 1930s, the federal government also began offering help to poor mothers with dependent children through the Social Security Act's Aid to Dependent Children section (the name was later changed to Aid to Families with Dependent Children). However, many states limited the eligibility of the mothers based on whether or not they were married, or were cohabiting with a man.

One of the most important legal cases involving welfare eligibility was *King v. Smith*. A Mrs. Smith of Alabama had been receiving welfare for herself and her four children, because the fathers of the children were dead or absent. In 1966, this aid was denied because welfare officials found out that she was having a sexual relationship with a man who visited her on the weekends. The man was not the father of her children, was not willing or able to support her and her children, and

was under no legal obligation to do so. Under Alabama law, however, a woman who cohabits with an able-bodied man was ineligible for government aid because it was assumed that the man—even if he was not the father of the children—should be supporting the children. Many other states also had similar provisions. Mrs. Smith approached a civil rights lawyer, who filed a case on her behalf. In 1968, the Supreme Court ruled that the Alabama law and other similar state laws were in conflict with the Social Security Act because they denied aid to eligible children simply on the basis of their mother's behavior. According to the court's opinion, "destitute children who are legally fatherless cannot be flatly denied federally funded assistance on the transparent fiction that they have a substitute father" (Kornbluh 2007, 67–68; *King v. Smith*; see Primary Document 41).

See also: Aid to (Families with) Dependent Children; Child Labor Laws—Supreme Court Cases; Minimum-Wage Laws—Supreme Court Cases; National Labor Relations Act

Sources

Hall, Kermit L., ed. *The Oxford Companion to the Supreme Court of the United States.* New York: Oxford University Press, 1992.

Jost, Kenneth, ed. *The Supreme Court A to Z.* Washington, DC: CQ Press, 2003.

Kornbluh, Felicia. *The Battle for Welfare Rights: Politics and Poverty in Modern America.* Philadelphia, PA: University of Pennsylvania Press, 2007.

Lewis, Thomas, and Richard Wilson, eds. *Encyclopedia of the U.S. Supreme Court.* Pasadena, CA: Salem Press, 2001.

PRIMARY DOCUMENT 41

Excerpt from *King V. Smith*, U.S. Supreme Court Case, 1968

It is interesting to compare this court decision with Theodore Roosevelt's 1909 speech in support of the Children's Bureau and mothers' pensions, in which he declares that only "deserving mothers" should receive support. In the opinion excerpted below, the court points out that denying aid to poor children is not a legal way to deal with issues of so-called immoral behavior on the part of the mother.

MR. CHIEF JUSTICE WARREN delivered the opinion of the Court.

Alabama, together with every other State, Puerto Rico, the Virgin Islands, the District of Columbia, and Guam, participates in the Federal Government's Aid to Families With Dependent Children (AFDC) program, which was established by the Social Security Act of 1935.... This appeal presents the question whether a regulation of the Alabama Department of Pensions and Security, employed in that Department's administration of the State's federally funded AFDC program, is consistent with Subchapter IV of the Social Security Act, and with the Equal Protection Clause of the Fourteenth Amendment. At issue is the validity of Alabama's so-called "substitute father" regulation which denies AFDC payments to the children of a mother who "cohabits" in or outside her home with any single or married able-bodied man....

I.

The AFDC program is one of three major categorical public assistance programs established by the Social Security Act of 1935.... The category singled out for welfare assistance by AFDC is the "dependent child," who is defined ... as a "needy child ... who has been deprived of parental support or care by reason of the death, continued absence from the home, or physical or mental incapacity of a parent, and who is living with" any one of several listed relatives. Under this provision, and, insofar as

relevant here, aid can be granted only if "a parent" of the needy child is continually absent from the home. Alabama considers a man who qualifies as a "substitute father" under its regulation to be a nonabsent parent within the federal statute. The State therefore denies aid to an otherwise eligible needy child on the basis that his substitute parent is not absent from the home.

Under the Alabama regulation, an "able-bodied man, married or single, is considered a substitute father of all the children of the applicant ... mother" in three different situations: (1) if "he lives in the home with the child's natural or adoptive mother for the purpose of cohabitation"; or (2) if "he visits [the home] frequently for the purpose of cohabiting with the child's natural or adoptive mother"; or (3) if "he does not frequent the home but cohabits with the child's natural or adoptive mother elsewhere." Whether the substitute father is actually the father of the children is irrelevant. It is also irrelevant whether he is legally obligated to support the children, and whether he does in fact contribute to their support. What is determinative is simply whether he "cohabits" with the mother.

The testimony below by officials responsible for the administration of Alabama's AFDC program establishes that "cohabitation," as used in the regulation, means essentially that the man and woman have "frequent" or "continuing" sexual relations. With regard to how frequent or continual these relations must be, the testimony is conflicting. One state official testified that the regulation applied only if the parties had sex at least once a week; another thought once every three months would suffice; and still another believed once every six months sufficient. The regulation itself provides that pregnancy or a baby under six months of age is prima facie evidence of a substitute father.

Between June 1964, when Alabama's substitute father regulation became effective, and January 1967, the total number of AFDC recipients in the State declined by about 20,000 persons, and the number of children recipients by about 16,000, or 22%. As applied in this case, the regulation has caused the termination of all AFDC payments to the appellees, Mrs. Sylvester Smith and her four minor children.

Mrs. Smith and her four children, ages 14, 12, 11, and 9, reside in Dallas County, Alabama. For several years prior to October 1, 1966, they had received aid under the AFDC program. By notice dated October 11, 1966, they were removed from the list of persons eligible to receive such aid. This action was taken by the Dallas County welfare authorities pursuant to the substitute father regulation, on the ground that a Mr. Williams came to her home on weekends and had sexual relations with her.

Three of Mrs. Smith's children have not received parental support or care from a father since their natural father's death in 1955. The fourth child's father left home in 1963, and the child has not received the support or care of his father since then. All the children live in the home of their mother, and except for the substitute father regulation are eligible for aid. The family is not receiving any other type of public assistance, and has been living, since the termination of AFDC payments, on Mrs. Smith's salary of between $16 and $20 per week which she earns working from 3:30 A. M. to 12 noon as a cook and waitress.

Mr. Williams, the alleged "substitute father" of Mrs. Smith's children, has nine children of his own and lives with his wife and family, all of whom are dependent upon him for support. Mr. Williams is not the father of any of Mrs. Smith's children. He is not legally obligated, under Alabama law, to support any of Mrs. Smith's children. Further, he is not willing or able to support the Smith children, and does not in fact support them. His wife is required to work to help support the Williams household.

II.

.... One of the statutory requirements is that "aid to families with dependent children ... shall be furnished with reasonable promptness to all eligible individuals...." As noted above, 406 (a) of the Act defines a "dependent child" as one who has been deprived of "parental" support or care by reason of the death, continued absence, or incapacity of a "parent." In combination, these two provisions of the Act clearly require participating States to furnish aid to families with children who have a parent absent from the home, if such families are in other respects eligible.

The State argues that its substitute father regulation simply defines who is a nonabsent "parent" under 406 (a) of the Social Security Act. The State submits that the regulation is a legitimate way of allocating its limited resources available for AFDC assistance, in that it reduces the caseload of its social workers and provides increased benefits to those still eligible for assistance. Two state interests are asserted in support of the allocation of AFDC assistance achieved by the regulation: first, it discourages illicit sexual relationships and illegitimate births; second, it puts families in which there is an informal "marital" relationship on a par with those in which there is an ordinary marital relationship, because families of the latter sort are not eligible for AFDC assistance.

We think it well to note at the outset what is not involved in this case. There is no question that States have considerable latitude in allocating their AFDC resources, since each State is free to set its own standard of need and to determine the level of benefits by the amount of funds it devotes to the program.... Further, there is no question that regular and actual contributions to a needy child, including contributions from the kind of person Alabama calls a substitute father, can be taken into account in determining whether the child is needy. In other words, if by reason of such a man's contribution, the child is not in financial need, the child would be ineligible for AFDC assistance without regard to the substitute father rule. The appellees here, however, meet Alabama's need requirements; their alleged substitute father makes no contribution to their support; and they have been denied assistance solely on the basis of the substitute father regulation. Further, the regulation itself is unrelated to need, because the actual financial situation of the family is irrelevant in determining the existence of a substitute father.

Also not involved in this case is the question of Alabama's general power to deal with conduct it regards as immoral and with the problem of illegitimacy. This appeal raises only the question whether the State may deal with these problems in the manner that it has here—by flatly denying AFDC assistance to otherwise eligible dependent children.

Alabama's argument based on its interests in discouraging immorality and illegitimacy would have been quite relevant at one time in the history of the AFDC program. However, subsequent developments clearly establish that these state interests are not presently legitimate justifications for AFDC disqualification. Insofar as this or any similar regulation is based on the State's asserted interest in discouraging illicit sexual behavior and illegitimacy, it plainly conflicts with federal law and policy.

A significant characteristic of public welfare programs during the last half of the 19th century in this country was their preference for the "worthy" poor. Some poor persons were thought worthy of public assistance, and others were thought unworthy because of their supposed incapacity for "moral regeneration." ... This worthy-person concept characterized the mothers' pension welfare programs, which were the precursors of AFDC.... Benefits under the mothers' pension programs, accordingly, were customarily restricted to widows who were considered morally fit.

In this social context it is not surprising that both the House and Senate Committee Reports on the Social Security Act of 1935 indicate that States participating in AFDC were free to impose eligibility requirements relating to the "moral character" of applicants.... During the following years, many state AFDC plans included provisions making ineligible for assistance dependent children not living in "suitable homes." ... As applied, these suitable home provisions frequently disqualified children on the basis of the alleged immoral behavior of their mothers....

In the 1940's, suitable home provisions came under increasing attack. Critics argued, for example, that such disqualification provisions undermined a mother's confidence and authority, thereby promoting continued dependency; that they forced destitute mothers into increased immorality as a means of earning money; that they were habitually used to disguise systematic racial discrimination; and that they senselessly punished impoverished children on the basis of their mothers' behavior, while inconsistently permitting them to remain in the allegedly unsuitable homes. In 1945, the predecessor of HEW produced a state letter arguing against suitable home provisions and recommending their abolition. Although 15 States abolished their provisions during the following decade, numerous other States retained them.

In the 1950's, matters became further complicated by pressures in numerous States to disqualify illegitimate children from AFDC assistance. Attempts were made in at least 18 States to enact laws excluding children on the basis of their own or their siblings' birth status. All but three attempts failed to pass the state legislatures, and two of the three successful bills were vetoed by the governors of the States involved. In 1960, the federal agency strongly disapproved of illegitimacy disqualifications.

Nonetheless, in 1960, Louisiana enacted legislation requiring, as a condition precedent for AFDC eligibility, that the home of a dependent child be "suitable," and specifying that any home in which an illegitimate child had been born subsequent to the receipt of public assistance would be considered unsuitable. In the summer of 1960, approximately 23,000 children were dropped from Louisiana's AFDC rolls. In disapproving this legislation, then Secretary of Health, Education, and Welfare Flemming issued what is now known as the Flemming Ruling, stating that as of July 1, 1961,

"A State plan ... may not impose an eligibility condition that would deny assistance with respect to a needy child on the basis that the home conditions in which the child lives are unsuitable, while the child continues to reside in the home. Assistance will therefore be continued during the time efforts are being made either to improve the home conditions or to make arrangements for the child elsewhere."

Congress quickly approved the Flemming Ruling, while extending until September 1, 1962, the time for state compliance. At the same time, Congress acted to implement the ruling by providing, on a temporary basis, that dependent children could receive AFDC assistance if they were placed in foster homes after a court determination that their former homes were, as the Senate Report stated, "unsuitable because of the immoral or negligent behavior of the parent."

In 1962, Congress made permanent the provision for AFDC assistance to children placed in foster homes and extended such coverage to include children placed in child-care institutions. At the same time, Congress modified the Flemming Ruling by amending 404 (b) of the Act. As amended, the statute permits States to disqualify from AFDC aid children who live in unsuitable homes, provided they are granted other "adequate care and assistance."

Thus, under the 1961 and 1962 amendments to the Social Security Act, the States are permitted to remove a child from a home that is judicially determined to be so unsuitable as to "be contrary to the welfare of such child." The States are also permitted to terminate AFDC assistance to a child living in an unsuitable home, if they provide other adequate care and assistance for the child under a general welfare program. The statutory approval of the Flemming Ruling, however, precludes the States from otherwise denying AFDC assistance to dependent children on the basis of their mothers' alleged immorality or to discourage illegitimate births.

The most recent congressional amendments to the Social Security Act further corroborate that federal public welfare policy now rests on a basis considerably more sophisticated and enlightened than the "worthy-person" concept of earlier times. State plans are now required to provide for a rehabilitative program of improving and correcting unsuitable homes; to provide voluntary family planning services for the purpose of reducing illegitimate births; and to provide a program for establishing the paternity of illegitimate children and securing support for them.

In sum, Congress has determined that immorality and illegitimacy should be dealt with through rehabilitative measures rather than measures that punish dependent children, and that protection of such children is the paramount goal of AFDC. In light of the Flemming Ruling and the 1961, 1962, and 1968 amendments to the Social Security Act, it is simply inconceivable, as HEW has recognized, that Alabama is free to discourage immorality and illegitimacy by the device of absolute disqualification of needy children. Alabama may deal with these problems by several different methods under the Social Security Act. But the method it has chosen plainly conflicts with the Act.

III.

Alabama's second justification for its substitute father regulation is that "there is a public interest in a State not undertaking the payment of these funds to families who because of their living arrangements would be in the same situation as if the parents were married, except for the marriage." In other words, the State argues that since in Alabama the needy children of married couples are not eligible for AFDC aid so long as their father is in the home, it is only fair that children of a mother who cohabits with a man not her husband and not their father be treated similarly. The

difficulty with this argument is that it fails to take account of the circumstance that children of fathers living in the home are in a very different position from children of mothers who cohabit with men not their fathers: the child's father has a legal duty to support him, while the unrelated substitute father, at least in Alabama, does not. We believe Congress intended the term "parent" in 406 (a) of the Act to include only those persons with a legal duty of support.

The Social Security Act of 1935 was part of a broad legislative program to counteract the depression. Congress was deeply concerned with the dire straits in which all needy children in the Nation then found themselves. In agreement with the President's Committee on Economic Security, the House Committee Report declared, "the core of any social plan must be the child." The AFDC program, however, was not designed to aid all needy children. The plight of most children was caused simply by the unemployment of their fathers. With respect to these children, Congress planned that "the work relief program and ... the revival of private industry" would provide employment for their fathers. As the Senate Committee Report stated: "Many of the children included in relief families present no other problem than that of providing work for the breadwinner of the family." Implicit in this statement is the assumption that children would in fact be supported by the family "breadwinner."

The AFDC program was designed to meet a need unmet by programs providing employment for breadwinners. It was designed to protect what the House Report characterized as "[o]ne clearly distinguishable group of children." This group was composed of children in families without a "breadwinner," "wage earner," or "father," as the repeated use of these terms throughout the Report of the President's Committee, 25 Committee Hearings 26 and Reports 27 and the floor debates 28 makes perfectly clear. To describe the sort of breadwinner that it had in mind, Congress employed the word "parent." A child would be eligible for assistance if his parent was deceased, incapacitated or continually absent.

The question for decision here is whether Congress could have intended that a man was to be regarded as a child's parent so as to deprive the child of AFDC eligibility despite the circumstances: (1) that the man did not in fact support the child; and (2) that he was not legally obligated to support the child. The State correctly observes that the fact that the man in question does not actually support the child cannot be determinative, because a natural father at home may fail actually to support his child but his presence will still render the child ineligible for assistance. On the question whether the man must be legally obligated to provide support before he can be regarded as the child's parent, the State has no such cogent answer. We think the answer is quite clear: Congress must have meant by the term "parent" an individual who owed to the child a state-imposed legal duty of support.

It is clear, as we have noted, that Congress expected "breadwinners" who secured employment would support their children. This congressional expectation is most reasonably explained on the basis that the kind of breadwinner Congress had in mind was one who was legally obligated to support his children. We think it beyond reason to believe that Congress would have considered that providing employment for the paramour of a deserted mother would benefit the mother's children whom he was not obligated to support.

By a parity of reasoning, we think that Congress must have intended that the children in such a situation remain eligible for AFDC assistance notwithstanding their mother's impropriety. AFDC was intended to provide economic security for children whom Congress could not reasonably expect would be provided for by simply securing employment for family breadwinners. We think it apparent that neither Congress nor any reasonable person would believe that providing employment for some man who is under no legal duty to support a child would in any way provide meaningful economic security for that child.

A contrary view would require us to assume that Congress, at the same time that it intended to provide programs for the economic security and protection of all children, also intended arbitrarily to leave one class of destitute children entirely without meaningful protection. Children who are told, as Alabama has told these appellees, to look for their food to a man who is not in the least obliged to support them are without meaningful protection. Such an interpretation of congressional intent would be most unreasonable, and we decline to adopt it. . . .

IV.

. . .. We think it well, in concluding, to emphasize that no legitimate interest of the State of Alabama is defeated by the decision we announce today. The State's interest in discouraging illicit sexual behavior and illegitimacy may be protected by other means, subject to constitutional limitations, including state participation in AFDC rehabilitative programs. Its interest in economically allocating its limited AFDC resources may be protected by its undisputed power to set the level of benefits and the standard of need, and by its taking into account in determining whether a child is needy all actual and regular contributions to his support.

All responsible governmental agencies in the Nation today recognize the enormity and pervasiveness of social ills caused by poverty. The causes of and cures for poverty are currently the subject of much debate. We hold today only that Congress has made at least this one determination: that destitute children who are legally fatherless cannot be flatly denied federally funded assistance on the transparent fiction that they have a substitute father.

Source

King v. Smith, 392 U.S. 309 (1968). Supreme Court Decisions, GPO Access. http://frwebgate5.access.gpo.gov/cgi-bin/TEXTgate.cgi?WAISdocID=4658 72455250+33+1+0&WAISaction= retrieve (accessed February 12, 2009).

T

TECUMSEH (1768–1813)

Tecumseh was a Shawnee leader who was active in the early 1800s. He spent years traveling across the continent, attempting to unite Native tribes against the U.S. government's efforts to remove them from their native lands. Tecumseh and other native leaders equated land with prosperity, and lack of land with poverty. Their attempt to keep their land was, in large part, an attempt to ensure that their people had adequate food, shelter, and other necessities.

Tecumseh was not the first American Indian leader to attempt to unite tribes against the white settlers and the U.S. government, and he was not the last, either. According to his biographer John Sugden, Tecumseh stands out among American Indian leaders because his goal was so vast.

> Tecumseh planned a mighty Indian confederation, from the Great Lakes to the Gulf of Mexico. . . . Whereas most Indian resistance in the three centuries after 1600 was relatively local, Tecumseh believed that the lands and cultures of all Indians were endangered by the advance of powerful white civilizations, and he worked on a national scale. (1998, 9)

Tecumseh was born in Ohio, in a village along the Scioto River. He may have been part white: his father's father was reported to have been an Englishman. Even during Tecumseh's childhood, Shawnee leaders were banding together with other Native American tribes against the white settlers who wanted their land. This trend continued as Tecumseh reached adulthood and became a warrior himself, fighting alongside American Indians of various tribes to keep their land out of the hands of the whites. However, after years of war, the confederacy of tribes began to fall apart. By 1795, about two-thirds of Ohio had been ceded, through treaties, to the U.S. government.

Tecumseh was the best known and most admired opponent of white frontier expansion. He combined military skill and oratory brilliance to fashion one of the biggest pan-Indian alliances. (Library of Congress)

Tecumseh moved west with a band of supporters and started a series of villages, finally settling on the White River in present-day Indiana. By 1800, Tecumseh's band was suffering from drunkenness, disease, and internal squabbling. It was harder to find game to hunt, because land was being enclosed into farms, causing wild animals to leave the area, and also because animals were being overhunted for the fur trade. Between 1802 and 1805, the governor of the Indiana Territory, William Henry Harrison, made several treaties with American Indians for their land, sometimes using bribery or threats to persuade American Indians to agree.

At this troubling time, Tecumseh's younger brother emerged as a prophet. He preached that to regain the favor of Waashaa Monetoo, the Great Spirit, the Shawnees must give up liquor, sorcery, murder, and warfare. They must not beat their wives and children. They must confess their sins, give up white men's ways, revitalize traditional ceremonies, and remain separate from the white culture and economy. If they did this, the Prophet said, then eventually Waashaa Monetoo would reward them by overthrowing the whites and restoring the American Indians to their former prosperity. The Prophet did not encourage American Indians to fight with the whites, but only to purify themselves internally in preparation for the Great Creator's actions (Sugden 1998, 145, 157).

In 1806, Tecumseh and the Prophet established a new town at present-day Greenville, Ohio, to unite many Shawnee bands. The Prophet invited other tribes to come and hear him preach. At times, hundreds of American Indians from nearby tribes streamed into Greenville to hear the Prophet's message. Eventually, the Prophet's religion reached west to the Dakota and Lakota Sioux, and south to present-day Mississippi, Alabama, and Florida.

Because of harassment from U.S. government officials, in 1808, Tecumseh and his brother moved west with their followers to the junction of the Wabash and Tippecanoe rivers in present-day Indiana. The settlement was known as Prophetstown. In September 1809, Indiana Territory Governor Harrison negotiated with a group of American Indians to buy 3 million acres of land. None of the American Indians who sold this land actually lived on the land.

EYE-WITNESS VIEW OF TECUMSEH

A white man, John Dunn Hunter, who was captured at a young age and lived for many years with the Osage tribe, describes Tecumseh's visit to the Osages. Tecumseh

> addressed them in long, eloquent and pathetic strains; and an assembly more numerous than had ever been witnessed on any former occasion listened to him with an intensely agitated, though profoundly respectful interest and attention.... I wish it was in my power to do justice to the eloquence of this distinguished man, but it is utterly impossible. The richest colors, shaded with a master's pencil, would fall infinitely short of the glowing finish of the original.... The unlettered Te-cum-seh gave extemporaneous utterance only to what he felt. It was a simple but vehement narration of the wrongs imposed by the white people on the Indians, and an exhortation for the latter to resist them.... This discourse made an impression on my mind which, I think, will last as long as I live. (43–44)

Source: Hunter, John Dunn. *Memoirs of a Captivity Among the Indians of North America, from Childhood to the Age of Nineteen.* London, UK: Longman, Hurst, Rees, Orme, Brown and Green, 1824. Viewed November 2007 online at: books.google.com.

This action spurred Tecumseh to travel across the country, trying to persuade American Indians of all tribes to join him in defending all American Indian lands from the U.S. government. Before the 1809 land sale, Tecumseh had been hoping to settle matters peacefully with the United States, but after the sale, he was prepared for war. He traveled east and may have reached as far as the Iroquois in New York. He then traveled west and south, to Minnesota, Illinois, and Missouri. He argued (as many American Indian leaders had argued before him) that American Indian land belonged to all the tribes, and that no one tribe or chief should be able to sell portions that many tribes depended on. He urged American Indians to stop fighting with each other and to give up the annuity fees and other provisions they received from the U.S. government as payment for their land.

Some tribes and warriors agreed to join him. Because of their poverty, it was difficult for many American Indians to agree to give up annuity fees and provisions. Back in Indiana, Tecumseh asked Harrison to put off bringing white settlers onto the lands that he had recently purchased, until the issue of landownership could be resolved. Tecumseh then traveled for six months through ten states in the southern United States. He told his audiences that the British government would help the American Indians fight the U.S. government. He also told them that the Great Spirit was on their side. Tecumseh managed to persuaded some to join him, although others refused, hoping to maintain peace with the U.S. government.

Harrison did not want to wait for Tecumseh's return and further negotiations. In 1811, while Tecumseh was away from Prophetstown in the southern United States, Harrison led troops against Prophetstown in the Battle of Tippecanoe. Prophetstown was

PRIMARY DOCUMENT 42

Excerpt from "Sleep No Longer, O Choctaws and Chickasaws," speech by Shawnee leader Tecumseh, 1811

In view of questions of vast importance, have we met together in solemn council tonight.... The whites are already a match for us all united, and too strong for any one tribe alone to resist; so that unless we support one another with our collective and united forces; unless every tribe unanimously combines to give check to the ambition and avarice of the whites, they will soon conquer us apart and disunited, and we will be driven away from our native country and scattered as autumnal leaves before the wind....

Sleep not longer, O Choctaws and Chickasaws, in false security and delusive hopes. Our broad domains are fast escaping from our grasp. Every year our white intruders become more greedy, exacting, oppressive and overbearing. Every year contentions spring up between them and our people and when blood is shed we have to make atonement whether right or wrong, at the cost of the lives of our greatest chiefs, and the yielding up of large tracts of our lands. Before the palefaces came among us, we enjoyed the happiness of unbounded freedom, and were acquainted with neither riches, wants nor oppression. How is it now? Wants and oppression are our lot; for are we not controlled in everything, and dare we move without asking, by your leave? Are we not being stripped day by day of the little that remains of our ancient liberty? Do they not even kick and strike us as they do their blackfaces? How long will it be before they will tie us to a post and whip us, and make us work for them in their cornfields as they do them? Shall we wait for that moment or shall we die fighting before submitting to such ignominy?

Have we not for years had before our eyes a sample of their designs, and are they not sufficient harbingers of their future determinations? Will we not soon be driven from our respective countries and the graves of our ancestors? Will not the bones of our dead be plowed up, and their graves be turned into fields? Shall we calmly wait until they become so numerous that we will no longer be able to resist oppression? Will we wait to be destroyed in our turn, without making an effort worthy of our race? Shall we give up our homes, our country, bequeathed to us by the Great Spirit, the graves of our dead, and everything that is dear and sacred to us, without a struggle? I know you will cry with me: Never! Never! Then let us by unity of action destroy them all, which we now can do, or drive them back whence they came. War or extermination is now our only choice. Which do you choose? I know your answer. Therefore, I now call on you, brave Choctaws and Chickasaws, to assist in the just cause of liberating our race from the grasp of our faithless invaders and heartless oppressors. The white usurpation in our common country must be stopped, or we, its rightful owners, be forever destroyed and wiped out as a race of people. I am now at the head of many warriors backed by the strong arm of English soldiers. Choctaws and Chickasaws, you have too long borne with grievous usurpation inflicted by the arrogant Americans. Be no longer their dupes. If there be one here tonight who believes that his rights will not sooner or later be taken from him by the avaricious American pale-faces, his ignorance ought to excite pity, for he knows little of the character of our common foe.

And if there be one among you mad enough to undervalue the growing power of the white race among us, let him tremble in considering the fearful woes he will bring down upon our entire race, if by his criminal indifference he assists the designs of our common enemy against our common country. Then listen to the voice of duty, of honor, of nature and of your endangered country. Let us form one body, one heart, and defend to the last warrior our country, our homes, our liberty, and the graves of our fathers.

Choctaws and Chickasaws, you are among the few of our race who sit indolently at ease. You have indeed enjoyed the reputation of being brave, but will you be indebted for it more from report than fact? Will you let the whites encroach upon your domains even to your very door before you will assert your rights in resistance? Let no one in this council imagine that I speak more from malice against the paleface Americans than just grounds of complaint. Complaint is just toward friends who have failed in their duty; accusation is against enemies guilty of injustice. And surely, if any people ever had, we have good and just reasons to believe we have ample grounds to accuse the Americans of injustice; especially when such great acts of injustice have been committed by them upon our race, of which they seem to have no manner of regard, or even to reflect. They are a people fond of innovations, quick to contrive and quick to put their schemes into effectual execution no matter how great the wrong and injury to us; while we are content to preserve what we already have. Their designs are to enlarge their possessions by taking yours in turn; and will you, can you longer dally, O Choctaws and Chickasaws?

Do you imagine that that people will not continue longest in the enjoyment of peace who timely prepare to vindicate themselves, and manifest a determined resolution to do themselves right whenever they are wronged? Far otherwise. Then haste to the relief of our common cause, as by consanguinity of blood you are bound; lest the day be not far distant when you will be left singlehanded and alone to the cruel mercy of our most inveterate foe.

Source

Vanderwerth, W. C. *Indian Oratory: Famous Speeches by Noted Indian Chieftains.* Norman, OK: University of Oklahoma Press, 1971, 62–66. Used with permission.

---

destroyed. After a brief return to Prophetstown, during which Tecumseh urged his followers to be peaceful until he could made the federation stronger, Tecumseh again began traveling and recruiting support from other American Indian tribes. By June 1812, Tecumseh may have had as many as 3,500 warriors as allies in the northern United States (Sugden 1998, 273).

In mid-June, the United States officially declared war on Great Britain, and the War of 1812 began. The United States was upset over Britain's interference in American sea trade. Tecumseh and his followers fought with the British. They believed that if the British won the war, the Englishmen would help protect American Indian homelands. Tecumseh died in the Battle of the Thames in October 1813.

His federation disintegrated after his death. The Prophet was not able to hold the coalition together, and neither was

Tecumseh's son, Paukeesaa. Soon after, the U.S. government passed the Indian Removal Act of 1830 and resumed its drive to remove American Indians from their homelands east of the Mississippi. American Indians of many tribes would not unite again until the 1940s, the beginning of the American Indian self-determination movement.

Tecumseh's speeches were occasionally written down by eyewitnesses. In the speech that appears in the accompanying sidebar, Tecumseh visited with the Choctaws and Chickasaws in Mississippi, hoping to convince them to join with his federation of American Indian tribes. Unfortunately, despite his eloquence, Tecumseh did not manage to convince the Choctaw chief, Pushmataha, to join him. Pushmataha hoped to continue peaceful relations with the U.S. government.

See also: Indian Removal Act of 1830; Indian Self-Determination

Source

Sugden, John. *Tecumseh: A Life*. New York: Henry Holt, 1998.

TEEN PREGNANCY PREVENTION

Teenaged women who give birth and choose to keep their babies almost always suffer from poverty. They generally do not have enough education to get a well-paying job, and they often choose not to marry, so must struggle along as single parents. In addition to being a cause of poverty, teen pregnancy is also often a result of poverty: young people who grow up in poor neighborhoods, and who experience family and community chaos, are at the highest risk for teenaged childbearing (Farber 2003, 67).

Pregnancy and childbirth among teenagers have been common for centuries. In the past, however, most of these teens were married by the time they gave birth. In addition, in earlier times, young people finished their education by the age of fifteen or sixteen, so pregnancy and childbirth in the late teen years did not interrupt education and hinder career opportunities, as it does today. In the late 1960s, births to unmarried teens began to go up, and governments grew concerned.

Since the 1970s, governments in the United States have been interested in preventing pregnancies among unmarried teens. State and local governments, as well as private organizations, have come up with a wide variety of programs to discourage teens from becoming pregnant. Programs include those that focus on sexuality, and those that do not. Programs that focus on sexuality include sex education classes in high school, birth control counseling at a health clinic, and the availability of contraception to teens. Programs that do not focus on sexuality, but that have had impact on reducing the teen pregnancy rate, include service-learning programs and early childhood education programs for disadvantaged children.

An ongoing argument in the government has to do with what teens should be taught about sexuality. Should they receive the message that abstinence from sex is the only acceptable choice? Or, should they receive objective information about pregnancy and birth control, with no values attached? Or,

ABSTINENCE-ONLY EDUCATION: THE FEDERAL GOVERNMENT'S DEFINITION

To receive funds for abstinence-only education, programs must adhere to all eight of the following principles, which first appeared in the 1996 Personal Responsibility and Work Opportunity Reconciliation Act.

For purposes of this section, the term 'abstinence education' means an educational or motivational program which—

(A) has as its exclusive purpose, teaching the social, psychological, and health gains to be realized by abstaining from sexual activity;

(B) teaches abstinence from sexual activity outside marriage as the expected standard for all school age children;

(C) teaches that abstinence from sexual activity is the only certain way to avoid out-of-wedlock pregnancy, sexually transmitted diseases, and other associated health problems;

(D) teaches that a mutually faithful monogamous relationship in context of marriage is the expected standard of human sexual activity;

(E) teaches that sexual activity outside of the context of marriage is likely to have harmful psychological and physical effects;

(F) teaches that bearing children out-of-wedlock is likely to have harmful consequences for the child, the child's parents, and society;

(G) teaches young people how to reject sexual advances and how alcohol and drug use increases vulnerability to sexual advances; and

(H) teaches the importance of attaining self-sufficiency before engaging in sexual activity.

Source: Personal Responsibility and Work Opportunity Reconciliation Act, Section 912, Abstinence Education.

should they be presented with something in between?

The federal government has been committed to abstinence-only education. Starting in 1981, the federal government began offering grants for demonstration and research programs for abstinence-only education, through Title XX (twenty) of the Public Health Service Act. In 1996, the Personal Responsibility and Work Opportunity Reconciliation Act made additional federal funds available for abstinence-only education. Section 912 of this law amended the Maternal and Child Health program to insert a specific definition of abstinence-only education. In 2000, the U.S. Congress added even more funds for abstinence-only education through the Community-Based Abstinence Education program (Howell and Keefe 2007).

Have government programs been effective at reducing the pregnancy and birth rates to teen mothers? At first they did not seem to be. The pregnancy

A high school health teacher leads a discussion with a group of students on sex education in Seattle, February 2006. Washington schools are not required to teach sex education; however, in the districts where the topic is taught, state law mandates that students be instructed on abstinence, not on birth control pills or other ways to prevent pregnancy. (AP/Wide World Photos)

rate for teens ages fifteen to nineteen rose from ninety-five per 1,000 in 1972, to 117 per 1,000 in 1990. Since then, however, the pregnancy rate has dropped. It reached 97.3 per 1,000 in 1995. The birth rates for teens ages fifteen to nineteen went down from sixty-two per 1,000 in 1991, to forty-one per 1,000 in 2005. However, in 2006, there was a slight uptick in the births to teens: forty-two per 1,000. As of 2000, about 40 percent of teen pregnancies were aborted (Farber 2003, 16, 19–20; Hamilton, Martin, and Ventura 2007, 9).

Douglas Kirby has surveyed studies of adolescent pregnancy prevention programs across the country to determine which programs have been most effective at preventing teen pregnancy and childbirth. Despite the federal government's insistence on abstinence-only

programs, such programs have not been shown to be particularly effective. By and large, they did not delay the first sexual experience or reduce the number of sexual partners. They also did not persuade more sexually active teens to return to abstinence. However, two-thirds of comprehensive sex education programs did show positive results in terms of delaying sex, reducing the number of sexual partners, increasing contraceptive use, persuading teens to return to abstinence, and reducing unprotected sex. These comprehensive programs emphasize abstinence as the best choice, but also stress that condoms and contraception should be used by teens who choose to have sex.

Other programs that work to prevent teen childbearing included providing emergency contraception to young women and one-on-one reproductive health counseling for young men. Among the programs that were not based on sexuality, a few showed promising results. Service learning programs combine after-school volunteer work with group discussion, journal writing, or some other kind of reflection or writing. These kinds of programs were found to delay sexual activity and reduce teen pregnancy rates. According to Kirby, researchers are not sure why these programs are effective. Year-round preschool programs for poor children have been found to reduce teen childbearing. When the young people who participated in the preschool programs became teens, they were much less likely to give birth than similar teens who had not been part of the preschool program (Kirby 2007, 15–19).

See also: Child Care and Early Childhood Education; Contraception and Abortion; Maternal and Child Health Services

Sources

Farber, Naomi. *Adolescent Pregnancy: Policy and Prevention Services.* New York: Springer Publishing Company, 2003.

Hamilton, Brady E., Joyce A. Martin, and Stephanie Ventura. "Births: Preliminary Data for 2006." National Center for Health Statistics, U.S. Department of Health and Human Services. *National Vital Statistics Report* 56, no. 7 *December 5, 2007).

Howell, Marcela, and Marilyn Keefe. "The History of Federal Abstinence-Only Funding." Washington, DC: Advocates for Youth, July 2007. http://www.advocatesforyouth.org/publications/factsheet/fshistoryabonly.htm (accessed October 2008).

Kirby, Douglas. "Emerging Answers 2007 Summary." Washington, DC: National Campaign to Prevent Teen and Unplanned Pregnancy, November 2007. http://www.thenationalcampaign.org/ea2007/ (accessed October 2008).

TEMPORARY ASSISTANCE FOR NEEDY FAMILIES

Temporary Assistance for Needy Families (TANF) is a federal program that provides cash aid to poor families. The assistance is "temporary" because families are eligible to receive this aid for only two years at a time, and for only five years during a lifetime. TANF was created by the Personal Responsibility and Work Opportunity Reconciliation Act of 1996. The TANF program replaced Aid to Families with Dependent Children (AFDC) in 1997. AFDC, a federal government program that started in 1935, had provided cash aid to all eligible families with no time limit.

After TANF was implemented, the number of poor families receiving cash aid declined dramatically. In 1994, 5.1 million families received AFDC; by 2003, 2 million families received TANF payments. Some of this decline was probably due to a strong economy and decreased unemployment. In addition, a great expansion of the Earned Income Tax Credit in 1993 provided low-income workers with added incentive to earn income. Medicaid was also expanded in 1997, to provide health insurance to children living above the poverty line, but still in lower-income families, and this probably enabled poor people to accept low-wage jobs that generally do not provide health insurance. Nevertheless, TANF policies probably did play a key role in helping to move people into the workforce (Lurie 2006, 21–22).

For decades, many people had wanted to reform "welfare," as AFDC was often called. Critics charged that

AFDC discouraged recipients from finding and keeping jobs. Since 1962, laws had attempted to encourage or require AFDC recipients to work and to stop relying on AFDC payments, but the result was the opposite: the AFDC rolls grew, with more and more people receiving benefits. In general, the federal and state governments did not devote enough money to the process of getting people into the workforce. There was not enough money to reach people, help them get jobs, and provide them with funding for other necessities such as child care.

TANF is different from AFDC because it is not an "entitlement." Under AFDC, every person who met the eligibility requirements was guaranteed the cash benefits, with no time limit. Under TANF, every eligible person will not necessarily receive benefits. The federal government provides TANF funding as a "block grant"—a lump-sum payment. States can decide when and how much cash assistance to provide. States are required to spend their own money on the TANF program. While some states call their cash assistance program TANF, other states have different names for their TANF programs, and many of these names emphasize work, such as the following: California Work Opportunity and Responsibility to Kids, Transitional Employment Assistance, Colorado Works, JOBS FIRST, and Employment First (Coven 2005).

The TANF law requires that a certain percentage of clients be required to participate in work activities. States can exempt certain clients from working, such as single parents with children under the age of one. Most states have emphasized quickly placing clients into jobs for which they are qualified. Clients who refuse to participate in work activities can have their cash benefit withdrawn. In general, people can receive TANF benefits only for two years in a row, and for five years during their entire lifetime, although states can choose to exempt up to 20 percent of their caseload due to hardship (Peterson, Song, and Jones-DeWeever 2003, 2).

As of 2008, single parents are required to participate in work activities for at least thirty hours a week, and two-parent families must work for thirty-five to fifty-five hours per week. If single parent with children under six cannot find child care, however, then the state cannot penalize them for failing to work. States are required to show that at least 50 percent of all families receiving TANF, and 90 percent of two-parent families, are participating in work activities. A "work activity" can include working, looking for a job (for up to four weeks in a row), providing community service, pursuing vocational training of up to twelve months, attending high school, or providing child care services to someone who is participating in community service (HHS, TANF Fact Sheet).

TANF has provided more money, in a more flexible format, than the AFDC program provided to the states. Because federal funding is provided as a block grant, and because this block grant has been generous, states have the ability to move money around and have had enough money to provide child care and transportation help to clients, which in turn enables them to look for and accept jobs (Lurie 2006, 16, 20).

What has happened to the people who left welfare? Since TANF is only

ENCOURAGING WORK

Welfare offices have changed their rules to emphasize work. For example, in Georgia (Temporary Assistance for Needy Families) TANF applicants must first search for a job before their welfare application is processed. In Michigan and Texas, welfare applicants must first attend a group session about work. Offices have also changed their decor to emphasize work. Here are slogans on some of the posters found in welfare offices in the year 2000:

"Welcome Job Seekers!"

"You Have A Choice, Choose A Job—Work First"

"Work First so that your child is not the next generation on welfare"

"Life works if you Work First!"

"There is a better alternative: Work First"

"Job Seekers Welcome!"

"Time Is Running Out/Welcome Job Seekers, Your Independence Is Our Success"

Source: Lurie, Irene. At the Front Lines of the Welfare System: A Perspective on the Decline in Welfare Caseloads. Albany, NY: Rockefeller Institute Press, 2006, 47, 55–56.

available for two years in a row, many people were forced to leave the program at around the turn of the century. Welfare offices around the country braced for an onslaught of needy people calling and pleading for help. In Cleveland, Ohio, social workers were given stacks of cash to hand out, in case they encountered clients with pressing emergencies. To their surprise, however, there was no emergency, because many former TANF recipients had already found jobs. The employment rate of low-income single mothers increased from 59 percent in 1996, to 68 percent in 2000. The income of the women who left welfare also rose about 25 percent over the TANF benefits they had been receiving. Still, many of these women continue to work low-wage occupations, such as sales, clerical, and service jobs (Peterson, Song, and

Jones-DeWeever 2003, x, 11; "From Welfare to Workfare" 2006).

Families with low incomes who are no longer eligible for TANF still may be eligible for other government programs such as food stamps, child care vouchers, housing vouchers, and Medicaid.

According to the Institute for Women's Policy Research, "increases in employment do not necessarily result in moving low-income single parents toward long-term economic self-sufficiency" (Peterson, Song, and Jones-DeWeever 2003, x). In other words, although TANF has been more successful than any other welfare-to-work program at encouraging work, poor women are still working for low wages.

See also: Aid to (Families with) Dependent Children; Earned Income Tax Credit;

Family Support Act of 1988; Food Stamp Program/Supplemental Nutrition Assistance Program; Housing—Low-Income; Medicaid; Mothers' Pensions; Personal Responsibility and Work Opportunity Reconciliation Act of 1996; Social Security Act; Welfare-to-Work Programs

Sources

Coven, Martha. "An Introduction to TANF." Washington, DC: Center on Budget and Policy Priorities, November 22, 2005. http://www.centeronbudget.org/1-22-02tanf2.htm (accessed September 2008).

"From Welfare to Workfare: Helping the Poor." *The Economist*, July 29, 2006, U.S. edition.

Lurie, Irene. *At the Front Lines of the Welfare System: A Perspective on the Decline in Welfare Caseloads*. Albany, NY: Rockefeller Institute Press, 2006.

Peterson, Janice, Xue Song, and Avis Jones-DeWeever. *Before and After Welfare Reform: The Work and Well-Being of Low-Income Single Parent Families*. Washington, DC: Institute for Women's Policy Research, 2003. http://www.iwpr.org/pdf/D454.pdf (accessed September 2008).

Web Site

HHS (U.S. Department of Health and Human Services). TANF Fact Sheet. http://www.acf.hhs.gov/opa/fact_sheets/tanf_fact-sheet.html (accessed September 2008).

TENNESSEE VALLEY AUTHORITY

The Tennessee Valley Authority (TVA) was an innovative New Deal agency designed to modernize a poor region of the country during the Great Depression: the area of 41,000 square miles in seven states, through which flowed the Tennessee River. The project had a number of different purposes, including regional planning, conservation, flood control, construction of a government-owned electrical power plant, river navigation, and economic stimulation by improving agriculture and making the area more attractive to industries. President Roosevelt signed the TVA in May 1933. The idea was to use the power of government and the innovation of business to plan and develop the area. Roosevelt called the TVA "a corporation clothed with the power of government but possessed of the flexibility and initiative of a private enterprise" (quoted in Davis 1986, 90).

Supporters had high hopes for the TVA when it first began. As Tennessee author James Agee wrote in an October 1933 article in *Fortune* magazine, "If TVA succeeds in its valley, it will be of significance not merely to the whole Southeast and not merely as a classic model for similar work in other valleys, but ultimately of importance to all the US" (p. 636).

However, the inspiring vision of the TVA did not last, although the project itself has continued to the present day. As sociologist Robert Leighninger notes, the TVA "still exists as a system of dams and reservoirs and as a producer of electricity, but as a vision of the American future it had evaporated within five years of its conception" (2007, 102).

When the TVA started, the area of the Tennessee Valley suffered from erosion and deforestation. James Agee describes the scene:

[C]areless fires and unregulated cutting have ruined and are ruining great stands of timber on watersheds where trees should have stood forever. Because natural resources which should have sustained local industries indefinitely have been shipped away in crude form and exhausted, whole

Construction of the Fort Loudon Dam in Tennessee by the Tennessee Valley Authority, 1942. Photo by Arthur Rothstein. (Library of Congress)

communities have been and are being pauperized, abandoned.... The waste land descends unimpeded into the river slowly but surely to choke the channels and to fill in great natural reservoirs that cannot be replaced. (2005, 633)

To remedy this situation, the TVA was set up as an independent government corporation, not part of any other federal government department. Dams were built to provide power, control flooding, and improve the navigability of the Tennessee River. Construction of the first dam, Norris Dam near Knoxville, Tennessee, was begun in 1933, and completed in 1936.

Included in the Norris Dam project were a series of parks and a community with housing, school, and shops. Some

cooperative businesses were also started. Workers on the Norris Dam labored five and a half hours per day, six days a week. In their free time, they had access to classes in academic and vocational subjects. Norris was meant to be a "model American community" and "a showcase for rural electrification, decentralized industry, and town planning," according to information on the New Deal Network Web site. Despite this idealism, however, the town of Norris was racially segregated: blacks were not allowed to live there. After the dam was completed, the workers left the town and it became simply a suburb of Knoxville. In 1948, the government sold the town to a private company.

Land that would be flooded once the dams were built was bought by the government, and the people were helped to move. The vast majority of people seemed happy with the government price for their land and were happy to move. The creation of the dams did break up communities, however.

In addition to bringing the Tennessee Valley into the future, the TVA made some attempt to preserve the past. The visitors' center at the Norris Dam sold locally made traditional crafts, such as furniture, metalwork, woven items, and baskets. Craft shops were also opened in Chattanooga and New York City.

Although one of the main goals of the TVA was to bring low-cost, government-run electricity to the area, the electricity delivery was delayed by court battles: private power companies challenged the constitutionality of the law. Once the law was upheld in 1938, the power started being delivered.

In addition to building dams, the TVA also planted trees, taught farmers how to decrease erosion on their lands, and eliminated malaria by getting rid of stagnant, standing water. Incomes went up: in 1929, the average person in the valley earned less than half of the national average, and by the early 1950s, they earned 79 percent of the national average. A fertilizer plant demonstrated new ways of making fertilizer (Leighninger 2007, 109–116).

One of the most innovative aspects of the TVA project has been its architecture. "The TVA was, in fact, an early platform for the development of modern architecture in the United States," says Christine Macy in a recent book on the architecture of the TVA. The chief TVA architect for its first eleven years, Roland Wank, favored a modernistic look for the dams, without the decorative elements that were popular at that time. Wank's plans, with their simple lines, emphasized the awesome size and power of the dams (Culvahouse 2007, 28, 41–47; Leighninger 2007, 107–109).

Despite its promising beginnings, like all New Deal projects, the TVA was overshadowed by the war effort during World War II. Since then, the TVA has been criticized for its environmental damage from coal-fired power plants that polluted the air and ruined the landscape when the coal was strip-mined. When the TVA added nuclear power plants, it was criticized for spending too much money (Biles 1991, 41–42).

As of 2009, the TVA is the nation's largest public (government-owned) power company. Since April 2000, the TVA has started to incorporate renewable energy in the form of solar power, wind energy generation, and methane gas. According to its Web site, the TVA's major role is as a source of cheap power: "The TVA's most important contribution is keeping power rates competitive. This helps attract industries that bring good jobs to the region. Low power rates also give Valley residents more money to spend on other goods and services."

While the TVA may not have lived up to the high hopes of its founders, it did succeed in lifting people out of poverty and jump-starting the economy in the Tennessee River Valley.

See also: Great Depression; New Deal; Roosevelt, Franklin Delano; Public Works Projects

Sources

Agee, James. "Tennessee Valley Authority," *Fortune*, October 1933. Reprinted in *James Agee: Film Writing and Selected Journalism*. New York: Library of America, 2005.

Biles, Roger. *A New Deal for the American People.* DeKalb, IL: Northern Illinois University Press, 1991.

Culvahouse, Tim, ed. *The Tennessee Valley Authority: Design and Persuasion.* New York: Princeton Architectural Press, 2007.

Davis, Kenneth S. *FDR: The New Deal Years, 1933–1937.* New York: Random House, 1986.

Leighninger, Robert D. Jr. *Long-Range Public Investment: The Forgotten Legacy of the New Deal.* Columbia, SC: University of South Carolina Press, 2007.

Web Sites

New Deal Network. TVA: Electricity for All: The Dams and Their Builders. http://newdeal.feri.org/tva/tva09.htm (accessed April 2008).

Tennessee Valley Authority. http://www.tva.gov/ (accessed April 2008).

TERMINATION AND RELOCATION

Termination and relocation were two federal government policies of the

1950s, regarding American Indians. These policies were supposed to relieve Native American poverty by assimilating American Indians into the larger mainstream culture. Instead, the policies caused even more poverty.

"Termination" referred to the idea that federal oversight over Native American tribes would be ended, or terminated. "Relocation" was the idea of moving Native Americans off the reservation and relocating them to urban areas, where they were supposed to find jobs.

The termination policy arose after the end of World War II. Congressional leaders wanted to end federal oversight of Native Americans because they believed many tribes had already achieved social and economic progress, and because supposedly significant cultural differences no longer existed between American Indians and the mainstream culture. Congressional leaders were looking for ways to save money, and cutting services to Native Americans seemed like a good idea. In addition, outsiders were eager to have access to federally protected American Indian land (Prucha 1984, 1043; 1985, 69).

Therefore, Congress passed the House Concurrent Resolution No. 108 in 1953, which stated that they intended to end the federal government supervision and control of American Indians. Congress then passed laws specifying termination procedures for various tribes.

The Menominee Tribe in Wisconsin was one of the first to be terminated. They were a relatively prosperous tribe, literate in English, and employing many tribal members in their forestry and lumber businesses. The tribe had recently won an $8.5 million judgment against the U.S. government because the government had mismanaged the tribe's forest resources. However, the payment of this judgment was held up until the Menominee agreed to termination. Under this pressure, the tribe voted in favor of termination. The reservation's land was taken over by a corporation. After termination, the sawmill laid off many tribal employees. The tribe's tax base could not support the schools and hospital. Instead of saving money, the federal and state governments ended up pouring in more funds to sustain the Menominees (Prucha 1984, 1051–1052, 1135–1136).

The Klamath tribe of Oregon had a similar experience. Before termination, they had paid for almost all their government services, including a hospital, using revenues from their 1.3 million acre reservation, which contained valuable timber and ranchland. The government believed that the Klamath was ready for termination because the tribe members were educated in public schools, intermarried with outsiders, and had a similar standard of living as their white neighbors. Congress terminated them in 1954. Most of the tribal land was sold to the U.S. government, and the proceeds were given to individual tribal members (Prucha 1984, 1053; Wilson 1999, 362–366).

According to James Wilson, the federal government came out the winner as a result of the termination policy. In terms of the Klamath reservation, "for $90 million [the federal government] acquired land and timber worth, by its own, very conservative reckoning, $120 million. In the twenty-five years following Termination, the former reservation, now largely incorporated in the Winnema National Forest, earned the United States close to $200 million" (1999, 366).

The Klamath Indians, in contrast, became impoverished after termination.

By 1966, because more and more of their members needed welfare or other government assistance, the federal and state governments ended up spending more than $6 million on termination and its aftereffects, whereas before termination, the Klamath had received just $144,000 per year from the government (Wilson 1999, 367, 376).

As these two cases became known to the public, the National Congress of American Indians and those who supported American Indians protested strongly against the policy of termination. One writer in an American Indian magazine pointed out that, without federal oversight, American Indians and their land were liable to be exploited by outsiders (Prucha 1984, 1056).

By the end of the 1950s, the policy of termination was no longer being followed. Although only about 3 percent of Native Americans had been subjected to termination, the policy created enormous fear among Native Americans. In fact, this fear was one factor that prompted Native American activists to take matters into their own hands and that prompted the drive toward American Indian self-determination that began in the 1960s (Prucha 1984, 1059).

In conjunction with the termination policy, the U.S. government also encouraged Native Americans to move off the reservation and get jobs in urban areas. The government's rationale for relocation was that, since American Indian populations were increasing, and since reservation land was not able to support more American Indians (because there was not enough land, or because the land was of poor quality), American Indians should be encouraged to leave the reservations and get jobs in other areas (Prucha 1984, 1080).

The government opened relocation offices in major cities. From 1953 to 1960, more than 30,000 American Indians were "relocated" from reservations to urban areas. Because about a third of the relocated American Indians ended up returning to the reservations, the government appropriated more and more money to help the American Indians adjust to their new environment. A study in Minneapolis in the mid-1950s showed that most American Indians arrived in the city without enough money, and with very little idea of how to find and keep a good job. They lived in overcrowded housing because they took in relatives from the reservation, and they sometimes succumbed to alcoholism. By the end of the 1950s, the government realized that the relocation program was not working as they had hoped (Prucha 1984, 1080–1084; Wilson 1999, 368).

See also: Indian Self-Determination

Sources

Prucha, Francis Paul. *The Great Father: The United States Government and the American Indians.* Lincoln, NE: University of Nebraska Press, 1984.

Prucha, Francis Paul. *The Indians in American Society: From the Revolutionary War to the Present.* Berkeley, CA: University of California Press, 1985.

Wilson, James. *The Earth Shall Weep: A History of Native America.* New York: Atlantic Monthly Press, 1999.

TITLE IX OF THE 1972 EDUCATIONAL AMENDMENTS

Women have historically suffered more poverty than men. One reason has been that women have been denied the opportunity to become educated to pursue well-paying careers. Although this cause of poverty was noted as far back as the early 1800s, by Mathew Carey, a Philadelphia bookseller and advocate for the poor, the U.S. government did not address the issue of gender discrimination in education until 1972.

Title IX of the 1972 Educational Amendments finally prohibited gender discrimination in any school or college that received federal funds. Because almost all schools and colleges do receive federal funds, this law has had a major impact on education nationwide.

Throughout the history of the United States, women have been denied admission to schools, colleges, and professional training. Colonial schools often taught only boys. Girls, if taught at all, were given instruction for a few hours in the early morning or late afternoon, or during the summer, when boys did not attend. When high schools became popular in the 1800s, sometimes they did not accept girls. Other high schools provided different classes and teachers for boys and girls. State-supported universities as well as elite private colleges refused to admit women during the 1800s and into the 1900s (Sadker and Sadker 1994, 15–35).

As late as the 1960s in high school, girls were routinely barred from shop classes, physics classes, and athletic programs. Women were denied admission to medical school, law school, and other professional schools. In 1966, the daughter of President Lyndon Johnson, Luci Baines Johnson, was denied admission to the school of nursing at Georgetown University because she was married—the school did not admit married women. As late as 1970,

Virginia state law barred women from admission to the University of Virginia's College of Arts and Sciences (*Title IX: 25 Years of Progress* 1997).

In 1971, Congresswoman Edith Green (D-OR) held hearings on gender discrimination in education. In the early 1970s, several members of Congress, including Green, introduced bills that would have prohibited gender discrimination in education. The controversial aspect of these bills was college admissions policies. Some members of Congress wanted to continue to allow colleges and universities to discriminate based on gender in terms of who they admitted to their institutions. The final bill prohibited gender discrimination in admissions at public colleges and universities (except for those that traditionally had been single-sex institutions), but allowed discrimination at private colleges and universities (Carleton 2002, 173–174).

During the 1970s, many schools did not comply with Title IX. After the law's passage, members of Congress continued to try to offer amendments and laws to weaken or disable the law, but none of these laws passed. The Health, Education, and Welfare Department took several years to come out with rules for implementing and enforcing the law. Meanwhile, girls continued to be barred from advanced math courses and certain traditionally male vocational classes. School districts spent much more money on boys' sports than on girls' sports. Colleges awarded many more scholarships to young men than to young women (Sadker and Sadker 1994, 36; Carleton 2002, 175).

One setback for Title IX was a 1984 Supreme Court decision, *Grove City College v. Bell*, in which the Court

---

"IT MADE PERFECTLY GOOD SENSE"

Educators Myra and David Sadker asked participants in their workshops to relate stories of sex discrimination in education before Title IX was passed. Here is one such story:

> I went to a large university in New England during the 1960s. I was called into the dean's office along with another senior, a young man named John. The dean congratulated us both on our academic performance. He told us there was one scholarship to graduate school available. Although I had a slightly higher grade point average, he decided to award the money to John who, he said, would have to support a family some day. What really gets me today, almost thirty years later, is that back then it all made perfectly good sense. Even though John came from a rich background and I came from a poor one, I agreed that the scholarship should go to John. Today I am the sole support of my two children, and I wish I had that graduate degree.

Source: Sadker, Myra, and David Sadker. *Failing at Fairness: How America's Schools Cheat Girls.* New York: Charles Scribner's Sons, 1994, 34–35.

---

ruled that the federal government could regulate only those education programs that directly received federal funds. In other words, Title IX did not apply to the entire school or college, but only to the specific program receiving the federal funds. In response, Congress passed the Civil Rights Restoration Act in 1988, making it clear that Title IX applied to schools and colleges as a whole, and not just to specific programs (Carleton 2002, 176).

Title IX has helped women to gain access to education opportunities. In 1971, 18 percent of women and 26 percent of men had completed four or more years of college. As of 1997, women accounted for a majority of college students and earned a majority of master's degrees. In 1966, just half a percent of engineering degrees were earned by women. By 1991, women earned 15 percent of engineering degrees. Title IX prohibits schools from expelling or discriminating against girls who become pregnant, and the law has helped lower the dropout rate of girls who do become pregnant in high school. From 2002 to 2006, the Office of Civil Rights at the Department of Education investigated and resolved more than 1,100 complaints brought under Title IX (*Title IX: 25 Years of Progress* 1997; "35th Anniversary of Title IX" 2007).

See also: Carey, Mathew

Sources

Carleton, David. *Landmark Congressional Laws on Education.* Westport, CT: Greenwood Press, 2002.

Sadker, Myra, and David Sadker. *Failing at Fairness: How America's Schools Cheat Girls.* New York: Charles Scribner's Sons, 1994.

Title IX: 25 Years of Progress. Washington, DC: U.S. Department of Education, June 1997. http://www.ed.gov/pubs/TitleIX/index.html (accessed August 2008).

"35th Anniversary of Title IX." Press Release. Washington, DC: U.S. Department of Education, June 2007. http://www.ed.gov/news/pressreleases/2007/06/06222007.html (accessed August 2008).

TOWNSEND MOVEMENT

The Townsend Movement was one of several movements for old-age pensions that occurred during the first decades of the twentieth century. As the American population grew more urban, it became harder for families to support their elderly parents and relatives. Many families no longer owned a farm that could easily make use of the limited labor and provide for the needs of the elderly. During the 1920s, the Fraternal Order of Eagles managed to push for passage of a few state old-age pension laws. The American Association for Old Age Security launched its campaign for old-age pensions in 1927. The Townsend Movement, which started in 1933, was the largest and most influential of the old-age pension movements.

The elderly were hit hard by the Great Depression, which started in 1929. About half of those over the age of sixty-five were not able to support themselves. State and private pension systems covered only a small proportion of people. Still, during the first years of the Depression, the federal government did nothing to support an old-age pension system. Many politicians still believed that old-age pensions should be provided by state governments. (Holtzman 1963, 20–24).

The Townsend Movement called for a payment of $200 per month to anyone over sixty years of age who agreed not to work. (This was a large amount of money—the equivalent to about $3,000 in 2007, based on the Consumer Price Index, the price of common goods and services). This was to be funded by a 2 percent tax on the sale of goods and other business transactions. Recipients of the money would be required to spend it within the month. This provision would ensure that the money would be used to stabilize the economy, according to its supporters (Amenta 2006, 1).

The Townsend Plan was popular and influenced the Social Security system established under President Franklin Roosevelt. According to Roosevelt's Secretary of Labor, Frances Perkins, who helped write the Social Security Act, "In some districts the Townsend Plan was the chief political issue, and men supporting it were elected to Congress. The pressure from its advocates was intense" (Perkins 1946, 279).

Francis Townsend was a physician in Long Beach, California. This part of California had experienced a 100 percent increase in its elderly population from 1920 to 1930, mainly due to people moving into the state. Townsend was born in 1867, and turned sixty in 1927. He thought of his plan not only as a way to help the elderly, but also as a way to end the Depression by putting money into people's hands (Holtzman 1963, 25–26, 32–33).

Townsend first publicized his plan through a letter in his local newspaper. Readers were so enthusiastic about his plan that the newspaper devoted pages to their letters. People visited his home to find out how to put his ideas into action, and Townsend decided to devote his time to promoting the plan. When people criticized the plan as

Townsend Plan supporter displays a sign at a rally in Columbus, Kansas, May 1936. Photo by Arthur Rothstein. (Library of Congress)

being too expensive, Townsend said he chose $200 per month because this amount, spent every month, would provide money for the employment of one person. Critics charged that the proposed tax to fund the plan could not possibly provide such a high monthly stipend to each person over sixty (Holtzman 1963, 35–39).

Despite the criticism, "Townsend Clubs" sprang up throughout the country, and at its height, the movement had 2 million members—about 20 percent of those sixty years and older. This was a large movement—"a size never reached by any organization in the civil rights or women's rights movement," points out Edwin Amenta, a sociology professor at the University of California (2006, 1).

When President Franklin Roosevelt set up his Committee on Economic Security in 1934 to come up with a plan for old-age pensions and other permanent social insurance programs, the committee received as many as 1,500 letters per day asking them to support the Townsend Plan. The committee, however, believed that Townsend's plan was not economically sound. They proposed a plan that would provide in the neighborhood of $30 per month to the elderly. When the Social Security bill was introduced into the U.S. Congress in January 1935, a congressman from Long Beach, California, introduced the Townsend bill. Administration officials and members of Congress criticized the Townsend bill, saying that it would cost half the nation's income. Townsend Plan supporters then rewrote their bill to specify that pensions would not exceed the money that the tax generated. Still, the bill was defeated, and the Social Security Act passed in August 1935 (Amenta 2006, 76, 81, 85, 90, 92).

Although the Townsend bill did not pass, the pressure exerted by Townsend Plan supporters probably helped to ensure the passage of the Social Security Act, because politicians knew that some sort of old-age pension plan had to be enacted. After the passage of the Social Security Act, the Townsend Movement continued to be strong until about 1941, and it probably helped to increase benefits levels in the 1939 amendments to the Social Security Act (Amenta 2006, 221–222).

See also: Great Depression; Social Security Act

Sources

Amenta, Edwin. *When Movements Matter: The Townsend Plan and the Rise of Social Security*. Princeton, NJ: Princeton University Press, 2006.

Holtzman, Abraham. *The Townsend Movement: A Political Study*. New York: Bookman Associates, 1963.

Perkins, Frances. *The Roosevelt I Knew*. New York: Viking Press, 1946.

Web Site

Measuring Worth (comparing the U.S. dollar value over history). http://www.measuringworth.com/uscompare/ (accessed May 2008).

U

UNEMPLOYMENT INSURANCE

The loss of a job is one of the major causes of poverty, and unemployment insurance is one of the most effective government programs to alleviate such poverty.

Unemployment insurance is part of the federal Social Security Act, passed in 1935. According to this law, each state is required to set up an unemployment insurance program. States can decide who is eligible (temporary and part-time workers may not be eligible), and how much money the unemployed workers can receive. States can also require unemployed people to register with the state employment service so they can find another job. Generally, programs provide benefits for twenty-six weeks to people who have lost their jobs through no fault of their own, and most states pay less than 50 percent of the average weekly wage in that state. During an economic depression, when unemployment is high, benefits may be continued for a longer time. The program is funded by federal and state payroll taxes (O'Leary and Wandner 1997, 681; National Academy of Social Insurance Web site).

For most of American history, unemployment was viewed as bad luck and as nothing that the government needed to get involved with. Workers were expected to save money when they were working, to tide them over during periods of unemployment. Those who suffered from frequent unemployment were often seen as lazy, unstable, or incapable of holding down a steady job (O'Leary and Wandner 1997, 3–4).

During the economic depression of the 1890s, some business and government leaders offered a few programs to help the unemployed, such as small-scale public works projects, or special unemployment funds, but these were temporary and generally only covered a small fraction of workers. Social scientists and economics urged businesses to plan their production to avoid having to lay off workers, but many businesses were unable or unwilling to do this. Employment services were also started by many state and city governments to help workers find jobs and get training for new jobs. However, these services were generally not successful because often employers did not want to hire workers from the government-run employment services. In the early 1900s, even some labor union leaders rejected the idea of government-sponsored unemployment insurance because they wanted the unions themselves to take care of the problem by negotiating for shorter work hours (so more people could work) and by setting up union unemployment insurance plans (Katz 1996, 202–205).

By the time of the Great Depression of the 1930s, it became clear to government leaders and labor union leaders that something more had to be done. It was apparent that unemployment was not just a problem affecting the individual worker, but something that affected the entire economy, because when a lot of people were out of work, they had no money to buy the things that industry produced. Businesses then earned less money and laid off more employees, and the downward economic cycle continued.

One government response to unemployment during the Great Depression was to create jobs. The federal government's New Deal program under President Franklin Roosevelt got involved for the first time in large-scale public works projects. The federal government provided billions of dollars and hired millions of unemployed people to build roads, bridges, schools, and parks; to prepare meals for schoolchildren; to sew clothes for the needy; and for many other projects.

Another response to unemployment was the passage of unemployment insurance laws. With the support of labor leaders, the first state to pass an unemployment insurance law was Wisconsin, in 1932. Four more states soon passed similar laws. These first laws provided low benefits for a limited amount of time—about ten weeks. In 1935, the federal Social Security Act made unemployment insurance mandatory for all states (Katz 1996, 205–206).

At first, agricultural, domestic, nonprofit, and government employees were excluded from this unemployment insurance, as were employees of businesses with fewer than eight workers. Workers had to wait three or four weeks before receiving payments, and benefits lasted an average of sixteen weeks. From the 1940s to the 1970s, as the economy improved and unemployment was low, benefits were extended for more weeks, the maximum benefit was increased, and the waiting period was decreased. As of amendments passed in 1976, the majority of workers are covered by unemployment insurance. One problem with unemployment insurance is that it has not kept up with the changing way people work. Compared with 1935, when the law was passed, more people are now self-employed or choose to work part-time, and generally unemployment insurance does not cover them (O'Leary and Wandner 1997, 669–675; National Academy of Social Insurance Web site).

Unemployment insurance has had a positive impact on family poverty rates as well as on the nation's economy. According to the Center for Budget and Policy Priorities, unemployment insurance is one of the top government programs to lift children above the poverty line (see Preface, figure 1, for more details). Unemployment insurance also helps stabilize the economy. A 1999 study commissioned by the U.S. Department of Labor found that economic recessions in the 1970s, 1980s, and 1990s would have been 17 percent deeper without the unemployment insurance program (Chimerine, Black, and Coffey 1999, 10–11).

See also: Great Depression; New Deal; Public Works Projects; Social Security Act

Sources

Chimerine, Lawrence, Theodore S. Black, and Lester Coffey (Coffey Communications, LLC). "Unemployment Insurance as an Automatic Stabilizer: Evidence of Effectiveness Over Three Decades," ed. Martha Matzke. Washington, DC: U.S. Department of Labor, July 1999 (study on unemployment insurance). http://wdr.doleta.gov/owsdrr/99-8/99-8.pdf (accessed May 2008).

Katz, Michael. *In the Shadow of the Poorhouse: A Social History of Welfare in America.* New York: Basic Books, 1996.

O'Leary, Christopher J., and Stephen A. Wandner, eds. *Unemployment Insurance in the United States: Analysis of Policy Issues.* Kalamazoo, MI: W.E. Upjohn Institute for Employment Research, 1997.

Web Site

National Academy of Social Insurance. Sourcebook on Unemployment Insurance. http://www.nasi.org/publications3901/publications_list.htm?cat_id=78 (accessed May 2008).

UNITED NATIONS HUMAN RIGHTS TREATIES

United Nations treaties are legally binding documents. Countries that sign and ratify these treaties are obliged to follow them. Some United Nations treaties deal with human rights issues, and some of these human rights include the alleviation of poverty. United Nations treaties are also called "conventions" or "covenants." The United Nations human rights treaties are based on the Universal Declaration of Human Rights, which was adopted by the United Nations in 1948.

The human rights treaties have positively affected the laws and actions of many countries that have ratified them. Many law schools teach international human rights law, based on the United Nations human rights treaties. Some countries have created new laws or constitutional amendments that incorporate the goals of the human rights treaties. Some countries have created "action plans" based on the treaties. Nongovernmental organizations publicize the requirements of the treaties and pressure governments to comply with them (Heyns and Viljoen 2002, 7–19).

The United States takes United Nations treaties seriously. Once ratified, treaties are considered to be law. However, the human rights treaties require additional "implementing legislation" to specify how the treaty will be interpreted by the courts (Walker, Brooks, and Wrightsman 1999, 38).

The United Nations has adopted dozens of human rights treaties. The following United Nations treaties deal, at least in part, with poverty as a human rights violation. While the United States has signed all of the following treaties, it has ratified only one of them. Signing a treaty indicates that a nation intends to ratify the treat. The treaty does not become binding until it is ratified or otherwise formally agreed to. In the United States, ratification involves a vote by the U.S. Senate.

International Convention on the Elimination of All Forms of Racial Discrimination (CERD)

This treaty was adopted by the United Nations in December 1965. It calls for an end to discrimination based on race, ethnicity, nationality, or color. Everyone is to have equality in terms of legal, political, economic, and social rights. Everyone should have the right to work, to receive fair pay, and to join labor unions. Everyone should have a right to housing, public services, medical care, and education. This treaty has been ratified by 173 countries as of August 2008. The United States signed this convention in September 1966, and ratified it in October 1994 (OHCHR, CERD Ratification).

International Covenant on Economic, Social and Cultural Rights (CESCR)

This covenant was adopted by the United Nations General Assembly on 1966 and is part of what is known as the International Bill of Human Rights, which also includes the Universal Declaration of Human Rights (adopted in 1948), and the International Covenant on Civil and Political Rights (adopted in 1966). The CESCR calls for the right to work, to be paid fair wages, and to have safe working conditions. Workers must have the right to join trade unions and to benefit from "social insurance" (government-sponsored insurance programs). The convention calls on countries to take steps to ensure that all people have an adequate standard of living, including appropriate food, clothing, shelter, and medical care. Primary (elementary) education should be required and free, and higher education should be made accessible to everyone. This treaty has been ratified or otherwise agreed to by 159 countries, as of September 2008. The United States signed this treaty in October 1977, but as of October 2008, has not yet ratified it (OHCHR, CESCR Ratification).

Convention on the Elimination of All Forms of Discrimination against Women (CEDAW)

This treaty was adopted by the United Nations in December 1979. It calls on governments to make sure that women have equal legal, political, economic, social, and cultural rights with men. In terms of economic rights, the convention specifies that women should receive equal pay for equal work, and they should have equal access to education and employment opportunities, as well as equal access to bank loans, mortgages, and other forms of credit. Countries should ensure that women have maternity leave with pay, or with benefits, and without loss of employment or seniority. This treaty has been ratified or agree to by 185 countries, as of February 2008. The United States signed this treaty in July 1980, but as of October 2008, has not yet ratified it (OHCHR, CEDAW Ratification).

Convention on the Rights of the Child (CRC)

This treaty was adopted by the United Nations in November 1989. This is a "bill of rights" for children, specifying their rights to a nationality, to be raised by their parents whenever possible, to have access to education and health care, and to have freedom of thought, religion, and peaceful assembly. In terms of economic rights, the treaty states that countries must "recognize the right of every child to a standard of living adequate for the child's physical, mental, spiritual, moral and social development" (UNHCHR, Convention on the Rights of the Child).

The CRC has been ratified by 193 countries as of February 2008. The United States signed this treaty in February 1995, but as of October 2008, is one of only two countries that has not yet ratified it. The other country is Somalia (which is not able to ratify because it has no recognized government) (OHCHR, CRC Ratification).

Enforcement

The United Nations human rights treaties are "enforced" mainly by public pressure. There is no permanent international police force that will come into a country and demand that they follow the treaties. However, once a treaty has been widely accepted around the world, countries that do not follow the treaty's provisions are often held up to public scrutiny. Countries that ratify human rights treaties are required to submit reports to the United Nations, detailing how their country is complying with the goals of the treaties. Also, each treaty has a separate committee of experts that monitors how the treaties are being implemented in each country. Some treaties allow individuals to make complaints to the committee against their countries, whereas other treaties do not have this provision.

Even countries that have not ratified the United Nations human rights treaties can be held accountable for their human rights violations. For example, sometimes the United Nations will set up temporary working groups or "special rapporteurs" to investigate and report on certain human rights violations in specific countries (*Rights of Women* 1998, 9–15).

While the United States has been a leader in terms of drafting human rights treaties, it has been reluctant to actually ratify them and make them part of U.S. law. Some members of Congress, as well as members of the American public, fear that United Nations treaties will supplant U.S. laws and cause a change in the American way of life. People fear that, by signing the United Nations treaties, the United States would be subject to control by the United Nations. During the Cold War years (mid-1940s to early 1990s), when the United States saw the Soviet Union, a Communist country, as its main enemy, some people believed the United Nations treaties to be pro-Communist.

Opposition to the treaties arose while the first treaties were still being written. In the 1940s and 1950s, the American Bar Association (a professional group of lawyers) opposed the United Nations treaties, and warned that these treaties would threaten the rights of Americans. In the 1950s, a constitutional amendment called the Bricker Amendment was considered. This amendment, proposed by Senator John Bricker of Ohio, stated that international treaties could not deny or abridge any rights in the Constitution. The Bricker Amendment also made it clear that international treaties could not supplant state laws.

In 1953, the administration of President Dwight Eisenhower made a commitment not to ratify the human rights treaties that were then being drafted in the United Nations. In 1954, the Bricker Amendment failed to receive the two-thirds majority needed for an amendment to the Constitution. Nevertheless, opposition to most United Nations human rights treaties has remained strong in the U.S. Senate (Kaufman 1990, 2, 20, 94–106).

In 1994, the United States finally did ratify CERD. The United States has submitted two reports to the United Nations in compliance with this treaty. In 2006, the United Nations issued an "Early Warning and Urgent Action Procedure" to the United States, in response to Native American tribes that asked the United Nations to take action, because, according to the complaint, Western Shoshone people were being denied access to their ancestral land. The United Nations Committee for the Elimination of Racial Discrimination urged the United States to open a dialogue with the Western Shoshone people; freeze plans to privatize their ancestral land; and stop imposing grazing fees, horse and livestock impoundments, and arrests, on the Western Shoshone people for using their ancestral land ("Early Warning" 2006).

See also: International Covenant on Economic, Social, and Cultural Rights; Universal Declaration of Human Rights

Sources

"Early Warning and Urgent Action Procedure: Decision 1 (68): United States of America." Committee for the Elimination of Racial Discrimination, April 11, 2006. http://www.unhchr.ch/tbs/doc.nsf/(Symbol)/25eeac288211bee9c1257181002a3cfb?Opendocument (accessed October 2008).

Heyns, Christof, and Frans Viljoen. *The Impact of the United Nations Human Rights Treaties on the Domestic Level.* The Hague, Netherlands: Kluwer Law International, 2002.

Kaufman, Natalie Hevener. *Human Rights Treaties and the Senate: A History of Opposition.* Chapel Hill: University of North Carolina Press, 1990.

Rights of Women: A Guide to the Most Important United Nations Treaties on Women's Human Rights. New York: International Women's Tribune Centre, 1998.

Walker, Nancy E, Catherine M. Brooks, and Lawrence S. Wrightsman. *Children's Rights in the United States: In Search of a National Policy.* Thousand Oaks, CA: Sage Publications, 1999.

Web Sites

United Nations Office of the High Commissioner for Human Rights. Committee on Economic, Social, and Cultural Rights (CESCR). http://www2.ohchr.org/english/bodies/cescr/ (accessed August 2009).

United Nations Office of the High Commissioner for Human Rights. Committee on the Elimination of Discrimination against Women (CEDAW). http://www2.ohchr.org/english/bodies/cedaw/ (accessed October 2008).

United Nations Office of the High Commissioner for Human Rights. Committee on the Elimination of Racial Discrimination (CERD). http://www2.ohchr.org/english/bodies/cerd/ (accessed August 2009).

United Nations Office of the High Commissioner for Human Rights. Committee on the Rights of the Child (CRC) http://www2.ohchr.org/english/bodies/crc/ (accessed October 2008).

United Nations Office of the High Commissioner for Human Rights. Convention on the Elimination of All Forms of Discrimination against Women. http://www2.ohchr.org/english/law/cedaw.htm (accessed October 2008).

United Nations Office of the High Commissioner on Human Rights. Convention on the Rights of the Child. http://www2.ohchr.org/english/law/crc.htm (accessed October 2008).

United Nations Office of the High Commissioner on Human Rights. International Covenant on Economic, Social and Cultural Rights. http://www2.ohchr.org/

english/law/cescr.htm (accessed October 2008).

United Nations Office of the High Commissioner on Human Rights. International Convention on the Elimination of All Forms of Racial Discrimination. http://www.www2.ohchr.org/english/law/cerd.htm (accessed October 2008).

UNIVERSAL DECLARATION OF HUMAN RIGHTS

The Universal Declaration of Human Rights (UDHR) was adopted by the United Nations General Assembly in December 1948. It represents the first time the countries of the world reached an agreement on a set of human rights objectives—including poverty alleviation—that every member country should strive to reach. It is not a legally binding "treaty," but it is the basis of the United Nations human rights treaties. International human rights law is also based on the UDHR. All countries have accepted the UDHR. According to the United Nations Office of the High Commissioner for Human Rights, "The Declaration represents a contract between governments and their peoples, who have a right to demand that this document be respected" (OHCHR Web site).

Some of the rights specified in the UDHR deal with the alleviation of poverty. These include the right to own property; the right to work, including free choice of employment, just working conditions and pay, and the right to join labor unions; and the right to rest and leisure, including holidays with pay. Article 25 states that

Eleanor Roosevelt holds a poster of the Universal Declaration of Human Rights, an international agreement that she played an important role in crafting in 1948. (Corel)

Everyone has the right to a standard of living adequate for the health and well-being of himself and of his family, including food, clothing, housing and medical care and necessary social services, and the right to security in the event of unemployment, sickness, disability, widowhood, old age or other lack of livelihood in circumstances beyond his control.

The UDHR was drafted during the late 1940s, soon after the founding of the United Nations. Eleanor Roosevelt, widow of the late U.S. President Franklin Roosevelt, was chair of the drafting committee. Socialist countries were especially interested in seeing economic rights, such as the right to a decent standard of living, included in the document. Asian, Latin American, and Middle Eastern countries were also in favor of the inclusion of economic rights. Roosevelt pushed for the inclusion of economic rights, even though some people in the United States accused her of being a Communist sympathizer for her stance. Some people in the United States would have preferred to limit "human rights" to civil and political rights, such as the right to vote, and to avoid the question of economic rights (James 2007, 144–147, 152).

John Humphrey of Canada, who drafted the first version of the UDHR, tells his version of the inclusion of economic rights:

Although most of the articles related to civil and political rights, economic, social and cultural rights were not neglected. I did not need to be told that the former can have little meaning without the latter. It is by no means certain that economic and social rights would have been included in the final text if I had not included them in mine. There was considerable opposition in the Drafting Committee to their inclusion. (Humphrey 1983, 407)

After the UDHR was accepted by the United Nations member countries, two human rights treaties were drafted based on the UDHR. These were the International Covenant on Civil and Political Rights, and the International Covenant on Economic, Social, and Cultural Rights. Adopted in 1966, these two treaties are binding legal documents for the countries that ratify them. Together, the UDHR and these two covenants make up what is called the International Bill of Human Rights.

Since that time, the United Nations has adopted numerous other human rights treaties, all of them based on the UDHR. The United Nations has held two world conferences to study and report on how countries are applying the UDHR. The first conference was held in 1968, in Tehran, Iran, and the second was in 1993, in Vienna, Austria.

See also: International Covenant on Economic, Social, and Cultural Rights; Roosevelt, Eleanor; United Nations Human Rights Treaties

Sources

James, Stephen. *Universal Human Rights: Origins and Development.* New York: LFB Scholarly Publishing, 2007.

Humphrey, John P. "The Memoirs of John P. Humphrey: The First Director of the United Nations Division of Human Rights." *Human Rights Quarterly* 5, no. 4 (1983): 387–439.

PRIMARY DOCUMENT 43

Universal Declaration of Human Rights

PREAMBLE

Whereas recognition of the inherent dignity and of the equal and inalienable rights of all members of the human family is the foundation of freedom, justice and peace in the world,

Whereas disregard and contempt for human rights have resulted in barbarous acts which have outraged the conscience of mankind, and the advent of a world in which human beings shall enjoy freedom of speech and belief and freedom from fear and want has been proclaimed as the highest aspiration of the common people,

Whereas it is essential, if man is not to be compelled to have recourse, as a last resort, to rebellion against tyranny and oppression, that human rights should be protected by the rule of law,

Whereas it is essential to promote the development of friendly relations between nations,

Whereas the peoples of the United Nations have in the Charter reaffirmed their faith in fundamental human rights, in the dignity and worth of the human person and in the equal rights of men and women and have determined to promote social progress and better standards of life in larger freedom,

Whereas Member States have pledged themselves to achieve, in cooperation with the United Nations, the promotion of universal respect for and observance of human rights and fundamental freedoms,

Whereas a common understanding of these rights and freedoms is of the greatest importance for the full realization of this pledge,

Now, Therefore THE GENERAL ASSEMBLY proclaims THIS UNIVERSAL DECLARATION OF HUMAN RIGHTS as a common standard of achievement for all peoples and all nations, to the end that every individual and every organ of society, keeping this Declaration constantly in mind, shall strive by teaching and education to promote respect for these rights and freedoms and by progressive measures, national and international, to secure their universal and effective recognition and observance, both among the peoples of Member States themselves and among the peoples of territories under their jurisdiction.

Article 1.

All human beings are born free and equal in dignity and rights. They are endowed with reason and conscience and should act towards one another in a spirit of brotherhood.

Article 2.

Everyone is entitled to all the rights and freedoms set forth in this Declaration, without distinction of any kind, such as race, colour, sex, language, religion, political or other opinion, national or social origin, property, birth or other status. Furthermore, no distinction shall be made on the basis of the political, jurisdictional or international status of the country or territory to which a person belongs, whether it be independent, trust, non-self-governing or under any other limitation of sovereignty.

Article 3.

Everyone has the right to life, liberty and security of person.

Article 4.

No one shall be held in slavery or servitude; slavery and the slave trade shall be prohibited in all their forms.

Article 5.

No one shall be subjected to torture or to cruel, inhuman or degrading treatment or punishment.

Article 6.

Everyone has the right to recognition everywhere as a person before the law.

Article 7.

All are equal before the law and are entitled without any discrimination to equal protection of the law. All are entitled to equal protection against any discrimination in violation of this Declaration and against any incitement to such discrimination.

Article 8.

Everyone has the right to an effective remedy by the competent national tribunals for acts violating the fundamental rights granted him by the constitution or by law.

Article 9.

No one shall be subjected to arbitrary arrest, detention or exile.

Article 10.

Everyone is entitled in full equality to a fair and public hearing by an independent and impartial tribunal, in the determination of his rights and obligations and of any criminal charge against him.

Article 11.

(1) Everyone charged with a penal offence has the right to be presumed innocent until proved guilty according to law in a public trial at which he has had all the guarantees necessary for his defence.

(2) No one shall be held guilty of any penal offence on account of any act or omission which did not constitute a penal offence, under national or international law, at the time when it was committed. Nor shall a heavier penalty be imposed than the one that was applicable at the time the penal offence was committed.

Article 12.

No one shall be subjected to arbitrary interference with his privacy, family, home or correspondence, nor to attacks upon his honour and reputation. Everyone has the right to the protection of the law against such interference or attacks.

Article 13.

(1) Everyone has the right to freedom of movement and residence within the borders of each state.

(2) Everyone has the right to leave any country, including his own, and to return to his country.

Article 14.

(1) Everyone has the right to seek and to enjoy in other countries asylum from persecution.

(2) This right may not be invoked in the case of prosecutions genuinely arising from non-political crimes or from acts contrary to the purposes and principles of the United Nations.

Article 15.

(1) Everyone has the right to a nationality.

(2) No one shall be arbitrarily deprived of his nationality nor denied the right to change his nationality.

Article 16.

(1) Men and women of full age, without any limitation due to race, nationality or religion, have

the right to marry and to found a family. They are entitled to equal rights as to marriage, during marriage and at its dissolution.

(2) Marriage shall be entered into only with the free and full consent of the intending spouses.

(3) The family is the natural and fundamental group unit of society and is entitled to protection by society and the State.

Article 17.

(1) Everyone has the right to own property alone as well as in association with others.

(2) No one shall be arbitrarily deprived of his property.

Article 18.

Everyone has the right to freedom of thought, conscience and religion; this right includes freedom to change his religion or belief, and freedom, either alone or in community with others and in public or private, to manifest his religion or belief in teaching, practice, worship and observance.

Article 19.

Everyone has the right to freedom of opinion and expression; this right includes freedom to hold opinions without interference and to seek, receive and impart information and ideas through any media and regardless of frontiers.

Article 20.

(1) Everyone has the right to freedom of peaceful assembly and association.

(2) No one may be compelled to belong to an association.

Article 21.

(1) Everyone has the right to take part in the government of his country, directly or through freely chosen representatives.

(2) Everyone has the right of equal access to public service in his country.

(3) The will of the people shall be the basis of the authority of government; this will shall be expressed in periodic and genuine elections which shall be by universal and equal suffrage and shall be held by secret vote or by equivalent free voting procedures.

Article 22.

Everyone, as a member of society, has the right to social security and is entitled to realization, through national effort and international co-operation and in accordance with the organization and resources of each State, of the economic, social and cultural rights indispensable for his dignity and the free development of his personality.

Article 23.

(1) Everyone has the right to work, to free choice of employment, to just and favourable conditions of work and to protection against unemployment.

(2) Everyone, without any discrimination, has the right to equal pay for equal work.

(3) Everyone who works has the right to just and favourable remuneration ensuring for himself and his family an existence worthy of human dignity, and supplemented, if necessary, by other means of social protection.

(4) Everyone has the right to form and to join trade unions for the protection of his interests.

Article 24.

Everyone has the right to rest and leisure, including reasonable limitation of working hours and periodic holidays with pay.

Article 25.

(1) Everyone has the right to a standard of living adequate for the health and well-being of himself and of his family, including food, clothing, housing and medical care and necessary social services, and the right to security in the event of unemployment, sickness, disability, widowhood, old age or other lack of livelihood in circumstances beyond his control.

(2) Motherhood and childhood are entitled to special care and assistance. All children, whether born in or out of wedlock, shall enjoy the same social protection.

Article 26.

(1) Everyone has the right to education. Education shall be free, at least in the elementary and fundamental stages. Elementary education shall be compulsory. Technical and professional education shall be made generally available and higher education shall be equally accessible to all on the basis of merit.

(2) Education shall be directed to the full development of the human personality and to the strengthening of respect for human rights and fundamental freedoms. It shall promote understanding, tolerance and friendship among all nations, racial or religious groups, and shall further the activities of the United Nations for the maintenance of peace.

(3) Parents have a prior right to choose the kind of education that shall be given to their children.

Article 27.

(1) Everyone has the right freely to participate in the cultural life of the community, to enjoy the arts and to share in scientific advancement and its benefits.

(2) Everyone has the right to the protection of the moral and material interests resulting from any scientific, literary or artistic production of which he is the author.

Article 28.

Everyone is entitled to a social and international order in which the rights and freedoms set forth in this Declaration can be fully realized.

Article 29.

(1) Everyone has duties to the community in which alone the free and full development of his personality is possible.

(2) In the exercise of his rights and freedoms, everyone shall be subject only to such limitations as are determined by law solely for the purpose of securing due recognition and respect for the rights and freedoms of others and of meeting the just requirements of morality, public order and the general welfare in a democratic society.

(3) These rights and freedoms may in no case be exercised contrary to the purposes and principles of the United Nations.

Article 30.

Nothing in this Declaration may be interpreted as implying for any State, group or person any right to engage in any activity or to perform any act aimed at the destruction of any of the rights and freedoms set forth herein.

Source

United Nations. http://www.un.org/Overview/rights.html (accessed October 2008). Used with permission.

Web Sites

OHCHR (United Nations Office of the High Commissioner for Human Rights). "Information Kit." Universal Declaration of Human Rights 60th Anniversary, 2007. http://www.ohchr.org/EN/UDHR/Pages/60UDHRIntroduction.aspx (accessed October 2008).

United Nations. "Universal Declaration of Human Rights," *Human Rights Today* (UN Briefing Papers). http://www.un.org/rights/HRToday/ (accessed October 2008).

United Nations. "Universal Declaration of Human Rights." http://www.un.org/Overview/rights.html (accessed October 2008).

UPWARD BOUND/ COLLEGE PREPARATION PROGRAMS

Higher education is one important ticket to a better-paying job. To help young people from low-income families enter college, the federal and state governments have instituted a number of college preparation programs. The first of these programs was Upward Bound. This program was started in the mid-1960s, by the Office of Economic Opportunity, which was created by the Economic Opportunity Act of 1964.

Upward Bound grew out of the Community Action Programs of the Economic Opportunity Act of 1964. A number of colleges submitted proposals to the federal government to start community action programs to help disadvantaged teens prepare for college. Inspired by these proposals, the Office of Economic Opportunity decided to start a nationwide program during the summer of 1965, to help poor youths prepare for college. At that time, while 40 percent of high school graduates overall entered college, only 8 percent of poor teens entered college (Levitan 1969, 166).

Upward Bound provides a six- or eight-week summer session at a college campus, during which time students take classes and participate in extracurricular activities. The program continues during the school year, with students traveling to college campuses once a week for tutoring or other activities. By 1966, there were 220 Upward Bound programs throughout the country. The federal government also initiated a few other services for poor youths: Talent Search, to identify and help disadvantaged youths with the potential to succeed in college; and Student Support Services, to provide support to undergraduate students to help them graduate from college. In 1968, these three programs were joined under the heading of TRIO. Since then, TRIO has grown to encompass several more programs, including Educational Opportunity Centers, which provide counseling and advice to disadvantaged adults who want to start or continue a college degree; and a program to prepare college graduates from disadvantaged backgrounds to seek higher degrees (Levitan 1969, 170–171; *A Profile of the Upward Bound Program* 2004, 1; U.S. Department of Education, History of Federal TRIO Programs).

Upward Bound students must either come from a low-income background (below 150 percent of the poverty line) or be a potentially first-generation college student (neither parent has a bachelor's degree). Some students are paid a stipend for participating in the summer program, to make up for the fact that they are not able to hold a job during that time. During the 2002–2003 school year, Upward Bound served more than 56,000 students. This is a small percentage of the eligible population. For example, according the U.S.

government census for 2000, there were about 20 million people ages fifteen to nineteen. Upward Bound estimates that about 62 percent of this population are potentially first-generation college students, and about 28 percent live below 150 percent of the poverty line, meaning that millions of young people who are eligible for Upward Bound are not being served (*A Profile of the Upward Bound Program* 2004, 2–4, 19–23; U.S. Census Bureau, Profile of General Demographic Characteristics, 2000).

Talent Search, which is a less intensive program than Upward Bound, served more than 380,000 students during 2002–2003. In 1998, the federal government started GEAR UP (Gaining Early Awareness and Readiness for Undergraduate Programs) to provide grants to states to set up programs in high-poverty middle schools and high schools. All students within those schools are provided with services to help them succeed in school and enter college. As of 2000–2001, GEAR UP served 200,000 students (Swail and Perna 2002, 19; *National Evaluation of GEAR UP* 2003, 5; *A Profile of the Upward Bound Program* 2004, 4; U.S. Department of Education, GEAR UP).

Some states have implemented their own college outreach programs. For example, after California voters outlawed affirmative action programs throughout the state, the University of California system began an outreach program to help disadvantaged young people get ready for college (Swail and Perna 2002, 16).

An ongoing study by the Department of Education has examined how successful Upward Bound has been in helping disadvantaged young people succeed in college. The results of this study show that students who had low education expectations before they entered Upward Bound benefited the most from the program. In addition, students who stayed the longest in Upward Bound had the greatest benefits. For all participating students, Upward Bound boosted the high school math credits taken by participants and increased enrollment in four-year colleges, but it did not have much effect on high school grades or postsecondary education enrollment (*The Impact of Regular Upward Bound* 2004, xvii–xviii).

See also: Affirmative Action; Community Action Programs; Economic Opportunity Act of 1964; Higher Education Act of 1965; Johnson, Lyndon

Sources

The Impact of Regular Upward Bound: Results from the Third Follow-Up Data Collection. Washington, DC: U.S. Department of Education, April 2004. http://www.mathematica-mpr.com/education/upbound.asp (accessed July 2008).

Levitan, Sar A. *The Great Society's Poor Law: A New Approach to Poverty.* Baltimore, MD: Johns Hopkins Press, 1969.

National Evaluation of GEAR UP: A Summary of the First Two Years. Washington, DC: U.S. Department of Education, 2003. http://www.ed.gov/rschstat/eval/highered/gearup.pdf (accessed July 2008).

A Profile of the Upward Bound Program, 2000-2001. Washington, DC: U.S. Department of Education, Office of Postsecondary Education, Federal TRIO Programs, August 2004. http://www.ed.gov/programs/trioupbound/ubprofile-00-01.doc (accessed July 2008).

Swail, Watson Scott, and Laura W. Perna. "Pre-College Outreach Programs: A National Perspective." In *Increasing Access to College: Extending Possibilities for All Students,* ed. William G. Tierney and Linda Serra Hagedorn. Albany, NY: State University of New York Press, 2002.

Web Sites

U.S. Census Bureau. Profile of General Demographic Characteristics, 2000. http://

factfinder.census.gov/servlet/QTTable?_
bm=y&-geo_id=01000US&-qr_name=
DEC_2000_SF1_U_DP1&-ds_name=
DEC_2000_SF1_U (accessed July 2008).

U.S. Department of Education. GEAR UP.
http://www.ed.gov/programs/gearup/index.
html (accessed July 2008).

U.S. Department of Education. History of the
Federal TRIO Programs. http://
www.ed.gov/about/offices/list/ope/trio/trio-
history.html (accessed July 2008).

U.S. Department of Education. Upward
Bound. http://www.ed.gov/programs/tri-
oupbound/index.html (accessed July 2008).

URBAN RENEWAL

Urban renewal refers to a process of clearing cities of slums (substandard housing used by the poor) and replacing the slums with higher-quality buildings and parks. This process is also called "urban redevelopment." Slum clearance has been a government priority since the early part of the twentieth century. While urban renewal has resulted in more healthful and beautiful cities, and higher-quality housing, it has also resulted in less housing for low-income people, because the government and private developers have not replaced the destroyed slum housing units with an equal number of public or low-income housing units. Urban renewal has been one of the causes of rising homelessness since the 1980s.

During the early twentieth century, housing reformers such as Jacob Riis and Lawrence Veiller publicized the crowded, unsafe, and unsanitary conditions of slum housing. Reformers recommended that slums be cleared and that the government pass housing standard laws to regulate fire safety and the amount of space, light, and air circulation in housing. However, the poorest people often could not afford to live in improved housing, and at that time, the government generally did not get involved in building housing for the poor.

During the Great Depression of the 1930s, a government housing survey showed that only 38 percent of the nation's housing was in good condition. About 2 percent of housing was deemed unfit for humans, and an additional 16 percent was in need of major repairs. In response, some programs of President Franklin Roosevelt's New Deal were aimed at constructing new and improved housing for the poor (Bellush and Hausknecht 1967, 4).

The federal government really began to get involved in urban renewal starting in 1949, with the passage of the Housing Act of 1949 and the formation of the Urban Renewal Administration. One impetus for this law was the 1940 housing census, which showed that in urban areas, 40 percent of housing was seriously defective—that is, needing major repairs, or lacking running water or private bathrooms. The goal of the 1949 Housing Act was "a decent home and suitable living environment" for all Americans (quoted in Lang and Sohmer 2000, 291). The law contained provisions for more public (government-funded) housing for the poor, as well as for increased homeownership and slum clearance. This law marked the first time the federal government became directly involved in slum clearance, which until that time was seen as an issue for local governments.

The Housing Act of 1949 helped millions of people to become homeowners. It also helped to increase the quality and size of homes. In 1949, the average new home had two bedrooms,

Protesters picket against the proposed destruction of the Lincoln Square neighborhood to build Lincoln Center, 1956. (Library of Congress)

one bathroom, no garage, and no air-conditioning; was heated by coal; and contained less than 1,000 square feet. The average new home in 1999 had three or more bedrooms, three bathrooms, a two-car garage, and central air-conditioning, and it contained 2,000 square feet.

However, the law also harmed poor people who were displaced when slums were cleared. While the law called for 810,000 new low-income housing units by 1955, this goal was not met: only a quarter of this number was built. By 1967, urban renewal had destroyed more than 400,000 housing units for the poor, and replaced them with only 42,000 public-housing units for the poor. Often, the clearance of one slum simply meant that poor families had to move to another slum (Bellush and Hausknecht 1967, 14; Lang and Sohmer 2000, 291–295; Katz, 2001, 51).

The slum clearance provisions—Title I of the law—did benefit some people. It helped private developers gain access to valuable land. Government loans were given to cities to purchase slum land. Cities then resold this land, usually for less money, to private developers. According to Jewel Bellush and Murray Hausknecht, "Title I subsidized the purchase of prime land by private entrepreneurs, with the federal government paying the lion's share of the subsidy" (1967, 12).

Urban renewal was not the only federal government program that destroyed poor neighborhoods. In 1956, the passage of two laws promoting highway construction—the Interstate and Defense Highway Act, and the Highway Revenue Act—also hastened the destruction of poor neighborhoods. Highways generally were built through poor neighborhoods and displaced the residents of these neighborhoods (Katz 2001, 53).

Amendments to the Housing Act in 1954, 1959, and 1961 allowed more and more urban renewal money to be spent on commercial projects, rather than on housing. These funds helped to expand universities and hospitals in urban areas. By the 1960s, advocates for the poor began to realize that urban renewal was harming, rather than helping, the poor, and they turned against it. In addition, the "renewal" aspect of urban renewal was proving a disappointment. Construction projects for slick new office buildings were sometimes delayed or left incomplete, or proved unprofitable once built.

In 1974, Congress combined urban renewal with the "model cities" program developed in the 1960s, under the administration of President Lyndon

Johnson. The new program was called the Community Development Block Grant. Congress passed the Urban Development Action Grant program in 1977 to complement the Community Development Block Grants. These programs aim to give cities more flexibility in how they use federal funds, although people with low and moderate incomes are supposed to benefit. Cities can use this money not only for slum clearance, but also for neighborhood centers, energy conservation, and private development designed to create new jobs. Although poor people are supposed to benefit, in reality, the money often has been used for fancy office buildings and shopping malls where, it is hoped, some of the poor might find work.

Since 1974, the federal government has provided much less money for these community development programs than had been provided through Title I of the Housing Act. According to historian Jon Teaford, the negative experience of urban renewal under Title I has turned many city planners away from the bulldozer approach—simply destroying poor neighborhoods—and toward a program of conserving and rehabilitating old neighborhoods. As Teaford remarks, "the chief product of Title I was a widely held commitment never to have another Title I" (Teaford 2000, 463, also see 443–462).

See also: Homelessness; Housing, Low-Income; Model Cities; Riis, Jacob; Veiller, Lawrence

Sources

Bellush, Jewel, and Murray Hausknecht, eds. *Urban Renewal: People, Politics and Planning.* Garden City, NY: Anchor Books, 1967.

Katz, Michael B. *The Price of Citizenship: Redefining the American Welfare State.* New York: Metropolitan Books, 2001.

Lang, Robert E., and Rebecca R. Sohmer. "The Legacy of the Housing Act of 1949: The Past, Present and Future of Federal Housing and Urban Policy." Fannie Mae Foundation, *Housing Policy Debate* 11, no. 2 (2000).

Teaford, Jon C. "Urban Renewal and its Aftermath." Fannie Mae Foundation, *Housing Policy Debate* 11, no. 2 (2000).

V

VEILLER, LAWRENCE (1872–1959)

During the Progressive Era of the first part of the twentieth century, Lawrence Veiller worked for better housing for poor people in New York City. His ideas and the laws he pushed for influenced housing legislation for poor people around the country. In his time, he was "the most important housing reformer in the country," according to historian Michael Katz (1996, 177).

Lawrence Veiller was born in Elizabeth, New Jersey, on January 7, 1872. His father was a businessman. After graduating from City College of New York, he worked as a volunteer for the local Charity Organization Society and for the University Settlement house, both of which were prominent private charitable organizations that aimed to help the poor. Veiller worked with poor people who lived in crowded tenement housing in the Lower East Side of Manhattan. He decided that improved housing was a key to improving the lives of the poor.

From 1895 to 1897, he was a plans examiner for the New York City buildings department. In 1898, he drew up plans to improve tenement buildings and convinced the president of the Charity Organization Society to support his plan. Veiller proposed fifteen amendments to the city's tenement laws, including larger air shafts to provide more light and air to tenement apartments. But the city government ignored his suggestions. Veiller then decided to appeal directly to the public. In 1900, he produced a two-week exhibition on tenement housing, including photographs, maps linking disease to tenement housing, plans for improved tenement housing, and a cardboard model of a block of tenements in the Lower East Side, illustrating the crowded conditions, lack of places to bathe, and lack of natural light.

Theodore Roosevelt, then governor of New York, agreed to support Veiller. He called for the formation of a state

PRIMARY DOCUMENT 44

Excerpt from *The Tenement House Problem*, edited by Robert de Forest and Lawrence Veiller

This report was prepared by the New York City Tenement House Commission, and published in 1903. Its findings and recommendations led to laws regulating tenement-house builders and to the creation of the New York City Tenement House Department to enforce these laws.

THE TYPICAL NEW YORK TENEMENT

Some knowledge of the prevailing kind of New York tenement house must necessarily precede any consideration of its evils and their remedies. It is known as the "double-decker," "dumb-bell" tenement, a type which New York has the unenviable distinction of having invented. It is a type unknown to any other city in America or Europe.

Although the housing problem is one of the leading political questions of the day in England, the conditions which exist there are ideal compared to the conditions in New York. The tall tenement house, accommodating as many as 100 to 150 persons in one building, extending up six or seven stories into the air, with dark, unventilated rooms, is unknown in London or in any other city of Great Britain. It was first constructed in New York about the year 1879, and with slight modifications has been practically the sole type of building erected since, and is the type of the present day. It is a building usually five or six or even seven stories high, about 25 feet wide, and built upon a lot of land of the same width and about 100 feet deep. The building as a rule extends back 90 feet, leaving the small space of ten feet unoccupied at the rear, so that the back rooms may obtain some light and air. This space has continued to be left open only because the law has compelled it. Upon the entrance floor there are generally two stores, one on each side of the building, and these sometimes have two or three living rooms back of them. In the centre is the entrance hallway, a long corridor less than 3 feet wide and extending back 60 feet in length. This hallway is nearly always totally dark, receiving no light except that from the street door and a faint light that comes from the small windows opening upon the stairs, which are placed at one side of the hallway. Each floor above is generally divided into four sets of apartments, there being seven rooms on each side of the hall, extending back from the street to the rear of the building. The front apartments generally consist of four rooms each and the rear apartments of three rooms, making altogether fourteen upon each floor, or in a seven-story house eighty-four rooms exclusive of the stores and rooms back of them. Of these fourteen rooms on each floor, only four receive direct light and air from the street or from the small yard at the back of the building. Generally, along each side of the building is what is termed an "air shaft," being an indentation of the wall to a depth of about 28 inches, and extending in length for a space of from 50 to 60 feet. This shaft is entirely enclosed on four sides, and is, of course, the full height of the building, often from 60 to 72 feet high. The ostensible purpose of the shaft is to provide light and air to the five rooms on each side of the house which get no direct light and air from the street or yard; but as the shafts are narrow and high, being enclosed on all four sides, and without any intake of air at the bottom, these rooms obtain, instead of fresh air and sunshine, foul air and semi-darkness. Indeed it is questionable whether the rooms would not be more habitable and more sanitary with no shaft at all, depending for their light and air solely upon the front and back rooms into which they open; for each family, besides having the foul air from its own rooms to breathe, is compelled to breathe the emanations from the rooms of some eleven other families; nor is this all, these shafts act as conveyors of noise, odors, and disease, and when fire breaks out serve as inflammable flues, often rendering it impossible to save the buildings from destruction.

A family living in such a building pays for four rooms of this kind a rent of from $12 to $18 a month. Of these four rooms only two are large enough to be deserving of the name of rooms. The front one is generally about 10 feet 6 inches wide by 11 feet 3 inches long; this the family use as a parlor, and often at night, when the small bedrooms opening upon the air shaft are so close and ill- ventilated that sleep is impossible, mattresses are dragged upon the floor of the parlor, and there the family sleep, all together in one room. In summer the small bedrooms are so hot and stifling that a large part of the tenement house population sleep on the roofs, the side-walks, and the fire-escapes. The other room, the kitchen, is generally the same size as the parlor upon which it opens, and receives all its light and air from the "air shaft," or such a supply as may come to it from the front room. Behind these two rooms are the bedrooms, so called, which are hardly more than closets, being each about 7 feet wide and 8 feet 6 inches long, hardly large enough to contain a bed. These rooms get no light and air whatsoever, except that which comes from the "air shaft," and except on the highest stories are

generally almost totally dark. Upon the opposite side of the public hall is an apartment containing four exactly similar rooms, and at the rear of the building there are, instead of four rooms on each side of the hallway, but three, one of the bedrooms being dispensed with. For these three rooms in the rear the rent is generally throughout the city from $10 to $15 a month. In the public hallway, opposite the stair, there are provided two water-closets, each water-closet being used in common by two families and being lighted and ventilated by the "air shaft," which also lights and ventilates all the bedrooms. In the newer buildings there is frequently provided, in the hall-way between the two closets, a dumb-waiter [small elevator to transport items] for the use of the tenants.

It is not to be wondered at, therefore, that with such a kind of tenement house repeated all over the different parts of this city, and forming practically the only kind of habitation for the great mass of the people, the tenement house system has become fraught with so much danger to the welfare of the community. The effect upon the city population of the form of congregated living found in our tenement houses is to be seen, not only in its results upon the health of the people, but upon their moral and social condition as well. The public mind is just now especially aroused over the manifestation of one special form of vice in tenement districts. It is not to be wondered at that vice in various forms should manifest itself in the tenements; the wonder is that there is not more vice in such districts.

The tenement districts of New York are places in which thousands of people are living in the smallest space in which it is possible for human beings to exist—crowded together in dark, ill-ventilated rooms, in many of which the sunlight never enters and in most of which fresh air is unknown. They are centres of disease, poverty, vice, and crime, where it is a marvel, not that some children grow up to be thieves, drunkards, and prostitutes, but that so many should ever grow up to be decent and self-respecting. All the conditions which surround childhood, youth, and womanhood in New York's crowded tenement quarters make for unrighteousness. They also make for disease. There is hardly a tenement house in which there has not been at least one case of pulmonary tuberculosis within the last five years, and in some houses there have been as great a number as twenty-two different cases of this terrible disease. From the tenements there comes a stream of sick, helpless people to our hospitals and dispensaries, few of whom are able to afford the luxury of a private physician, and some houses are in such bad sanitary condition that few people can be seriously ill in them and get well; from them also comes a host of paupers and charity seekers. The most terrible of all the features of tenement house life in New York, however, is the indiscriminate herding of all kinds of people in close contact, the fact, that, mingled with the drunken, the dissolute, the improvident, the diseased, dwell the great mass of the respectable working-men of the city with their families.

Source

De Forest, Robert Weeks, and Lawrence Veiller, eds. *The Tenement House Problem: Including the Report of the New York State Tenement House Commission of 1900.* New York (State) Tenement House Commission. New York: Macmillan & Co., Ltd, 1903, 7–10.

Tenement House Commission. Veiller was appointed secretary of this commission and did much of the work, which involved studying the results of previous investigations of tenement houses. The commission came out with a 1,000-page report, *The Tenement House Problem.* This report found that the vast majority of tenement houses currently being constructed were violating at least one law. Tenement builders often failed to install fire escapes and left less than the mandatory ten-foot yard at the backs of buildings, for example. Veiller also surveyed the housing situation in other cities as part of this report (Lubove 1962, 140; Jackson 1976, 112–120).

As a result of this study, the Tenement Law of 1901, which Veiller wrote, was passed to regulate tenement-house builders and require them to make accommodations for more light and air, install better fire exits and more fire-proofing, and include a toilet in every apartment. The Tenement House Department was created to enforce this law. Although Veiller was not the head of this department—he was the deputy—he in fact did most of the work to run this department. Meanwhile, as a result of Veiller's influence, other city governments and Charity Organization Societies were investigating housing for the poor (Lubove 1962, 132–136, 140–144; Jackson 1976, 122–125).

Veiller resigned from his government position in 1904, when a new mayor took office. He continued to work on housing reform as a member of the Charity Organization Society's Tenement House Committee. In 1910, he helped found the National Housing Association to help cities across the country pass and enforce housing laws for the poor. He served as director of this organization from 1911 to 1936. His advice and his books on housing law influenced almost all state and local housing laws until 1920 (Lubove 1962, 144–145).

Although Veiller believed government must regulate private builders, he never believed that the government should actually build housing for the poor or provide the money for such construction, because he assumed, like many others at that time, that government was too inefficient to accomplish this task. The result of the laws he helped pass, however, was that many of the tenements built to conform with these laws ended up being too expensive for the poorest families. Builders who adhered to the new laws charged higher rents to cover their increased expenses. Although it became clear that private builders could not build decent housing that was affordable to the very poor and still make a profit, Veiller continued to oppose government-funded housing, even after the start of the Great Depression of the 1930s. At that time, the federal government began building housing for the poor, and Veiller's ideas were no longer popular (Lubove 1962, 180–182).

See also: Great Depression; Housing, Low-Income; Progressive Era; Scientific Charity; Settlement Houses

Sources

Jackson, Anthony. *A Place Called Home: A History of Low-Cost Housing in Manhattan.* Cambridge, MA: The MIT Press, 1976.

Katz, Michael. *In the Shadow of the Poorhouse: A Social History of Welfare in America.* New York: Basic Books, 1996.

Lubove, Roy. *The Progressives and the Slums: Tenement House Reform in New York City, 1890–1917.* Pittsburgh, PA: University of Pittsburgh Press, 1962.

VOCATIONAL EDUCATION

Vocational education refers to classes that train people for jobs or careers that do not require a four-year college degree. Vocational education has been especially targeted to people who do not wish to go to college, and who otherwise might be at risk of poverty because of unemployment or a low-wage job. Vocational education, it is argued, can help such people improve their skills and earnings. Vocational education has also been called "industrial" education, "occupational" education, and "technical" education.

The earliest kind of vocational education in the United States was apprenticeships, programs in which teenagers and young adults lived and worked with "masters" and were taught a craft or trade. Apprenticeships were common in early America, but the tradition had faded by the late 1800s.

In the late 1800s, some educators began arguing that the American education system was too focused on academic learning. "Manual training" classes were started in many states, to engage all students in working with their hands. Drawing, woodworking, metal work, sewing, and cooking were seen as especially valuable for the urban poor, but useful for all young people, as a balance to intellectual learning.

Soon, however, educators began to realize that simple manual training was not going to prepare students for actual jobs. The idea of vocational training, which would prepare students for specific jobs, became popular between 1890 and 1910. Business groups, education groups, and labor organizations were in favor of vocational education. Businesses believed they would have better employees if more occupational training classes were available. Educators felt that vocational education classes would help those who dropped out of high school. Labor unions were the most cautious about supporting vocational education. They liked the idea of more education opportunities for workers. However, they feared that vocation education might create a two-tier education system, with privileged people pursuing academic training leading to higher-paying jobs, and children of the working class relegated to vocational education, leading to lower-paying jobs. Still, the American Federation of Labor, a major labor union, eventually did support the idea of industrial education. Several states established vocational schools at this time, including Connecticut, Massachusetts, New Jersey, New York, and Wisconsin (Lazerson and Grubb 1974, 13–20; McClure, Chrisman, and Mock 1985, 38–39).

In 1917, the U.S. Congress passed the Smith-Hughes Act, which provided federal funding to states to help them start vocational education programs. States had to spend an equal amount of money to receive a federal grant. Federal money could be used to pay salaries of teachers and supervisors, and could also be used to train teachers. As a result of federal aid, states started many part-time vocational schools—by far the most popular type of occupational education. By 1924, 92 percent of students who attended federally funded training programs, were in part-time programs (Lazerson and Grubb 1974, 32; McClure, Chrisman, and Mock 1985, 64).

Some labor leaders and educators were still concerned that vocational education would lead to a second-class education for poorer people. In fact, from 1913 to 1920, Chicago considered a proposal to divide the city's education system into two divisions, starting with seventh grade. One group of children would continue with academic education, whereas the other group would be taught industrial skills. Business leaders were in favor of this approach, but educators were opposed, and the law never passed (Lazerson and Grubb 1974, 36–37).

During the Great Depression of the 1930s, which caused widespread unemployment, the federal government set up some job-training programs for young people, including the National Youth Administration. During the 1940s, while the United States was involved in fighting in World War II, vocational training was often linked to the defense industry. In the early 1960s, there was renewed interest in vocational education, and a new law was passed: the Vocational Education Act of 1963. This increased federal funding for occupational education allowed states more flexibility in how they used the money and focused on people who were poor or who lacked education (Lazerson and Grubb 1974, 42–45).

In 1984, the 1963 law was amended with the Carl D. Perkins Vocational Education Act. This law aimed to increase access by adults to vocational education and to expand the program to other populations (such as the disabled) that were not being served. The Perkins Act was reauthorized in 1998 and 2006. Instead of separating vocational students and academic students, the law aims to make sure that vocational students focus on academics as well, and that all students are held to the same academic standards. During the 1990s, students who concentrated on vocational education also took an increasing number of academic classes, and increased their reading and math test scores. In addition, vocational education courses are available to all students, and 97 percent of high school students take at least one vocational education class (Van Horn and Schaffner 2003, 165; Silverberg et al. 2004, 2, 18–19).

Vocational classes lead to careers in a variety of fields, such as agriculture, health care, business, food service, child care, printing, mechanics, electronics, construction, aeronautics, and cosmetology. According to a 2004 report assessing whether vocational education helps students increase their earnings, seven years after graduation, students earned 2 percent more for each vocational education course they took. This economic benefit extends to men and women, as well as to people from poor families and to disabled people (Silverberg et al. 2004, xix–xx, 22).

See also: Apprenticeship; National Youth Administration; Public Schools; Welfare-to-Work Programs

Sources

Lazerson, Marvin, and W. Norton Grubb, eds. *American Education and Vocationalism: A Documentary History, 1870–1970.* New York: Teachers College Press, Columbia University, 1974.

McClure, Arthur F., James Riley Chrisman, and Perry Mock. *Education for Work: The Historical Evolution of Vocational and Distributive Education in America.* Cranbury, NJ: Associated University Presses, 1985.

Silverberg, Marsha, Elizabeth Warner, Michael Fong, and David Goodwin. *National Assessment of Vocational Education Final Report to Congress.* Washington, DC: U.S. Department of Education, 2004.

Van Horn, Carl E., and Herbert A. Schaffner. *Work in America.* Santa Barbara, CA: ABC-CLIO, 2003.

VOTING RIGHTS

Poor people, among other Americans, have been denied the right to vote in the United States. This has been due to rules that in the past prohibited voting by poor people, as well as rules that make it more difficult for the poor and uneducated to vote.

In 1776, the signers of the Declaration of Independence insisted that governments derive "their just power from the consent of the governed." One might think this would imply that all adults in the country should have the right to vote. In fact, the U.S. Constitution says virtually nothing about the right to vote. The American colonies and states each made their own rules about who was eligible to vote. In the colonial era and the early United States, many states allowed voting only by white males who owned property. In 1790, ten out of thirteen states had property requirements for voters. As late as 1855, three out of thirty-one states still had some sort of property requirements for at least some voters. Some states replaced their property requirements with tax-paying requirements, which also barred poor people from voting. As late as the early 1900s, several states had tax-paying requirements for at least some elections (Keyssar 2000, appendix tables A.3, A.10).

During the colonial era and in the early United States, voting was seen as a privilege, not a right. Leaders assumed that voters should be men who were not economically dependent on anyone else. Because voting in early America was often conducted in a public manner, and not by secret ballot, it was assumed that anyone who was not economically independent could be pressured to vote a certain way.

During the 1800s, as the population of states grew, more and more men found themselves disenfranchised because they were laborers, merchants, or farmers who did not own enough land. They pressured states to change voting laws. In addition, new political parties were created, and some of these parties wanted to enfranchise more people to gain votes. Americans also came to believe that all white men, regardless of their economic status, ought to have the right to vote. Therefore, states stopped imposing economic barriers to voting, such as property-owning or tax-paying requirements (Keyssar 2000, 34–42).

However, as states got rid of their property and tax-paying requirements, they also instituted prohibitions against voting by people who were receiving aid to the poor. From 1792 to the late 1800s, twelve states denied voting to poor people. As late as 1901, New Hampshire excluded from voting all persons who had received aid for the poor within ninety days of the election (Keyssar 2000, 61, appendix table A.6).

During the 1800s and early 1900s, as economic barriers to voting fell, states began excluding from voting American Indians, free blacks, and women. Some states even excluded Catholics and Jews. These populations tended to be poor and uneducated. In the late 1800s and early 1900s, states also began to pass laws that, although they did not target people of a certain race, had the effect of disenfranchising blacks, non-English speakers, and poor people. As a result of these laws and rules, voter turnout for presidential elections dropped from about 70 percent of eligible voters in the late 1800s to less than 50 percent by 1920 (Piven and Cloward 2000, 48, 66).

After the Civil War of the 1860s, which ended slavery, blacks were able to exercise their right to vote during the Reconstruction Era. However, after 1877, southern states passed laws to restrict blacks from voting. These laws included "poll taxes" (taxes that had to be paid at the voting booth) and literacy tests. Poor, uneducated blacks could not afford the tax and could not read. Such rules disenfranchised many poor, uneducated southern whites. By 1924, almost no blacks voted in southern states, and even white voter turnout dropped to 32 percent (Piven and Cloward 2000, 86).

In northern states, educated, native-born men sought to discourage immigrants from voting. Eleven states repealed laws that had allowed immigrants to vote if they said they intended to become citizens. Between 1890 and 1928, eleven northern and western states instituted literacy tests for voting, which kept non-English speakers and illiterate people from voting. More and more states began requiring voter registration. By 1929, all but three states required some form of voter registration. This

African Americans vote in Alabama for the first time. (National Archives)

extra step in the voting process tended to disenfranchise the poor, who might not have the time to make an extra trip to a perhaps far-away location to register. Some states even required people to reregister in person each year. These voter registration requirements account for an estimated 30 to 40 percent decline in voter turnout (Piven and Cloward 2000, 88, 90, 92).

In the second half of the twentieth century, voting rights were expanded for southern blacks. As a result of the Voting Rights Act of 1965, southern blacks regained their right to vote. However, from 1964 to 1980, voting went down among all groups of people except for southern blacks. Voting went down the most among the unemployed and uneducated. One reason for this decline is perhaps that political parties

were not actively reaching out to new voters (Piven and Cloward 2000, 124).

Criminals account for another group of people who have been barred from voting. To this day, people who have been convicted of a felony are barred from voting in many states—even after they have completed their prison terms. Because poor people are more likely to be convicted of a felony, this means that a significant percentage of poor people have become disenfranchised.

In the 1980s, activists for the poor started a movement to make voter registration easier for the poor. This movement aimed to allow voter registration at offices that provide public assistance to the poor, as well as at drivers' license bureaus and through the mail. The National Voter Registration

Act was passed in 1993. As a result of this new law, 73 percent of eligible voters were registered in 1996—the highest percentage of voter registration since 1960, when records were first kept. The law may also account for the fact that voter turnout increased from about 52 percent of eligible voters in the 1992 presidential election, to 60 percent in 2004, and to 62 percent in 2008 ("Executive Summary" 1997; U.S. Election Project, Voter Turnout).

See also: Criminal Justice System and Poverty; National Voter Registration Act of 1993; Reconstruction Era; Segregation Laws; Voting Rights Act of 1965

Sources

Keyssar, Alexander. *The Right to Vote: The Contested History of Democracy in the United States.* New York: Basic Books, 2000.

Piven, Frances Fox, and Richard A. Cloward. *Why Americans Still Don't Vote, and Why Politicians Want It That Way.* Boston, MA: Beacon Press, 2000.

"Executive Summary of the Federal Election Commission's Report to the Congress on the Impact of the National Voter Registration Act of 1993 on the Administration of Federal Elections." June 1997. http://www.fec.gov/votregis/nvrasum.htm (accessed October 2008).

Web Site

U.S. Election Project Voter Turnout. http://elections.gmu.edu/voter_turnout.htm (accessed October 2008).

VOTING RIGHTS ACT OF 1965

African Americans gained the right to vote in 1870, with the ratification of the Fifteenth Amendment to the U.S. Constitution. However, starting in the 1890s, southern states created laws to deny blacks the right to vote. For example, states required voters to pay a tax before voting (many blacks were poor and could not pay the tax); they administered literacy tests (blacks were disproportionately uneducated, and might not pass such a test); or they disqualified voters who were deemed immoral. These laws were sometimes applied selectively to blacks and not to whites.

Over the years, federal courts struck down some of these laws, but southern states passed new laws. In response to the civil rights movement which began in the 1950s, Congress passed laws in 1957, 1960, and 1964 in an effort to help blacks regain their right to vote. However, these laws required each individual voting jurisdiction to be sued, making it difficult to enforce the law (U.S. Department of Justice, Civil Rights Division, Voting Section).

In 1964, soon after the passage of the Civil Rights Act of 1964, civil rights activists such as Martin Luther King, Jr. turned their attention to the voting situation in the southern United States. King and other civil rights leaders believed that the right to vote was a key factor to enable blacks to address their needs for decent jobs and education opportunities. In 1957, King said in a speech, "give us the ballot and we will no longer have to worry the federal government about our basic rights" (King 1998, 108).

In December 1964, King talked with President Johnson about introducing a voting rights bill, but Johnson discouraged him, saying that there were other bills he wanted to concentrate on. To pressure the president and the U.S. Congress to pass a strong law protecting the voting rights of blacks, King and civil rights groups planned demonstrations in Selma, Alabama, starting in early 1965. Selma was in Dallas County, where only 350 of the eligible 15,000 blacks were registered to vote. King and civil rights leaders led thousands of blacks in marches to the courthouse to register to vote. Hundreds of demonstrators were arrested and jailed, but no one was able to successfully register to vote. King noted that "there were many more Negroes in jail in Selma than there were Negroes registered to vote" (King 1998, 276).

The media covered the demonstrations and arrests. During one demonstration in nearby Marion County, police beat and shot at demonstrators, one of whom died. As demonstrators walked on March 7, 1965, to Montgomery, Alabama, to deliver a petition to the governor, state troopers rode horses through the crowd and released tear gas. In response, sympathy marches began all over the country. A week later, President Johnson agreed to introduce voting rights legislation into Congress (Patterson 1989, 141–150).

Johnson signed the Voting Rights Act of 1965 in August. The law prohibited the use of voting practices that discriminated on the basis of race. The law targeted certain areas of the country where discrimination had been the worst. In these areas, jurisdictions could not make any changes that affected voting until the federal government made sure the changes would not result in racial discrimination. The U.S. attorney general could appoint federal examiners and federal observers to monitor voter registration and elections.

As a result of the Voting Rights Act, federal examiners began conducting voter registration, and many more blacks registered to vote. In Alabama in March 1965, only 19.3 percent of blacks were registered to vote, compared with 69 percent of whites. By November 1988, the percentage of blacks registered to vote had increased to 68.4 percent, compared with 75 percent of whites. In Mississippi in March 1965, only 6.7 percent of blacks were registered to vote, compared with 70 percent of whites. By November 1988, 74 percent of blacks were registered to vote, compared with 80.5 percent of whites. Many other southern states show similar dramatic increases in the percentage of blacks registered to vote (U.S. Department of Justice, Civil Rights Division, Voting Section).

See also: Civil Rights Act of 1964; Civil Rights Movement; Great Society; Johnson, Lyndon; King, Martin Luther, Jr.; Voting Rights

Sources

King, Martin Luther, Jr. *The Autobiography of Martin Luther King, Jr.,* ed. Clayborne Carson. New York: Warner Books, 1998.

Patterson, Lillie. *Martin Luther King, Jr. and the Freedom Movement.* New York: Facts on File, 1989.

Web Site

U.S. Department of Justice. Civil Rights Division, Voting Section. http://www.justice.gov/crt/voting/intro/intro.htm (accessed July 2008).

VOUCHERS

Vouchers are a type of government subsidy that helps people pay for certain necessities, such as child care or housing. It is a type of certificate or coupon worth a certain amount of money, which can only be spent on specific services.

Parents rally in support of school vouchers outside the Supreme Court in Washington, D.C., February 2002. (AP/Wide World Photos)

Vouchers give poor people more flexibility than some other methods of government assistance. For example, instead of being forced to live in government-subsidized housing in a certain part of town, housing vouchers allow low-income people to choose from a wider variety of housing, and to use their vouchers to pay for part or all of the cost. Vouchers give the governments control over how low-income people spend their money. Instead of providing cash that might not be used for the intended services, governments can provide vouchers, which can be used only to pay for specific things.

Vouchers are commonly used to help low-income people pay for food, housing, child care, and transportation to and from work. Many states use vouchers as part of their "general assistance" program to help poor people who are not eligible for federal aid.

Vouchers are used for a variety of smaller programs. In Cleveland, Ohio, low-income students in kindergarten through third grade can use vouchers to pay for after-school tutoring. In Pasco County, Florida, vouchers are available to help low-income parents pay for prescription drugs for their children (Steuerle et al. 2000, 504–513).

Sometimes, the use of vouchers is controversial. For example, a few city and state governments have experimented with vouchers to help low-income families pay for tuition at private schools. Some people argue that this use of vouchers is unconstitutional, because it could result in government payments to religious schools (if parents chose to send their children to religious schools), and the U.S. Constitution requires the separation of church (religion) and state (government). Others argue that providing vouchers to some students takes money away from already struggling public school systems (Howell and Peterson 2002, 28–31).

One of the first widespread voucher programs was the food stamp program, which first started in the late 1930s. The food stamps, or coupons, were felt to be more flexible than simply handing out surplus food once a month (a commonly used method of feeding the hungry at that time). With food stamps, people can choose their own food and can buy their food more frequently, so that storage was not a problem. The vouchers can be used for almost any kind of food. The food stamp program has been successful in terms of making sure poor people meet their nutritional needs. However, the food stamp benefits are low, and recipients often run out before the end of the month.

Another food program that uses vouchers is the Special Supplemental Nutrition Program for Women, Infants and Children (WIC), which started in 1972. This program provides vouchers to poor pregnant women and young children. Unlike the food stamp program, the WIC vouchers can be used only to buy specific, high-nutrition foods, such as iron-fortified cereal and orange juice.

Housing vouchers were first used in 1965, with the passage of the Housing and Urban Development Act of 1965. The use of housing vouchers was controversial at that time, because they would allow poor black families the choice of moving into white neighborhoods. From the 1930s until the introduction of vouchers, poor people were housed in units specifically built for them. Vouchers gave people more freedom in terms of choosing their own housing. The 1974 Housing Act renewed the federal government's support for housing vouchers. Poor families are required to pay 30 percent of their income for the housing, and the government pays the rest, up to a certain limit. The housing voucher is actually a subsidy paid directly to the landlord. In some cases, families may use these vouchers to purchase a home.

The housing vouchers are not "entitlements"—that is, they are not given to every poor person. A limited number of vouchers are available, and they generally go first to single-parent families with children. Only about 10 percent of poor people actually receive a voucher (Salins 1987, 24–25; Andrew 1998, 133–134; Wright, Rubin, and Devine 1998, 90; Office of Housing Choice Vouchers Web site).

Child care vouchers became common with the passage of the Child Care and Development Block Grant in 1990, which required states to offer child care vouchers or certificates so low-income parents could pay for child care. Vouchers allow poor parents more flexibility in choosing their child care. Before vouchers became common, low-income parents had to send their children to specific government-funded child care centers, which may not have been conveniently located. With vouchers, low-income parents have the choice to find care that is located near their home and that fits their work schedule. They also can choose to pay other family members for child care (Steuerle et al. 2000, 196–203).

See also: Child Care and Early Childhood Education; Food Stamp Program/Supplemental Nutrition Assistance Program; General Assistance; Housing, Low-Income; Special

Supplemental Nutrition Program for Women, Infants and Children; Welfare-to-Work Programs

Sources

Andrew, John A. III. *Lyndon Johnson and the Great Society.* Chicago, IL: Ivan R. Dee, 1998.

Howell, William G., and Paul E. Peterson. *The Education Gap: Vouchers and Urban Schools.* Washington, DC: Brookings Institution Press, 2002.

Salins, Peter D., ed. *Housing America's Poor.* Chapel Hill, NC: University of North Carolina Press, 1987.

Steuerle, C. Eugene, Van Doorn Ooms, George E. Peterson, and Robert D. Reischauer, eds. *Vouchers and the Provision of Public Services.* Washington, DC: Brookings Institution Press, 2000.

Wright, James D., Beth A. Rubin, and Joel A. Devine. *Beside the Golden Door: Policy, Politics and the Homeless.* New York: Aldine de Gruyter, 1998.

Web Site

Office of Housing Choice Vouchers. http://www.hud.gov/offices/pih/programs/hcv/ (accessed August 2008).

W

WALD, LILLIAN
(1867–1940)

In 1893, Lillian Wald started the first secular visiting nurse service in the United States to serve poor people in the Lower East Side of New York City. She started one of the first settlement houses in the United States. She led the creation of city playgrounds for poor children, and along with fellow settlement-house worker Florence Kelley, she pushed for the formation of the federal Children's Bureau.

Lillian Wald was born in March 10, 1867, in Cincinnati, Ohio. Her parents had been born in Europe, and had come to the United States as children. Her father sold optical supplies. The family was Jewish, but they were "Reform" Jews, and as such tried to assimilate into the mainstream culture, even welcoming Christian ministers to preach at their temple (Siegel 1983, 7).

Wald attended a prestigious high school and, at the age of sixteen, she applied to Vassar College, but was rejected because she was too young. She continued her high school studies and then did clerical work for a few years. In 1889, while fetching a nurse to help her sister through a difficult pregnancy, Wald asked the nurse about her training and career, and decided that she, too, wanted to be a nurse (Siegel 1983, 8–9, 14–15).

She began her training that same year at the School of Nursing at the New York Hospital in New York City, and then enrolled in the Women's Medical College to deepen her theoretical knowledge. One morning a week, she taught a health class to immigrant women. One day, a weeping child entered the classroom to let Wald know that the child's mother could not attend class because she was ill. Wald left the class and followed the child home, where she found a family of seven living in two rooms. The mother, who had given birth two days before, was covered in dried blood. Wald washed the mother, the baby, and the other

---

A DAY IN THE LIFE OF A VISITING NURSE

Lillian Wald wrote periodic reports of her activities to her benefactor, Jacob Schiff. The following is from one of her early letters to him, on July 25, 1893:

Dear Mr. Schiff,

My first call was on the Goldberg baby whose pulse and improved condition had been maintained after our last night's care. After taking the temperature, washing and dressing the child, I called on the doctor who had been summoned before, told him of the family's tribulations and he offered not to charge them for the visit. Then I took Hattie Isaacs, the consumptive, a big bunch of flowers and while she slept I cleaned out the window of medicine bottles. Then I bathed her, and the poor girl had been so long without this attention that it took me nearly two hours to get her skin clean. She was carried to a couch and I made the bed, cooked a light breakfast of eggs and milk which I had brought with me, fed her, and assisted the mother to straighten up and then left....

Next, inspecting some houses on Hester Street, I found water closets which needed chloride of lime [a disinfectant].... In one room, I found a child with running ears, which I syringed, showing the mother how to do it, and directed her to Dr. Koplick of the Essex Street Dispensary for further attention. In another room there was a child with "summer complaint" [diarrhea] to whom I gave bismuth and tickets for a sea-side excursion.

After luncheon I saw the O'Briens and took the little one, with whooping cough, to play in the back of our yard. On the next floor, the Costria baby had a sore throat for which I gave the mother borax and honey and little cloths to keep it clean.

Source: Coss, Clare, ed. *Lillian D. Wald: Progressive Activist.* New York: The Feminist Press at the City University of New York, 1989.

---

children, scrubbed the floor, and promised to return (Siegel 1983, 23–26).

That experience changed her life. "That morning's experience was a baptism by fire," she wrote in her autobiography, *The House on Henry Street.* "Deserted were the laboratory and the academic work of the college. I never returned to them" (1915, 7). She convinced a fellow nurse, Mary Brewster, to work with her in starting a visiting nurse service for the poor immigrants of the Lower East Side. "We were to live in the neighborhood as nurses, identify ourselves with it socially, and, in brief, contribute to it our citizenship" (1915, 8–9).

They found two benefactors willing to cover their living expenses and nursing supplies: Jacob Schiff and his mother, Betty Loeb. Although what they wanted to do was very much in line with the new settlement-house movement, Wald had not yet heard of settlement houses. She soon would: she and Brewster found rooms with a group of women who had started the College Settlement on the Lower East Side. From here, they roamed the neighborhood, dressed in dark blue uniforms, visiting apartments, giving out advice on sanitation and caring for the sick (Wald 1915, 2, 10; Siegel 1983, 28–32).

In September 1893, they found an apartment of their own and continued their ministrations. They were pioneers: Wald's biographer Beatrice Siegel notes that, at that time, in the entire country there were only twenty visiting nurse services, all of them tied to a particular church or charity (1983, 35).

In her autobiography, Wald details the principles of their service. It was to be secular; it would not be connected with any particular doctor or dispensary, but it would respond to calls from all doctors and from patients themselves. She and Brewster also decided to charge a small fee for their services, if the patient's family could pay. In this way, the service would not have the stigma attached to a free service only for the poor (Wald 1915, 27–29).

In 1895, to expand the service, Jacob Schiff bought a house at 265 Henry Street. Several more nurses moved in to join Wald (by this time Mary Brewster was ill and had to end her involvement in the venture). This was the beginning of the Henry Street settlement house. By 1900, fifteen residents were living at the house, and by 1902, the settlement had added three more buildings on Henry Street. Wald's biographer Beatrice Siegel points out that Wald and her nurses were developing the concepts of preventive care and community health care, whereas until that time poor people generally took no action regarding their health until things reached at a critical stage. The nurses linked

> health to home conditions, sanitation, food, employment, and mental and

emotional stress. A nurse might recommend a job for an unemployed husband, or a change of jobs; look into a child's problems at school or with the police; often they dipped into their purses to supply money for food and rent. (Siegel 1983, 42–43, 47–48)

Wald soon reached beyond nursing and beyond her local neighborhood in her quest to help the poor. Realizing that poor children often had no safe place to play, Wald created a playground by combining the Henry Street backyard with two adjacent yards. In 1898, she was one of the founders of the Outdoor Recreation League, to prod the city to create neighborhood parks. She urged public schools to appoint school nurses, because often children with contagious diseases attended school and spread illness; and she fought to convince schools to serve lunches, arguing that hungry children could not learn well. In 1905, she and fellow settlement-house worker Florence Kelley began working with President Theodore Roosevelt (who was a friend of Wald's) to form the federal Children's Bureau, which was to collect health statistics on infants and children. She also worked on behalf of laws to end child labor. Realizing that women were often poor because of low pay, Wald helped form the Women's Trade Union League (Siegel 1983, 53–63, 70–71).

In 1933, Wald retired as head worker of Henry Street settlement, but continued to serve on its board of directors. Both the Henry Street settlement and the visiting nurse service continue today, although in 1944, the visiting nurse service separated from the settlement house, and is now the Visiting Nurse Service of New York (Siegel 1983, 164; Henry Street Settlement Web site).

See also: Children's Bureau; Kelley, Florence; Playgrounds; Sanger, Margaret; Settlement Houses

Sources

Siegel, Beatrice. *Lillian Wald of Henry Street*. New York: Macmillan Publishing Company, 1983.

Wald, Lillian. *The House on Henry Street*. New York: Henry Holt, 1915.

Web Sites

Henry Street Settlement. www.henrystreet.org (accessed June 2008).

Visiting Nurse Service of New York. http://www.vnsny.org/ (accessed June 2008).

WELFARE CAPITALISM

When businesses provide benefits and services to their workers to attract and keep good employees, this is termed "welfare capitalism." Such benefits and services can include health insurance or medical care, company housing, athletic facilities, nursery schools or day care facilities, stock options, pension plans, and so forth.

According to history professors Edward Berkowitz and Kim McQuaid, at the beginning of the twentieth century, some American businesses were ahead of the government in terms of providing benefits and service to the American people. At a time when government old-age pensions did not exist, when not even the elderly or poor had government health insurance, when cities may not have provided public parks, tennis courts, or swimming pools, some American businesses

A company housing project on the outskirts of steelmill property, Homestead, Pennsylvania, 1907. (Corbis)

provided these to their employees. The actions of these businesses influenced governments to provide such services to the American public, according to Berkowitz and McQuaid: "we believe that during the formative years of the American welfare state the private sector provided the conceptual models and administrative capacities upon which public sector programs were based" (1992, x).

The welfare capitalism movement began in the late 1800s and early 1900s. Some companies began providing housing, food, medical care, and sometimes even funeral services and cemeteries. Colorado Fuel and Iron Company offered schools for children of its employees, as well as adult classes in cooking, sewing, and English (for immigrants), and a company library. U.S. Steel provided nineteen company swimming pools. Hershey Chocolate had a museum and zoo (Brandes 1976, 4–5).

One reason that businesses provided these extra benefits was to make sure their workers were happy, and would do good work. Unhappy workers could and did quit their jobs, or even destroy or sabotage the product or service of the company. So it was in a company's best interest to make sure workers were satisfied. In addition, businesses wanted to blunt the impact of unions and the labor movement. At the same time that some companies offered extra benefits, many companies refused to hire union workers, and kept private police forces to end strikes—sometimes violently, for example, by shooting at striking workers (Brandes 1976, 1–7).

Business owners also hoped to keep American government small by providing services themselves that, in European countries, were being provided by governments. They believed that, with a small and weak government, business would have more power. By the 1920s, welfare capitalism was widespread: thousands of companies offered such benefits to millions of workers. Companies wanted to keep their good workers once they trained them, and so benefits were designed to encourage workers to remain with the same company for life.

However, the Great Depression of the 1930s put an end to this, at least temporarily. As profits fell, companies cut wages and benefits. The federal government eventually stepped in with its New Deal program, providing government pensions (Social Security), unemployment insurance, workers' compensation, and public recreational facilities built by workers on public works projects. The government even passed a law to help workers unionize—the National Labor Relations Act (Jacoby 1997, 4–5).

However, welfare capitalism did not disappear. After the Great Depression,

when prosperity returned to the United States in the 1940s and after, a few nonunionized businesses again began offering benefits and services to their employees. In the 1960s and 1970s, welfare capitalism grew and spread. At this time, unions were declining somewhat in strength, and businesses hoped to attract and keep a more educated workforce. In the 1990s, as the economy changed and many previously large and stable companies began laying off thousands of workers, some companies adopted a two-tier standard for welfare capitalism: some employees (often the less educated ones) got few benefits, while other, more valued employees received a lot of benefits. As fewer workers joined unions, and more workers held temporary or part-time jobs, fewer workers at the end of the twentieth century received the benefits of welfare capitalism. According to public policy professor Sanford Jacoby, "Corporations today are less willing to shoulder risks for their employees than in earlier years." Furthermore, many young, educated workers do not want to remain in the same job for life: they prefer the freedom of choosing new jobs every few years to gain new experiences and skills (Jacoby 1997, 9, 261–264).

See also: Great Depression; Labor Unions; National Labor Relations Act; New Deal; Progressive Era

Sources

Berkowitz, Edward, and Kim McQuaid. *Creating the Welfare State: The Political Economy of 20th-Century Reform.* Rev. ed. Lawrence, KS: University Press of Kansas, 1992.

Brandes, Stuart. *American Welfare Capitalism, 1880–1940.* Chicago, IL: University of Chicago Press, 1976.

Jacoby, Sanford. *Modern Manors: Welfare Capitalism Since the New Deal.* Princeton, NJ: Princeton University Press, 1997.

WELFARE RIGHTS MOVEMENT

The welfare rights movement began in the 1960s, as a protest against the poverty experienced by blacks who had left the agricultural south for northern cities, could not find jobs, and were living in poverty. In the opinion of sociologists Frances Fox Piven and Richard Cloward, the welfare rights movement was an important part of the civil rights movement and

> in a sense the most authentic expression of the black movement in the postwar period. The many hundreds of thousands who participated were drawn from the very bottom of the black community.... It was, in short, a struggle by the black masses for the sheer right of survival. (1977, 264–265)

In the 1960s, as the civil rights movement won political rights for southern blacks and an end to racial segregation, blacks continued to suffer high rates of unemployment both in rural, agricultural areas, and in urban areas. In the 1960s, in certain urban areas, 24 to 41 percent of blacks were unemployed. The civil rights movement began turning its attention to economic issues. Welfare rights groups began in 1963, in several cities—one of the first was organized by Johnnie Tillmon in Los Angeles, called the Aid to Needy Children Mothers. Dozens of riots in cities around the country were started by angry and frustrated poor blacks,

and some of these protests were staged at welfare offices. Partly in response to the riots, the community action programs started through President Johnson's Economic Opportunity Act of 1964 were being proactive about educating poor blacks around the country about their right to government aid and helping them apply for such aid. Government lawyers on behalf of the poor were helping to expand eligibility rules by taking cases to court. From 1960 to 1966, the number of people applying for government aid doubled, and a larger percentage of applicants were being approved for relief (Piven and Cloward 1977, 267, 271–274; National Welfare Rights Union, History of the Welfare Rights Movement).

In 1967, local welfare rights groups joined together to form the National Welfare Rights Organization (NWRO). The group was founded by George Wiley, a civil rights leader, with help from Frances Fox Piven and Richard Cloward, two university professors who were interested in helping the poor to organize. Its first chair was Johnnie Tillmon, who had started the welfare rights group in Los Angeles.

The NWRO's goals were decent jobs with adequate pay, and adequate income for those who could not work. They limited their voting membership mostly to poor people, because they did not want middle-class members to dominate the organization, as had happened with civil rights organizations. They attracted members by offering to help members apply for government benefits that were not well-publicized. At its height, the NWRO had 540 local chapters and up to 30,000 members. According to history professor Felicia Kornbluh, the NWRO was "the largest national organization of poor people in the history of the United States." However, as it became easier to apply for and receive benefits, many members dropped out (West 1981, 39–41; Kornbluh 2007, 2).

During its seven-year existence, the NWRO lobbied against antiwelfare bills in Congress. The NWRO led thousands of marchers to demand better benefits for the poor, and it fought against cuts in benefits in various states. They publicized the skimpy menus with which the welfare recipients had to make do. In 1970, they staged a takeover of the Department of Health, Education and Welfare, in which welfare recipient Beulah Sanders became "acting secretary." The group occupied the building for nine hours (Kornbluh 2007, 1, 139–140; National Welfare Rights Union, History of the Welfare Rights Movement).

The NWRO worked with other groups such as the City-Wide Coordinating Committee of Welfare Groups, a New York City organization that staged demonstrations and demanded consumer credit for poor people. They also worked with Martin Luther King's Poor People's Campaign, which started in 1968. Some NWRO leaders did not trust King at first because he came from a middle-class background; however, they insisted on meeting with King—not his representative—and after questioning him, agreed to work with him. Welfare rights groups from around the country participated in the Poor People's Campaign's six-week encampment in Washington, D.C., in 1968 (Nadasen 2005, 71–72; Kornbluh 2007, 1, 100–101, 123).

As government welfare budgets continued to be cut, the NWRO began advocating for a "guaranteed adequate income" (also termed "guaranteed minimum income" or "guaranteed annual income")—an income that would cover the basics of life. In 1970, they publicized a plan featuring $5,500 as a basic annual income. This figure did not cover such middle-class necessities as a car, long-distance phone calls, out-of-town travel, or dry cleaning. The plan included work incentives. This program would replace all existing public assistance programs. Senator Eugene McCarthy introduced the NWRO basic income bill into Congress in 1970 (Kornbluh 2007, 142–143; National Welfare Rights Union, History of the Welfare Rights Movement).

The NWRO was forced to close in 1974 because of lack of funds, and because the political tide had turned more conservative. When Richard Nixon took office as president in 1969, he resolved to dismantle the Great Society programs that President Johnson had put in place to combat poverty and other social ills. By 1975, as Felicia Kornbluh states, "the welfare rights era was over.... The welfare rights campaign lost its mainstream legitimacy and visibility; public aid recipients lost most of their ability to place new ideas on the national agenda" (Kornbluh 2007, 183–185). The public, and politicians, were again eager to believe that welfare recipients were lazy and ignorant (West 1981, 352–354).

According to Piven and Cloward, who had helped to start the NWRO, the welfare rights movement "failed" because it did not continue to help more eligible people to apply for aid. Instead, it shifted emphasis to lobbying in Congress, where the organization had little influence. "Had it pursued a

PRIMARY DOCUMENT 45

"Welfare Is a Women's Issue," by Johnnie Tillmon

Johnnie Tillmon was the first chair of the National Welfare Rights Organization. This essay was first published in 1972 in Ms. *magazine and has since been widely reprinted and quoted.*

I'm a woman. I'm a black woman. I'm a poor woman. I'm a fat woman. I'm a middle-aged woman. And I'm on welfare.

In this country, if you're any one of those things you count less as a human being. If you're all those things, you don't count at all. Except as a statistic.

I am 45 years old. I have raised six children. There are millions of statistics like me. Some on welfare. Some not. And some, really poor, who don't even know they're entitled to welfare. Not all of them are black. Not at all. In fact, the majority-about two-thirds-of all the poor families in the country are white.

Welfare's like a traffic accident. It can happen to anybody, but especially it happens to women.

And that's why welfare is a women's issue. For a lot of middle-class women in this country, Women's Liberation is a matter of concern. For women on welfare it's a matter of survival.

Survival. That's why we had to go on welfare. And that's why we can't get off welfare now. Not us women. Not until we do something about liberating poor women in this country.

Because up until now we've been raised to expect to work, all our lives, for nothing. Because we are the worst educated, the least-skilled, and the lowest-paid people there are. Because we have to be almost totally responsible for our children. Because we are regarded by everybody as dependents. That's why we are on welfare. And that's why we stay on it.

Welfare is the most prejudiced institution in this country, even more than marriage, which it tries to imitate. Let me explain that a little.

Ninety-nine percent of welfare families are headed by women. There is no man around. In half the states there can't be men around because A.F.D.C. (Aid to Families With Dependent Children) says if there is an "able-bodied" man around, then you can't be on welfare. If the kids are going to eat, and the man can't get a job, then he's got to go.

Welfare is like a super-sexist marriage. You trade in a man for the man. But you can't divorce him if he treats you bad. He can divorce you, of course, cut you off anytime he wants. But in that case, he keeps the kids, not you. The man runs everything. In ordinary marriage, sex is supposed to be for your husband. On A.F.D.C., you're not supposed to have any sex at all. You give up control of your own body. It's a condition of aid. You may even have to agree to get your tubes tied so you can never have more children just to avoid being cut off welfare.

The man, the welfare system, controls your money. He tells you what to buy, what not to buy, where to buy it, and how much things cost. If things-rent, for instance-really cost more than he says they do, it's just too bad for you. He's always right.

That's why Governor [Ronald] Reagan can get away with slandering welfare recipients, calling them "lazy parasites," "pigs at the trough," and such. We've been trained to believe that the only reason people are on welfare is because there's something wrong with their character. If people have "motivation," if people only want to work, they can, and they will be able to support themselves and their kids in decency.

The truth is a job doesn't necessarily mean an adequate income. There are some ten million jobs that now pay less than the minimum wage, and if you're a woman, you've got the best chance of getting one. Why would a 45-year-old woman work all day in a laundry ironing shirts at 90-some cents an hour? Because she knows there's some place lower she could be. She could be on welfare. Society needs women on welfare as "examples" to let every woman, factory workers and housewife workers alike, know what will happen if she lets up, if she's laid off, if she tries to go it alone without a man. So these ladies stay on their feet or on their knees all their lives instead of asking why they're only getting 90-some cents an hour, instead of daring to fight and complain.

Maybe we poor welfare women will really liberate women in this country. We've already started on our own welfare plan. Along with other welfare recipients, we have organized so we can have some voice. Our group is called the National Welfare Rights Organization (N.W.R.O.). We put together our own welfare plan, called Guaranteed Adequate Income (G.A.I.), which would eliminate sexism from welfare. There would be no "categories"-men, women, children, single, married, kids, no kids-just poor people who need aid. You'd get paid according to need and family size only and that would be upped as the cost of living goes up.

As far as I'm concerned, the ladies of N.W.R.O. are the front-line troops of women's freedom. Both because we have so few illusions and because our issues are so important to all women-the right to a living wage for women's work, the right to life itself.

Source

Johnnie Tillmon. "Welfare Is a Women's Issue (1972)." *Ms.* Magazine, Spring 2002. http://www.msmagazine.com/spring2002/tillmon.asp (accessed January 2009).

---

mobilizing strategy, encouraging more and more of the poor to demand welfare, NWRO could perhaps have left a legacy of another million families on the rolls. Millions of potentially eligible families had still not applied for aid, especially among the aged and working poor" (1977, 363).

On the other hand, history professor Premilla Nadasen believes that the welfare rights movement was successful in that it "influenced welfare policy and helped shape the debate about welfare in the 1960s." The movement gained higher monthly benefits and grants for special items, and empowered the poor to fight for their right to basic necessities (2005, 231–232).

The NWRO was revived in 1987 as the National Welfare Rights Union. In 1997, they began an "Economic Human Rights" campaign that gathered evidence of economic human rights violations across the country, and presented these violations to the United Nations (National Welfare Rights Union, History of the Welfare Rights Movement).

See also: Aid to (Families with) Dependent Children; Civil Rights Movement; Community Action Programs; Economic

Opportunity Act of 1964; Great Society; Guaranteed Annual Income; Johnson, Lyndon; King, Martin Luther, Jr.; Legal Services for the Poor; Poor People's Campaign; United Nations Human Rights Treaties; Universal Declaration of Human Rights

Sources

Kornbluh, Felicia. *The Battle for Welfare Rights: Politics and Poverty in Modern America.* Philadelphia, PA: University of Pennsylvania Press, 2007.

Nadasen, Premilla. *Welfare Warriors: The Welfare Rights Movement in the United States.* New York: Routledge, 2005.

Piven, Frances Fox, and Richard A. Cloward. *Poor People's Movements: Why They Succeed, How They Fail.* New York: Pantheon Books, 1977.

West, Guida. *The National Welfare Rights Movement: The Social Protest of Poor Women.* New York: Praeger Publishing, 1981.

Web Site

National Welfare Rights Union. History of the Welfare Rights Movement. http://www.nationalwru.org/prod02.htm (accessed July 2008).

WELFARE-TO-WORK PROGRAMS

The word "welfare" has generally referred to cash payments to poor mothers. These cash payments were originally provided in the form of "mothers' pensions" by states in the early part of the 1900s. At that time, their purpose was to allow the mother to stay at home with her children and to alleviate her need to work. In 1935, Aid to Dependent Children (ADC) was created as part of the Social Security Act. This provided federal funding for cash payments to poor mothers, and again, the purpose was to allow poor mothers to stay at home with their children.

However, as society changed and came to accept the idea of mothers working outside the home, so too did the attitude toward poor mothers who received welfare payments. By the 1960s, the general public as well as politicians had come to the conclusion that these mothers ought to work and earn money.

Poor men were always supposed to work, unless they were disabled. In the late 1800s, some city governments started public works projects to provide jobs to unemployed men. Starting in the 1930s, the federal government began a massive program of job creation as part of the New Deal to lift the country out of the Great Depression. Many of these jobs targeted men who had families, although some women also benefited from these jobs. However, many of these programs barred women from participating if their husbands were employed. Women made up only one-sixth of the total workers with the Works Progress Administration and the Federal Emergency Relief Administration (Rose 1995, 41).

During World War II, unemployment virtually disappeared as the government created jobs in the war industry. After World War II, poor mothers continued to be able to rely on ADC. At that time, government work programs were not geared specifically toward poor mothers who received ADC, but the poorest mothers—black women—were often denied welfare to force them to accept low-wage work. For example, some southern states had rules that mothers could not receive aid as long as jobs were available in the cotton fields. Louisiana was the first state to implement such a rule, in 1943. The Louisiana rule was sometimes applied to children as young as seven, who were expected to work alongside their mothers in the fields. In 1952, Georgia passed a law stating that mothers with children over one year old were expected to find work, and as long as jobs were available, they could be denied aid. In Arkansas, mothers and older children were expected to work, whenever work was available (Bell 1965, 46, 82, 107; Rose 1995, 73–74).

In 1962, the U.S. Congress renamed ADC the Aid to Families with Dependent Children (AFDC). The emphasis shifted from providing aid to single mothers to helping families become self-supporting. The Community Work and Training Program emphasized putting unemployed fathers to work, but the program was optional for states, and only thirteen states chose to participate. Also in 1962, the Manpower Development and Training Act was a federal program that emphasized job training for men, although women could participate as well—45 percent of trainees were women. This program was successful at placing clients in jobs, but it was criticized because it was tightly controlled by the federal government, and states wanted more control over the funds.

The passage of the Economic Opportunity Act in 1964 made more federal money available for job training for unemployed parents. Poor mothers also were provided with money for child care, transportation, and job placement assistance. In 1967, the federal government's Work Incentive (WIN) program required that employable AFDC clients—including mothers—be referred to jobs. However, the law did nothing to create jobs. Of those

who attended WIN employment training, only 24 percent of men and 18 percent of women were able to find jobs, and these jobs generally paid low wages.

The Comprehensive Employment and Training Act (CETA) was passed in 1973. This program did emphasize job creation. Over half the participants were women, and the training did help women to increase their earnings. However, CETA was dogged by rumors of fraud and misuse of money. Funds for this program were cut after 1980, and this program ended in 1983 (Rose 1995, 83–84; Katz 2001, 64–65; Lurie 2006, 4–14).

Starting in the early 1970s, several states developed Community Work Experience Programs, which required some AFDC recipients—fathers in two-parent families, and single parents with children over the age of six—to work in community service jobs in exchange for their benefits. They were required to work for up to eighty hours per month in nonprofit organizations or government jobs. The goal was to provide work experience and work training. Only a very small percentage of AFDC recipients ended up participating in these programs. Critics complained that the programs were too expensive and too inefficient, and that they did not ultimately help people to get permanent jobs (Rose 1995, 105–106, 137).

In 1988, the Family Support Act was passed, which required parents receiving AFDC to work sixteen hours per week in a work program in exchange for benefits. While the federal government provided some funding for this program, states were required to put in 40 percent of the money for job training, and many states did not have the money. States thus were not able to reach every AFDC recipient and require them to participate in a work program. By 1992, only 7 percent of all adults receiving AFDC were participating in a work program, and by 1995, 20 percent were participating. And after people found jobs in the private sector, the government did almost nothing to help them afford child care (Katz 2001, 75–76; Lurie 2006, 7, 12).

Federal and state governments had been trying for decades to reduce their welfare rolls and get people into jobs, but instead, the welfare rolls continued to grow. In the 1990s, things started to come together. In 1993, the Earned Income Tax Credit (EITC) was greatly expanded, to ensure that anyone who worked forty hours per week, and had a child, would be living above the federal poverty line. This expansion of the EITC made it easier for poor families to support themselves with low-wage work. In 1996, Congress passed the Personal Responsibility and Work Opportunity Reconciliation Act of 1996, which created the Temporary Assistance for Needy Families program and provided money to states to help poor families. States now had enough money to provide child care and transportation help to poor families, thus enabling them to accept jobs.

In addition, Medicaid (health insurance for the poor) was made available to more poor and low-income families. This helped families accept low-wage jobs that did not provide health insurance, since the government was providing the health insurance. As a result of the Personal Responsibility and Work Opportunity Reconciliation Act, the expansion of the EITC, the expansion of Medicaid, and the provision of child-care vouchers, welfare rolls have dropped, and more parents are working.

See also: Aid to (Families with) Dependent Children; Comprehensive Employment and Training Act; Earned Income Tax Credit; Federal Emergency Relief Act; Full Employment; Great Depression; Manpower Development and Training Act of 1962; Medicaid; Mothers' Pensions; New Deal; Personal Responsibility and Work Opportunity Reconciliation Act of 1996; Public Works Projects; Temporary Assistance for Needy Families; Vouchers; Works Progress Administration

Sources

Bell, Winifred. *Aid to Dependent Children.* New York: Columbia University Press, 1965.

Katz, Michael B. *The Price of Citizenship: Redefining the American Welfare State.* New York: Metropolitan Books, 2001.

Lurie, Irene. *At the Front Lines of the Welfare System: A Perspective on the Decline in Welfare Caseloads.* Albany, NY: Rockefeller Institute Press, 2006.

Rose, Nancy E. *Workfare or Fair Work: Women, Welfare, and Government Work Programs.* New Brunswick, NJ: Rutgers University Press, 1995.

WOODWARD, ELLEN SULLIVAN (1887–1971)

During the New Deal of the 1930s, Ellen Sullivan Woodward headed the women's public works projects of the Civil Works Administration (CWA), the Federal Emergency Relief Administration (FERA), and the Works Progress Administration (WPA). At a time when poor single women were often overlooked, and at a time when many people believed that married women ought not to work, Woodward encouraged all women to get jobs. She often worked closely with First Lady Eleanor Roosevelt to achieve her goals. During the 1940s, after the New Deal was over, she served as one of the three members of the Social Security Board.

Ellen Sullivan Woodward was born on July 11, 1887, in Oxford, Mississippi. Her father was a lawyer and served in the U.S. Congress for a short time. Her mother died when she was eight years old. She completed her formal education at the age of fifteen, married at nineteen, and gave birth to a son in 1909. Her husband was a lawyer, politician, and judge. Until after her husband died when she was thirty-seven, she held no paid job. She was a leader of a local women's club, which helped work for civic improvements such as sidewalks, better roads, and electric lights. In the 1920s, she helped initiate a citywide cleanup campaign in Louisville, Mississippi. In 1925, after her husband's death, she agreed to run for his seat in the Mississippi House of Representatives. She won and completed his term, which ended in 1928.

She then accepted a job—her first paid job—with the Mississippi State Board of Development, with the goal of expanding the state's industry and agriculture, and marketing its products across the country. The Great Depression started in 1929, and Mississippi's people suffered from the economic depression as well as from a drought. In 1932, Woodward was appointed as the only woman member of the new Mississippi State Board of Welfare. When Franklin Roosevelt ran for president in 1932, Woodward organized the women of the state to support his bid.

Roosevelt appointed Woodward to head the women's division of the

Ellen Sullivan Woodward, head of women's public works projects during the New Deal. (Library of Congress)

FERA, an agency that gave money to states for job creation and poor relief. Eleanor Roosevelt hosted a White House Conference on the Emergency Needs of Women to gather ideas about works projects for women. Fifty prominent women leaders attended the conference. Harry Hopkins, head of the FERA, admitted that he did not know what kinds of work to create for women. Everyone at the conference seemed to adhere to fairly traditional views regarding appropriate work for women: they agreed that women could not work on the construction projects that men were being assigned to, and that women should not be asked to leave home to take up a job. Woodward noted that it would be more difficult to find 500,000 jobs for women, than to put 4 million men to work. The women at the conference suggested such work projects as sewing rooms, canning centers, clerical and domestic work, public health work, nursery schools, music programs, public library services, and teaching (Ware 1981, 106–107; Swain 1995, 40–44).

Hardly had Woodward begun her work with FERA, however, when Roosevelt created a new temporary agency, the Civil Works Administration (CWA), to put 4 million "men" to work during the winter of 1933–1934. Woodward was concerned because Roosevelt's directive used the word "men," and state administrators were taking this literally. "It took weeks of effort and thousands of wires and letters to correct the erroneous impressions," Woodward noted in a letter to Eleanor Roosevelt (Ware 1981, 108).

Woodward instructed states to get the help of voluntary women's organizations to set up sewing rooms, nursery schools, canning centers, and other workplaces for women. By January, about 300,000 women were employed at CWA jobs. One problem was that wages for women were generally lower than wages for men, because women worked for the Civil Works Service division, which was required to pay at least $0.30 per hour, whereas men generally worked on CWA construction projects and received about $1 per hour. Woodward managed to assign some women to construction projects as clerical workers, nurses, statisticians, and even as day laborers, so they could be paid more (Swain 1995, 45–46; Cook 1999, 87).

The WPA, started in 1935, also had a women's division, which Woodward headed. The public continued to be hostile to the idea of married women working. Woodward responded by pointing that the hours of WPA jobs were not long and that a married woman could take care of her home as well as hold a WPA job: "The self-respect engendered by her work responsibilities and her security wages will make her a happier, more energetic, and enthusiastic homemaker than if she were obliged to try to make both ends meet for herself and her family on a dole based on her budget deficiency." She even supported the right of women with small children to work, even though other prominent New Deal women leaders were against it, such as Secretary of Labor Frances Perkins and Children's Bureau administrators, who believed that mothers should be paid to stay at home with their children. Woodward's idea carried the day when Harry Hopkins issued an executive order that women were to be hired for WPA jobs even if they had small children at home (Swain 1995, 63).

Woodward tried to diversify the kinds of work women were assigned to do. Although more than 50 percent of WPA women workers were still in sewing rooms, women also rode packhorses to deliver books to rural areas; public health nurses provided immunizations; and women kept books in New York City. Woodward was pleased that the WPA employed women regardless of marital or motherhood status (Cook 1999, 275–276).

Despite the efforts of Woodward and Eleanor Roosevelt, women's work projects never achieved much support in the Roosevelt administration. According to Eleanor Roosevelt's biographer Blanche Wiesen Cook, "women's projects were continually demeaned. ER and Woodward had few, if any, real supporters among their male allies. Hopkins never endorsed the principle of equal work for equal pay, and despite ER's efforts, FDR never spoke out in favor of women's work" (1999, 88).

After resigning from the WPA in 1938 (toward the end of the New Deal), Woodward served on the Social Security Board until 1946, when it was abolished. She worked to educate women about Social Security benefits and to push for women to be more fully covered by Social Security.

See also: Children's Bureau; Civil Works Administration; Federal Emergency Relief Act; Great Depression; New Deal Women's Network; Perkins, Frances; Roosevelt, Eleanor; Roosevelt, Franklin Delano; Social Security Act; Works Progress Administration

Sources

Cook, Blanche Wiesen. *Eleanor Roosevelt, Volume Two: 1933–1938.* New York: Viking Press, 1999.

Swain, Martha H. *Ellen S. Woodward: New Deal Advocate for Women.* Jackson, MS: University Press of Mississippi, 1995.

Ware, Susan. *Beyond Suffrage: Women in the New Deal.* Cambridge, MA: Harvard University Press, 1981.

WORKERS' COMPENSATION

The injury or death of a household breadwinner is liable to throw a family into poverty. Workers' compensation pays workers who are injured on the job, and pays money to the dependents of workers killed on the job.

Workers' compensation (originally termed "workmen's compensation") was the first widespread social insurance program in the United States. States began passing workmen's compensation laws in 1911, and by 1920,

forty-three states had such laws in place. According to University of Arizona economics professors Price Fishback and Shawn Everett Kantor, workmen's compensation laws were a prelude to the many other forms of social insurance laws that federal and state governments have passed in the twentieth century, such as unemployment insurance, the Social Security Act, and Medicare (2000, 1).

Most workers in the United States are covered by state compensation laws. Federal government employees are covered by a federal law. Under most laws, workers receive up to two-thirds of their wages while they are injured and unable to work, as well as medical costs associated with the injury or disease. Depending on the state, employers can buy workers' compensation insurance through a state fund or private insurance companies. During the 1990s, workers' compensation accounted for twice as much benefits (cash and medical expenses) paid to employees, compared with unemployment insurance (Fishback and Kantor 2000, 1).

After the Industrial Revolution made dangerous work common, workers were often seriously injured or killed by factory machines or in industrial accidents. Between 1888 and 1908, about 35,000 American workers were killed on the job, and 536,000 were injured. In 1916, 10 percent of railroad workers were injured on the job. The laws at that time allowed business owners to get out of paying compensation for the injury, if they could ascribe a worker's injury to his or her own carelessness or the negligence of another employee. Owners could fault workers for continuing to work in a situation that they knew was dangerous. Workers rarely were able to collect any money, even if they were disabled and unable to earn a living in the future.

In the late 1800s and early 1900s, some states began modifying laws to make it easier for injured workers, or the dependents of dead workers, to win lawsuits against employers. As a result, more and more injured workers began to sue their employers and win. Still, pursuing a case in court against an employer was expensive and time-consuming, and often the payments received were small (Katz 1996, 198–199).

Reformers attacked this problem in two ways: by working for the passage of state workmen's compensation laws, and by promoting safety in factories and industrial work. Both employers and employees were in favor of workmen's compensation laws. Labor unions and organizations like the American Association for Labor Legislation (an organization of economists and political scientists) and the National Association of Manufacturers worked for the passage of workmen's compensation laws. To receive benefits under these laws, a worker had only to prove that he or she was injured on the job. No fault was assigned. Although under these laws, employers were required to pay benefits to many more workers, still they were protected from the occasional huge award if by chance an employee's lawsuit was successful under the old system. So with workmen's compensation laws, employers had somewhat more control over the amount of money they might be required to pay, and workers were more assured of getting a fair amount to tide them over the period of injury (Lubove 1986, 53–57; Fishback and Kantor 2000, 88–89).

The original workmen's compensation laws generally excluded certain classes of workers, such as domestic and agricultural workers, and those working in nonhazardous occupations. Over the years, more classes of workers have been included, so that by 2002, about 98 percent of workers were covered, according to the National Academy of Social Insurance Web site.

Starting in 1915, states also began offering coverage for occupational diseases and, by the 1980s, all states covered occupational diseases. Recently, some states have also offered coverage for disabilities caused by psychological stress. At the same time that more and more workers have been covered by workers' compensation laws, workplace injuries and deaths have declined (Workers' Compensation History on Economic History Web site).

In addition to workers' compensation benefits, those who are disabled for at least a year and are unable to work (whether or not the disability was caused on the job) are eligible for federal Social Security disability payments. In 2002, Social Security paid more than $65 billion to disabled workers, while workers' compensation paid more than $53 billion in cash and medical benefits (National Academy of Social Insurance Sourcebook).

See also: Industrial Revolution; Medicare; Progressive Era; Social Security Act; Unemployment Insurance

Sources
Fishback, Price V., and Shawn Everett Kantor. *A Prelude to the Welfare State: The Origins of Workers' Compensation.* Chicago, IL: University of Chicago Press, 2000.

Katz, Michael. *In the Shadow of the Poorhouse: A Social History of Welfare in America.* New York: Basic Books, 1996.

Lubove, Roy. *The Struggle for Social Security, 1900–1935.* Pittsburgh, PA: University of Pittsburgh Press, 1986.

Web Sites

National Academy of Social Insurance. Sourcebook on Workers' Compensation and Disability. http://www.nasi.org/publications3901/publications_show.htm?slide_id=1&cat_id=79 (accessed May 2008).

Workers' Compensation History on Economic History. http://eh.net/encyclopedia/article/fishback.workers.compensation (accessed May 2008).

WORKS PROGRESS ADMINISTRATION

The Works Progress Administration (later called the Works Projects Administration, WPA) was the largest New Deal agency and was designed to provide work to the unemployed. It was created in April 1935, when President Franklin Roosevelt realized that the Great Depression was not ending as quickly as everyone hoped it would. He had ended or was about to end the temporary federal aid and works projects (the Federal Emergency Relief Administration [FERA] and the Civil Works Administration), yet people were still unemployed, hungry, and in need of help. The National Youth Administration, another part of the Works Progress Administration designed to help poor young people, was created in June 1935.

The WPA was one part of the federal government's attempts to more permanently help the unemployed and needy. The other part was the Social Security Act, signed in August 1935 by President Roosevelt, which set up a national program for old-age pensions, unemployment insurance, and aid to the disabled and dependent children (Brown 1940, 301).

The WPA's initial goal was to employ 3.5 million people. In the end, after eight years of existence, it had employed a total of 8.5 million people and spent about $10.5 billion. Its workers built or repaired roads, water and sewer systems, and schools and other public buildings, as well as sewing clothes for the needy, cooking lunches for schoolchildren, providing immunizations, teaching adult education classes, and compiling statistics on chronic diseases, housing, and unemployment. WPA workers constructed some of the most well-known and enduring landmarks in the country, such as the Cow Palace arena in San Francisco, La Guardia Airport in New York City, National Airport near Washington, D.C., and River Walk in San Antonio, Texas (Hopkins 1936, 166–168, 173; Taylor 2008, 2–3).

Although building upon their work, the WPA was also somewhat different from its predecessors, the Civil Works Administration and the FERA. While the Civil Works Administration had taken only 50 percent of its workers from relief rolls (the rest being hired from anyone who applied), the WPA hired 90 percent of its workers from relief rolls—those whom the states said were already receiving aid to the poor, or were eligible to receive it. The program hired only one member of every family—usually the head of the family. The wages and hours of workers under the WPA were slightly different than under the FERA. Whereas FERA

Works Progress Administration artist painting a mural, ca. 1933–1941. (Library of Congress)

workers received the "prevailing wage" of jobs in that area (the wage normally paid for that kind of work), and then were limited in the amount of hours they could work so as not to go above a certain monthly limit, the WPA workers were required to put in 120 hours per month for their pay-check—so they made more money but often worked more hours, too (Hopkins 1936, 167; Meriam 1946, 375–376; Taylor 2008, 197).

Because the main goal of the WPA was to provide employment, they looked for projects that would employ the most people, with little outlay needed for equipment or other nonlabor costs. According to Harry Hopkins, the administrator of the program, the first things WPA considered when choosing

projects were the number of eligible workers in an area, and their skills; projects that would be useful to the community were secondary. "Thus, for instance, although a town may need a school badly, WPA will not build it unless the local labor reserve contains enough skilled construction workers," explained Hopkins. The WPA did not want to compete with private busi-nesses, so all projects had to involve government buildings, land, or services. In addition, the WPA did not want to simply take over existing state and local government functions, such as routine maintenance, repair, and con-struction, but rather it wanted to create new jobs that the states or cities could not or would not do for themselves. Despite these limitations, the WPA

GUIDEBOOKS TO AMERICA

The Federal Writers' Project, part of the Works Progress Administration (WPA), produced state travel guidebooks at a time when there were very few up-to-date guidebooks available. Thomas Fleming was one of the people who worked on the California guidebook. After he was forced to drop out of college due to lack of money, he applied for a WPA job and started work installing sewer lines, until someone told him that, since he had attended college for two years, he could be hired as a white-collar worker for more money. He was assigned to research California history at a library on the campus of the University of California–Berkeley.

> Each morning he rose at [his rooming house] in Berkeley, ate a bowl of cereal in the common kitchen, and walked to campus.... where Fleming signed in and picked up his day's assignment. Then he went to the fourth floor.... In the stacks under the eaves, Fleming was learning the details of California's past. At the end of each day, he turned in his handwritten paragraphs at the desk he had checked in at in the morning.

Source: Taylor, Nick. *American-Made: The Enduring Legacy of the WPA: When FDR Put the Nation to Work.* New York: Bantam Books, 2008, 299–302.

found projects in "almost every type of work imaginable," says Donald Howard. "So vast have the WPA's achievements been that attempts to present them in quantitative terms only stagger the imagination" (Hopkins 1936, 167; Howard 1943, 126; Meriam 1946, 366).

By the time it ended, WPA workers had constructed or improved about 640,000 miles of roads; built or improved 124,000 bridges; constructed or renovated almost 40,000 schools; built or improved 28,000 parks and playgrounds; installed or repaired almost 20,000 miles of water mains; installed or improved 27,000 miles of storm and sanitary sewers; and built or renovated almost 2.5 million sanitary privies. WPA workers had built libraries, tunnels, auditoriums, gymnasiums, swimming pools, golf courses, band shells, hospitals, office buildings, armories, firehouses, jails, airports, fish hatcheries, water and sewer treatment plants, and pumping stations. They repaired 80 million books, sewed 300 million garments, and prepared more than 900 million school lunches. Thousands of WPA-staffed nursery schools served tens of thousands of children, and a million adults were enrolled in adult education classes taught by WPA teachers. Concerts, plays, puppet shows, and circuses were performed by WPA artists and seen by 180 million people. Artists and writers produced 475,000 works of art and 276 books (Leighninger 2007, 78–79; Taylor 2008, 523–524).

"Such numbers convey almost no impact by themselves," observes Nick Taylor. "They are silent on the transformation of the infrastructure that occurred, the modernizing of the country, the malnutrition defeated and educational prospects gained, the new horizons opened" (2008, 524).

Despite its enormous accomplishments, the WPA was the most criticized New Deal agency. "Its workers were mocked as shiftless shovel leaners," says Nick Taylor. "Its projects gave rise to a mocking new word: 'boondoggles'" (which meant a waste of public money). Critics attached the word "boondoggle" to an elaborate WPA-built dog shelter in Memphis, complete with showers; a monkeyhouse in the Little Rock, Arkansas, oo; and the WPA arts program. In response, President Roosevelt replied, "If we can boondoggle ourselves out of this depression, that word is going to be enshrined in the hearts of the people for many years to come." There were occasional mistakes: a lake was dug in North Carolina which turned out not to have a water source, for example. Nevertheless, according to Nick Taylor, "for the most part the WPA was being run efficiently and free of scandal" (Taylor 2008, 2, 216–218).

A national appraisal of the WPA conducted in 1938 determined how well the WPA did in providing jobs to those who had none. Using surveys sent to cities, the appraisal found that local governments would have liked even more help from the federal government to employ more people. Half the replies from smaller cities said that the WPA programs had provided enough jobs for all the unemployed who were capable of work, and only one-third of the replies from larger cities felt that the WPA had been able to employ every unemployed person who could work. So despite the vast scope of the WPA, even more help was needed (Howard 1943, 607).

See also: Civil Works Administration; Federal Emergency Relief Act; Great Depression; Hopkins, Harry; Indian New Deal; National Recovery Administration; National Service; National Youth Administration; New Deal; Public Works Projects; Roosevelt, Franklin Delano; Social Security Act; Woodward, Ellen Sullivan

Sources

Brown, Josephine Chapin. *Public Relief 1929–1939*. New York: Henry Holt, 1940.

Hopkins, Harry. *Spending to Save: The Complete Story of Relief*. Seattle, WA: University of Washington Press, 1936.

Howard, Donald S. *The WPA and Federal Relief Policy*. New York: Russell Sage Foundation, 1943.

Leighninger, Robert D., Jr. *Long-Range Public Investment: The Forgotten Legacy of the New Deal*. Columbia, SC: University of South Carolina Press, 2007.

Meriam, Lewis. *Relief and Social Security*. Washington, DC: Brookings Institution, 1946.

Taylor, Nick. *American-Made: The Enduring Legacy of the WPA: When FDR Put the Nation to Work*. New York: Bantam Books, 2008.

Index

About the Author

JYOTSNA SREENIVASAN has a Master's degree in English literature. She worked for many years with nonprofit organizations in Washington, D.C. She is the author of three books for children, and her short fiction has been published in numerous literary magazines. She is also the author of the ABC-CLIO book, *Utopias in American History* (2008).